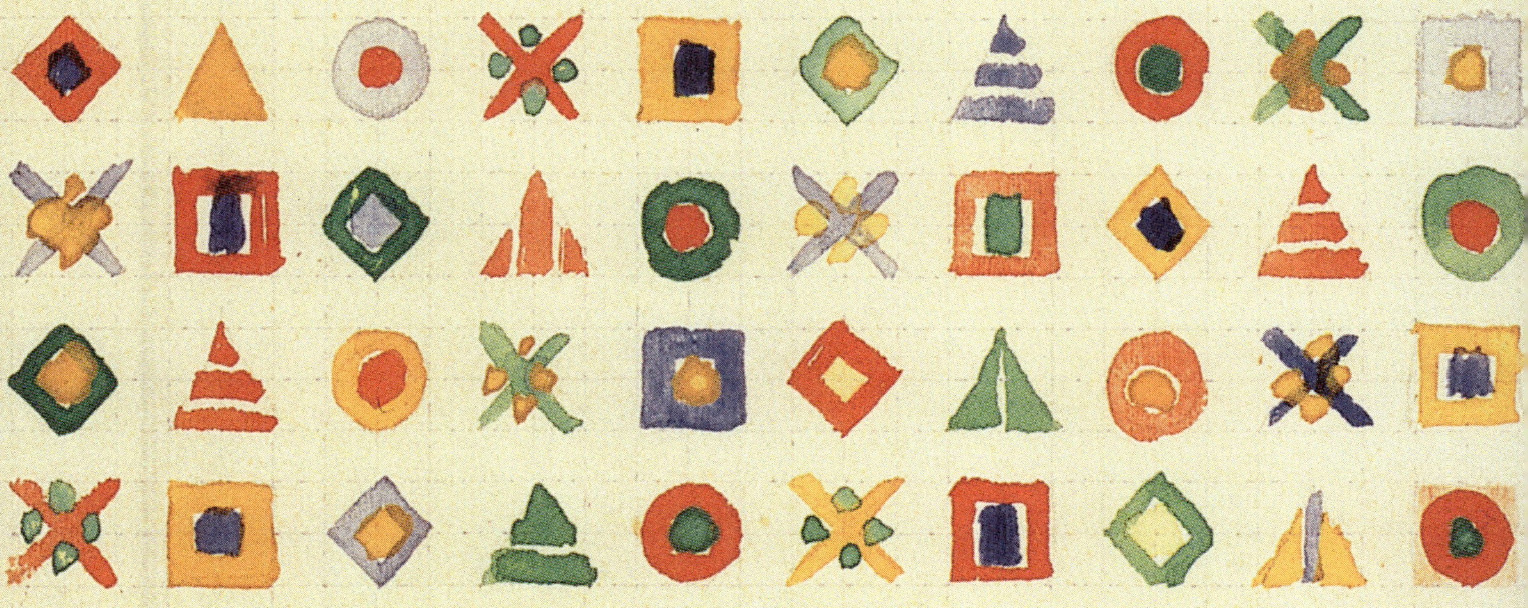

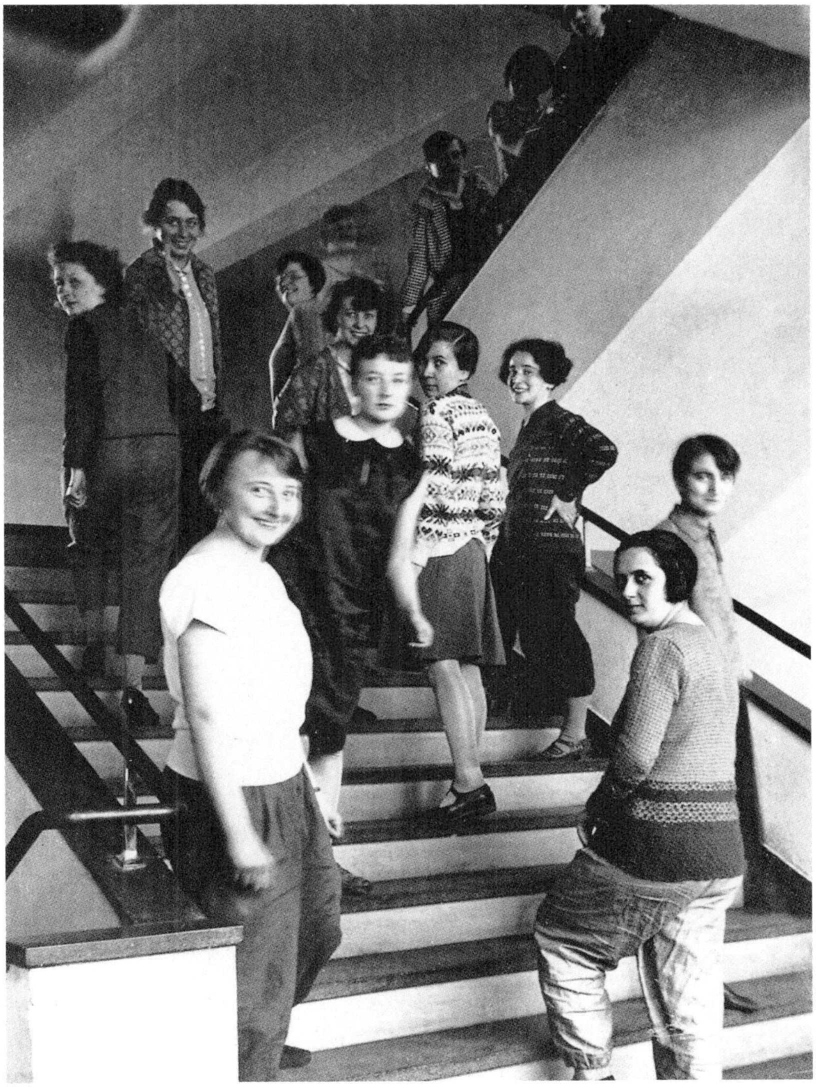

Translated from the German by Emer Lettow and Sarah Kane (pp. 22–33 and 36–49)
Design: Kuni Taguchi
Copyediting: Philippa Hurd
Typesetting: Barbara Kekus
Proofreading: Chrisoula Petridis
Color Separation: Quat'coul
Printed in Malaysia

Distributed in North America by Rizzoli International Publications, Inc.

Originally published in German as *Bauhaus-Frauen: Meisterinnen in Kunst, Handwerk und Design*

English-language edition

editions.flammarion.com

09 10 11 3 2 1

ISBN-13: 978-2-08-030120-8
Dépôt légal: 10/2009

Thanks

to Ingrid Radewaldt, Hamburg, for her competent and patient cooperation,
to Sandra Kemker, Bremen, for her articles on Marianne Brandt and Lucia Moholy,
to Renate Häselbarth, Weimar, for her article on Anni Albers,
to Sabina Frank, St. Gangloff, for retouching several portraits,
to Bettina Straube, Bad Berka, for her research on Helene Börner,
to Renate Scheper, Berlin, for information on and photos of Lou Scheper and Florence Henri,
to Eva Müller, Landeszentrale für politische Bildung, Thüringen for her long term support for the *Bauhaus Women* project,
to the Thüringer Ministerium für Wissenschaft, Forschung und Kunst, Bereich Literaturförderung, for a small author scholarship that made the preliminary work for this book possible,
to Elke Eckert, Dokumentenarchiv im BHA Berlin, for her experienced and helpful input on archive material,
to the Archive of v. Bodelschwinghschen Anstalten for the generous loan of picture material on Benita Otte,
to Monika Dittmar, Ofen- und Keramikmuseum Velten, for generous access to text and picture material on Margarete Heymann-Loebenstein-Marks.

Ulrike Müller

BAUHAUS WOMEN

Art • Handicraft • Design

With the collaboration of Ingrid Radewaldt
and Sandra Kemker

Flammarion

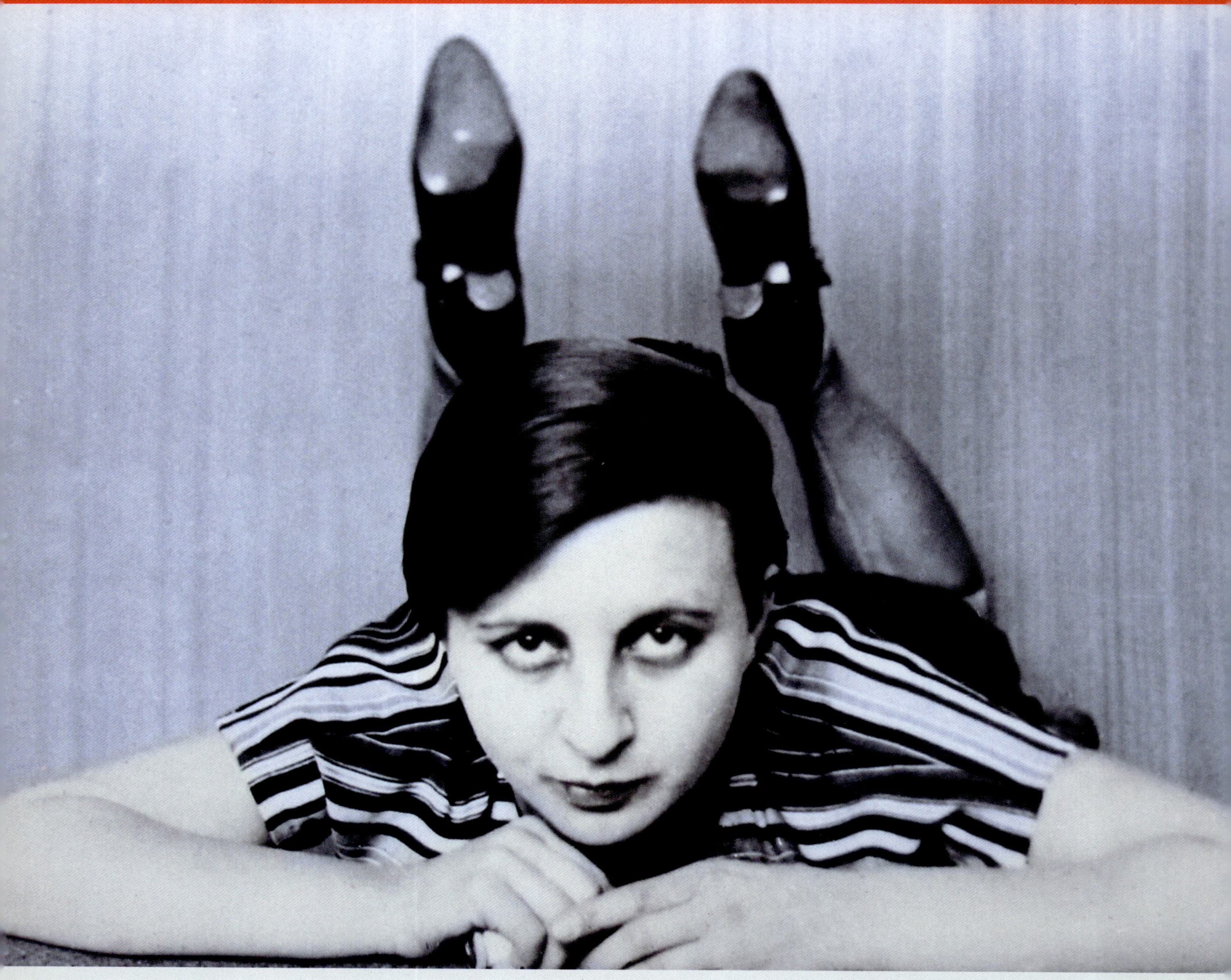

Contents

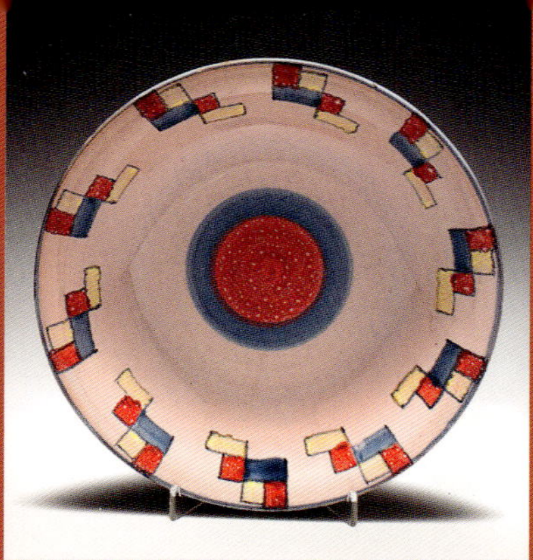

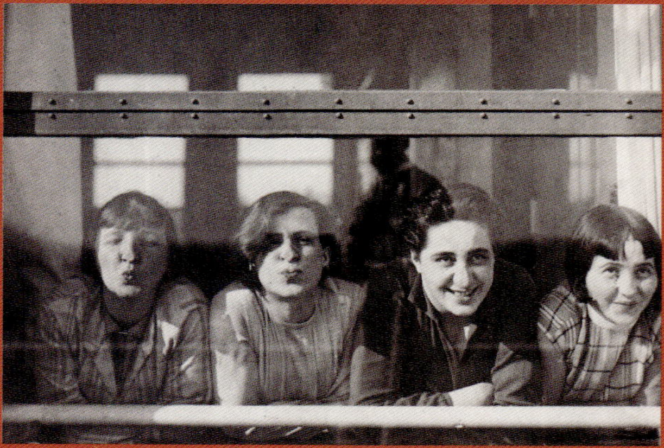

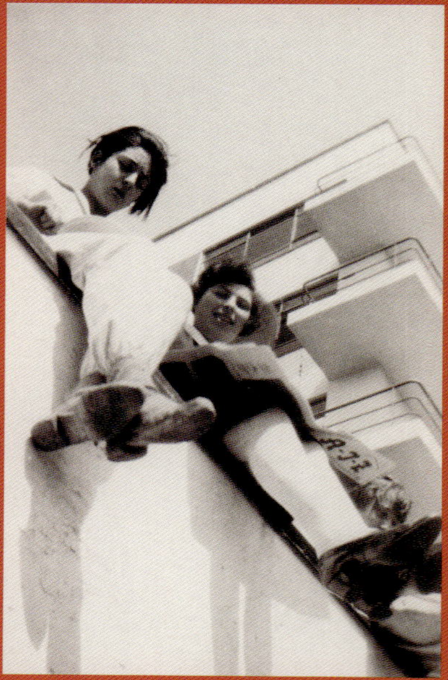

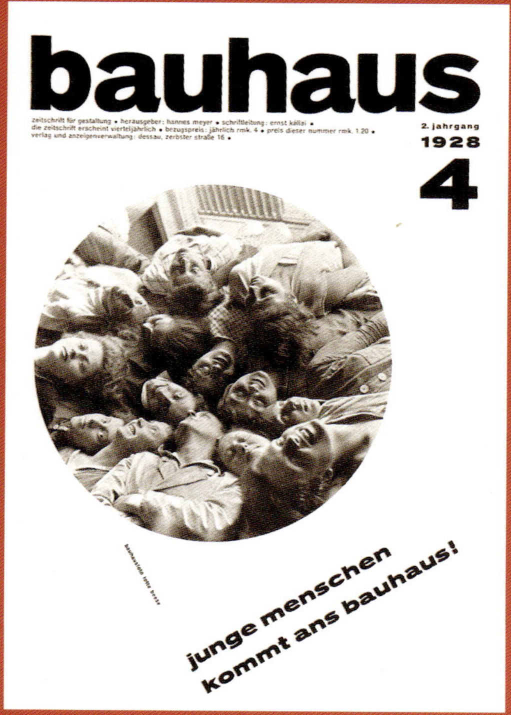

bauhaus

zeitschrift für gestaltung • herausgeber: hannes meyer • schriftleitung: ernst kállai •
die zeitschrift erscheint vierteljährlich • bezugspreis: jährlich rmk. 4 • preis dieser nummer rmk. 1.20 •
verlag und anzeigenverwaltung: dessau, zerbster straße 16 •

2. jahrgang
1928
4

junge menschen
kommt ans bauhaus!

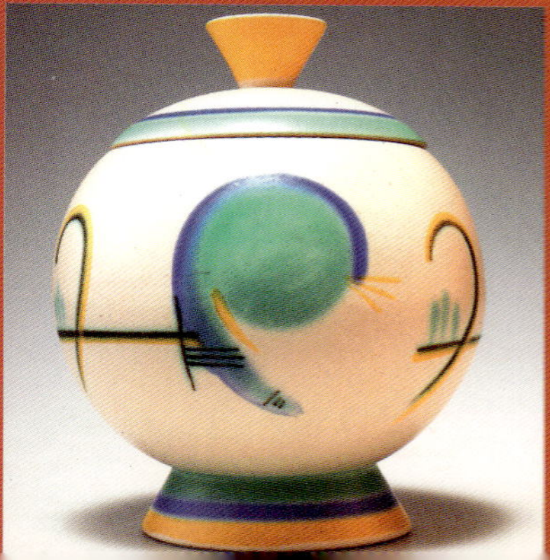

Early Modernism, the Bauhaus, and Bauhaus Women

The history of painting, sculpture, architecture, photography, craft, and design in the first third of the twentieth century is also the story of female awakenings in art. When the State Bauhaus opened its doors to both male and female applicants in 1919, there were more female than male applicants for the first semester. Things were not always made easy for these women, and in retrospect, one can attribute much of the innovative potential of the Bauhaus to them.

This book presents a range of important women—teachers, designers, artists—who taught or studied at the Bauhaus, or who, as Bauhaus masters' wives, developed their own profiles and carried the ideas and works of the Bauhaus forth into the world. Their achievements and life-stories are part of the art-historical process of early Modernism, which had flourished up to World War I, achieved a second high point in the 1920s, and came to a premature, violent end in Germany because of National Socialism.

The artistic avant-garde developed out of opposition to the frosty, "stiff-upper-lip", authoritarian climate in the German Empire at the beginning of the 1920s. They wanted to reform life completely in favor of reality, simplicity, naturalness, and wholeness. The young Turks shook up the prudery, conventions, bureaucratic order, and class barriers of the Empire. Ties were left unknotted, corsets unhooked and discarded, the body was rediscovered at sunrise, sensually and reflectively, naked in the park, in gymnastic exercises, close to the cosmos, in celebration. The different sexes and cultures danced toward each other, old and new art forms from painting to music to photography or interpretive dance formed unusual alliances. A new perception of time came with this new period. Machines, automobiles, and railways increased the speed of life in the cities. Devices like slow-motion, flashbacks, slowness, and simultaneousness were increasingly used in film and literature. Women discovered their enjoyment of self-portrayal and self-representation. The stage became a rehearsal room for experimenting with the *Gesamtkunstwerk*. The new art got rid of the decorative and strived to understand reality. Design elements for the abstraction of reality were taken from basic tones, basic shapes, and basic colors towards "the spiritual in art" (Kandinsky). The zeitgeist of many reform movements, which were taking place simultaneously, and spanning countries, was reflected in developments in the teaching of art and music. In Geneva in 1902, the Swiss musician Émile Jacques-Delcroze introduced his concept of rhythmic education, from which the Berlin singer and music teacher Gertud Grunow, among others, developed her practical theory of the relationship between sound, color, and movement. From 1920 on, she was the only woman to teach as a form master at the Weimar Bauhaus. As a result of the Secession movement, art school reforms, and the new understanding of form at the Wiener Werkstätte, Vienna became an important center of artistic innovation

• *Margarete Heymann-Loebenstein-Marks, Bowl, c. 1930; Four young women from the weaving workshop; Bauhaus women, 1930–31; Title page of* Bauhaus *magazine, 1928; Margarete Heymann-Loebenstein-Marks, Lidded jar, c. 1930.*

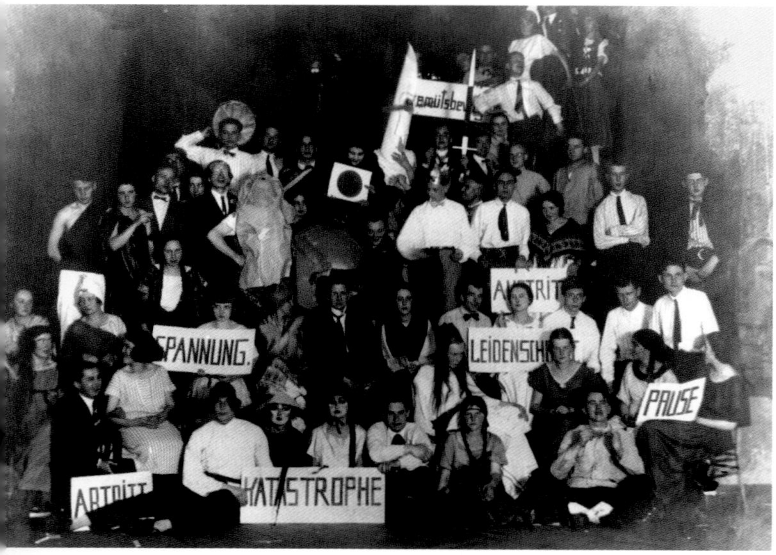

in the first decade of the twentieth century, alongside cities such as Berlin, Dresden, and Munich.

The educational reformers included Franz Ciszek and Johannes Itten. Itten was later to become a Bauhaus teacher, and founded an art school with the new educational concept of free learning in Vienna in 1917. Apart from a few exceptions, women did not have access to study art at academies in the nineteenth century. They could only take private lessons and had to pay much more for these lessons than men. The Grossherzogliche Sächsische Kunstgewerbeschule (Grand Ducal Saxon School of Arts and Crafts) in Weimar was among the few academies which accepted female students before the founding of the Weimar Republic. In the winter semester 1912–13 there were fifty-five women registered and ninety-nine men. These were not only aristocratic ladies who sketched in the countryside, but numbered among them the avant-garde artist Ella Bergmann-Michel, who experimented with constructivist and Dadaist collages well before Schwitters.

At the end of the nineteenth century there were more places for women in art schools than in academies. This was due above all to economic reasons. Art was up-and-coming and due to the further development of industry, employees were sought. A window was opened to the calls from women's rights movements and groups for school and vocational education for women, with the help of which women had been kept away from universities and academies until 1919. The expression "decorative artist" or "decorative arts" apart from its neutral, objective meaning was applied, as demonstrated by the art historian Magdalena Droste, in a pejorative, segregating manner to mean "female" (superficial or dilettante) Even Bauhaus director Gropius warned of "decorative arts dilettantism." The first crafts training school for women was geared towards amateur, high-ranking daughters and governesses. The Lette-Verein (1865) became one of the most important training institutions, which, apart from painting, sculpture, and drawing, offered subjects such as "illumination of cards and pictures" and pattern sketching, and also soon founded an embroidery school. This association cleverly and successfully oriented its syllabus according to the prevailing demands of the labor market. Since drawing had become a compulsory school subject in Prussia in 1872, preparation courses for the examination to become a drawing teacher were also offered. Then, in 1890, the Lette-Verein founded a photographic training institute for women. The number of craft schools that accepted women is estimated to have been about sixty in 1910. Twelve of these were exclusively reserved for women or were founded for women. In a further twenty-three schools, access for women was subject to special conditions of acceptance, four allowed women only probationary access or access on a trial basis, ten separated female students into "Ladies Departments"; in six, women were given separate classes for life studies. The remainder tended towards mixed instruction. The Reimann School in Berlin, founded in 1902, was one of the most progressive training schools. Albert and Klara Reimann's practical, educational reform, a synthesis of craft and art, demonstrated a relationship with the Bauhaus, which was still another seventeen years away. A class for interior design was established there in 1912.

• *Bauhaus party at a country guest house, Ilmschlößchen, near Weimar, June 1924.*

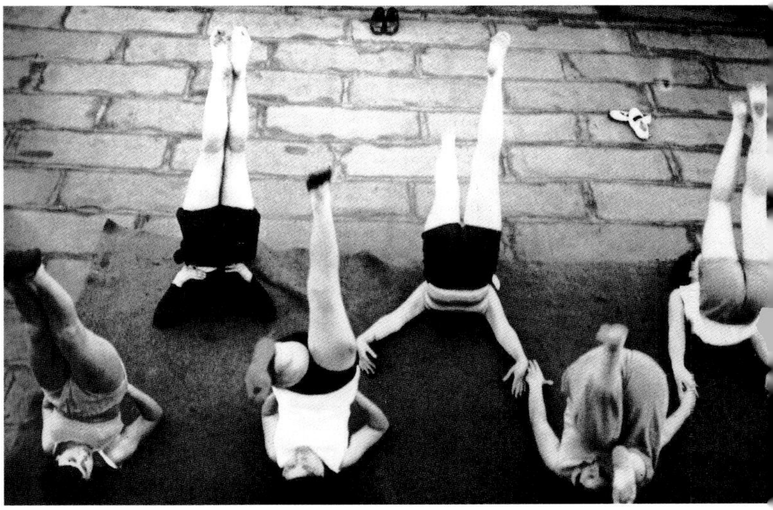

Important impetuses for the concept of interaction between art and crafts, implemented at progressive schools and workshops, came from the English Arts and Crafts movement, which had in the last third of the nineteenth century declared war on academic art on the one hand, and on mass-production of crafts on the other, and which aspired to a synthesis between painting, architecture, and crafts. The most famous representative of this movement was William Morris, a country-house builder and wallpaper designer who countered the established school of thought by which textile work was dismissed as "mere" female activity. The Arts and Crafts movement inspired Richard Riemerschmid, Henry van de Velde, and Josef Hoffmann, among others, and female designers in their sphere such as Else Unger, Else Oppler, and Lilly Reich. Architect and practical theorist Hermann Muthesius and his wife, the musician, Anna Muthesius were important agents in promoting the English reforms in Germany. In contrast to Morris, the Deutscher Werkbund (German Work Federation) founded in Munich in 1907 by Muthesius among others, aimed at overcoming the contrast between art and mass production. *Sachlichkeit* (which was known as *Neue Sachlichkeit* (New Objectivity) after World War I) and functionality were central ideas of these new aspirations. In 1920 the first woman interior designer, and later Bauhaus teacher Lilly Reich, was elected to the board of directors of the Werkbund.

Walter Gropius incorporated the Werkbund's fundamental requirements into his program for founding the Bauhaus. Although his training regulations were very modern for the time, they were based on medieval crafts regulations, a tradition with deeply patriarchal structures: the community of pupils (apprentices) and teachers (masters) united under the roof of the Bauhaus (derived from the medieval *Bauhütte* (building shed).

At the beginning of the Weimar Republic, women gained the franchise and academic freedom. When Walter Gropius opened the State Bauhaus in Weimar in 1919, he boldly announced in the program: "any respectable person whose talent and previous education is deemed suitable by the Masters' Council may be accepted as an apprentice at the Bauhaus, irrespective of age or sex." The designated gender-specific tuition fee regulation, according to which gentlemen were to pay 150 marks and ladies 180 marks, was no longer applicable in the provisional budget for 1919–20. Most young women, who began their studies at the Weimar Bauhaus in 1919, had already completed a training course in a craft or educational subject. Eighty-four female and seventy-nine male applicants registered at the Bauhaus in the summer semester of 1919, attracted by the visionary character of the school and the possibility of acquiring a concrete occupation. In his first speech, Gropius proclaimed: "No difference between the beautiful and the strong sex. Absolute equality but also absolutely equal obligation to the work of all craftsmen."

Ideas of gender which were presented in modern Bauhaus teaching by most of the masters were generally consistent with the ideas of the late Enlightenmement as represented by Rousseau and further reinforced by Nietzsche on the threshold of modernism: man was the intelligent bearer of culture; woman a creature of nature defined by feeling. As the art historian Anna Baumhoff

• *Students during floor exercises on the roof of the Preller House in Dessau, c. 1930.*

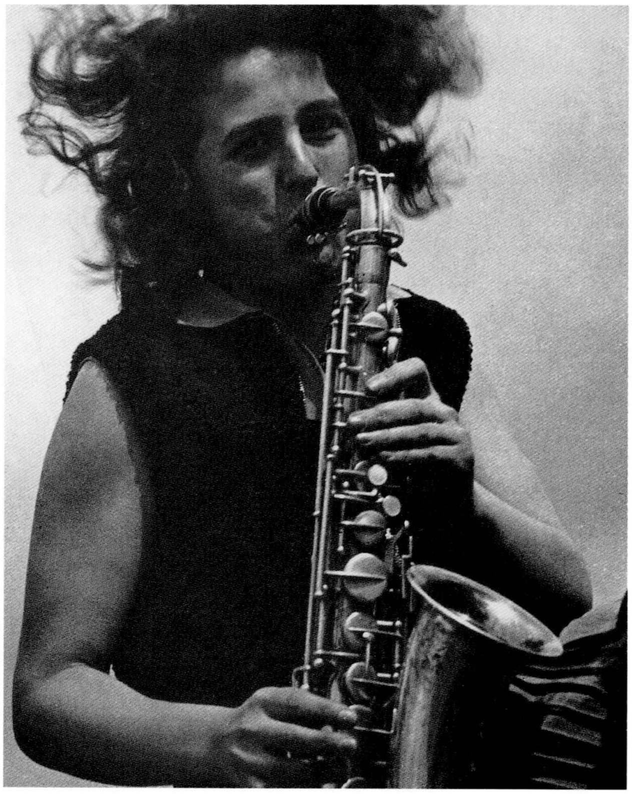

has demonstrated in detail, the ideas of the Bauhaus ranged from the allocation of the notions of the triangle, the color red, and the intellect to masculinity and the square, blue, and matter to femininity (Gropius), to the assertion that women are born with the capacity to see two-dimensionally and they should therefore work with surfaces (Itten), or the conviction that genius is masculine (Klee), and creativity is generally identifiable with masculinity (Schlemmer, Kandinsky). Gropius feared early on that the large number of women would harm the school's reputation and recommended not to undertake "any more unnecessary experiments," and made the recommendation that "immediately following acceptance, an exact selection be made, above all among those of the more strongly represented female sex." Gerhard Marcks, ceramics form master, argued clearly in favor of "accepting as few women as possible in the pottery workshop, in both their interest and in the interest of the workshop." Carl Zaubitzer, head of graphic printing, likewise thought it better "for the future, to keep the female sex away from the printshop." The gifted artist Johanna Hummel was successfully ousted from the metal workshop following her application by being forbidden to sell her works herself, although it was obvious that she needed the income to live on. It was clear that the masters feared that female students would take valuable employment away from their male counterparts. Some women nevertheless succeeded in achieving positions in these male domains, for example, Dörte Helm and Lou Scheper in mural painting, although the workshop master Carl Schlemmer fundamentally rejected female participation in architectural projects. His famous brother Oskar coined the following saying in Dessau: "Where there is wool, there is a woman who weaves, if only to kill time." His mockery hit upon the core of the prejudices which had given rise, in Weimar, to weaving being declared a "women's class" as of 1920. As handweaving was generally classed as a craft and took last place in the hierarchy of art and craft, it seemed logically consistent that this workshop be led by a woman. The Masters' Council hoped in vain that the women's class would solve the "female problem." The weaving workshop soon became one of the most productive workshops and also had such commercial success that it took on a representative character for the entire Bauhaus. Again the "good reputation" of the school was in danger.

The majority of Bauhaus women, even exceptional artists such as Gunta Stölzl, did not question the traditional female image but others, like Dörte Helm, contradicted it in their actions. Life events and new beginnings such as separations, divorces, multiple marriages, conscious decisions to live alone or without men, mark the female struggle for independence as women and as artists. Marianne Brandt and Florence Henri examined the subject of the "New Woman" and the female image of their time in their photographic works. Grete Stern and Ellen Auerbach investigated a new equal artistic relationship

• *The American Bauhaus student Lotte Gerson with saxophone, the only woman to have played in the Bauhaus band, c. 1929.*

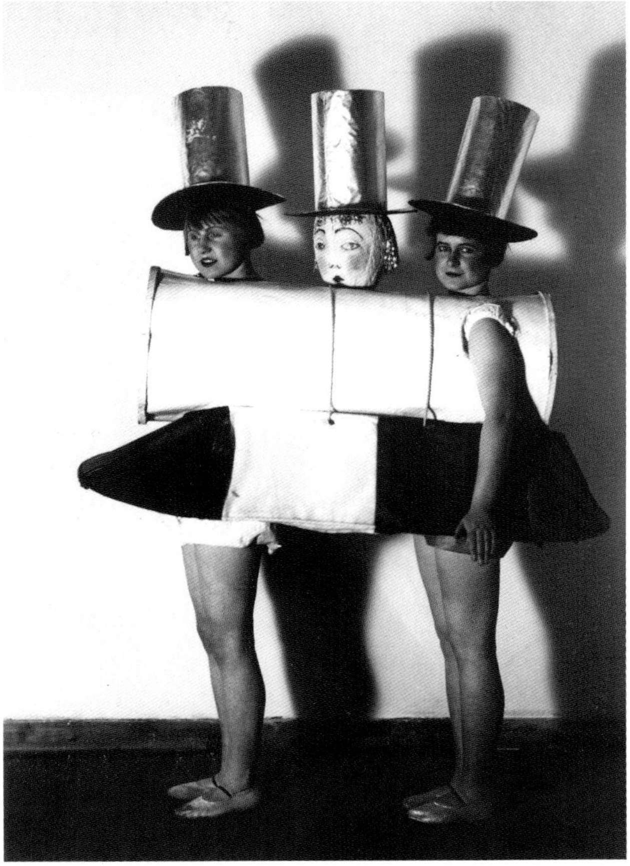

as the photographic couple "ringl + pit." In her biographical fragment, *Frau des 20. Jahrhunderts* (Twentieth-Century Woman), Lucia Moholy in retrospect criticized the "cult of the master" and the resulting inferior evaluation of female achievements in the Bauhaus, especially those of the female masters: "It would not be absurd, if someone were resolved to do so, to write about the role of the masters' wives, those who had no official status and yet played a decisive role in the aftermath of the Bauhaus . . . too much has been written about the masters themselves to have to discuss them here."

The fact that the majority of female students and teachers were to be found in the handweaving area, appears at first, to be in accordance with the training structure and the traditional female image. However, the ideas and innovations which they unleashed there were anything but traditional. They led to a surge in development in industrial design and to an artistic re-evaluation of textile art. Photography was the second-largest field involving women at the Bauhaus. Undeterred by centuries-old patriarchal baggage, this modern medium offered artistically ambitious women an experimental field in which to examine themselves and their time, as well as a concrete earning potential.

Among the artists Gropius was able to win over for the school, some played a great role as instigators, mentors, and artistic role models for the female students, irrespective of their consistently antiquated image of women. These numbered Itten and, above all, Klee, but also Schlemmer, Moholy-Nagy, Kandinsky, and later Walter Petermans. The ideas of the youth and lifestyle reform movements connected to art and everyday life, communal experience and at the same time individual artistic freedom in form and design, which played a central role in the early Bauhaus in its "romantic phase," promoted a free exchange between teachers and students, be they male or female, which went beyond all prejudices and reservations, and developed its creative dynamic at the numerous Bauhaus parties in particular.

Added to this, the catastrophic financial situation of many of the students promoted social solidarity through common facilities such as the Bauhaus canteen, a communal garden for cultivating vegetables, and stalls at the Christmas market. The content and structure of training changed at the Bauhaus in Dessau. What Gropius had already begun in the previous years in Weimar became part of the curriculum in Dessau from 1925: "Art and technology, a new entity!" Cooperation with industry was promoted, designing for mass production was professionalized. Improvization and spontaneity gave way to systematic teaching; instead of religiously utopian life plans, the sciences and technology gained importance, and a sober attitude was established. There was no longer a ceramics workshop.

• *"New Objectivity" party; joint party with the Bauhaus and the* Kunstgewerbeschule Halle *at Schloß Giebichenstein, 1925.*

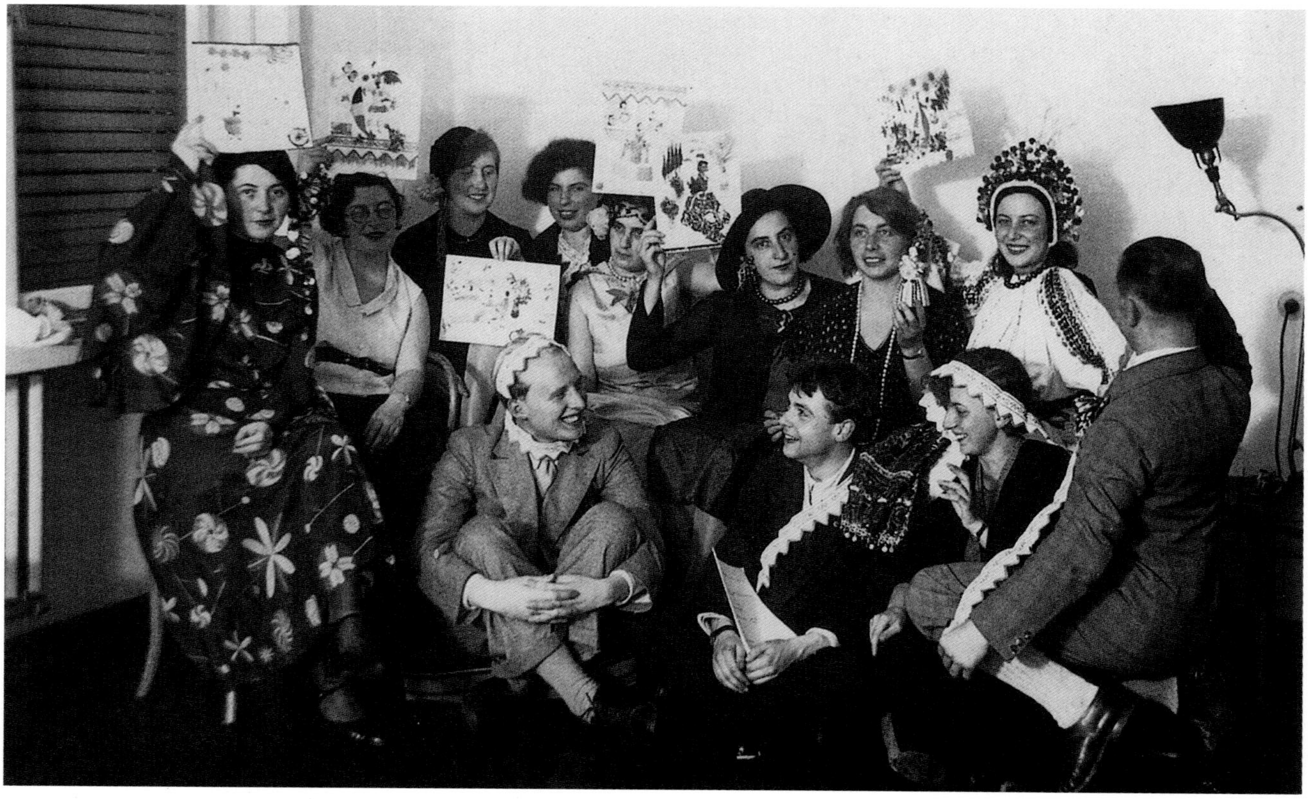

Women who did not wish to participate in the dogmatic journey from artwork to product left the Bauhaus. Some moved to the nearby college of applied arts at Schloß Giebichenstein in Halle. Benita Otte became leader of the weaving workshop; Marguerite Friedlaender led the ceramics workshop. Along with the Bauhaus, this college was considered to be one of the most progressive German training institutes in its field in the 1920s, with a romantically inclined but also industry-oriented avant-garde. The schools maintained strong contact with each other.

The dual model of form master and workshop master was also disposed with in Dessau.

"Young masters," former first-generation students, such as Josef Albers, Hinnerk Scheper, Marcel Breuer, and Gunta Stölzl now led the new workshops; "old masters" such as Klee and Kandinsky additionally offered free artistic courses. However, the lack of a sense of duty among the established elders, and the young men's endeavors to increase their own profiles changed the social climate. Ise Gropius mentions expectations of entitlement and egocentrism among the young masters.

The Bauhaus women, with few exceptions, such as Grete Reichardt and Lilly Reich, behaved in a less career-conscious manner than the men. In accordance with their socialization, they had internalized the collective idea in a far stronger way, and paid less attention to their own work. The disappearance of artistic performance in favor of the big picture was especially evident among the wives of the masters. Gifted students also achieved fewer high positions at the Bauhaus and in the subsequent period, and became less well-known. Marianne Brandt, who ran the metal workshop and developed prototypes for industry with great success, was bullied out of the workshop by her younger fellow-student, Hin Bredendiek. He then took on a professorship in Chicago during the Nazi period. She disappeared into domestic "emigration" at her parents' house in Chemnitz.

In time, the number of female students at the Bauhaus dropped. In the summer semester of 1922 there were fifty-two women and ninety-five men; in the winter semester 1924–25, thirty-four women and sixty-eight men. This can certainly be attributed to the Bauhaus's

• *Celebrating the first Bauhaus diplomas in the weaving workshop, 1929.*

move away from crafts and towards technical experiments. However, some of the women, among them Alma Buscher, Marianne Brandt, Otti Berger, and Anni Albers, were delighted to follow the new path and were very successful with their industrial prototypes. Under the directorship of Swiss architect Hannes Meyer, who pushed through the rejection of an artistic elite, and had models made at the school for "standard products" that many classes of the population could afford, a great many new women came to the Bauhaus, among them many from Eastern Europe. The number of foreign female students was over twenty-five percent by the end of the 1920s.

The focus on architecture and the dismantling of the workshop system under the authoritarian leadership of Mies van der Rohe finally led to a further drop in female student numbers. In the winter semester of 1932–33 there were only twenty-five women and ninety men at the Bauhaus in Berlin. In 1933 a professional disqualification was issued against many female teachers at the Bauhaus. They were pursued by the National Socialists because they were of Jewish descent, had been politically active—the Bauhaus had a reputation for this—came from enemy countries, or their works were considered to be "degenerate art." There were also, however, students who came to an agreement with the National Socialists during their studies and libelled their fellow students. Still others took part in important Nazi projects following the seizure of power in order to further their own careers. Six women were murdered in concentration camps, including Friedl Dicker and Otti Berger. Alma Buscher was killed in bombing. Many, including Marianne Brandt, Gertrud Arndt, and Ilse Fehling, survived under difficult conditions in Germany. A great number of artists such as Margarete Heymann-Loebenstein-Marks, Margaret Leischner, Lucia Moholy, and Grete Stern were able to travel to England. Further emigration destinations were Switzerland, Holland, France, Palestine, Mexico, Argentina, South Africa, and the United States. The Bauhaus was introduced to these host countries not only by men such as Paul Citroën, Josef Albers, Walter Gropius, László Moholy-Nagy, and Herbert Bayer, but also by women. Gunta Stölzl ran a handweaving workshop in Switzerland; Anni Albers took on a teaching position at the Black Mountain College, North Carolina in 1933; Marli Ehrmann became head of the textile department at Moholy-Nagy's School of Design in Chicago in 1939. Marguerite Friedlaender was one of the founders of the art center, Pond Farm, near San Francisco. Ise and Walter Gropius were a point of contact for the scattered emigrant community after World War II. They established relief operations for those who had survived National Socialism in Germany. The idea of setting up an archive came early and they began collecting Bauhaus documents and works. The Busch-Reisinger-Museum at Harvard University in Cambridge, Massachusetts, became home to a comprehensive Bauhaus collection. In Germany, Bauhaus ideas and methods were adopted again and continued after the war at the Hochschule für angewandte Kunst (College of Applied Arts) in Berlin-Weißensee and the Hochschule für Gestaltung (College of Design) in Ulm, among others.

ULRIKE MÜLLER, WEIMAR FEBRUARY 2009

Between Craft Tradition, Educational Reformism, and Free Art

Teachers and Students of the First Generation

Among the approximately forty-five Bauhaus teachers in Weimar and the thirty-five in Dessau, there were in each case six women, including teachers. A mere three of these women held leading positions in the weaving workshop during the entire Bauhaus period. The teachers of the first generation were Helene Börner, workshop master in Weimar; Gunta Stölzl, a teacher of the second generation as young master in Dessau; and Lilly Reich, externally appointed head of weaving and development in Dessau and Berlin. Lilly Reich was, among twelve male colleagues, the only woman in Berlin. Production contracts were made with students such as Anny Wottitz, Marianne Brandt, Anni Albers, Otti Berger, and Margaret Leischner. They gave professional training or took on provisional administrative roles mostly on the basis of badly paid, temporary positions.

Bauhaus founder Walter Gropius had based his new teaching concept on the structure and vocabulary of medieval craft regulations, which were traditionally deeply patriarchal. Legacy, education, authority as well as job-satisfaction, money, and fame through their own work were the preserve of men. Women were not present in the hierarchy of apprentice, journeyman, and master. "Frau Meisterin" as a rule meant the master's wife. The restrictions on women at the various academies were later as great as those in artisan fields. With a few exceptions, no women were accepted as art students until the early twentieth century. The fact that Ida Kerkovius was allowed to teach at the Stuttgart Academy from 1911 was a great exception.

From the end of the nineteenth century, industrialization had brought the development of a new area of training, in which more women learned, taught, and led in arts and crafts. Women could receive short occupational training courses in textiles, decoration, in the printshop, bookbinding, and photography as well as drawing, and could also teach in these subjects. When the Belgian architect van de Velde founded the Kunstgewerbliche Seminar (Craft Seminar) in Weimar in 1905, he included training for women. The metal and jewelry designers Erica von Scheel, Dora Wibira, and Dorothea Seeligmüller taught metalwork and enamelwork, and the study of color and ornamentation from 1906 to 1915; the weavers Li Thorn and Helene Börner taught various classes in the textile field for over ten years.

What were the conditions under which the first Bauhaus women taught? Gropius's grandiose if half-hearted promise of equal rights and duties for both sexes remained theoretical in the teaching field. Only male artists were appointed to the position of form master. Dora Wibiral received a lectureship in lettering in the

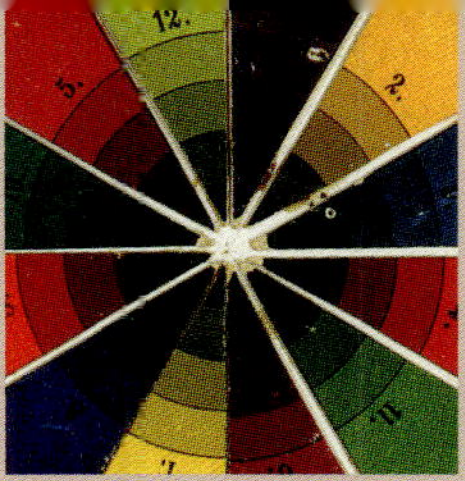

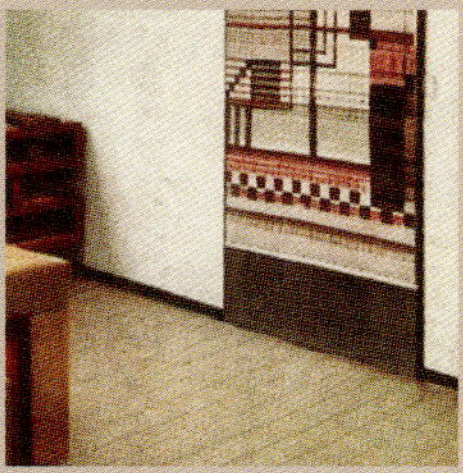

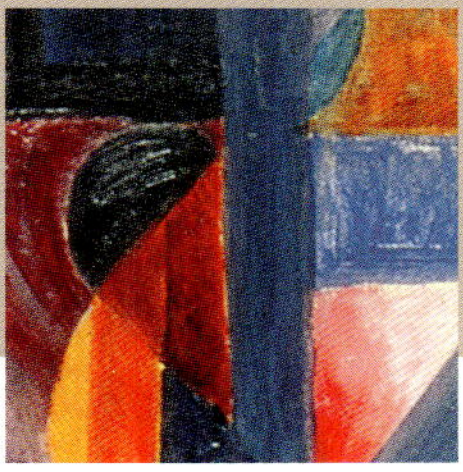

winter semester of 1919–20 which was not renewed. Helene Börner, the only Bauhaus workshop master remained in the weaving shop, which had been declared a women's domain, until the school moved to Dessau. Very little is known about her, which is why we will introduce her in this chapter. She was rejected by most of the female students because, as a former craft teacher, she embodied traditions that younger students, such as Anni Albers, had rejected in their mothers' generation. They no longer wanted cross-stitch blankets but craved artistic challenges. By contrast, music and dance teacher Gertrude Grunow, who at fifty was almost the same age, was well accepted. She propounded her own theory and gave modern holistic and experimental classes. Her teaching influenced the early Bauhaus curriculum. She was, however, fobbed off with a lectureship although she carried out the duties of a form master. When in 1923 a master's position finally came vacant, she was fired. In Dessau there was to be no more self-exploration or exploration of the senses, but concrete, physical toughening-up. The young Karla Grosch was hired as physical education teacher for this purpose. Something else was missing in Dessau, which the Weimar Bauhaus had provided: garden design. Thekla Mulert, who was officially hired as a gardener, not only cared for the cultivation of the Bauhaus gardens but also taught hungry students to grow vegetables. Many students of the first generation were, when they arrived, of similar age to their teachers. A large number of these women born in the 1870s and 1880s gave up their studies after one or two semesters. The majority of them had come to the Bauhaus from the Grand Ducal Saxon School of Arts and Crafts. The eldest of them, Marie Ullrich from Erfurt, was in the class of 1867. The students of a second group often came from far afield, and had already completed study programs, had artistic experience, and had consciously decided in favor of the Bauhaus. We will also discuss the eldest of this group, Ida Kerkovius. As this highly gifted painter began studying at the Bauhaus in in the second half of her life, she wanted to take new artistic paths and learn crafts from which she could make a living. Here she discovered a new artistic passion—weaving.

Finally, we should mention the oldest female Bauhaus student (statistically) of the second generation. In 1927 and 1928 Hamburg-born Leonore Maas, at nearly fifty years old, studied for two semesters at the Bauhaus in Dessau.

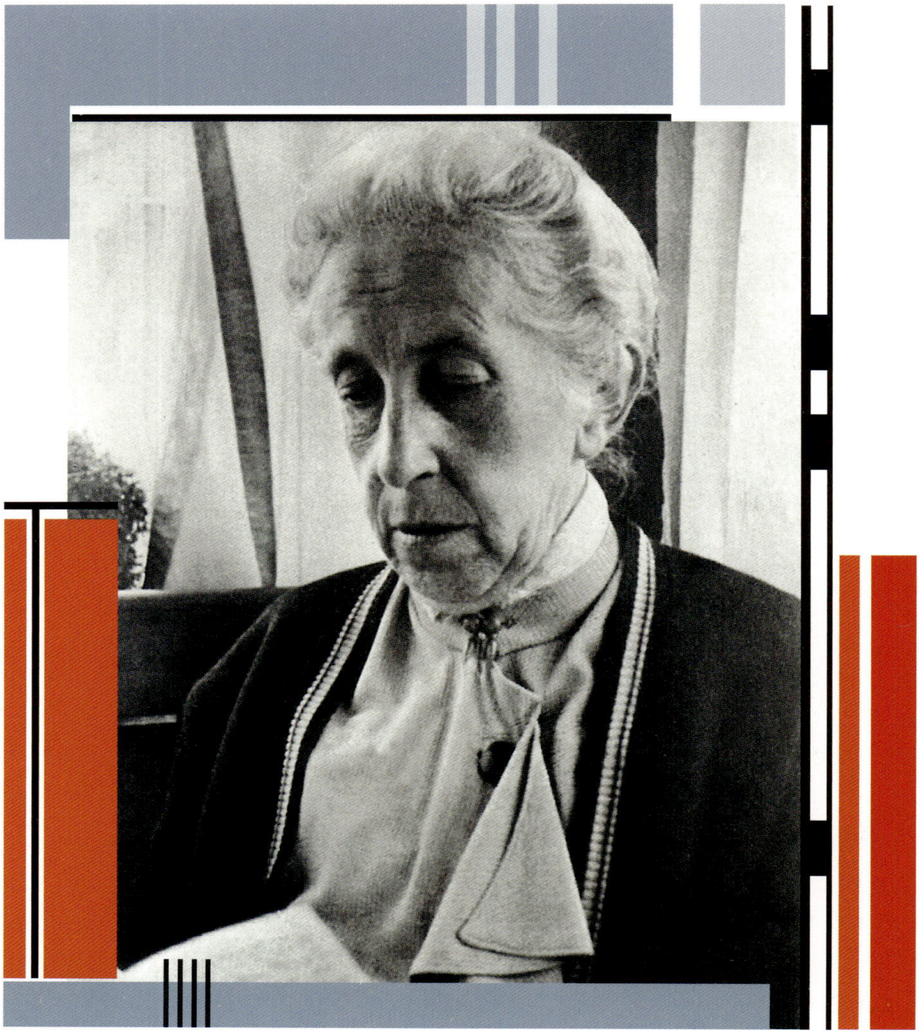

GERTRUD GRUNOW 1870–1944

"The inner peace for which people of our time are longing can be found. Our own misfortune is the misfortune of our fellow man. If we understand our own laws, we understand our fellow man in his. Peoples learn to understand, respect, and love other peoples. If we understand the laws of the macrocosm, we in turn understand the laws of the microcosm within ourselves, and both should be in harmony."

Gertrud Grunow in Der Gleichgewichtskreis *(The Circle of Balance)*

Gertrud Grunow was the only female form master at the Bauhaus. With her holistically oriented philosophical plan and the rhythmic musical exercises in her classes, she had a great influence on the early Bauhaus. Unfortunately, her contribution remains underestimated.

In the fall of 1919, the almost fifty-year-old teacher received a lectureship at the Weimar Bauhaus on recommendation of the preliminary course teacher Johannes Itten. He had heard her in Jena and was impressed by her teaching, the basic points of which concurred with his own ideas. Gertrud Grunow was, like Itten, of the opinion that only those who lived in harmony with the environment could be creatively active, that every person carried this harmony within them and could tap into it by way of exercises, transporting it from the unconscious to the conscious. In his concept of organic form, which he developed in 1916, and is described in his Organic Design Theory of 1923 which he implemented in his Bauhaus curriculum, didactics and the training structure of the Bauhaus aim at an organic development of the students, encompassing all their senses. The subject which Getrud Grunow was to teach, the Practical Harmony Course, soon renamed Practical Harmonizing Course, entailed training in perception and expression, which served to sensitize, reawaken, and reintegrate neglected sensory organs and thereby "heal" the individual.

Grunow's name appeared in connection with teaching at the Bauhaus for the first time in a letter from Itten to his friend, the Viennese musician Josef Matthias Hauer (1883–1959). Well before Schönberg, Hauer had already been experimenting since 1908 with composition using the twelve-tone method. His ideas connected insights from music theory with those of philosophy and mysticism. Itten had examined Hauer's model of the

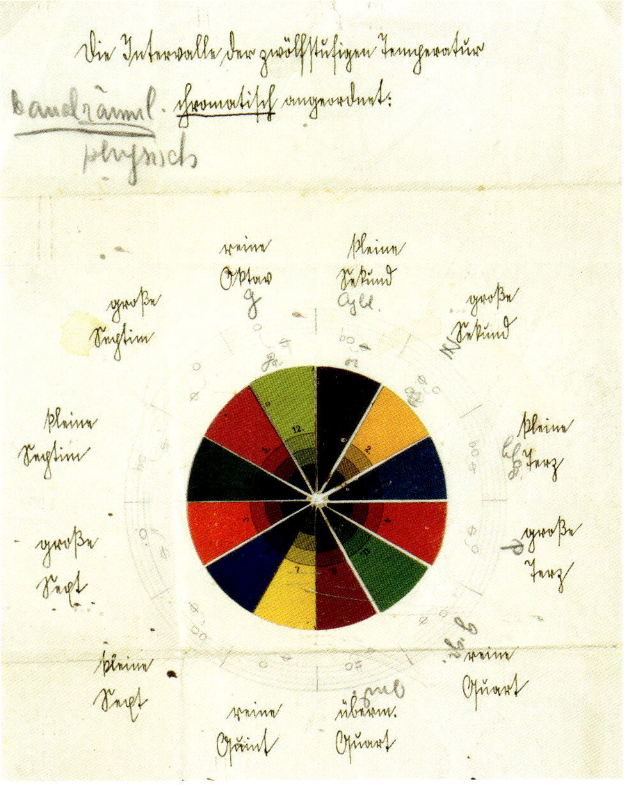

Klangfarbenkreis (circle of sound and color) when developing his preliminary course. He may have introduced the idea of harmonics to the Bauhaus. He wrote to Vienna from Weimar in November 1919: "A few weeks ago, a certain Fräulein Grunow came to me ... she wished to give a lecture at the Bauhaus on education through the eye and ear. After a much deliberation, I decided to encourage my students to take a course with her. I now attend her lectures myself and find many aspects very good."

Grunow had lived with her assistant Hildegard Heitmeyer since the spring of 1921, sharing the same house as Lily and Paul Klee. Klee had previously written in a letter: "Fräulein Grunow, Itten's guardian angel, will live above us, with a nice young lady, the guardian angel's assistant." From the summer semester of 1921, the harmonizing course was conceptually directly connected with the teachings of the preliminary course. The art historian Magdalena Droste points out that in the new version of the Bauhaus statutes from January 1921, published in June 1922, one of the greatest changes

• *Facing page: Gertrud Grunow, 1936.*

• *Above: Twelve-part color circle from Matthias Hauer, 1919.*

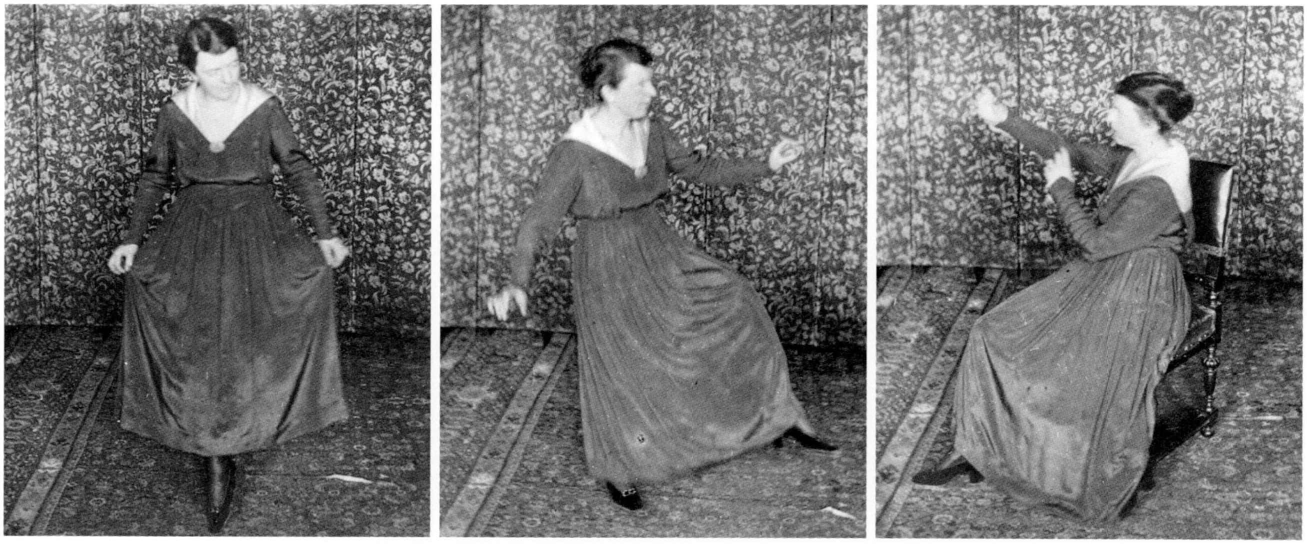

involved Gertrud Grunow, about whom was written: "For the whole duration of the training, a practical harmonizing class will be given, on the common basis of sound, color and form, the aim of which is to balance the physical and psychic characteristics of each." In 1923 Grunow's teaching was of central importance to the newly formulated Bauhaus program. Gropius even developed his definition of the character of its structure from her concept of harmonized powers. His description of the "Idea and Construction of the State Bauhaus" was supplemented by her contribution on the "Composition of Animate Form through Form, Color, and Tone." Her basic thesis was, "The highest law, upon which every system is built, is called balance. Thus, the ear plays a central role in perception, as it is connected with the organ of balance. The strong effect of sounds on people is due to balance."

She developed her practical theory from this position: "Every living force, every color, represents a system of laws, a sound." Hildegard Heitmeyer elucidated: "Gertrud Grunow ascertained that the movements which are set off in us when experiencing a sound or a color, arise from very particular nerved areas, and that sound and color have particular roots in the physical make-up of a person.... Twelve particular colors, in which the strength lives, to bring forth a simple, natural, balance in the entire human being. They represent the twelve tones of the chromatic scale." From this, Gertrud Grunow developed her course exercises.

Information about Gertrud Grunow's life and intellectual development is scarce. She was born in Berlin in 1870. She studied music in her hometown under Xaver and Phillip Scharwenka, and also with Hans Guido von Bülow and Giovanni Battista Lamperti, who came from the tradition of bel canto. Gertrude Grunow came to her musical experiments by freely using bel canto principles: absolute beauty, rounding and fullness in the single tone as well as in the flow of the melody. The Grunow expert Cornelius Steckner followed up the beginnings of her teaching: "More than likely during singing classes in 1908 she noticed ... at the piano the effect of certain single tones and colors, which promoted expression. At first she had the physiological effect on the larynx examined. The insights she gained in this period defined her life's course from there on."

Her specialist field comes under the heading of synesthetic musical education. Synesthetic means the melding of many sensual impressions. One sense unfolds via its relationship to another, to the whole, and vice versa. This pedagogic theory aims at a corresponding "systemic" balance between equal, different entities, e.g., between sound and color or intuition and intellect. Gertrude Grunow first introduced her teaching and visualization system in public lectures in Berlin and Jena in

• *Dancers in Gertrud Grunow's class, c. 1918.*

1919. She then not only taught all students at the Weimar Bauhaus but also masters such as Paul Klee and Johannes Itten until 1924.

How must Grunow's classes have looked? Her most important tool was her grand piano. Her admirer, the publishing director Eugen Diedrichs from Jena described one group class to his readers in the May 1920 issue of his magazine, *Die Tat*: "One shuts the eyes, a short period of inner closure follows. Then comes the instruction to imagine either a colored ball and then to feel it, prodding the fingers into it; or to imagine a note that is struck on the piano. In no time nearly all those present are moving. . . . A youth stands up, forcefully jabbing arm over arm in the air as if he were passing up slates on a building site, while his feet slide forcefully over the floor in a kind of dance rhythm. . . . One is . . . totally amazed at the expressive sign language of the girls' hands." At over ninety years old in an interview in 1980, the weaver and former Bauhaus student Else Mögelin remembered the tricky moments in class when those present received the unavoidable instruction from Gertrud Grunow: "And now, dance the color blue!"

At the end of every preliminary course, Getrud Grunow advised the students on their choice of artistic direction and on which corresponding workshop to take. She was a strict judge in the evaluations which she regularly made about the development of each and every student, but she also stood up for her students. She was obviously very well regarded. Her classes were considered interesting and original; her opinion as an expert was valued and held sway with the Masters' Council. The Bauhaus master Lothar Schreyer wrote in his memoirs in 1956: "She . . . appeared to us to be like one of the great intellectuals of antiquity. The intellectual connections between color, form, and tone arose to her from an inner clairvoyance. Thus, she brought people inwardly and outwardly into 'balance.'"

In the Bauhaus prospectus of June 1922 and in the official overview of the teaching body for the exhibition in 1923, Gertrud Grunow receives equal mention as a form master alongside men such Feininger, Itten, and Klee. Officially, she worked until the summer of 1923 as an assistant on a freelance basis. This situation in no way reflected the complexity and success of her work. She was the only woman among her mostly younger colleagues and the only "mere teacher" which, unfortunately, fitted with the prevailing gender-role cliché. Her work was about forming the personality. She did not publicize any of her own works of art and did not run a workshop. As an educational reformer, she was an asset; she was not, however, an aggressive proselytiser of modernism, and had no sense of cultivating her own image. Her silent disappearance from the faculty of the Weimar Bauhaus, and the long-standing disregard for her importance to the academic image of the Bauhaus, most probably result from this. The decisive arguments that Grunow's achievements were "not visibly" reflected in the students' performances made it easy for those who wished to abolish the harmonizing classes immediately following Itten's departure at Easter 1933. Although she was officially hired as a faculty member in June 1923, she was not given the status of the other form master, but was offered a separate contract as extraordinary teacher. She lost her most important colleague and strongest ally at the school when Itten left, with the result that in the fall of 1923 her classes suffered an unstoppable decline.

The minutes of the form masters' meeting of October 18, 1923 read succinctly: "It is generally to be observed that a definite, tangible effect of this course

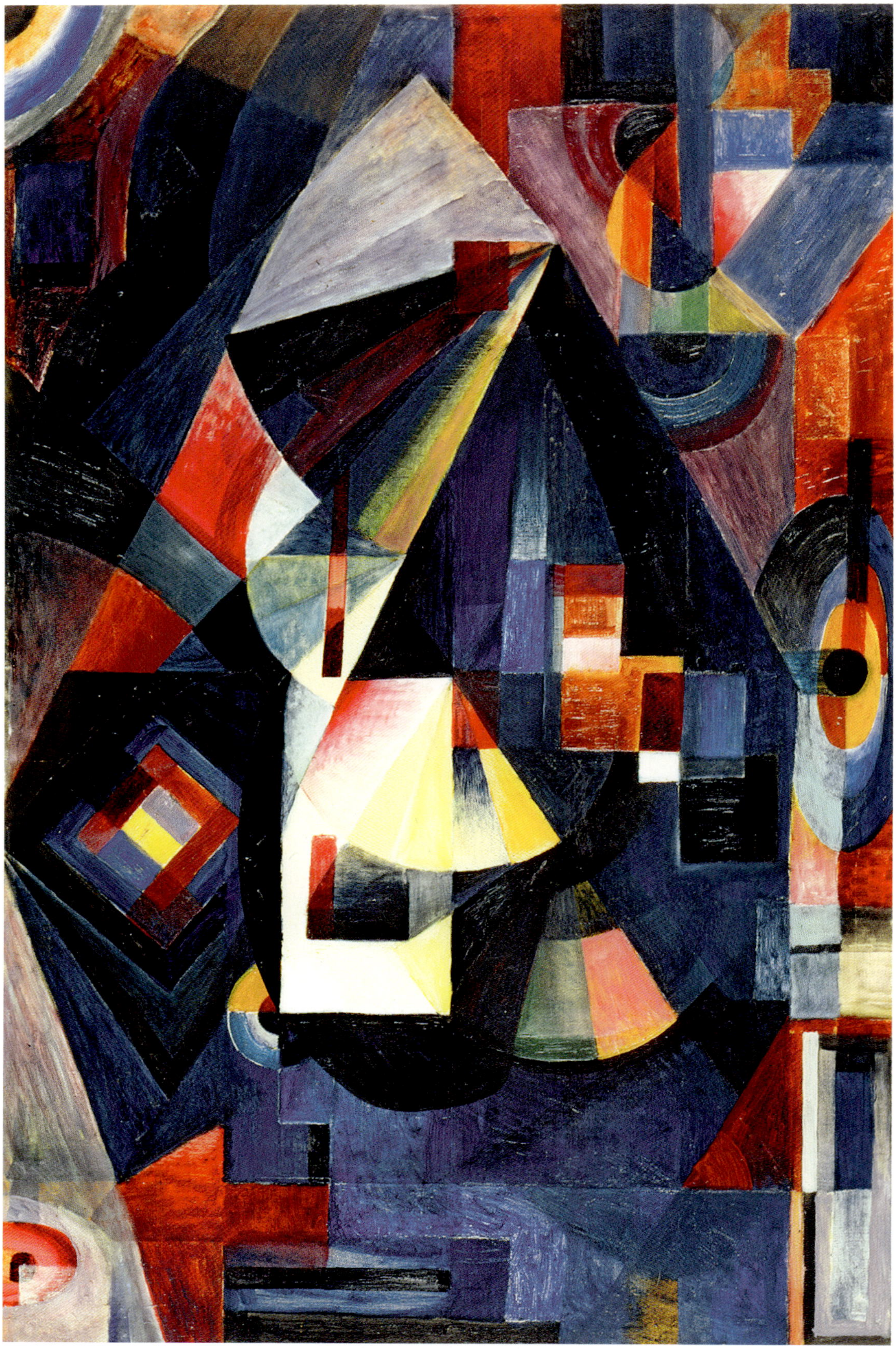

• Komposition in Blau (*Composition in Blue*), *painting by Johannes Itten, 1918.*

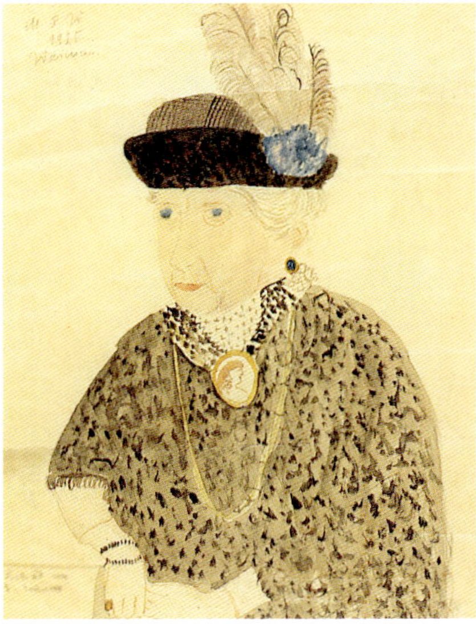

within the framework of Bauhaus aspirations has not been recognized over the past three years. The majority of masters (6:2) therefore considers perpetuation of the harmonizing course in the official syllabus unnecessary. Fräulein Grunow's discharge as of April 1, 1924 was therewith decided." Grunow gave her last course in the spring of 1924. Stecker writes that, above all at this time, the political and public attacks on Bauhaus opponents concentrated on her—was this also a reason for her dismissal?

Following the closure of the Weimar Bauhaus in 1925, Gertrud Grunow did not move to Dessau but took up a teaching post at the University of Hamburg until 1934. There she worked with Ernst Cassirer, Gertrud Bing, and William Stern as well as with Victor von Weizsäcker and the two young employees Wolfgang Müller-Kranefeld and Anni Adler until well into the 1930s.

Gertrud Grunow's teaching opened up connections to Gestalt psychology, Zen Buddhism, autogenic training, and to the principles of music therapy. The relationship between her teaching and the philosophical ideas of antiquity, as taught by Pythagoras, is also fascinating. His idea of a harmoniously oscillating cosmos, whose system reflects itself in the relationships between sound and numbers of tones to each other, is evident in the world-views of famous thinkers such as Hypatia of Alexandria (fourth century C.E.) and Hildegard von Bingen (11th century). Regarding the question of the basic meaning of tones in the micro- and macrocosmic systems, Gertrude Grunow's teaching shows clear parallels to Hildegard von Bingen.

When most scientists with whom Grunow had worked had to give up their positions after 1933, she lost her sphere of influence in Germany, and spent many months of the year teaching in England and Switzerland. She could no longer stay abroad during the war and returned to Germany in 1940. The last years of her life were wretched. She was caught in bombing in Düsseldorf in 1942. She moved to be with relatives in Leverkusen and died there two years later of a heart ailment on June 11, 1944, at the age of seventy-four.

In her last years in Leverkusen, Gertrud Grunow attempted to bring together her essays and ideas as her complete works. The final draft, however, was not completed. The surviving manuscripts made it to Weimar in 1996 and were published there in 2001. Hildegard Heitmeyer honored her teacher once more in an essay in 1967. She wrote: "Gertrud Grunow's life's work encompassed a great and rich research field on the elementary powers, sound, and color, which revealed totally new perspectives and systems that form the basis of our intellectual, emotional, and physical existence."

ULRIKE MÜLLER

• *Gertrud Grunow, drawing by Max Peiffer Watenphul, 1920.*

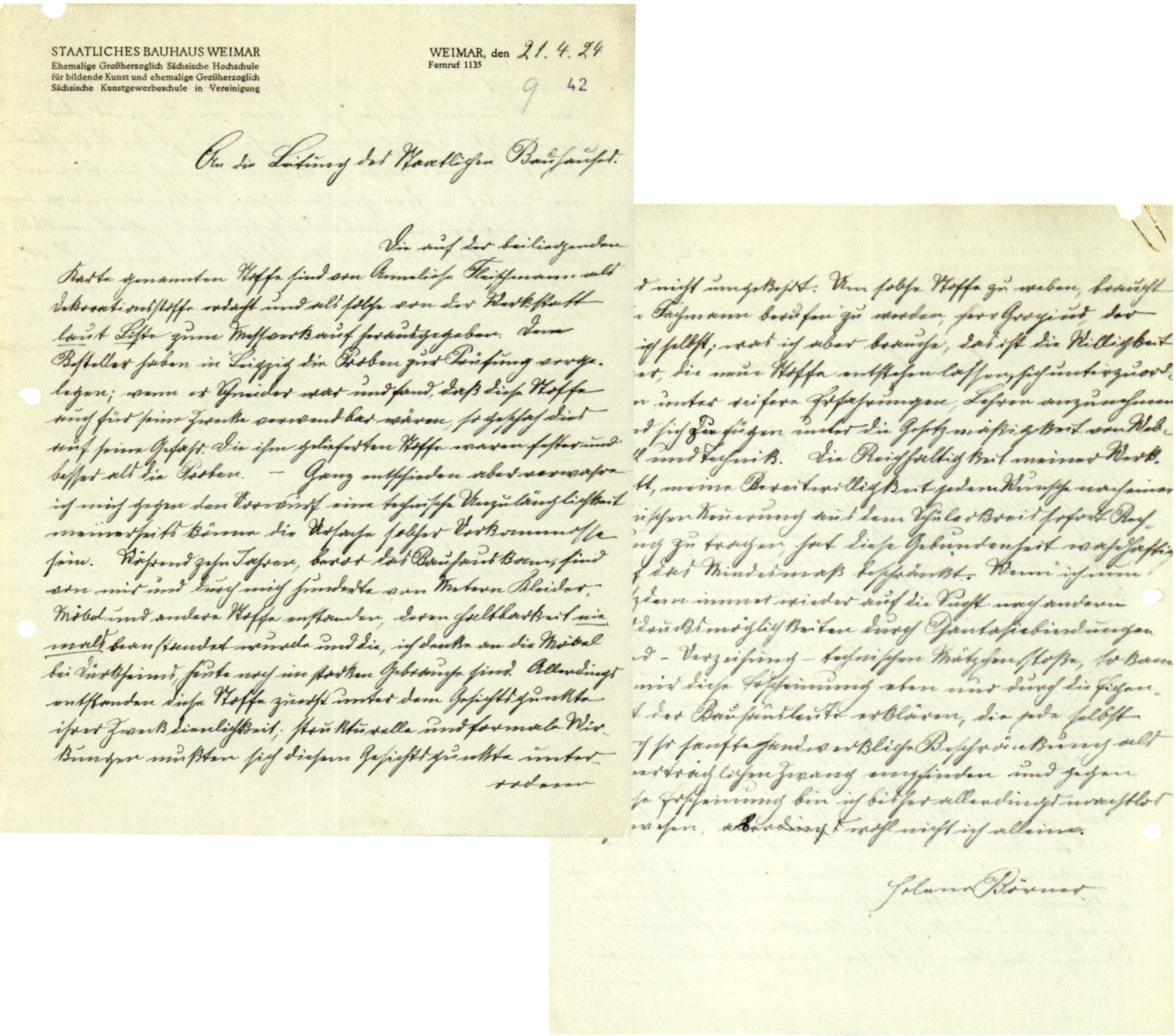
STAATLICHES BAUHAUS WEIMAR
Ehemalige Großherzoglich Sächsische Hochschule für bildende Kunst und ehemalige Großherzoglich Sächsische Kunstgewerbeschule in Vereinigung

WEIMAR, den 21. 4. 24
Fernruf 1135

HELENE BÖRNER c.1870–c.1938

"To the management of the State Bauhaus:
Over the course of ten years, before the advent of the Bauhaus, I produced and oversaw the production of hundreds of meters of clothes, pieces of furniture, and other materials whose durability was never questioned and . . . which even today are heavily used. . . . To weave such materials, no expert needs to be appointed, Herr Gropius, I myself am that person; what I do need, though, is the willingness of those who produce new fabrics to submit to more mature experiences, to accept instruction, and to show deference to the legitimacy of technology and of the loom."

Helene Börner, master of the weaving workshop, in a letter of April 21, 1924

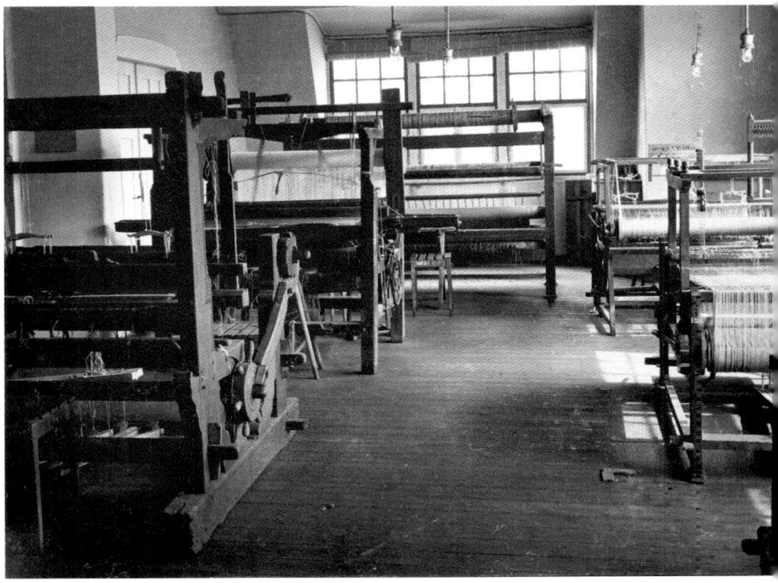

The only woman who belonged to the Weimar State Bauhaus from the first to the last day of its existence was workshop master Helene Börner, whose life and influence were intimately bound up with the history of the Bauhaus weaving workshop. Over the past years much has been documented and written about this period, so it is all the more surprising that so little is known about Helene Börner herself. Neither her exact date of birth nor the place of her birth (possibly Weimar) have come down to us, nor do we have any specific details concerning her professional training. She would presumably have trained as a needlework teacher, which was the usual education around 1900 for daughters from well-to-do homes, academic study not yet being open to women in Germany. In the Weimar directory of 1901 her profession is given as "seamstress."

The weaving workshop led by Helene Börner stood in a long Weimar tradition. As early as 1876 a group of dedicated Weimar ladies had founded a Verein für weibliche Handarbeit (Association for Women's Handicrafts) for women and girls of all social classes, which three years later was renamed Verein für weibliche Kunstindustrie (Association for Women's Art Industry). Its aim was to offer poorer women the opportunity to sell crafts that they had made themselves. Later the association changed its name yet again, this time to the Paulinenstiftung für gewebliches Hausfleiss (Pauline's Endowment for Commercial Home-Based Industry) after its patroness, the dowager Grand Duchess Pauline. In the report marking the twenty-five-year existence of the association reference is made to the fact that from 1899 the association was able to operate a hand-weaving workshop because the princess had donated five Swedish looms: these were the "building blocks" of the future Bauhaus weaving workshop. From 1905 till the middle of the 1920s Helene Börner ran the association. The Belgian architect Henry van de Velde had already approached her in 1904 presumably because he was seeking qualified teaching staff and equipment for his arts-and-crafts workshop and for the Kunstgewerbeschule (Craft School) that he planned to establish in Weimar under his own leadership. He offered the association an exchange: he would make available classrooms in the new school and shoulder the heating costs in exchange for the provision of lessons and appliances. The association put three looms at van de Velde's disposal; from October 1906 Helene Börner taught Swedish weaving and embroidery. In 1909 she also took over the running of the carpet workshop from its then head, the Swede Li Thorn, who left to get married. Looms and equipment remained in the possession of the Paulinenstiftung.

World War I forced the school to close in 1915, but the workshop in the rooms of the Kunstgewerbeschule (today the Van-de-Velde-Bau) remained fully equipped and Helene Börner continued to run it on a private basis. When van de Velde left Weimar in 1917, he suggested that Walter Gropius take over the headship of the school. In 1919 Gropius amazed the government by uniting the Kunstgewerbeschule with Weimar's fine arts college, the Kunsthochschule, to form the "State Bauhaus" under his own leadership. There was no official act of foundation,

• *Facing page: Helene Börner's letter to the management of the State Bauhaus of April 21, 1924.*

• *Above: Weaving workshop at the Bauhaus, 1923.*

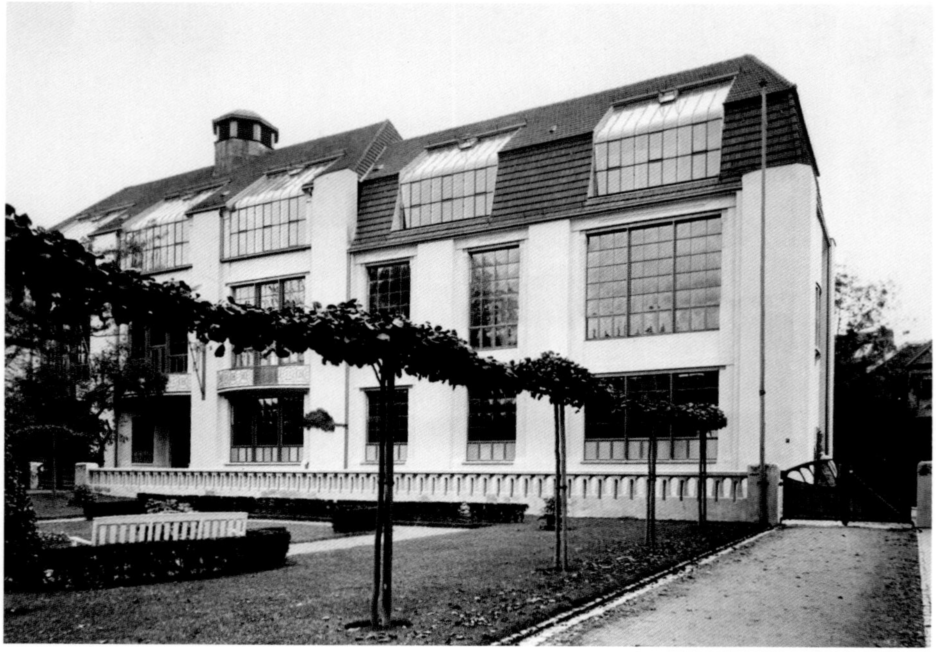

no sharp delineation, but rather a gradual process that saw changes made to both facilities and regulations. Thus it was that Helene Börner's workshop was taken over by the Bauhaus in its old form. The first craftspeople appointed by the Bauhaus, Helene Börner and Otto Dorfner (printing workshop), effectively operated their own workshops as before while being contractually bound to the Bauhaus. As early as October 1, 1919, a contract was drawn up between the Bauhaus and Helene Börner, and shortly afterwards female students who were interested in experimental weaving first made contact with Börner.

From the years after 1919 there are merely a handful of Helene Börner's notes and letters among the workshop and Bauhaus papers and a very few statements from contemporaries on which to base a picture of this very enthusiastic, loyal, and indeed technically highly competent woman. Although often criticized by the students and tending to remain in the shadows, her work was by no means unsuccessful or without impact. A letter from Helene Börner to Kämmer of October 27, 1919 documents, on the one hand, the somewhat uncomfortable studying conditions in the first winter semester at the Bauhaus and, on the other, this teacher's high degree of motivation and application where her pupils were concerned: "Dear Mr. Secretary! I myself am generally very sorry that I cannot carry on with the lessons; but completely apart from the fact that my pupils are not able to endure it and many of them have caught colds, you will see from Eberle's certificate that I myself am unable to function with the current temperature levels. I only sincerely hope that the heating will soon be fixed, as my young girls and I have a burning desire to be able to return to our normal activities."

When in May 1920 a separate women's department came into being which was housed in room 10 of the Van-de-Velde-Bau, Gropius suggested in the Masters' Council meeting " that the supervision and management of material . . . be taken over by the textile workshop" (ThStA Weimar, doc. no. 114). Helene Börner remained craft master, Johannes Itten was responsible for the artistic side, and Gunta Stölzl—soon to be one of the most important students of the weaving workshop—took on a supervisory function. In the meantime, the consumption of materials in the women's department had risen so sharply that Helene Börner also made available to her students materials from her own stocks. Thus Gunta Stölzl, later one of Börner's fiercest critics, wove several textiles with the finest thread from Börner's own private store.

In Itten's view craft education in the workshops should be completely subordinated to spiritual improvement. The management of the workshops, originally conceived as a cooperation between the craft masters and the form masters, was now experienced by the former as patronizing, in addition to which it was felt that an

• *Grand Ducal Saxon School of Arts and Crafts, Weimar, 1906 (architect: Henry van de Velde), home of the Weimar State Bauhaus from 1919 till 1925.*

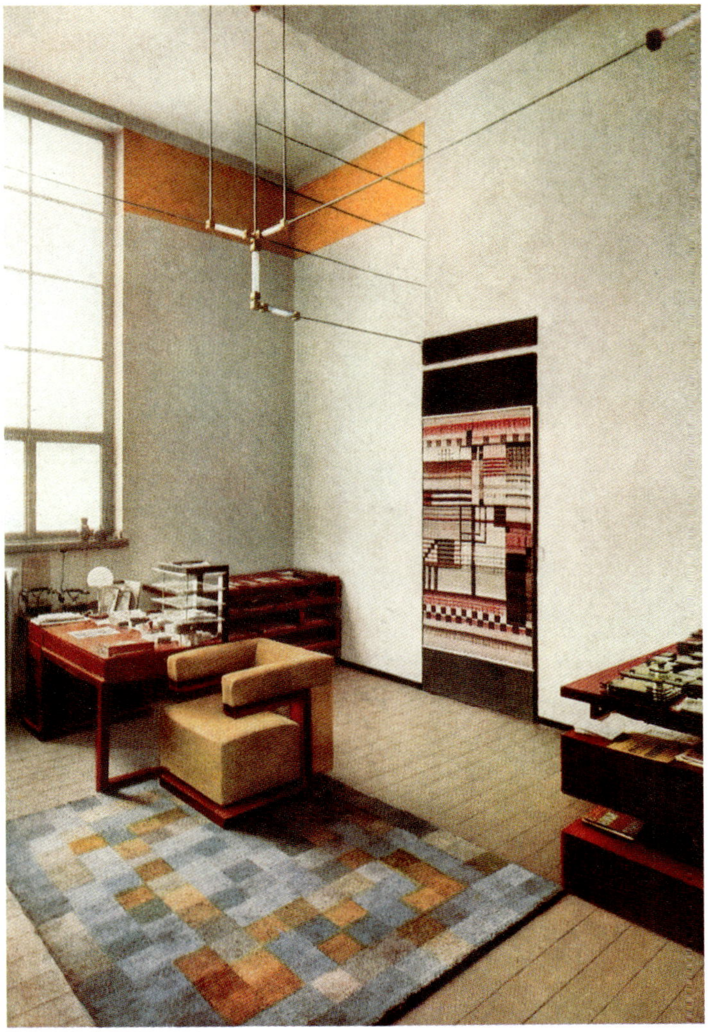

emphasis on artistic individualism hampered the smooth course of a craft apprenticeship. At this time there seem to have been increasing disagreements between Helene Börner and Gunta Stölzl—probably also an expression of a generational conflict. Stölzl and her fellow students accused Börner of having no knowledge of weaving technologies and being able to teach them little; maybe an unfair charge against Börner's long years of professional practice. At the heart of these charges lay a rejection of hand-me-down craft forms as unartistic and homespun and a desire to break away from the conventional through new experimental works—to break away, too, from Jugendstil, Börner's point of origin. Gunta Stölzl later referred to Börner as "a needlework teacher of the old school," from whom Weimar girls learned to embroider "birds, butterflies, the usual stuff on a pre-woven background."

On March 15, 1921, the Masters' Council noted: "The weaving workshop (women's department) has . . . made progress and has completely, of its own accord, developed into a women's department." Nevertheless, no apprenticeship certificates were issued in the women's department because the Weimar chamber of trade did not award these for the craft of weaving. This also meant that it was not possible for the women to register with the chamber of trade for the journeyman's or master's diploma, which again represented a serious handicap in terms of their future professional life.

The Bauhaus workshops were supposed to fund themselves through production and sales, the learning and practice phases thus being correspondingly short. The aim was to achieve independence from state contributions through a maximum of orders. In spring 1922 the first exhibition of work by Bauhaus students took place. The weaving workshop was at that time the best-staffed workshop, with seven journeywomen and fourteen apprentices then working there. It therefore became necessary to put its finances in order. Signed by the new form master, Georg Muche, an extremely detailed plan which presumably Gunta Stölzl, Benita Otte, and Helene Börner had helped to shape was presented in October 1922. At the beginning of 1923 an exhibition of Bauhaus works took place in Zurich and afterwards, from August to September, the great Bauhaus Exhibition. The weaving workshop made carpets and curtains for the Haus am Horn show home and for Gropius's office. Because the orders became more and more numerous, for example for the Gerson company in Berlin and for the Leipzig trade fair, Helene Börner had constantly to look for new assistants and for material. Gropius wrote a detailed

• *Director's study in Weimar, after a design by Walter Gropius, tinted black-and-white photo by Lucia Moholy, 1923.*

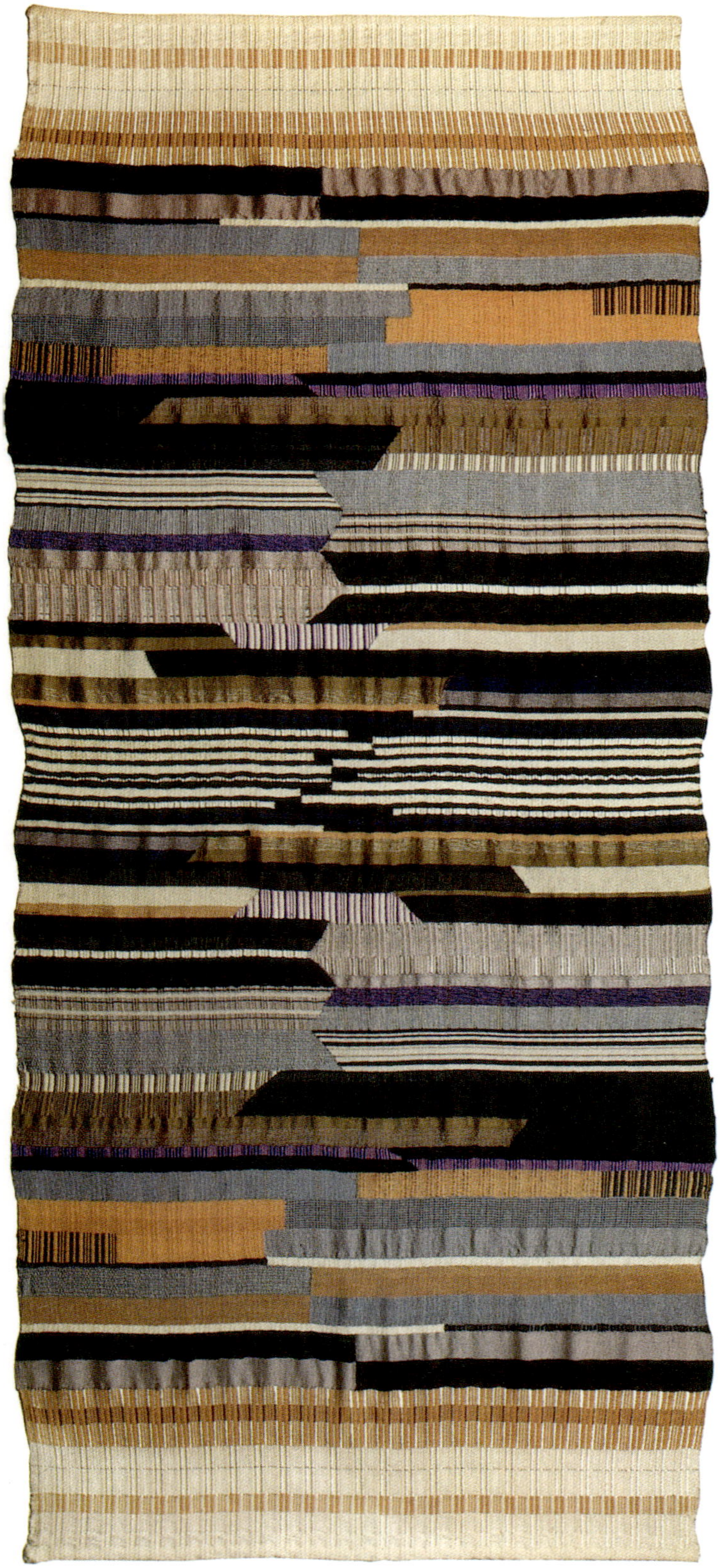

report on the successful work of the weaving workshop which ends with the words: "The weaving workshop can be called the best-equipped handweaving m ll in Germany." A workshop minute book from after 1923 reveals that in this highly productive period of the weaving workshop's history the Bauhaus owned "only four out of the twenty-one running looms, the others being the property of Fräulein Börner who has purchased the necessary looms over the last few years from her own funds because of the continuing lack of capital" (ThStA Weimar, doc. no. 183). Max Mielke, the caretaker hired by the Bauhaus who was very actively involved with Helene Börner's workshop, had built looms from materials which she paid for, and had also produced, at her expense, the spare parts that were indispensable for their routine maintenance. Mielke and Börner must have been close friends, for it is clear from a leave application made by the workshop master to the Bauhaus management that the pair traveled together to visit Mielke's dying mother.

In 1924 Helene Börner was forced to face up to allegations concerning a complaint. The syndic Emil Lange, for whom the never-ending dependence of the Bauhaus on Helene Börner and her "private property" was a thorn in the side, had some swatches independently tested by a famous handweaving mill. It was nevertheless established that as far as the materials were concerned it could be said to be perfectly woven craftwork and that the reproaches against the weaving workshop were unjustified. Days before the arrival of the certificate, Börner had already, on April 21, taken a masterful stance in a letter to Gropius: "I vigorously reject the accusation that a technical shortcoming on my part could be the cause of such occurrences.... To weave such materials, no expert needs to be appointed, Herr Gropius, I myself am that person."

• *Reversed woven 1925 reproduction by Helene Börner of Gunta Stölzl's original wall hanging with turned shuttles, 1923.*

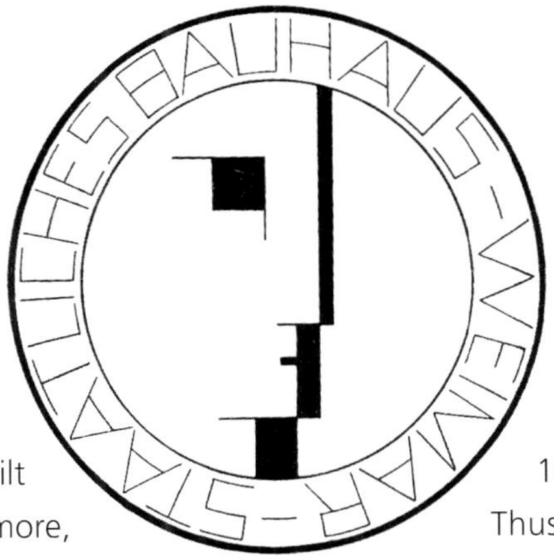

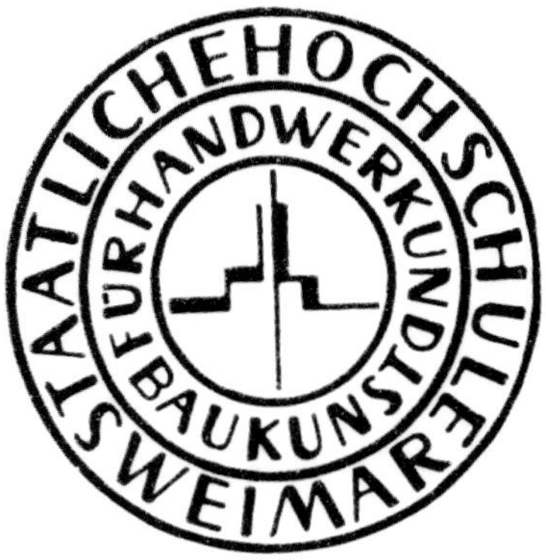

During her whole time at the Bauhaus Helene Börner always put all her energies into championing the workshop. A letter to El Muche, the wife of Georg Muche, conveys an impression of her commitment: "My dear Frau Muche! . . . I am sending you a pretty new quilt . . . and warmly ask you to try to sell one or more, because the Bauhaus coffers are emptier than ever. . . . I would certainly not bother you if we did not have to help out by all possible means. Sincerest greetings, Fräulein Börner." Helene Börner was also concerned about the lot of individual students. A later assessment by Bauhaus master Lothar Schreyer shows Helene Börner once again to be an especially kind teacher. He tells how a pupil in love with Itten came to see him in a state of despair and how he recommended that she go and work in the weaving workshop. "We went . . . into the workshop building . . . to Fräulein Börner, who at a glance from me led us into her small room. 'I have brought someone along who would very much like to work with you,' I said. 'Yes, my child, you come to me!' she said. Then she looked at me and again at the girl, 'What would you like to make?' 'A small cloth perhaps?' 'A little handkerchief?' she asked . . . with disarming kindness and stroked the girl's hand. 'Then we must first sketch something out. Please do this here in my room. And act as if my little kingdom were your home'."

After the enforced closure of the Weimar Bauhaus on March 31, 1925, Gropius moved the school to Dessau. The Bauhaus had rights to at least nine hundred different textile pieces: Gropius and Dr. Wilhelm Köhler, director of Weimar's art collections, had to agree on how they would be divided up, four major pieces being claimed by both sides. It was decided that Helene Börner should weave copies of these works for the Weimar collections. She executed the copies in 1925 and was also paid for them. Thus in a certain way the Bauhaus weaving workshop in Weimar came to a bizarre end: the innovative pupils left Weimar, while their teacher who had been criticized for incompetence stayed on and produced outstanding reproductions that showed a perfect mastery of technique. Helene Börner pursued her career at the Hochschule für Handwerk und Baukunst (Craft and Architecture College) under Otto Bartning. Her name is found in college documents up until 1926.

During the course of researching into Helene Börner informative details keep cropping up again and again. It is documented that in 1921 Börner joined the cooperative which had been formed to plan and execute the Bauhaus estate known as "the Horn." She evidently had a close interest in this residential project, so cannot therefore have been as old-fashioned as is often made out. Because the plan was thwarted, however, by the Weimar authorities, the cooperative was dissolved in 1930. The 1929 directory lists Helene Börner's address as Schloß Tiefurter and no longer gives an occupation for her; in the years from 1934 to 1937 she appears as "Börner, Helene" with a new address, now with the note "pensioner". Finally, in the directory of 1939–40, no entry is found. Thus the date and the circumstances of her death also remain to this day shrouded in mystery.

INGRID RADEWALDT

• *Above, left: Bauhaus* Profile *emblem by Oskar Schlemmer, 1922.*

• *Above, right: Emblem of the Staatliche Hochschule für Handwerk und Baukunst (State College of Craft and Architecture), 1926–30.*

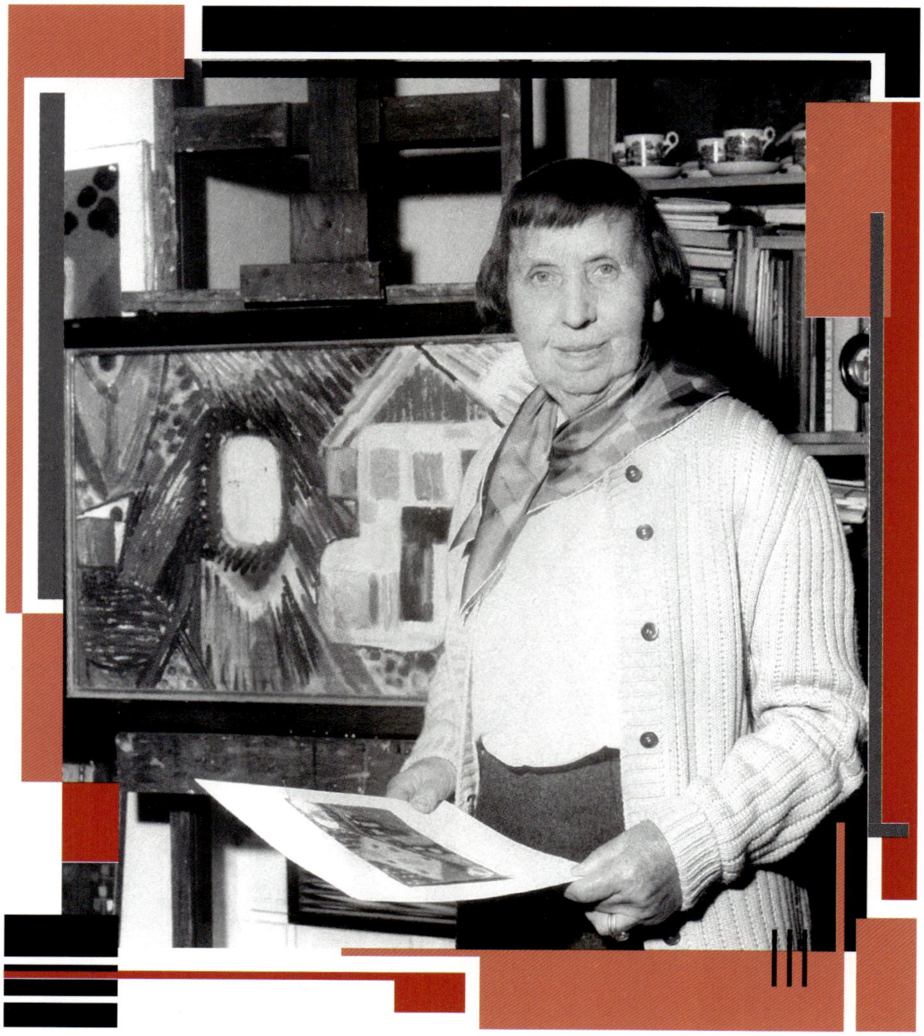

IDA KERKOVIUS 1879–1970

"The further I come, the clearer I see that work derived from artistic means is the key thing and is the most likely to lead to results; the personal must withdraw, but can never be wholly silenced. Klee has illuminated all these things for me anew, basically echoing what Hölzel always says. One must keep repeating these things because one forgets, unfortunately, so much and so fast."

Ida Kerkovius to Hanna Bekker vom Rath, 1922

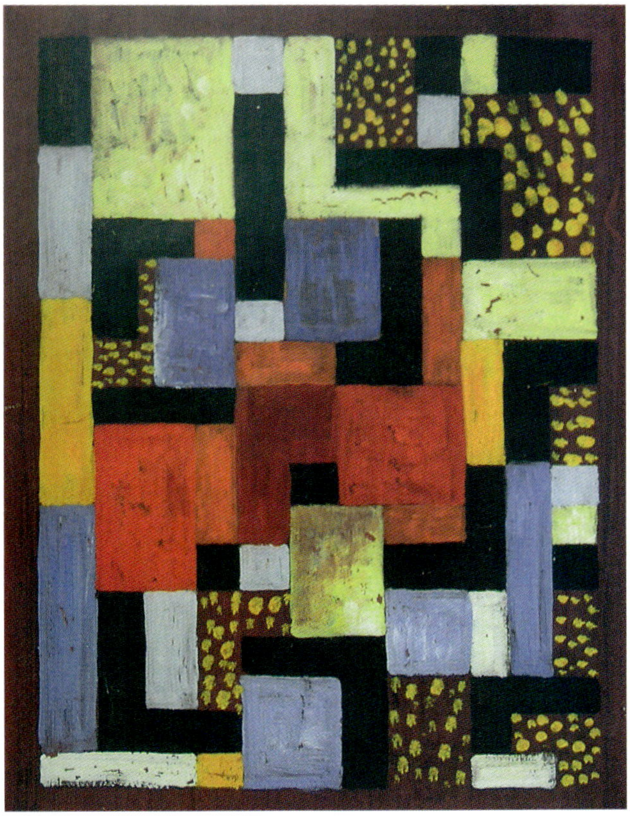

When Ida Kerkovius was accepted at the Weimar Bauhaus in the winter semester of 1920, she was already forty-one years old and thus one of its oldest students. She came out of curiosity "to see what the teaching is like there, and to receive new artistic stimuli."

In 1920, two weeks after her arrival in Weimar, she wrote to her friend Hanna Bekker vom Rath: "The Bauhaus this winter is more interesting than ever. As novelties, the characters Schreyer and Klee really liven things up and are a tremendous asset. Klee spoke about the function of the line—it was very good. I am noting everything down and will tell you everything when I have the opportunity."

The most important teacher at this time, however, was Johannes Itten, whose *Vorkurs* (foundation course) with its studies of the nude and of contrast opened up a new world for her. She carried out rhythm exercises and analysed the Old Masters "so as to understand the deep power of these pictures, which resides in their rhythm."

She was deeply entranced by Itten's teaching, which in every sense inspired new impulses in her, even with regard to the employment of different materials and their qualities. These "material studies" were not supposed to be likenesses; it was rather about grasping the nature of a material, an activity which suited her "penchant for things material."

Ida Kerkovius nevertheless found the work at the Bauhaus to be very exhausting: "So as to completely absorb the teaching, I take part in everything as if I were not able to count to ten (i.e., I work for myself alone, having lessons only on one day a week which, however, take up the whole day and make the biggest demands on mind and nerves). I am quite shattered by it each time and need two days afterwards to recover, so gripped am I by Itten's way of explaining things, which seems compelling and irrefutable. I am getting to know him from this perspective, namely as a teacher, for the first time and I must say that my expectations have been greatly exceeded."

The fact that she put herself under this pressure is all the more astonishing as just ten years earlier Itten had been her pupil. Itten had wanted to study at Stuttgart's Kunstakademie (Fine Arts Academy) under Adolf Hölzel, whose theory of artistic methods had by then achieved great recognition, but he was not offered a place. Since Hölzel was not allowed to give private lessons, he referred Itten to his star pupil Ida Kerkovius, who had been his assistant since 1911 and maintained a master's studio where she introduced newly enrolled students to Hölzel's pictorial theory. "When Itten came to my studio," she later reported, "he was highly surprised to find that he was to be taught by a woman. Nevertheless, when he saw my pictures he stayed." Itten was extremely impressed by Ida Kerkovius's teaching and later integrated many elements into his own classes. Ida Kerkovius

• *Facing page: Ida Kerkovius at the easel in her Stuttgart studio, 1959.*

• *Above: Ida Kerkovius, Rug design, gouache, 1920–23.*

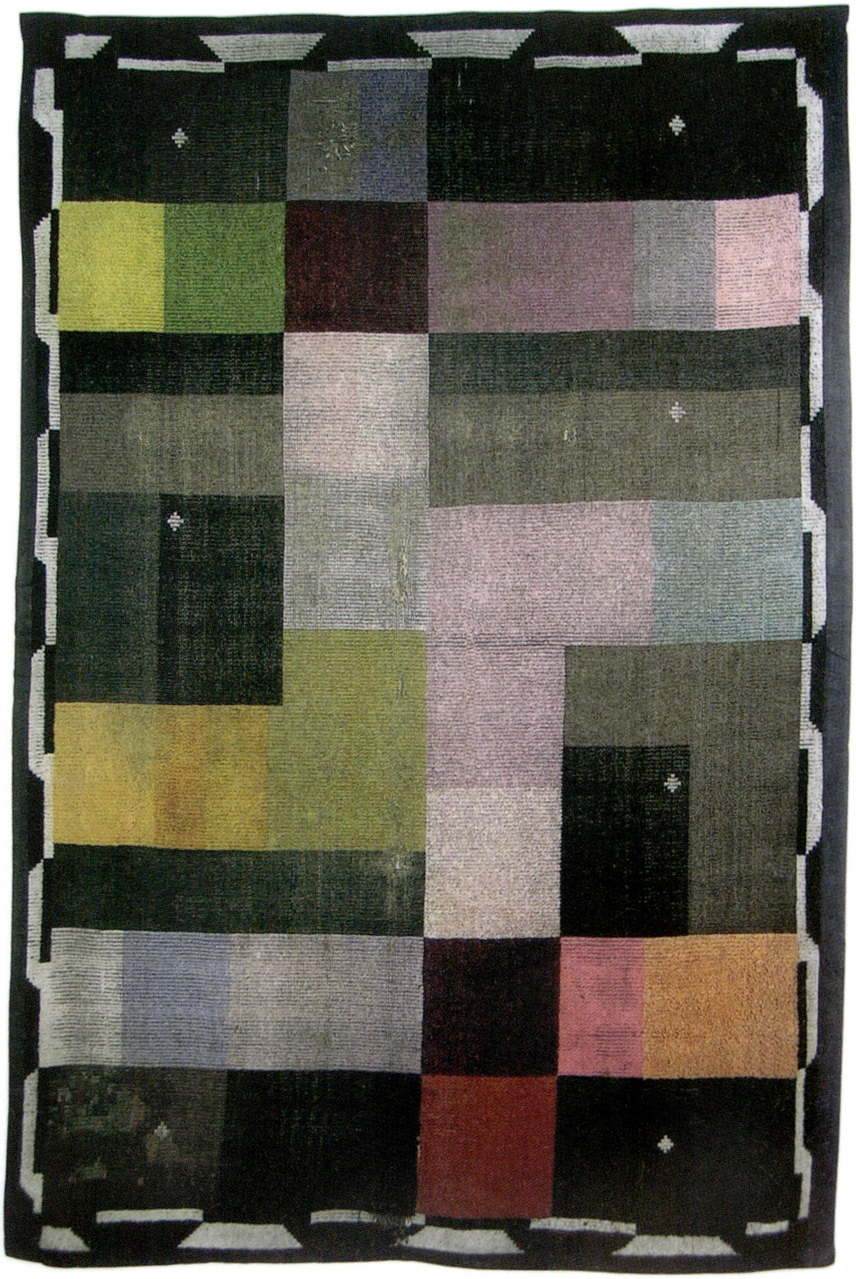

landscape painting. The pictorial quality which she had discovered in the works of this pupil of Hölzel awoke in her the desire for a new, more modern form of expression. As early as 1902 she decided impulsively—on the way back from an educational trip with relatives—to become Hölzel's pupil in Dachau and was set by him on the path towards abstract painting. Hölzel instructed his pupils to build up their pictures logically starting with the color; everything extraneous to the subject matter should dissolve in the composition. "The teachings which impressed me deeply took place in Dachau on the one hand in front of nature . . . and, on the other hand, in the studio." Hölzel taught his pupils how to see: flat forms were identified that were able to transfer three-dimensional nature to the picture plane.

Ida Kerkovius had to break off this intensive work with Hölzel after five months because her parents summoned her back to Livonia. When she exhibited her Dachau studies in Riga in 1904, she received praise in the *Rigasche Rundschau* of November 13 for her determined talent and sure grasp of the essentials.

Only in 1908 was she able to resume her education, this time in Berlin, but she soon rejected it as too academic. In the same year she moved to Stuttgart where Adolf Hölzel had taken up a teaching post in 1906 at the Kunstakademie. In 1911 she became his assistant.

apparently represented Hölzel's theory very persuasively, fostering a close, almost symbiotic respect for Hölzel which lasted up until his death.

Ida Kerkovius had already got to know Hölzel's working method in 1901 through the exhibition of one of his female pupils. She was then twenty-two years old and leading the life of a high-born German landowner's daughter in Riga. She attended a private painting school in Riga and received a solid basic education in still-life and

• *Ida Kerkovius, Bauhaus carpet, 1923.*

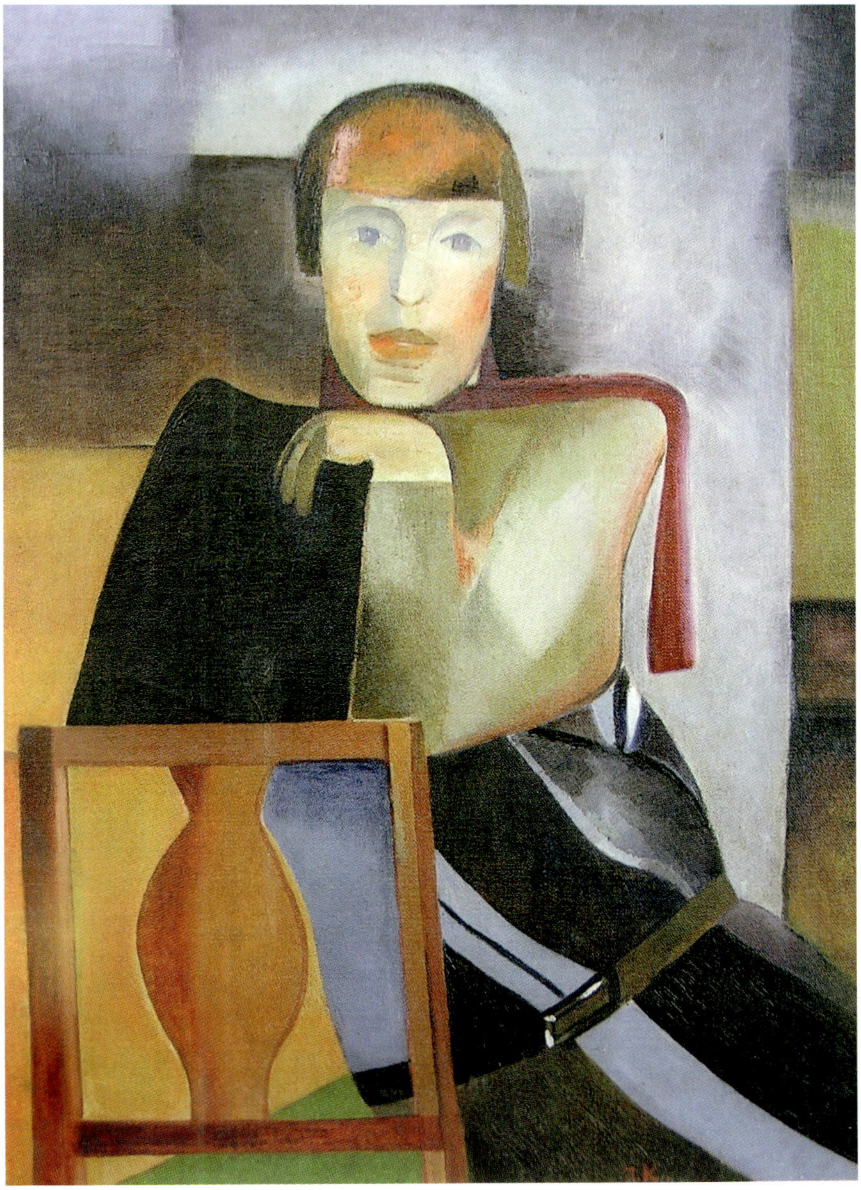

The outbreak of World War I in 1914 had serious consequences for Ida Kerkovius. As a Baltic German she was forced to adopt Russian citizenship and her family also lost large parts of its assets and were forced to surrender ownership of their land. After the death of her parents in 1915 she was obliged to earn her own living, yet as a foreigner she was no longer allowed to teach at the academy in Stuttgart. She also lost her master's studio—moreover, as a Swiss citizen, the student Johannes Itten had to leave the academy, too. Ida Kerkovius now transferred her classes to a private studio. One of her private school pupils, Hanna Bekker vom Rath, became her lifelong friend and patron. The latter acquired many of her works and later acted as her dealer, organizing exhibitions and promoting the sale of her works.

When Ida Kerkovius came to the Bauhaus in 1920, she set her sights not only on deepening her artistic knowledge, but also on the possibility of learning a craft that promised income: "Completely aside from the fact that I have a penchant for things material, I am obliged to create a new source of income for myself, because what should become of me in the future, since we have lost everything," she wrote to Hanna Bekker vom Rath on Easter Friday 1921.

In the weaving workshop her talent quickly became evident, having already in 1920 completed her first animal wall hanging using complicated forms. In 1922 she wove a rug from strips of fabric with meandering light-and-dark forms in a strictly rectangular arrangement. This rug was intended by Itten for the anteroom of Gropius's office and was planned in black, white, gray, ocher, and blue—Ida herself had provided an old black-and-white photograph with these color details and declared it to be her first Bauhaus carpet produced in 1920. However, it must surely be of a later date, since in two letters of April 1922 to her friend Hanna she is obviously referring to the production of this carpet, which Gropius published in his Bauhaus book of 1925: "Even I am very pleased with my

• *Ida Kerkovius,* Self-Portrait, *oil on canvas, c. 1929.*

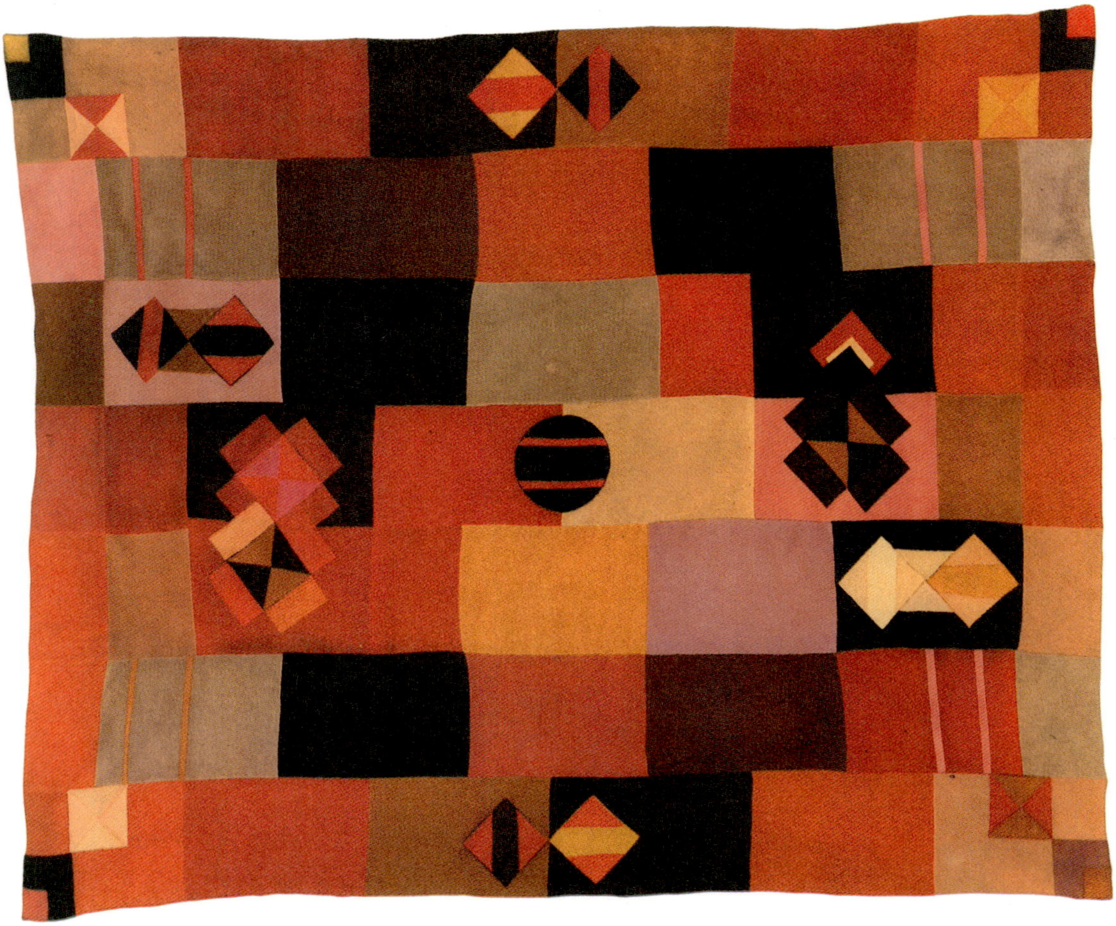

work. I am weaving a large rug, two meters (twenty feet) square. It is intended for a room in the Bauhaus: Gropius's reception room. This room is being designed by Itten, i.e., he is directing the different people who are working on it. Wall decorations and other such pieces are all to be in keeping with one another. He commissioned me to produce the carpet. First I made the life-size design in situ and it met with approval. I have already been weaving for one-and-a-half months and will soon have half of it ready, it's turning out very well, it also gives me great pleasure. Square forms only were prescribed and I was instructed to base my design more on the contrast between light and dark than on color. Different shades of gray play against each other, from pure white to the deepest black." And a little while later she reported to her friend that the work seemed to her insurmountably difficult, but that everybody was very much in favor of the carpet and found it very beautiful. "Klee even said it would have a lasting value. That pleased me very much. A party was also held in honor of this carpet."

Lothar Schreyer wrote about that occasion in his book *Erinnerungen an Sturm und Bauhaus*, which appeared in 1956: "We had marvellous parties at the Bauhaus, both large and small. Whenever a particularly fine piece of work was completed this was celebrated by the workshop in question. When Ida Kerkovius finished her first big carpet in the weaving workshop, we celebrated this in my small attic flat in the house by the park that used to belong to Frau von Stein. The carpet was very fine indeed and, at four square meters, almost filled the entire room. We surrounded it with burning candles and squatted around it on the floor chatting happily and quietly, while the fountain bubbled away under the window."

Another outstanding textile by Ida Kerkovius is a machine-sewn felt appliqué work in which the dominant

• *Ida Kerkovius, Felt appliqué work, c. 1921.*

tones are red. Basic geometrical forms are playfully scattered about—some of them artfully interlocking. This work, measuring 6 ¾ feet (2.1 meters) in length and 5 ¼ feet (1.6 meters) in width, might have been intended as a bedspread, but it was used by Hanna Bekker vom Rath as a wall hanging. Obviously Ida Kerkovius had tried out all textile techniques then offered at the Bauhaus. Thus a pane of material known as Jacquard fabric has also survived: such fabrics were very complex and labor-intensive to produce and only exist in a few examples among Weimar textiles from 1922 onwards.

In the last year of her stay at the Bauhaus in 1923 Ida completely devoted herself to carpet making. The preliminary sketches already testify to the high creative quality of these pieces, which are composed of richly contrasting right-angled forms and are surrounded by an ornamental black-and-white border. The large-size "Bauhaus rug" was shown at the Bauhaus Exhibition immediately after its completion where it met with great approval. Ida Kerkovius herself, in a letter of January 20, 1964 in the Bauhaus Archives, declared it self-confidently to be the most beautiful there.

Kerkovius wove another carpet with basic geometrical forms for Paul Klee in 1923. In her memoirs she wrote: "Paul Klee had a high regard for weaving, which he compared to music making, and I was delighted when he ordered for himself a carpet of the brand 'Kerko.'" In return she received from Klee a watercolor from 1920 which hung in her study until her death: today it is in the Metropolitan Museum of Art in New York. In 1924 Ida Kerkovius, now a German citizen, returned to Stuttgart. The proceeds from the sales of the Bauhaus carpet enabled her to acquire a big carpet loom on which over the following decades she was able to carry out numerous orders and thus guarantee herself a means of earning a living. In addition, her friend Hanna procured her commissions for costume designs.

She was also a painter and her pictures were shown at famous exhibitions. On the occasion of one of these exhibitions—in the Blaues Haus in Hofheim—Alexej von Jawlensky said of Ida: "She is all art."

During this period Ida Kerkovius undertook numerous trips, some of them together with Adolf Hölzel to whom she retained a lifelong connection but from whom she freed herself artistically, as Hölzel himself also commented: "She has taken on board my ideas, but in a curious fashion, she does things quite differently."

Ida Kerkovius never married, although she had many lifelong friends and sponsors, who not only secured orders for her, but who also, after her home was bombed out at the beginning of 1944, gave her a place to live as well as somewhere to work.

In 1958 she was appointed professor and founding member of the Baden-Württemberg artists' alliance. In 1964, the year that she turned eighty-five, she was at the height of her success: private collectors showed great interest, and art critics reacted very positively to the only remaining living German artist, besides Gabriele Münter, from the age of classical modernism. Her works became known through more than seventy gallery shows in Germany.

After her death in 1970 interest in Ida Kerkovius's art waned. Only since the 1990s has her work started to be seen again in exhibitions. Even her early work and the Bauhaus-inspired pieces show a mature composition and a remarkably masterful handling of color. Ida Kerkovius herself once said: "What moves me most is the final balancing out—a sort of equilibrium of form and color."

INGRID RADEWALDT

Women—A Class of their Own

The Artist Weavers

The weaving workshop is the one in which by far the most women had their practical training at the Bauhaus. It was thus not easy to make a choice for this chapter: with portraits of other textile artists such as Grete Reichardt, Monica Bella-Broner, Katja Rose, and Marli Ehrmann one could easily fill another book.

The first female Bauhaus students chose this women's workshop, and only then was it declared a "women's department." In her portrayal of the Bauhaus women, Magdalena Droste points out that both men and women viewed working with textiles as an activity naturally suited to women, thereby perpetuating the segregation of work according to sex which had taken hold since the nineteenth century at the latest. Some of the women artists were forced to join, although they actually had totally different desires. Some like Ida Kerkovius or Anni Albers quickly discovered their talent in this field and in the end even taught a few men such as Max Peiffer Watenphul to weave.

The Bauhaus women in the weaving workshop were the source of important developments for individual textile art as well as for modern industry, not just in Germany but also in countries such as Switzerland, England, Israel, and the United States. Droste tells us that weaving technique was of the most highly industrialized standard, thus providing the best conditions for the Bauhaus's aims.

Supported by fairly unsystematic teaching, and continuous trial and error, they created works with completely new patterns, shapes, and color combinations created from the basic shapes of triangle, circle, square, and basic colors such as yellow, red, and blue, or striped patterns in shades of black and white. The design ideas were chiefly communicated by form masters, such as Johannes Itten and Paul Klee, whose background was free painting. The narrative illustrated carpet, which flourished in the art deco period, was now replaced by two-dimensionally constructed designs with no recognizable subject, as taught in Wassily Kandinsky's and László Moholy-Nagy's classes.

Helene Börner and the form master of the weaving workshop, Georg Muche, soon turned to the task of extending the training to cover production as well. Already in March 1924 patterns were being offered and contracts negotiated at the Leipzig Trade Fair. Production was, however, repeatedly impeded by lack of materials. The Bauhaus bought the works of many students and thereby acquired the rights to market them.

Some weavers such as Benita Otte and Else Mögelin rejected this development of creating patterns for industrial production and thus did not go to Dessau in 1925. The development towards industrial design was brought to fruition at the Dessau Bauhaus. The design process

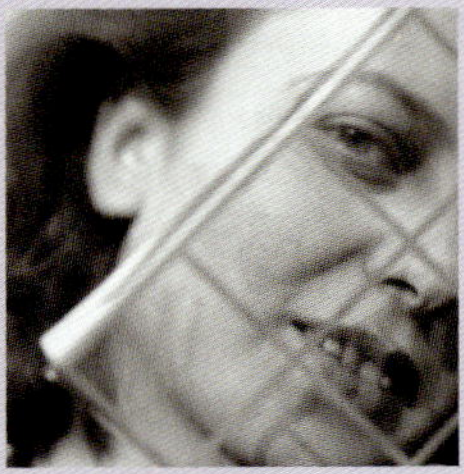

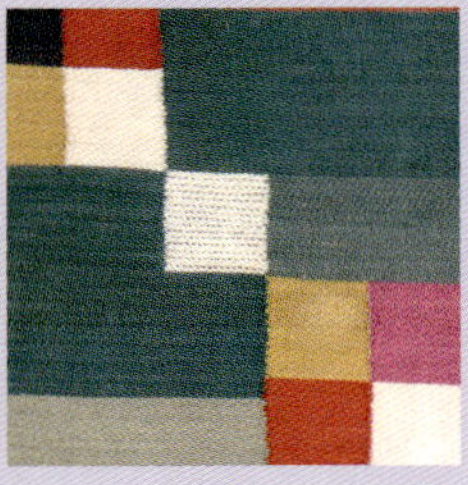

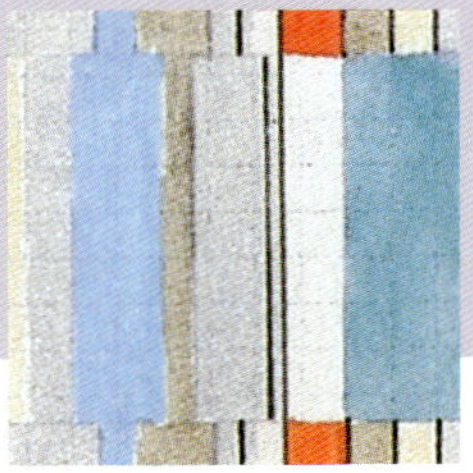

was systematized, the woven fabrics were priced and measured, and they were numbered. The students learned about the entire production processes, from colors to weaving and ordering fabric, and now had excellent knowledge and experience of work in industry. However, the majority of the female Bauhaus weavers would still have preferred independent work in their own craft businesses.

A shortcoming in the Weimar training was that women weavers could not sit a recognized examination at the Handwerkskammer (Crafts Council). This changed in Dessau. Upon completion of their Bauhaus education, they now received a diploma.

When Gropius left the Bauhaus and Hannes Meyer became the new director in April 1928, the women weavers too grappled with his new social utopian ideas. Now the functional material was to become more important. Carpets were no longer the focal point but "floor coverings"; artistic and aesthetic design criteria took a back seat. Systematic experiments on the characteristics of materials were extended to include synthetics and stretch fabrics, and tubular steel furniture or translucent curtain fabrics were developed. Anni Albers managed to create a fabric which was sound absorbent on one side and reflected light on the other. Jacquard looms were used, which optimized the production process. In 1930 cooperation began with the Berlin company, Polytex, which was licensed to recreate and sell Bauhaus patterns.

Günta Stölzl, who in effect ran the workshop as of 1925—officially as young master from 1927—resigned in 1931. This suited Ludwig Mies van der Rohe, the new director, very well. He could now fill the position with the interior designer and textile designer Lilly Reich, with whom he had worked and lived for years. Lilly Reich's creative direction, designing patterns for fabric prints and creating collections for companies, fitted exactly with Mies's plan to restructure the Bauhaus as a training institute for architecture. Application of the fabric prints soon followed, together with the Bauhaus wallpaper patterns. The textile department created many pattern books for curtain material, furniture covering, and children's clothing.

With the forced closure of the Bauhaus by the Nazis in 1933, the history of the textile workshop and the weaving workshop after 1919 was abruptly ended, but the story of the Bauhaus women weavers continued.

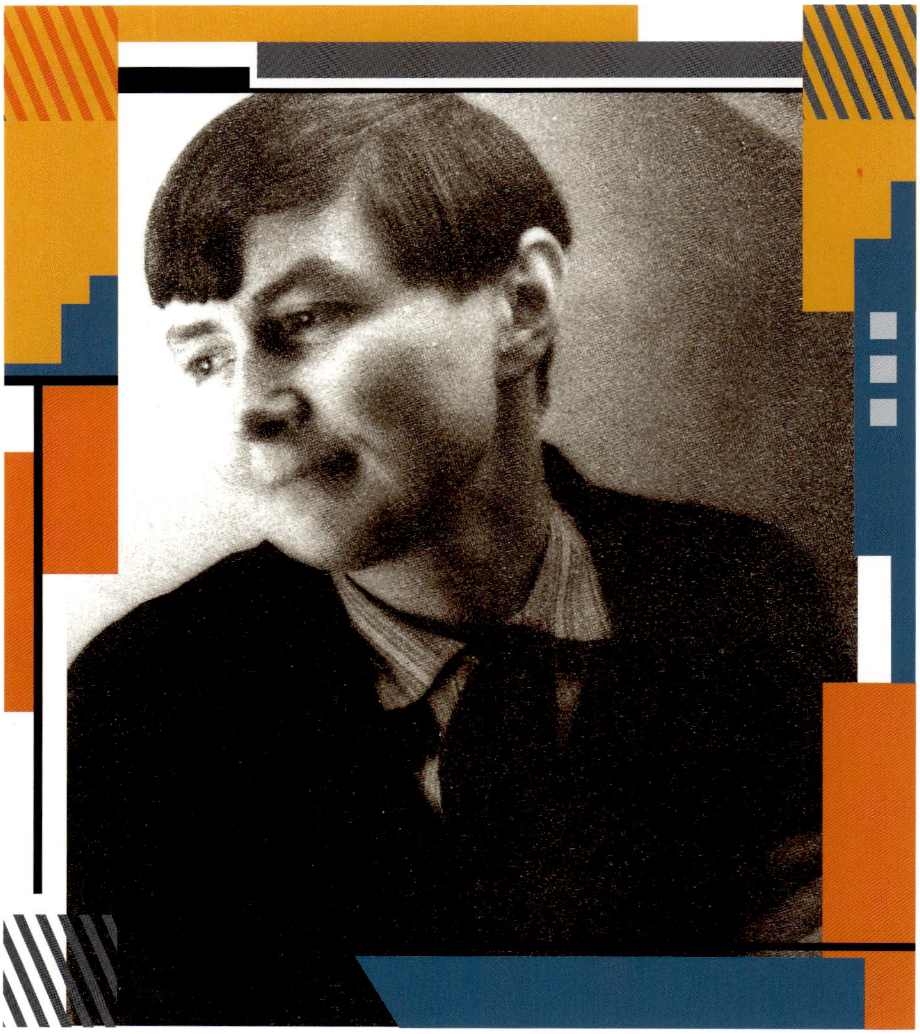

BENITA OTTE 1892–1976

"It was not just about the lessons—it was simply about life itself. Talks, discussions, exchange, pleasure in the work of others. Something was always going on because one took part in the whole and was oneself a part of the whole. It was ... an incredibly exciting time. Political attacks from outside, inside a tension between very different views of the world and of art. ... This great freedom, which often faced serious challenges, was the venture upon which Gropius embarked."

Benita Otte in Farblehre und Weberei, *1972*

Benita Otte was twenty-eight years old when she came to the Weimar Bauhaus in 1920. She had already passed two state exams as a drawing teacher and gym instructor, and a third in 1915 as a needlework teacher at Berlin's renowned Lette-Verein. She had taught for five years at the girls' grammar school in Uerdingen am Rhein, where her parents lived, and she was now a student once again, beginning work in the women's class. Her memoirs reveal nothing about the reasons for this new start in Weimar, but she was certainly attracted by the rich opportunities for experimentation which the Bauhaus program promised. In her contribution to the 1972 exhibition catalogue she states: "Our imagination was allowed to play with the most diverse material. It was about feeling, weighing, selecting, in order to come up with the greatest possible variety of combinations—contrasting?—or similar?—or?—or?—This happened in the context of Itten's lessons. . . . With us novices he began with 'relaxation exercises.' We drew standing up, with soft charcoal on big sheets of paper, often with closed eyes, on specific subjects: falling and climbing, military assault. Robbed of our vision, intensely focussed on just one idea, we drew differently. The results were often highly expressive. We drew rhythmical proportions, composed material scales, e.g., from hard to soft, from loose to dense, from rough to fine, from smooth to coarse, which could be read like a musical scale with the same differences of pitch. I remember long conversations with the clever Bittkow about how we could continue such beginnings."

Benita Otte came from a middle-class background and, according to the art historian Sigrid Wortmann-Weltge, "positively blossomed in the atmosphere of the Bauhaus and won the friendship of her fellow students and masters alike; she was particularly close to Marcks, Itten, Klee, and Schlemmer." There was soon a close bond of friendship between Benita Otte and Gunta Stölzl, which was to last a lifetime. They both started to experiment freely in the women's department in the area of weaving without letting themselves be led by the rules of the craft: "It was good that we started to experiment from the very first with such uncluttered minds, naively and without real expertise," wrote Benita Otte. "The rich possibilities of the most basic crossover of threads allowed the imagination and the creative will enough leeway for the strong impulses which we came to know." One of these strong impulses for her was the meeting with Paul Klee, who arrived at the Bauhaus in 1921. Among the many assignments that Klee set the students, some were particularly suitable for the weaving workshop; these included exercises with stripes, either with a succession of steps between the poles of black and white or which also showed transitions from black via gray to white. Such exercises trained the students' eye for nuances, but also for proportions. Many early striped fabrics made in the textile workshop can be traced back to these exercises. For the handling of color there were similar stripe exercises. To achieve exact color nuances, Klee frequently applied the technique of scumbling: the superimposition of layers of increasingly thin watercolor made

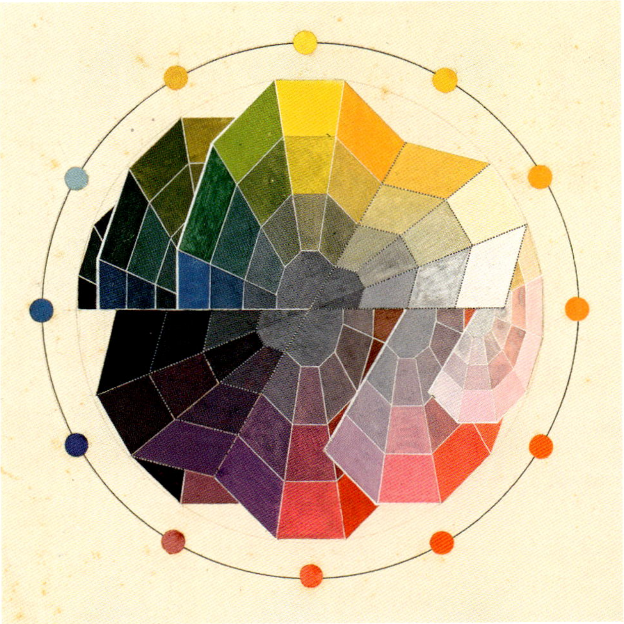

• *Facing page: Benita Otte, 1920s.*

• *Above: Benita Otte, Color swatch, c. 1925.*

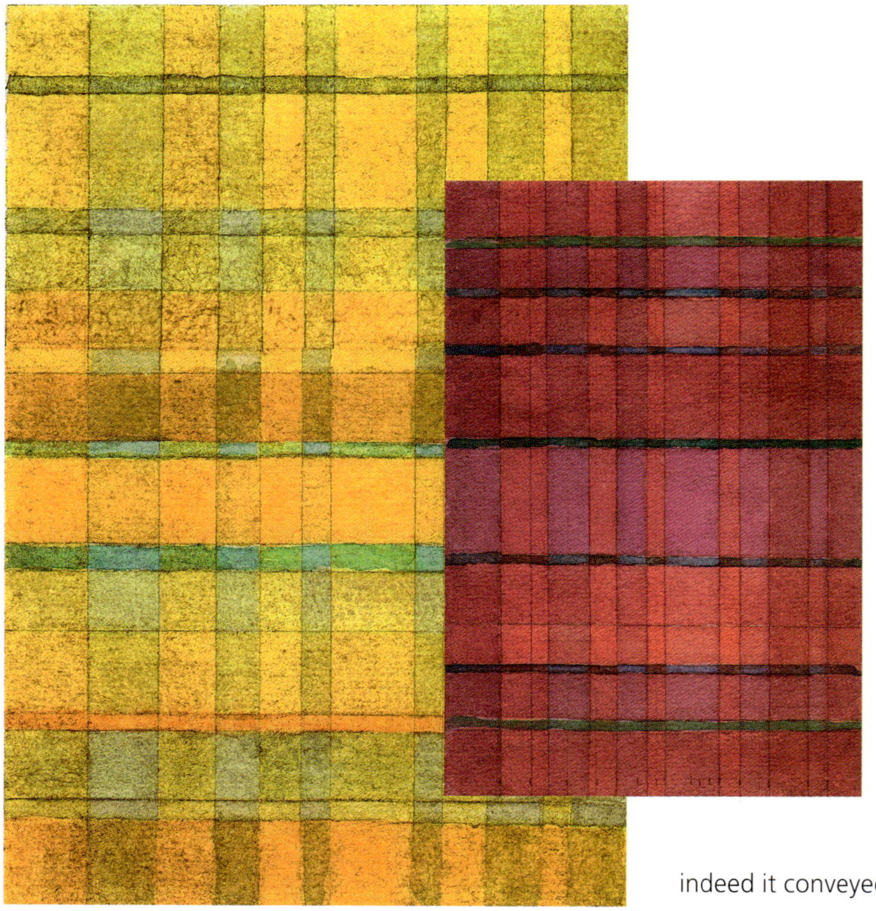

reality ascent is always followed by descent if the gravitational pull of the earth on a slower course increasingly overtakes the upward trajectory. Thus the curve of the earth ends up as straight (theoretically at the earth's center).' I have a vivid picture of that period: Klee is on his feet, speaking at the same time, he draws in the air, on the board. We follow the movement, its beginning, the energy of the rise, the tragic moment of 'no further,' the unavoidable 'back to earth' and, finally, the impact. This sounds very simplistic, if indeed it conveyed all there is to say. However, behind it was Klee, Klee himself. Intuitively I started to anticipate what one would later read in his diary. . . . At the temporal level I am not at all tangible, for I am just as much at home among the dead as among the unborn. A little closer to the heart of creation than usual, and yet still not close enough!' . . . If I was asked to say what Klee's teaching has meant for me, I would not know how to express it in words as I might with Itten, whose method stimulated me very directly. Klee reaches much deeper layers, unknown layers, conjures up in us the unconscious and the unknown, to which we listen intently. This stays with one throughout one's whole life."

the colors steadily more intense. Klee himself led the way with his own square and fugue pictures, and it is astonishing how many designs and finished textiles there are with square structures, by others such as Benita Otte, Gertrud Arndt, and Anni Albers. The experimentation with color gradations and blendings was especially important for the students of the weaving workshop, because the variety of available threads in all hues and the versatility of weaves made it possible to obtain many different tones in textile art. One particularly ingenious representation of secondary colors is a color swatch that Benita Otte developed out of the color wheel. It could be used as a color thermometer in weaving compositions and as a mixing aid.

Klee remained Otte's most important inspiration and she used his teachings much later to develop her own color theory. Otte highlighted her recollections of Klee with a central sentence from Klee's *Der Pfeil*: "'In earthly

Klee's influence on Benita Otte's work is reflected particularly in her work for her journman's exam of 1923. This wall hanging, executed in many different shades and in high-quality material has echoes in pictures from Klee's *Reise nach Kairouan* (1914). The center of the work consists of many-sided, compartmentalized square forms; towards the periphery the forms become calmer and more

• *Benita Otte, Class exercises, watercolor, 1920s.*

generous. There are layers of color with rich gradations which, together with triangular forms, are suggestive of landscape and architecture and take on the character of watercolor. This fine journeyman's piece would not have been possible without a long period of experimentation.

The economic crisis at the beginning of the 1920s forced even the Bauhaus to take unusual measures: thus vegetables were grown and vegetarian food cooked in the in-house canteen with the support of willing students such as Benita Otte and Gunta Stölzl. Schlemmer commented on this in a diary entry of 1921: "One positive thing for example is the canteen, in which with the help of some female pupils (who have voluntarily had to give up some of their artistic activities) food is prepared following Mazdaznan recipes (vegetarian, naturally), for pupils and masters. . . . It is nice that the girls appreciate these economic necessities and devote themselves ungrudgingly and of their own free will to the cause. In any case, the question of girls and women is integral to the problems of the Bauhaus; I mean equal rights, tolerance, or exclusion." It is moreover absolutely clear from this statement how conservative Schlemmer's own views of women still were—contrary to all the Bauhaus leadership's assurances about achieving equal rights. The women themselves hardly seemed aware of this attitude; most of them accepted their role and at the same time made use of their new freedoms.

From as early as 1920 big one-off textile pieces were increasingly produced at the Bauhaus, characterized by a daring handling of color and simple geometrical forms. The tapestry became the art form that best communicated and disseminated a still unusual abstract visual language, because, as art historian Magdalena Droste has explained, "while abstract art was often rejected, the wall hangings, carpets, and textiles of the Bauhaus almost always attracted interest, indeed favor, because critics did not expect the sort of meaning in textiles which they failed to find in abstract paintings." The first exhibition of work by students of the Weimar Bauhaus took place in April–May 1922. Otte moreover worked on a series of delicate red-and-green wall hangings in which she cleverly used threads to transform Klee's theories of color and form into a transparent textile.

In winter 1922 planning had already begun on a big Bauhaus exhibition, as the Thuringian government was demanding evidence of their achievements. Although Gropius considered the exhibition to be premature, he bent to the pressure and appointed a planning committee consisting of masters and pupils under the chairmanship of Georg Muche. Muche planned a show home, the Haus am Horn, and commissioned Benita Otte to draw the elevation and the isometric projection. In February

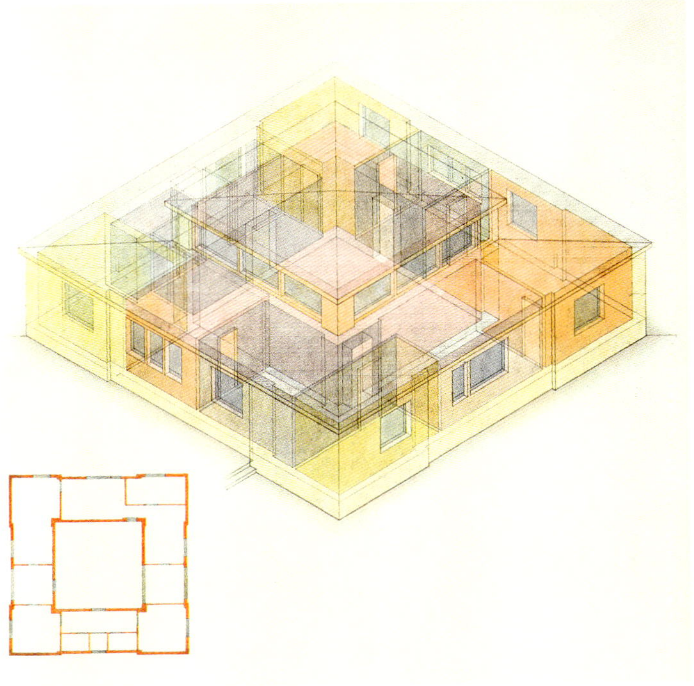

• Benita Otte, *Isometric projection, Haus am Horn, 1923.*

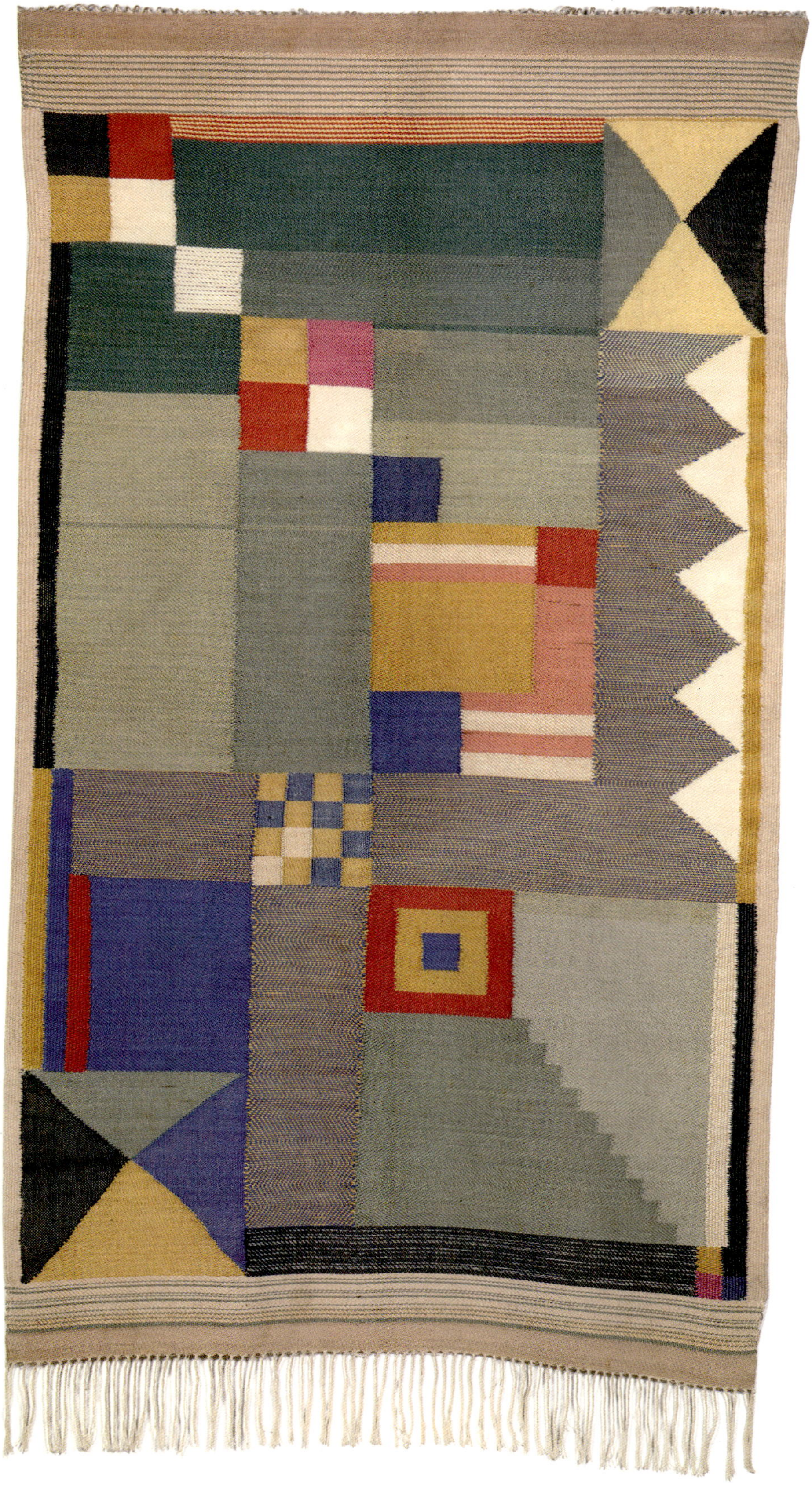

1972 Muche wrote looking back on this: "From the very first Benita Otte achieved forms of great beauty and in the spatial perspective of her architectural drawing she made—in colored layers of tone—both the external form and the interiors simultaneously transparent. Artistic talent, practical sense, and clarity in every way defined her being, her conduct as an individual." Benita Otte was also involved in the fitting out of the house accordingly. Thus, in cooperation with Ernst Gebhardt, she had sketched out a highly functional kitchen which became the prototype of its age. For the children's room she designed a washable floor carpet which corresponded to her notion of what children required in terms of color and form: on a pastel-colored ground brightly colored squares with different subdivisions made it look as if toys had been scattered over the carpet. The carpet was an ideal complement to the cubic room furnishings, which were simple yet carefully thought out in every detail.

Opportunities for exhibiting increased in 1923. Compositions with inlaid forms were produced on the low warp loom, woven wall hangings on the high warp loom, and various double weaves. Gunta Stölzl remembered: "Formally as well as technically we 'invented' incessantly. With these

• *Benita Otte, Rug for the children's room, Haus am Horn, 1923.*

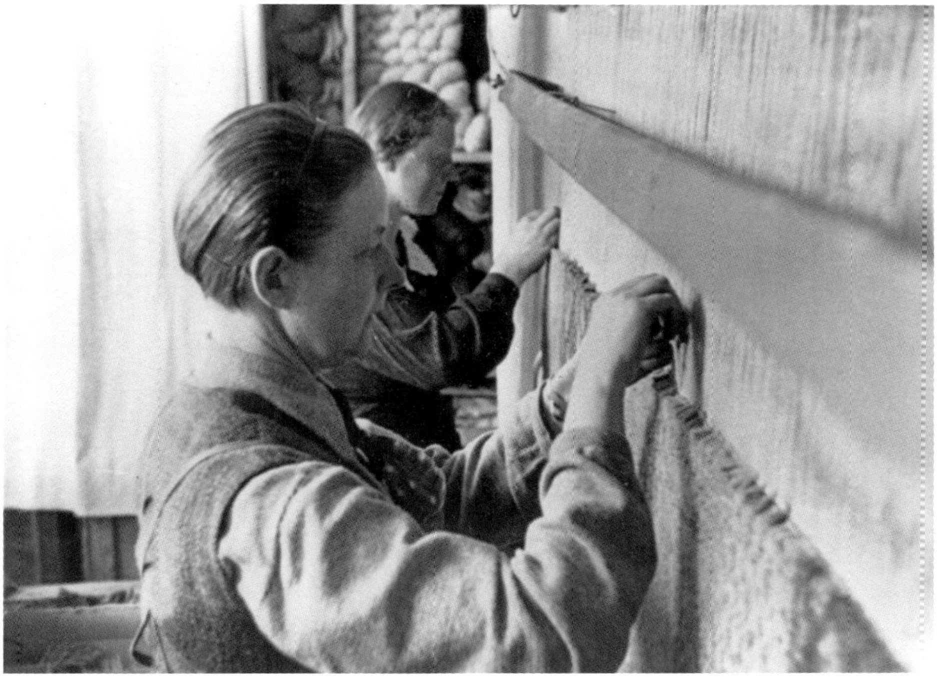

works we tried our luck at the Leipzig Trade Fair in 1924. The success we had there was considerable and pointed us in the direction of consumables, meter goods (curtain and furniture fabrics)."

On March 31, 1925, the members of the Bauhaus were dismissed, and the Bauhaus had to move to Dessau for political reasons. Benita Otte became head of handweaving at Giebichenstein *Kunstgewerbeschule* in Halle, where she took over the training and production workshop. She went, so the sculptor Gerhard Marcks wrote on December 31, 1971, in a letter to Wulf Herzogenrath "with several Bauhaus members of the old crew, who pledged allegiance to craft and who as 'romantics' did not want to take part in the trend towards technology."

Nevertheless, in 1933 all former Bauhaus members were relieved of their posts even in Halle. In 1929 Benita Otte had married the interior designer and photographer Heinrich Koch and now tried to start a new life with him in Prague. However, after her husband's tragic accidental death, she decided to go to the Bodelschwingh charitable foundation in Bethel near Bielefeld, where in September 1934 she took up a post as artistic and economic adviser to the whole weaving workshop.

Here she could fully realize what she had already begun in Halle, developing a design education programme which was firmly rooted in Klee's color theory, but which also included elements of Itten's preliminary course teaching at the Bauhaus. The representation of the color exercises shows a living, deeply felt, enthusiastic, but still very exact language. The abstract is connected with the concrete. The classical handweaving workshop as well as classes in work therapy also belonged to the evolving areas of responsibility under her management. With her educational talent Otte was able to develop the creativity of her male and female patients. As she had already done at the Weimar Bauhaus she now also set up a dyeworks for the workshops in Bethel. In order to be able to put the training on a professional footing, she belatedly took her master's certificate, so that trainees in Bethel could also sit the journeyman's exam. Until her retirement in 1957 she ran a big handweaving mill, and until 1969 she continued to explore color theory and put the exercises to the test in a number of watercolors that recall the paintings of Paul Klee. Looking back, her friend Gunta Stölzl said of her in the same year: "I always admired Otte's high degree of understanding for every aspect of a person, their work, their achievement, their destiny—all this has sealed our friendship."

Benita Koch-Otte died in 1976 in a nursing home near Bielefeld. In the Bethel textile workshop fabrics are still to this day produced and sold using her designs.

INGRID RADEWALDT

• *Benita Otte at the loom in the Bethel weaving workshop, 1950s.*

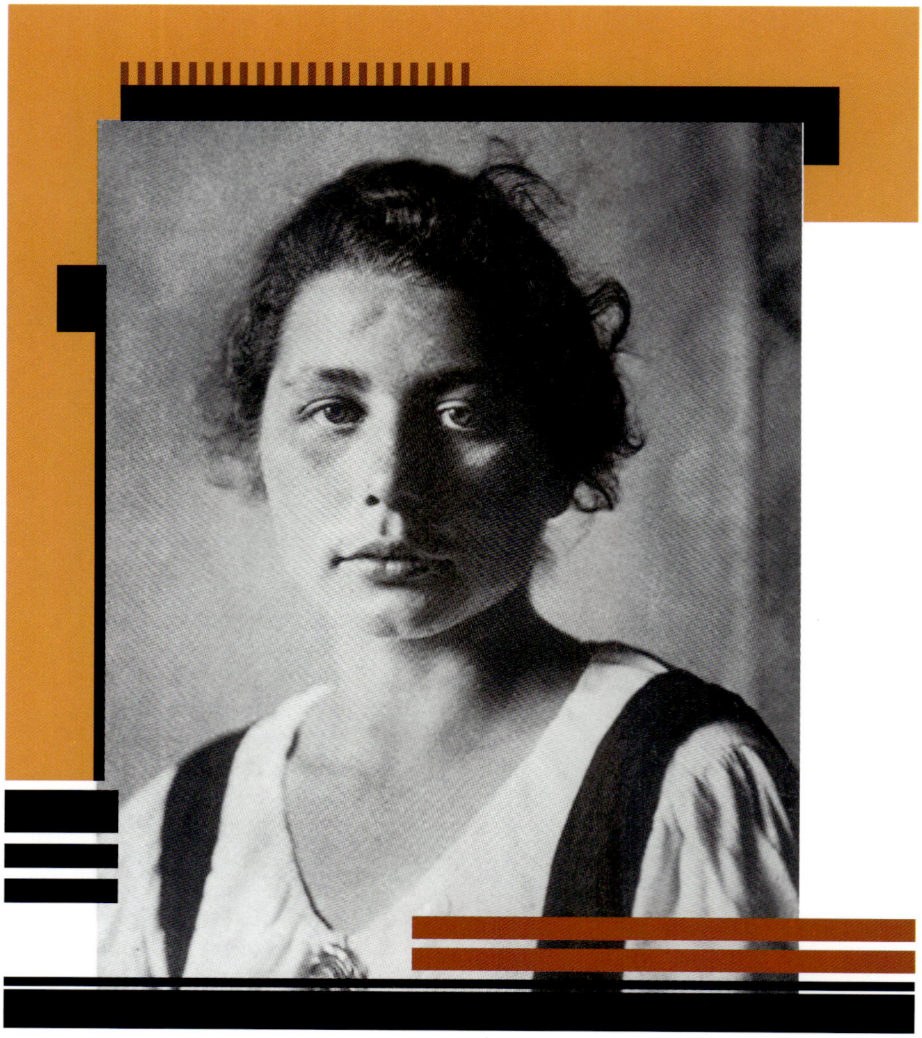

GUNTA STÖLZL 1897–1983

"We wanted to create living things with contemporary relevance, suitable for a new style of life. Huge potential for experimentation lay before us. It was essential to define our imaginary world, to shape our experiences through material, rhythm, proportion, color, form."

Gunta Stölzl, reflecting on her time at the Weimar Bauhaus in Bauhaus. Zeitschrift für Gestaltung, *July 2, 1931*

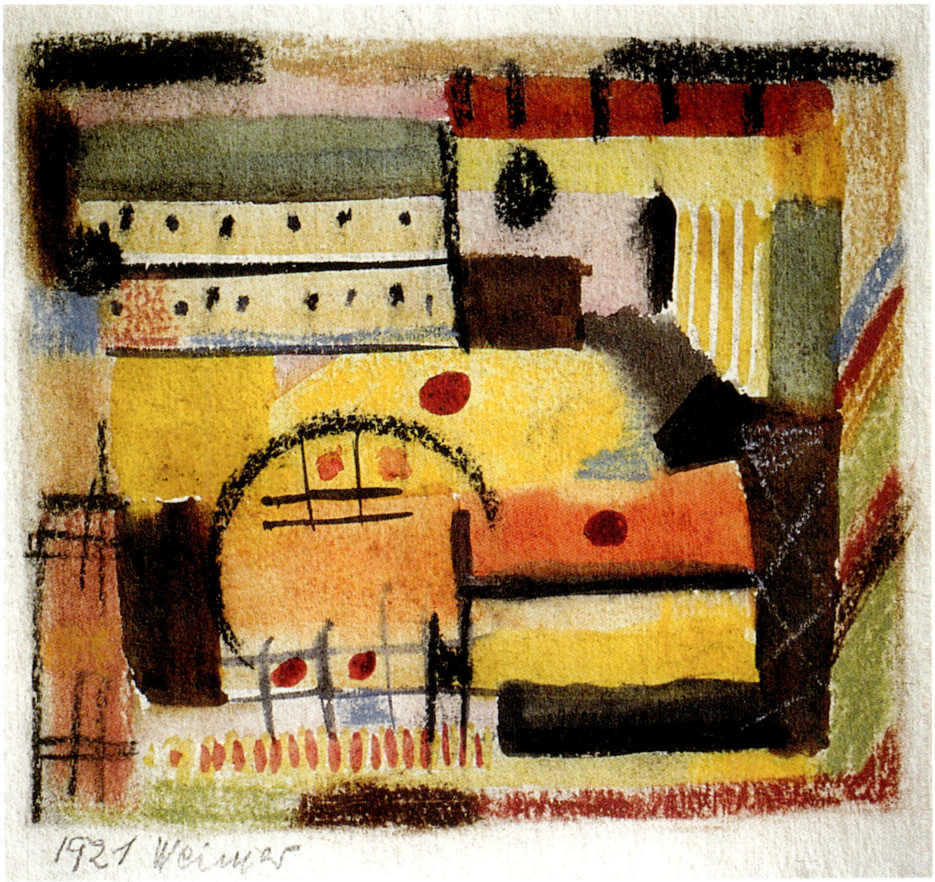

Gunta Stölzl was one of the most successful women to emerge from the Bauhaus and was perhaps more than any other synonymous with the work of the weaving workshop. She was the only woman full young master at the school, and was thus one of the very few women to achieve a management position at the Bauhaus at all.

Adelgunde Stölzl, known as Gunta, came from Munich. Her great-grandfather was a weaving master and her father a teacher who was deeply committed to the progressive education movement. The family lived very close to nature, and at the same time placed great value on a comprehensive education. Gunta was able to attend the girls' grammar school where in 1913 she took her school-leaving certificate—an exception at that time. When she arrived at the Weimar Bauhaus in 1919, she was twenty-two years old and no longer a novice in the artistic arena. She had already spent seven semesters studying at the Munich Kunstgewerbeschule, as women were still not being admitted to the fine arts academy at that time. The head of the school and Gunta's most important teacher was Richard Riemerschmidt, a holistically minded reformer in all areas of design. In 1919 Gunta Stölzl had applied to Walter Gropius, head of the Bauhaus, with a portfolio which contained work produced during her studies as well as free works and drawings, principally from the period when she served as a Red Cross nurse during World War I. These powerful drawings show her talent for observation and empathy, but also her grief and dismay at the destruction and cruelty of the war. Gropius immediately offered Stölzl a place.

Gunta Stölzl had always written a lot in her youth, and had taken great pleasure in writing. Her diaries and letters reflect her joy in the experience of nature, her wrestling with religious and existential questions, and her lifelong critical efforts to achieve real feelings and truthfulness—coupled with her capacity for exuberant enthusiasm. At the same time they also paint a sophisticated picture of the period that spanned her years of study in Weimar.

Gunta Stölzl's motives for going to the Bauhaus were manifold: the shattering, catastrophic experiences of World War I made the Munich Kunstgewerbeschule seem parochial and conservative, while the Bauhaus on the other hand promised in its manifesto a new ideal of life and work—for women too. It awoke in Gunta Stölzl hope for a truly fresh start. She began her first semester in ecstatic mood. In October 1919 she wrote in her diary: "There is nothing restrictive in my external life, I can organize it as I

• *Facing page: Gunta Stölzl, 1919.*

• *Above: Gunta Stölzl, Untitled, watercolor and colored chalk on thick paper, 1921.*

wish. Oh, how I dreamt of this so often and now it has really come true, I can still hardly believe it." And a few days later she wrote: "A new start. A new life begins."

From the outset parties were at the center of community life at the Bauhaus, having almost the same status as lessons. "On the first evening there was a wonderful party to celebrate the opening of the canteen, from which one instantly got a sense of the kind of spirit that blows through the place. A big hall with white-covered tables, green walls, music, and joyful playing pervades the air. All the people who have come with serious creative intentions are still quite unfamiliar to one another, but they want to get closer to one another, and what better way than with happy, aimless being together, dancing, and playing music? . . . Then came serious words from Gropius: 'We stand before a vacuum, it must be filled, it must be built up, and every hand is needed for the job'" (diary, October 8, 1919).

The winter of 1919 was an extremely busy one for Gunta Stölzl, and she began to make new friendships. Her diaries as much as her memoirs are dominated by eager, idealizing descriptions of the parties, but as early as 1920 there is a particular emphasis on the disputes, which she tries to analyze in her diary: "I arrived in Weimar just in time for some tough fights. It began with the first evening at the Bauhaus for Else Lasker-Schüler, the evening itself was wonderfully pure eastern Jewish. The challenging behaviour of Jews incited some pupils that evening to spoil for a fight. At first it almost looked as if the conflict would degenerate into anti-Semitism, but the danger passed. The racial issue though remains of course center-stage, but the Bauhaus ideal must rise above it." Gunta Stölzl was one of the first to take a critical stand against racist altercations in the early years of the Bauhaus, while it was only towards the end of the Weimar period that such disputes were reported in the press.

Conditions did not allow the teaching system at the Bauhaus to run terribly smoothly at first. There were no functioning workshops as yet and thus Gropius tried to realize his idea of the connection between art and craft by involving Weimar craftsmen. Gunta Stölzl began work with a glass painter, but soon became concerned that she would only learn "stale old craft" there. She switched to scene painting, whose highest goal she saw in fresco. The reality however was sobering. The work consisted in the renovation of the Bauhaus building. Initially there was hardly any structured tuition, and also little supervision, which is why creativity and personal initiative were required, these being reflected in the new spatial arrangement. In Gunta Stölzl's script for a broadcast on German radio in 1969 she wrote: "So a studio is already formed, the bed is painted ultramarine, the table is vermilion, the impossible chairs are burned, we sit on boxes, colorfully painted, on the walls

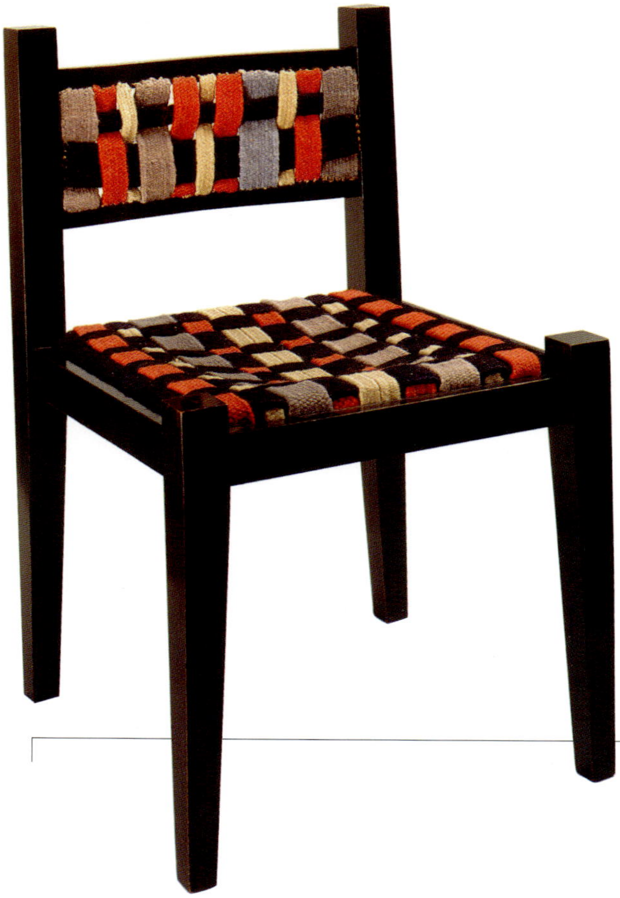

• *Chair by Marcel Breuer with woven band cover by Gunta Stölzl, 1921.*

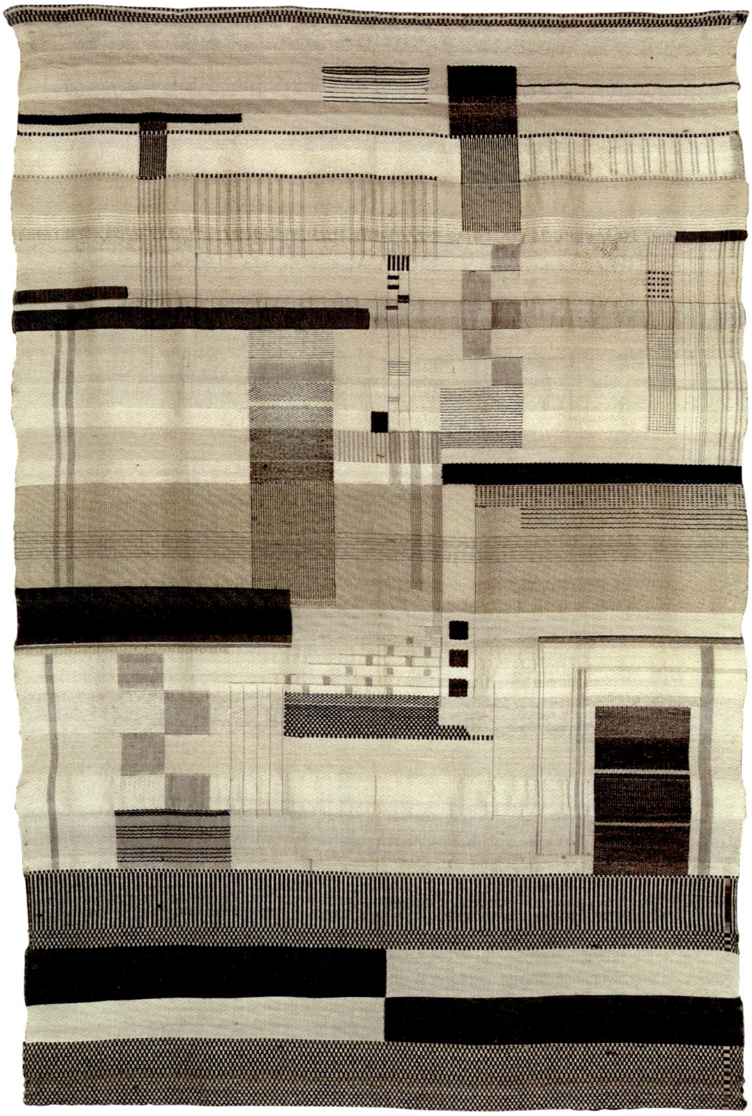

hang etchings, woodcut, and linocuts, watercolors, in the studio window an image leaded with colored glass, bottoms of bottles, and shards, quite abstract."

This kind of interior design can be traced back in essence to the suggestions of Johannes Itten who in 1919 was already giving regular classes, and for whom Gunta Stölzl had a particularly high regard because he appealed to all the senses and promoted her individual strengths. In her diary entry of October 8, 1919, she described these lessons: "Secrets, great connections made visible. . . . One must first train one's hand . . . we do finger exercises, just as a pianist does. . . . Drawing is not the reproduction of what is seen, but making whatever one senses through external stimulus flow through one's entire body, only to re-emerge as something entirely personal."

In 1920 room 10 of the workshop building saw the development of a special women's class, supported by Gropius, who, as documented in one set of Masters' Council minutes, had been unsettled by the large number of women at the Bauhaus. The technologies of this workshop, which was soon to be called the Weberei (weaving workshop), were initially somewhat limited. Alongside appliqué work and embroidery, wall-hanging technique and straightforward flatweaves, knotting techniques were also used. For this the styling was new, geometrical forms and abstract picture compositions predominated, the color scheme was sensitively taught, and the choice of material was unconventional. In spite of the lack of vocational instruction, there was a high level of enthusiasm and receptiveness. Bauhaus artist Anni Albers, who studied with Gunta Stölzl in Weimar, remembered it thus: "There was no proper teacher for textile work, we had no proper classes. Today people say only: 'They learnt all this at the Bauhaus!' At the beginning we learnt nothing at all. I learnt a lot from Gunta, who was a fantastic teacher. We sat there and simply tried things out." From 1920 the work in the weaving workshop was more tightly organized, and a six-hour working day agreed upon. The motives behind this were primarily economic ones, as it was necessary to sell the products in order to reduce the costs of the Bauhaus.

In winter 1920 Gunta Stölzl's tuition fees were waived, and later she also received a scholarship, which was certainly attributable to the very particular nature of her involvement in the weaving workshop. In 1921 Paul Klee arrived at the Bauhaus, and Gunta Stölzl immediately took up his theory of pictorial forms. Later she appreciated him as a teacher, to whom she owed "more

• *Gunta Stölzl,* Black-White, *wall hanging, 1923–24, reversed woven 1925 reproduction by Helene Börner, half-gobelin, plain weave, flatweaving with turned shuttles.*

profound, conceptually elaborated issues concerning form, relationships, and color values." In many of Gunta Stölzl's works from the early Weimar period it becomes clear how well she grasped the principles of her teacher, whose works she understood without copying them.

In spite of the intensity of her artistic work Gunta Stölzl's desire for happiness in her private life became all-important. In spring 1920 she fell in love with the painter Werner Gilles and after just a few days was sure she had found the man of her life. At Easter 1920 they got engaged. In lyrical letters and enthusiastic diary entries they described their love—which, however, was not destined to last. Gilles was soon wracked by doubt, and Stölzl ended the relationship. As a way out of her crisis she chose, as she had previously done in earlier years, to take a long trip, during which she gradually found her feet again and began to look very critically and pragmatically at her life's goals: "Our generation has simply not yet found the form for love and marriage. The same quest that expresses itself in all our works is just the desperate yearning for a new form of life. All marriages fail or are unhappy, Gropius is getting divorced, Feininger torments himself, Itten is controlled by a vampire (diary, shortly before May 28, 1920).

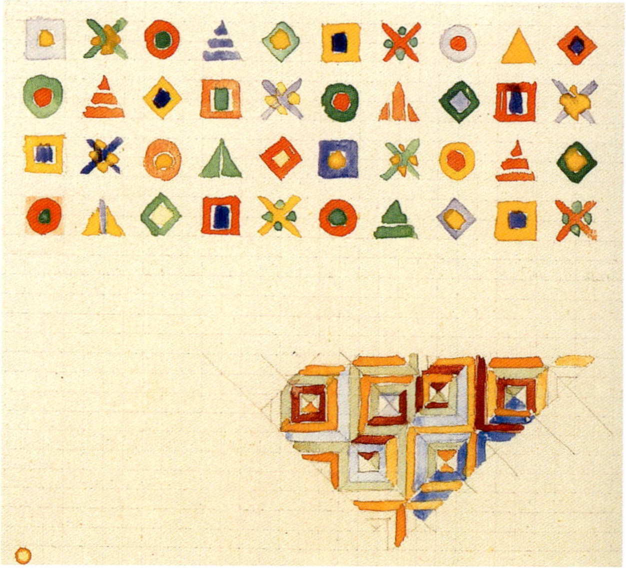

• *Gunta Stölzl, Sheet of pattern designs, Bauhaus Dessau, undated; transformed into carpeting from the preparatory design, 1994.*

Gunta Stölzl resolved from now on to channel all her energies into her work at the Bauhaus. Her thoughts on this were set out in a long—and final—diary entry: "I have had to busy myself with so many things this week that I have not willingly jumped on this tightrope of activity, but I also feel it was no coincidence that Gropius me on, and it also makes me really happy to have responsibility. . . . I now have the feeling that I can no longer separate my life and destiny from the Bauhaus and that is a great source of strength." In actual fact Gunta Stölzl did walk the "tightrope of activity" and proceeded to work on many major projects in the following period. Indeed she now became the defining personality of the textile workshop.

Together with Marcel Breuer, one of the cabinetmaking workshop's most creative students, she developed seat coverings, first in free abstract weaving, then with tight bands in just a few colors. These works were the beginning of a fertile collaboration between the weaving and cabinetmaking workshops, which resulted in the development of covering fabrics for modern slatted and tubular steel chairs. The year 1922 saw the production of the first large-scale pictorial wall hanging, now lost. This was followed by a ten foot by ten foot (three meter by three meter) knotted carpet which the form master Lothar Schreyer described as "blossoming like the spring meadow of a brighter world." This carpet was recognized by the Bauhaus as journeyman's quality and was presented in one of the first Bauhaus exhibitions in Weimar.

In 1923 the Bauhaus went public with a comprehensive exhibition. For the Haus am Horn, the show home that was planned especially for the exhibition, Stölzl wove one of the most notable carpets. Another exhibition piece, a

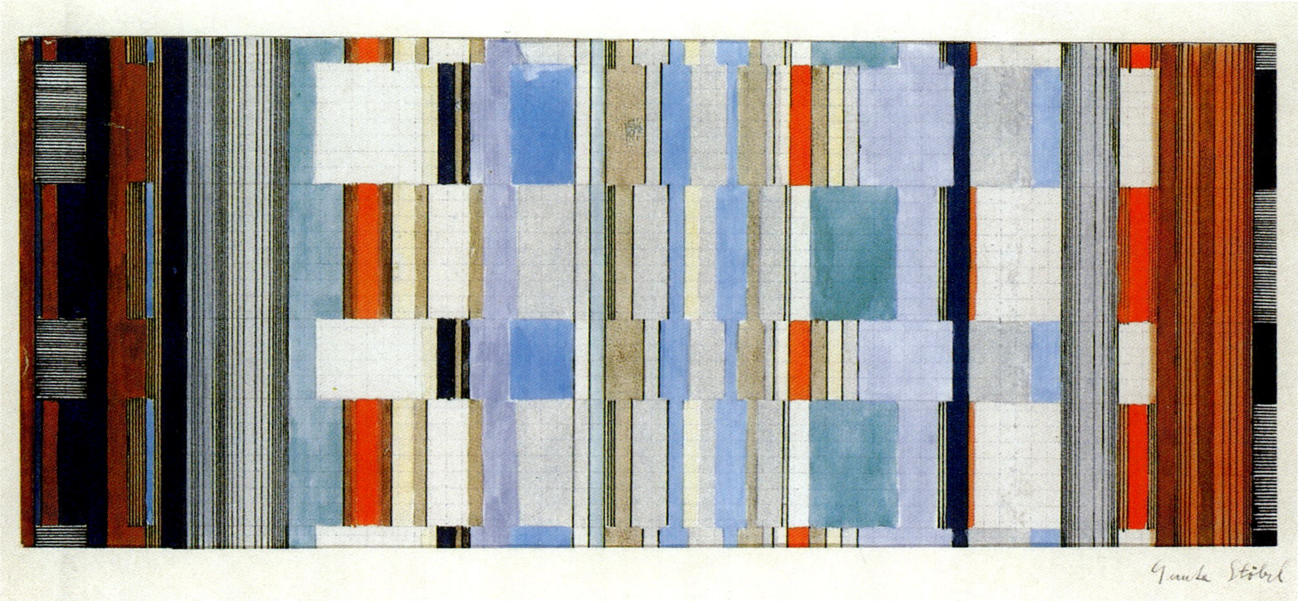

twenty foot (six-meter) long knotted carpet with abstract motifs, was acquired during the exhibition by an architect, who also bought her diploma piece. The year 1923 also witnessed the creation of three of the surviving big wall hangings of the Weimar period, which today are in museums in Basel, New York, and Cambridge, Massachusetts; in the years leading to 1925 Gunta Stölzl wove a series of wall hangings with striped patterns, some of which have remained in Weimar. In fall 1924 she was promoted to journeywoman in the Bauhaus weaving workshop, something that was quite exceptional among women at the Bauhaus.

In the production section of the weaving workshop meter goods were also being made, some of which were already being sold as prototypes for industry. The first companies started ordering Bauhaus fabrics. A path to modern textile design was forged, which was then continued and expanded at the Dessau Bauhaus. In Weimar right-wing political forces denied further support to the Bauhaus, which meant that Gropius was forced to close down his school. The move to Dessau began, and in 1927 Gunta Stölzl was bound to the new Bauhaus as a work master in the weaving department by the terms of an official contract with the city council of Dessau. After Georg Muche had left as a result of serious differences with the weaving students, Gunta Stölzl took over the whole running of the weaving workshop at the newly built Bauhaus in Dessau, where she was the first female member of the teaching staff. In her 1931 article in *Bauhaus* she commented on the school's artistic re-orientation: "we tried to simplify things, to rein in resources, to become more certain of our purpose . . . the slogan of this new age: a model for industry!"

Gunta Stölzl developed new syllabuses in Dessau, since the opening of the architecture department in 1927 demanded of the weaving workshop technically perfect modern products. The workshop took on ever-bigger orders, for example the fitting out of the theater café in Dessau with curtains and wall coverings. Alongside this, identical blankets were woven for the students' hall of residence according to a design by Gunta Stölzl, furniture fabrics were produced for Marcel Breuer's tubular steel chairs, and later the new Gewerkschaftsschule (Trade Union School) in Bernau was also furnished. Selling exhibitions also took place at the Leipzig trade fairs, which meant that the workshop had to cope with an extremely heavy workload. Gunta Stölzl wrote to her brother in 1927: "there is always a lot going on here—and one is mentally so caught up in the tempo of the place that one can't actually get round to one's own work. sometimes it is intolerable, particularly these last weeks. I don't know any way out—my time is completely eaten up with organization."

• *Gunta Stölzl, Design for a wall hanging, c. 1926.*

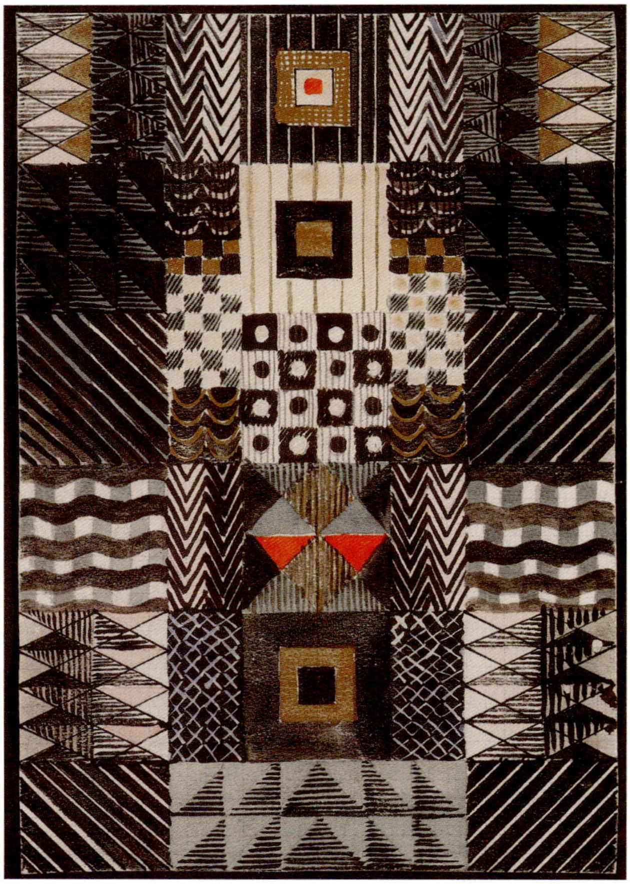

Gunta Stölzl's life would fundamentally change on a trip to the international architecture congress in Moscow in May 1928, where she fell in love with Arieh Sharon, who had been a student at the Bauhaus since 1926. He was a Jew, originally from Galicia, and had lived in Palestine for six years before enrolling in the architecture department. In 1928 Hannes Meyer assigned him the post of leading architect in the construction of the Gewerkschaftsschule in Bernau. In August Stölzl and Sharon were married. She had to give up her German nationality and adopt Palestinian citizenship. In October their daughter Yael was born in Berlin. The couple were together in Dessau only at weekends, because Sharon was still working in Bernau. She wrote to her brother: "We are a happy family! But what will become of the work at the bauhaus is still puzzling to me, for the moment it is eating me up."

In the meantime, internal difficulties were building up at the Bauhaus. Right- and left-wing forces were squaring up to one other, and the whole political situation was changing. Hannes Meyer, known as a "red," was dismissed without notice, Sharon lost his job. There was also an increasing amount of intrigue in the weaving workshop. Three students—Herbert von Arend, Ilse Voigt, and Margaretha Reichardt—supported by the teacher Walter Peterhaus, were critical of Stölzl, her private life, and her teaching, at first covertly, then openly. She had largely lost her support, since many of her old students, as well as colleagues Klee and Hannes Meyer, had left the Bauhaus. The protesting students took advantage of the change of directors and registered their accusations. Mies van der Rohe was keen to achieve a compromise, as former students recalled in a letter: "It was not about apportioning blame but rather about restoring peace."

In a letter of October 28, 1930, those same students consolidated and intensified their accusations, which became ever more absurd: "frau sharon has completely failed in educational, artistic, and organizational terms. she is absolutely unsure and ignorant on all technical points, e.g., the study of materials, and is unable to distinguish wool from cotton. This criticism of the fabrics would be governed only by antipathies and sympathies, in other words it was entirely personal and human, artistic judgement being completely absent. . . . frau sharon takes care of important organizational matters connected with the workshop only in terms of tea and coffee" (letter of October 28, 1930, Getty Museum, Los Angeles).

Stölzl felt powerless in the face of the students' personal hunger for power and their petty jealousies, not to mention the anti-Semitism—in the morning she would find a swastika fixed to her door—but she saw no possibility of working elsewhere, either in another college or in industry. At the beginning of January 1931 Stölzl was vindicated with regard to Herbert von Arend's complaint: he was instructed not to enter the workshop until

• *Gunta Stölzl, Design for a Jacquard wall hanging, 1927.*

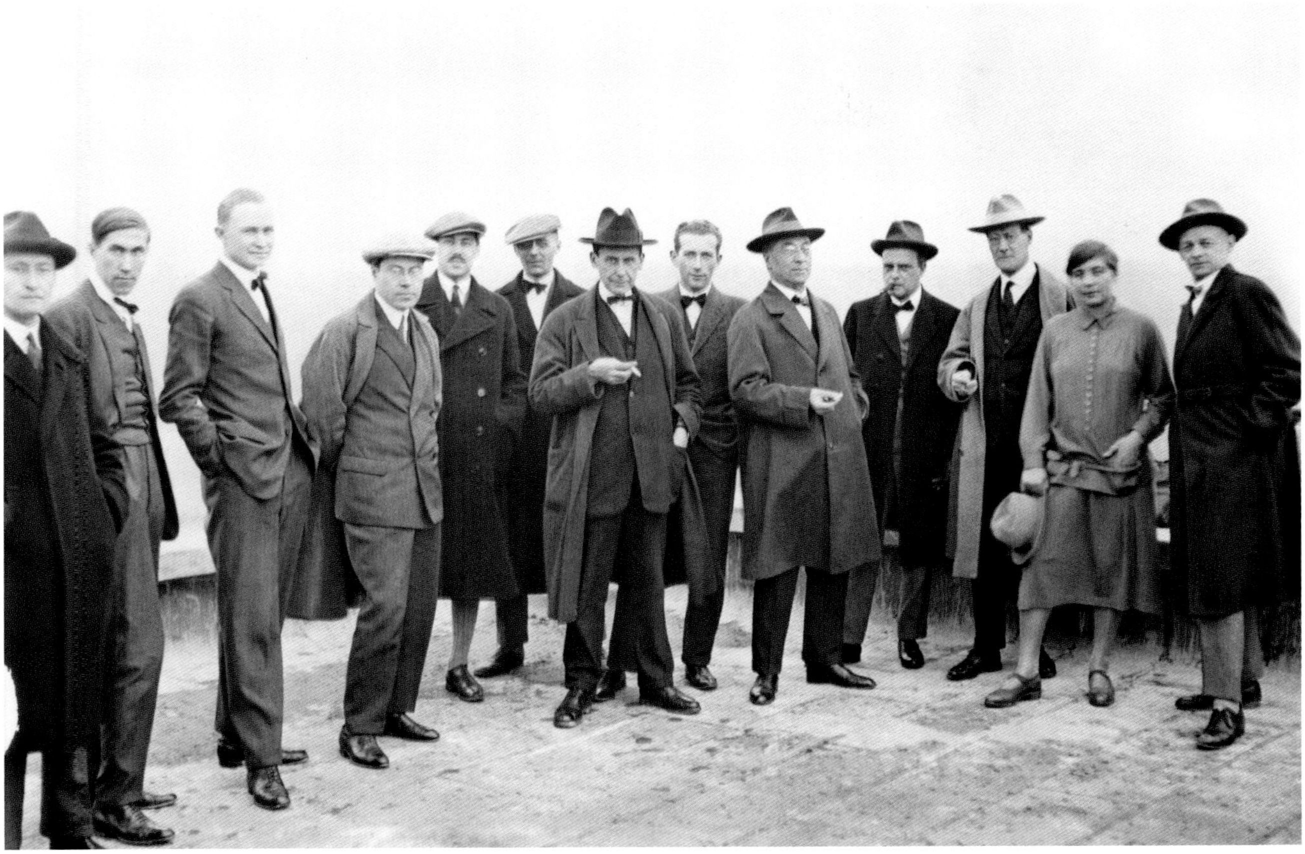

the issues had been cleared up. In March 1931 the situation reached such a point that she turned to her brother for legal advice: "this girl's father has not calmed down and has submitted to the administration a complaint against me, which is above all an attack on my personal life, apparently slandering me in the sexual realm . . . i myself also think that it would be smartest to resign and look for a new position. and i would very gladly leave — the whole job and especially the human side of it are not very pleasant here any more."

Her brother advised her to pursue an action for slander and to demand recompense for the harm done, telling her that she would not be able to fight against a dismissal. Gunta Stölzl drew only one conclusion from her brother's legal advice. She tendered her resignation that very same day, before she could be dismissed.

In May 1931 the Communist student group tried once again to have the accusers expelled from the Bauhaus. The text of KoStuFra (the Communist students' faction) drew satirically on the Nazis' propagandistic language in order to show the political dimension of the affair. Nevertheless, against the vote of the students the accusers were accepted back at the Bauhaus. Gunta Stölzl wrote to her brother about this so-called settlement: "For the first time now I am glad to get out of this gossipy and corrupt community. The students threw out the three agitators. Mies also removed them, and all the masters signed his action and posted it on the Bauhaus notice board. Then the mayor came along with a Nationalist (Nazi), the father of one of the female accusers, and they were taken back again! This is how powerful politics is and I have just unfortunately become a victim of it." Gunta Stölzl never read the eighty-page indictment of her, which has never been found in the Bauhaus documents. On July 7, 1931, Gunta Stölzl left Dessau for good.

She emigrated to Switzerland, where she ran her own handweaving mill until the age of seventy. She died in Küsnacht in 1983 at the age of eighty-six.

INGRID RADEWALDT

• *Bauhaus masters on the roof of the Bauhaus in Dessau, on the occasion of its opening on December 5, 1926. From left: Josef Albers, Hinnerk Scheper, Georg Muche, László Moholy-Nagy, Herbert Bayer, Joost Schmidt, Walter Gropius, Marcel Breuer, Wassily Kandinsky, Paul Klee, Lyonel Feininger, Gunta Stölzl, and Oskar Schlemmer.*

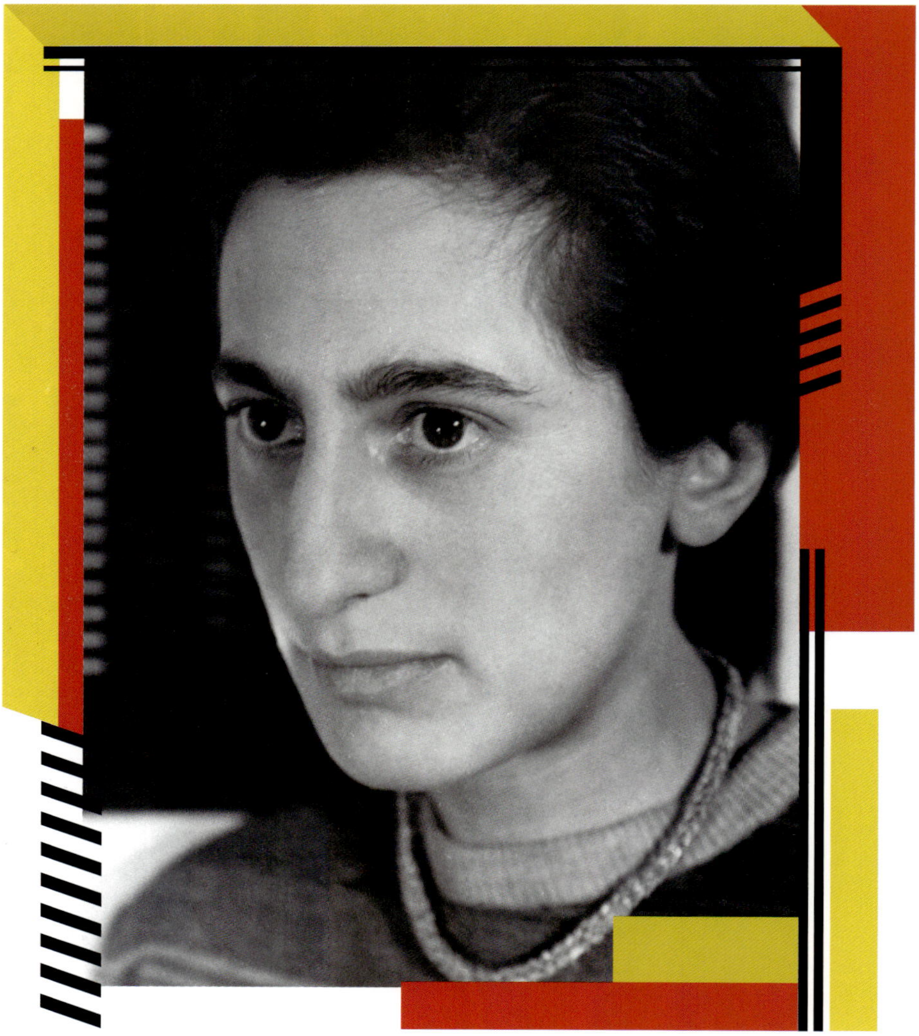

ANNI ALBERS 1899–1994

"Every beginner should be afforded this freedom of creativity. Courage is a key factor in every form of artistic creative process, it can best unfold when it is not curtailed too early by knowledge."

Anni Albers, Die Werkstatt der Weberei *(The Weaving Workshop)*

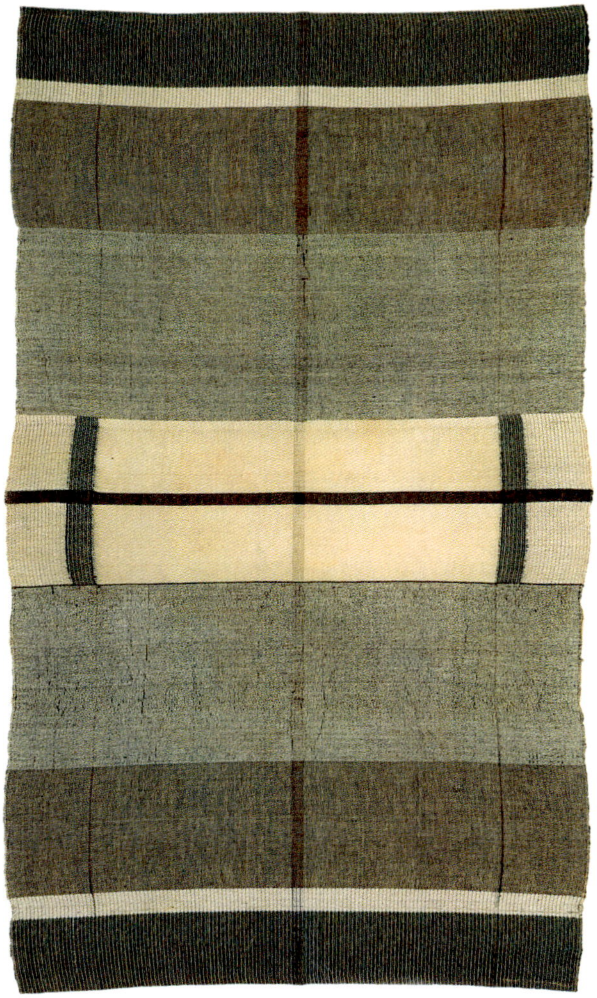

She was an artist who designed patterns for industry; she was an art collector and professor and she gave lectures and wrote books. If it can be said of one Bauhaus woman that she made a career for herself, then that woman was Anni Albers. She consistently merged the crafts from the weaving workshop, industrial textile production, and the abstract art of the modernist period, and brought them to a new unity. The persecution caused by the National Socialists, which gave rise to so much terrible suffering took an unexpectedly positive turn for Anni and her husband, the Bauhaus artist Josef Albers. They were able to continue their artistic work almost seamlessly having being forced to leave Germany in 1933. They remained in the United States and imported many Bauhaus ideas.

Anneliese Fleischmann was born on June 12, 1899, in Charlottenburg, Berlin to a bourgeois family and baptized in the Protestant faith. Her mother, Toni Fleischmann-Ullstein, belonged to the German-Jewish publishing family Ullstein. Her father, Siegfried Fleischmann, was a furniture manufacturer. As an adolescent Anni received home tutoring from an art teacher. Sten Nadoly wrote in his *Ullsteinroman*: "Anni . . . was the most difficult of the Fleischmann family. She was also the most beautiful, a first rate femme fatale. . . . She wanted to be a bohemian, a revolutionary, an artist." At the same time, she was highly sensitive with fluctuating self-confidence. She is said to have considered herself unattractive despite her beauty. At seventeen she began training with the Impressionist painter Martin Brandenburg. An attempt at lessons with Oskar Kokoschka failed. He was of the opinion that she would have been better off as a housewife and mother. She tried the Kunstgewerbeschule in Hamburg and was bored for two semesters on an embroidery course. Then she heard of the Bauhaus. Her father showed little understanding, yet she determinedly set off for Weimar.

She rented a simple room in Weimar, applied to the Bauhaus and was, however, at first turned down. Nevertheless, she stayed and fell in love with "a haggard half-starved ascetic from Westphalia, with irresistible blonde hair," as she always liked to describe him in later years—Josef Albers, who had studied at the Bauhaus since fall 1920. He was eleven years her senior, a trained artist, hailing from Bottrop in the Ruhr, and had not exactly grown up in the lap of luxury. She convinced him to help her in a second attempt, and it worked.

Anni Fleischmann began her studies at the Weimar Bauhaus on April 21, 1922. She received basic instruction from Muche and in the second semester took Itten's preliminary course and introduction to artistic design.

• *Facing page: Portrait of Anni Albers, 1929.*

• *Above: Anni Albers, Wall hanging, 1924.*

In the third semester she turned up in the "Women's Department," the weaving workshop, and felt out of place. "I considered weaving too womanish. I was looking for the right occupation and so I began weaving without any great enthusiasm, as this choice caused the least comment."

The working conditions in the weaving workshop were less than ideal, as she later remembered: "There was no proper teacher for textile work, and we didn't have proper classes. . . . We learnt absolutely nothing at the beginning. . . . We just sat there and practised." However, she knew to use this freedom to her advantage. In her contribution about the weaving workshop in Ise and Walter Gropius's book about the Bauhaus, she wrote: "This game with the material . . . brought astonishing results, novel weaves, stunning in their color texture and structure, which sometimes had an almost barbaric beauty."

Above all, she learned from and with her fellow student Gunta Stölzl, who had already taken on administrative duties in the textile workshop. The first of Anni's typical works were created in this period—large wall hangings and meter fabrics with abstract motifs strictly reduced to their basic geometric forms. In 1924 she assisted in the dye works and published two essays. In her piece *Wohnökonomie* (Living Economy) she was critical: "The conventional style of living is a used-up machine, which makes the woman a slave to the house," and she canvassed for the new purposefulness to which the Bauhaus aspired. In Bauhausweberei (Bauhaus Weaving Workshop) she explained: "Work today has to be experimental . . . we must re-visit manual and technical possibilities . . . we can then understand industry and work for it . . . so the way leads both to the individual item and to mass production."

The Bauhaus moved to Dessau in the spring of 1925 and in May, Anni and Josef married in a Catholic ceremony. Josef Albers, who had finished his training in the glass workshop, was by now a Bauhaus master and gave the preliminary courses. He is described as a good teacher, level-headed, and at one with himself albeit somewhat stubborn at times. The Albers shared a great passion for fabrics, materials such as metal and glass, and also plastics, as well as for geometric shapes and the reduction and abstraction of metaphorical language. Anni wove wall hangings for Gropius's new master's residence and turned to creating tapestries. With vertical and horizontal interwoven threads she created a strict geometric pattern, which corresponded closely with Josef's glasswork. Anni worked on a Jacquard loom for the first time in 1926 when Gunta Stölzl became the new head of the weaving workshop. She used this loom to transfer her geometric designs to fabric, with the desired precision. She also experimented with various synthetic materials.

Anni Albers's most important artistic teachers at the Bauhaus were Wassily Kandinsky and Paul Klee. From 1925, she studied artistic design techniques under Kandinsky, which she continued under Klee in the winter semester of 1927–28. Paul Klee was her "god." When the textile workshop chartered a small plane from the nearby Junkers factory to throw presents from the air in celebration of the adored Klee's fiftieth birthday, Anni Albers sat in the cockpit. Twice in 1929, she took on acting leadership of the textile workshop. She completed her studies at the Bauhaus and was awarded her diploma in February 1930. Her exam piece was a soundproof, light-reflecting wall-hanging, which could also be used as a curtain. The piece was created for the aula of the Gewerkschaftsschule (Trade Union School) in Bernau, which had been designed by Hannes Meyer. To reinforce

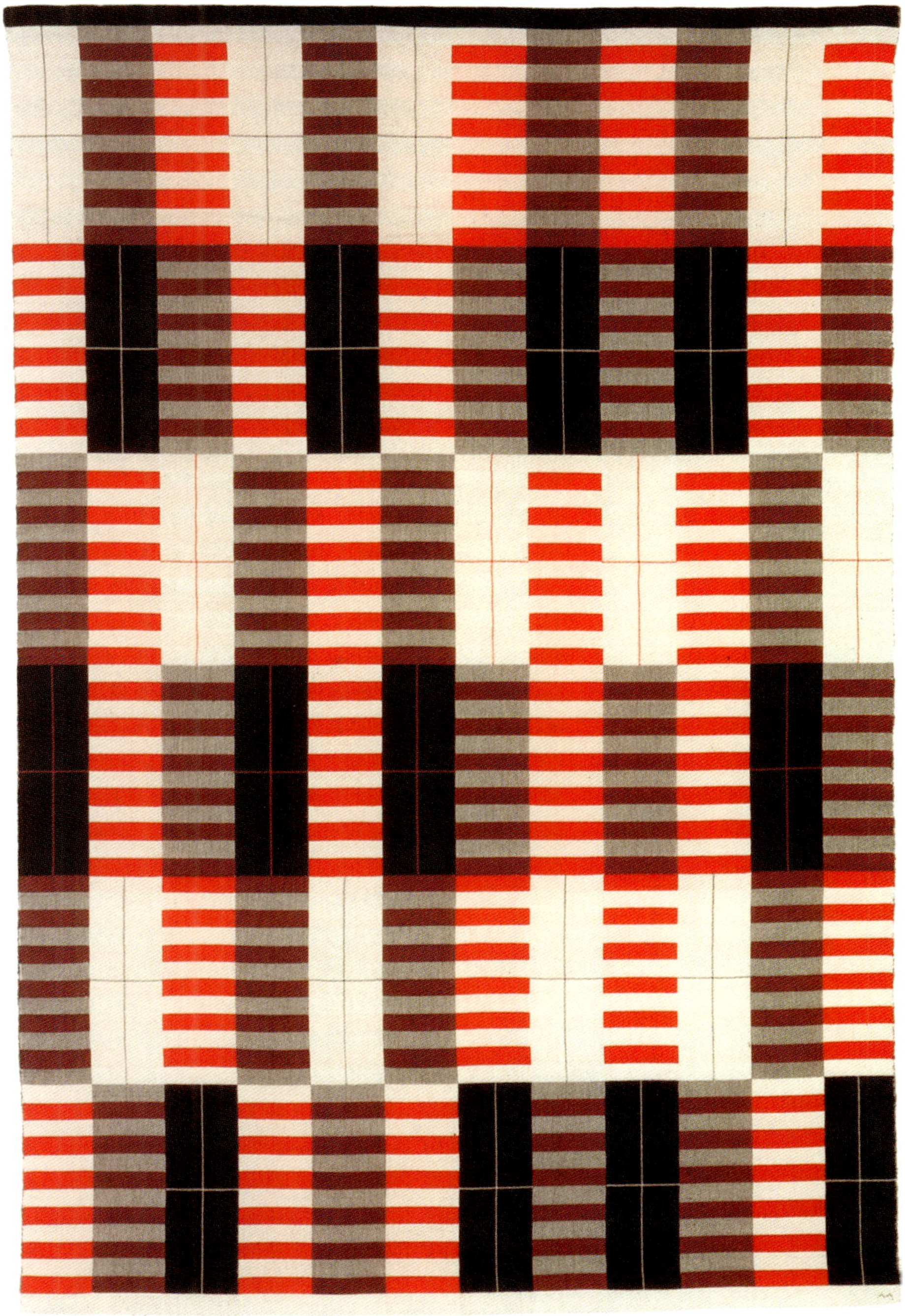

the light reflection, she used cellophane on the front and sound-absorbing chenille at the back.

After completing her studies, Anni Albers was hired as an ex officio teacher for theoretical instruction in the weaving workshop. In fall 1931, she took over the running of the weaving workshop until Lilly Reich took up the position. Anni took part in the exhibition *Deutsche Bauausstellung* in Berlin in the same year, for which she received an award of honor.

The Bauhaus was finally forced to close in 1933 by the National Socialists. Anni, whose Jewish descent had not played any major role up to this point, saw herself in increasing danger because of rising anti-Semitism. The architect Philip Johnson, who had visited the Bauhaus in 1927, became her knight in shining armor. He invited the couple to teach at the newly founded Black Mountain College in North Carolina, a college for modern art and education. The Albers arrived in New York in 1933, where they were lauded in the press as "representatives of European modernity." There was no language barrier for Anni as she had learned English from her Irish nanny. She began to build up the weaving workshop in the Black Mountain College in 1934 and was assistant professor of art at the college until 1949. Apart from that, she designed fabrics for large firms such as Rosenthal and Knoll. For her, the future of textile work was in industrial production, but she in no way sacrificed material experiments in her individual craftwork, to which she attached great importance. "The material itself is full of suggestions for its use," she wrote in her 1959 work *On Designing*.

• *Anni Albers, Wall hanging, 1926/1964.*

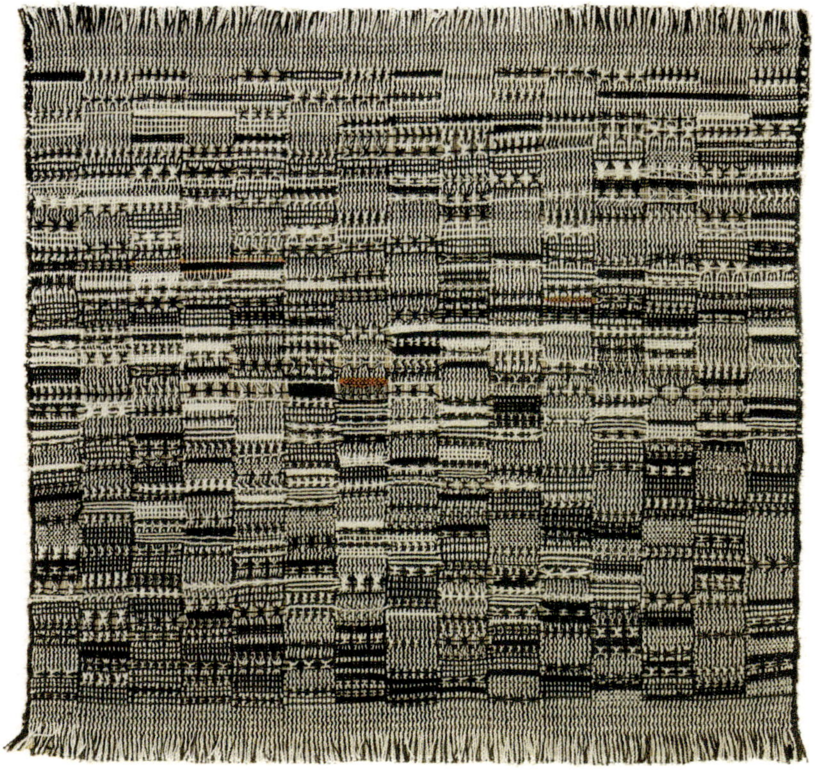

In his essay "Begegnung mit Anni Albers" (Encounter with Anni Albers) Nicholas Fox Weber, founder and director of the Josef & Anni Albers Foundation, refers to a small woven picture from 1948 in the Museum of Modern Art in New York, which exemplifies the work of these years: "Despite its smallness, every thread appears to carry boundless energy, the basic units of the composition connect and cross over each other with an inexhaustive liveliness as if they wished to express their existence to themselves and simultaneously their belonging to the bigger picture."

A philosophical, religious dimension oscillates through Anni Albers's work, to which she herself often referred. The work can offer many points of access to the endless varieties of creation, as the materials, motifs, and patterns offer new possibilities to perception over and over again. Indeed, at first they appear symmetrical, next asymmetrical, next they form a surface, then a space. Some of Anni's patterns are reminiscent of the drawings of a mandala, others of writing, still others of technical processes. Many works from the 1950s had titles which allude to writing as in the pictorial weave, *Open Letter* (1958). Anni Albers was anxious to allow threads, fabrics, structures, lines, colors, shapes, light, and space to create their own effect, not to enforce her own will on them. For her, this was the motor of activ ty, of experimentation, and also the source of humility. One could never know where the journey would lead.

Anni and Josef Albers led a disciplined life, the central point of which was work. Their studios are said to always have been tidy, the art business and bohemia were anathema to them, according to Nicolas Fox Weber in his article *Gemeinsames Leben, gemeinsame Arbeit* (Shared Lives, Shared Work, 1998). There was, however, some turbulence and power struggle in the relationship. Both competed time and again with the other and a robust insult was more the order of the day than mutual admiration. Anni's feelings of rivalry were additionally fed by the fact that, for a long time she was, in public, merely the artist's spouse and only thereafter appreciated as an artist in her own right.

This was all the more annoying for her since she invested more energy in the "day-to-day stuff," which made married life possible. In interviews following Josef's death in 1976 she gave differing statements on the subject of the artistic pecking order. In 1985 she said in an interview that he had definitely influenced her work, but she had definitely not influenced his.

An element of the couple's artistic life in the United States was Anni's enthusiasm for pre-Columbian art.

• *Anni Albers,* Open Letter, *pictorial weaving, 1958.*

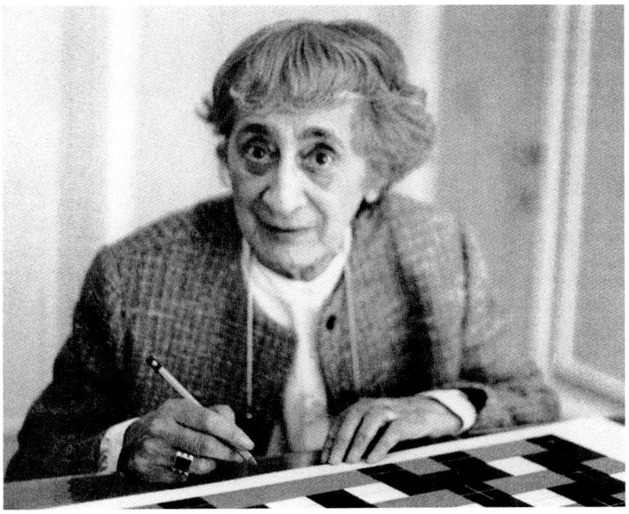

Between 1935 and 1967 she undertook several long journeys to Mexico, Peru, and Bolivia, and slowly built up an important collection of historical artefacts. In the art of the Maya and the Aztecs they both admired that to which they had both striven in their Bauhaus time—its beauty, a connection between rational order, simplicity, and economy. They discovered fascinating connections to abstract modern art. "The pre-Columbian culture also made it clear to us that one does not need to live in affluence to create great art. One should actually ask whether the exact opposite is true," was Anni Albers's conclusion in a later article. And yet she still liked to live well.

Anni's first international success was in 1949 when she was the first woman weaver ever to have an exhibition devoted to her at New York's Museum of Modern Art. "Her Weaving becomes a Modern Art," was the headline of a newspaper article about Anni Albers. She worked as a freelance weaver and extraordinary professor at Yale University, until 1962. She and her husband were honored with numerous awards and exhibitions in the 1950s and 1960s. Anni collated her knowledge in the field of textile design in the books *On Designing* (1959) and *On Weaving* (1965). She was commissioned by the Jewish Museum in New York to create a memorial work for the victims of the Holocaust in 1965. The piece, *Six Prayers*, was to be her last great textile work. From then on she turned her attentions to abstract print graphics. When the couple moved to Orange, near New Haven, Anni finally gave up her looms. In 1975 her works were on show in the Kunstmuseum, Düsseldorf and the Bauhaus Archive, Berlin—the first retrospective in Germany since 1933. The most comprehensive retrospective of her work to date was at the Renwick Gallery of the Smithsonian Institution in Washington in 1986.

Anni Albers died in Orange on May 9, 1994, aged ninety-four. To the end, she viewed her life and work as temporary: "Whatever I say or do appears to me as a real 'perhaps.'" This was her last sentence in a press conference in which she participated at the age of ninety, together with Dorothee Müller and Maximilian Schell. She also formulated the positive quintessence of the early Bauhaus in no uncertain terms: "What still interests me today is that this great quest bore fruit in great freedom—and not where a language is already spoken."

ULRIKE MÜLLER

• *Anni Albers in July 1983.*

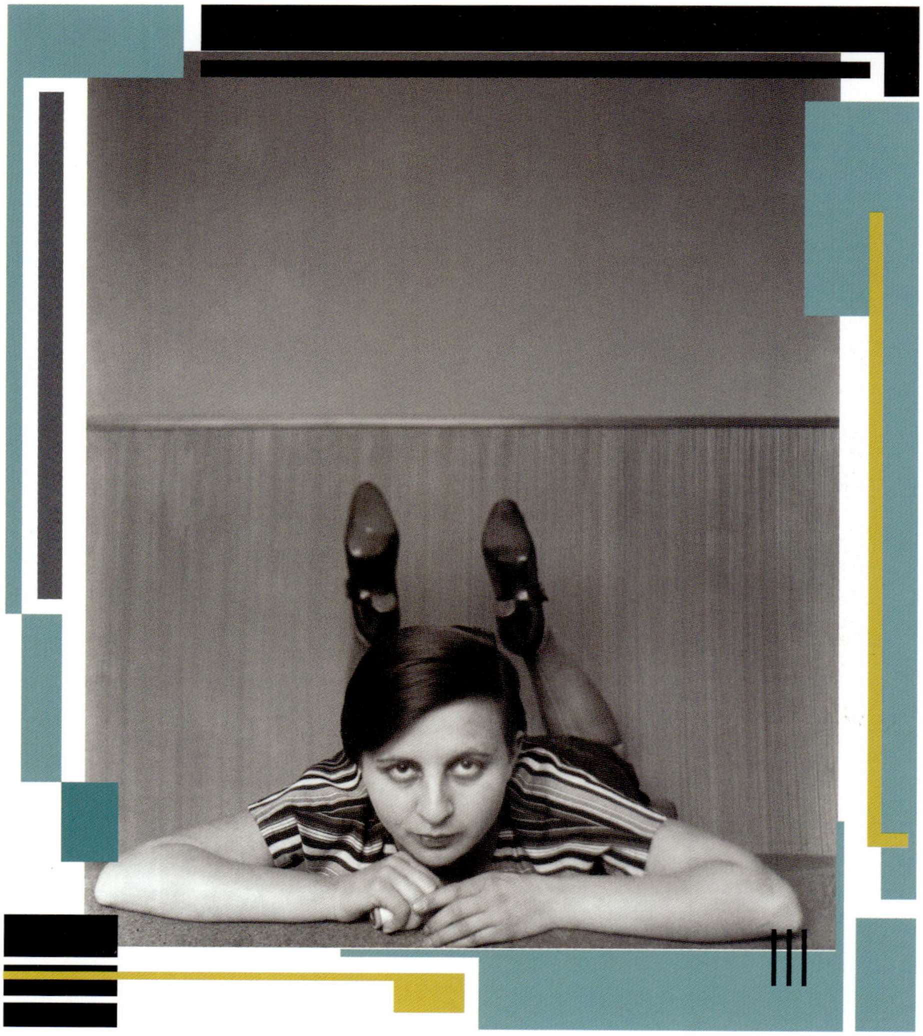

GERTRUD ARNDT 1903–2000

"They all went to the weaving workshop, whether they wanted to or not. Yes, that was simply the way out. . . . I never wanted to weave. It was absolutely not my aim. No, not at all. All those threads, I didn't want that. No, that was not my thing."

Gertrud Arndt

Gertrud Hantschk, born in Ratibor, Upper Silesia in 1903, attended the Kunstgewerbeschule in Erfurt until 1923 before being officially accepted at the Bauhaus in the winter semester of 1923. She participated in the preliminary course with Moholy-Nagy as well as in Klee's color and form classes, whose system especially interested her. She meticulously noted Klee's theories on fourteen handwritten pages with fine sketches in ink and watercolors on themes such as *Grau ist Norm* (Gray is the Norm), *Bewegung und Gegenbewegung* (Movement and Counter-Movement), or *Grundformenvergleiche* (Comparisons of Basic Shapes). The theme of the "square" which Klee himself made variations on in many of his works, became a leitmotif for many of her later designs, and her differentiating way with color could also be traced back to Klee. In 1994, at ninety-one, in a conversation with Monika Stadler, Gunta Stölzl's daughter, and Ingrid Radewaldt she recalled: "Artistically, we were with Klee and Kandinsky. They were our heroes." In the preliminary semester, she created, apart from her sketches, many designs whose quality and quantity would decide one's acceptance at a workshop. "It had to work. Either you were accepted or not."

Gertrud wanted to go on to study architecture but she was the only woman on the construction course and, according to her own statement, felt lost there. And Georg Muche had judged her composition drawings from the preliminary course with the words: "Let's make a rug out of it."

So she joined the weaving workshop. She viewed training in this workshop as her only possibility of continuing at the Bauhaus, as a woman. She began with the creation of a rug design for Gropius's office in Weimar, which had already been redesigned for the great Bauhaus exhibition of 1923. Beyer's isometric design sketch shows a strictly divided cubic room with an inner cube as a seating area. Gertrud Hantschk accentuated this cubic character with her knotted rug of blue and yellow squares, which matched the right-angled, yellow seating. The design sketch and twelve colored thread swatches survived, so that the rug for the reconstructed director's room in Weimar could be remade (see p. 25). A further meticulously painted rug design from 1924 was especially difficult to realize due to the thirty-seven colors, as the threads were no longer available to buy: "I had to dye all the wool myself—without knowledge and without help. It was awful," she remembered in her biography for the Vorwerk company brochure in 1993.

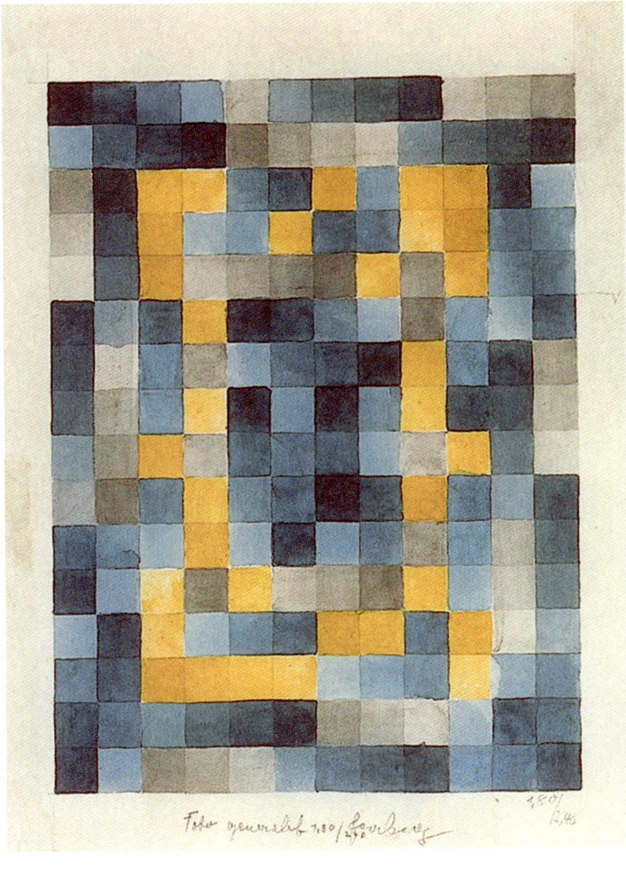

• *Facing page: Gertrud Arndt,* Selbstporträt mit Garnrolle *(Self-Portrait with Spool of Thread), Dessau, 1926.*

• *Gertrud Arndt, Design for a rug for Walter Gropius's director's room (see p. 25), 1923.*

The terrible economic situation at the beginning of the 1920s was especially tough for many Bauhaus members, including Gertrud Hantschk. "We were all malnourished, I weighed eighty-two pounds," she wrote in 1993 and said in an interview: "I paid for my room with a loaf of bread and half a pound of butter per week. And she (the landlady) was delighted to get the bread. . . . If you were given money in the evening, it was worth nothing by the following morning." In 1924, Gertrud Hantschk applied to have her workshop fees of twenty marks per month waived, and her request was granted. Director Gropius wrote in his explanation on January 22, 1925: "As the parents themselves do not have any great income, Fräulein Hantschk receives only meager financial support. She has to earn her own keep, for the most part." One possibility to earn money was contract work in the workshop or the production of exhibition pieces, for example for trade fairs. In light of this, it is remarkable that in 1927 Gertrude Hantschk, together with Mila Lederer, protested against the school exhibiting pieces marked "Bauhaus" without mention of the individual student's name. Otti Berger objected much later. In the meantime, Gertrud Hantschk worked on many samples for cut goods, often with stripes in reserved tones, which were recreated by the Stock company in 1979 because of their clear simplicity.

Gertud Hantschk took her journeywoman's examination at the Weaver's Guild in Glauchau with three other Bauhaus students on March 4, 1927. It is assumed that she created numerous larger pieces for the examination, such as a double-weave with varying light and dark tones. This work, declared a "wall hanging," became a prototype for the so-called "Bauhaus style." Similar fabrics were later created as cut goods. A further brilliant work was the knotted rug *Thost No. 4*, which was designed and created, also with square features, for a Hamburg shipping company owner. Colored fabric samples still exist from this and another rug from 1927. Students were already expected to calculate the sale prices of products for public sale strictly according to prevailing economic criteria, and to include all production and accommodation costs. Thus an exact calculation for Gertrud Hantschk's rug exists: she calculates 645 work hours at a price of 30 pfennigs and 45 hours at 50 pfennigs; the materials according to weight and price as well as 30 percent workshop costs and 50 percent general expenses. The result is two different prices: one for the sale of the rug itself—2,000 marks (written in ink) the other for the sale of the design—1,455 marks (written in pencil).

In 1927 Gertrud Hantschk married Bauhaus student Alfred Arndt. He had passed his journeyman's examination in 1924 and had since lived and worked as a freelance architect in Probstzella, where he created the largest (until 1927) surviving Bauhaus ensemble, the Haus des Volkes (House of the Nation) in Thuringia. He worked and took his master's exam at the Bauhaus in 1928. In 1929, the couple moved to Dessau where

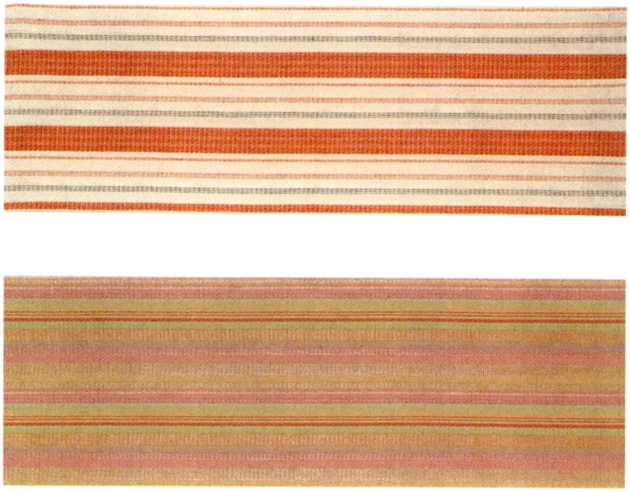

• *Gertrud Arndt, Curtain fabrics, 1926–27.*

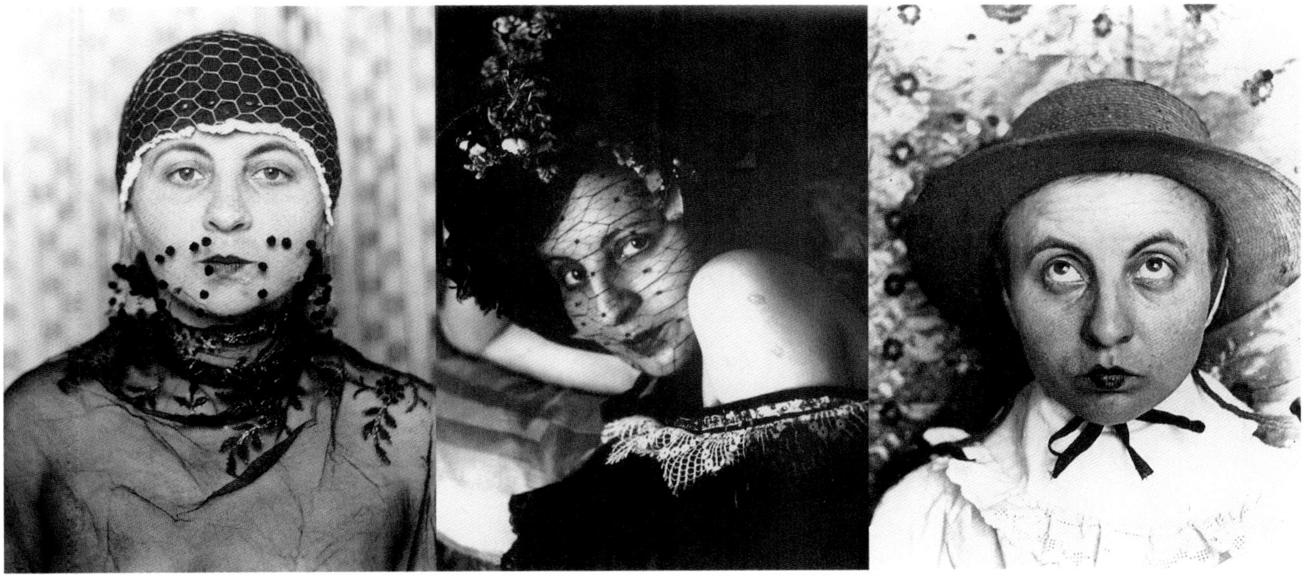

Alfred Arndt became full-time Bauhaus master in the construction workshop.

Gertrud Arndt was, apparently, not interested in a permanent position following her marriage. She worked on a few textile objects, but dedicated herself increasingly to photography. She took part in Bauhaus events and also took the photography course which had been newly established by Walter Peterhans in 1929, but was not fully integrated in the day-to-day work. She had time and leisure "to sit at home doing nothing, so to speak, and I began to take these photos out of boredom," she remembered in a conversation with Sabina Leßmann in 1993. She did not attribute any artistic meaning to her pictures at this time. Photography was first and foremost for personal documentation or arose from personal adventurousness. It was not until the rediscovery of the Bauhaus after World War II that her photographs were published and exhibited. One part of these works clearly shows that she was totally proficient in the *Neues Sehen* (New Vision). During her time in Erfurt, Gertrud Arndt had already bought a camera and carried out initial experiments, none of which have survived. There is, however, a comprehensive photograph collection from the years 1926 to 1932. This comprises of the now famous series of forty-three self-portraits in various costumes, titled *Maskenporträts* (Mask Portraits) by Gertrud Arndt herself. In 1979 she described their creation, which took only a few days: "I sat opposite the camera, on a stool about two meters away from the window. A broom handle leaned against the stool from behind, to which a page with small print was affixed. I focussed sharply on this . . . I did not have an automatic shutter release, which is why I fixed a line of thread to the release button, stretched it vertically to the floor under an object, which let the thread through and was so heavy that the camera could not fall down. I took the end of the thread in my hand and pulled—it was very easy." These transformation photographs, which she described as her relaxation, appear to relish in defying all requirements of modern photography: no extreme angles or details, no constructivist mirroring, no reduction to geometric basics. Instead, we find a buoyant opulence of design accessories from grandma's time; fabric and paper flowers, collars, veils, hats and gloves, feathers and lace with the help of which the inner personality is coaxed out in the most varied stage-setting. As Sabina Leßmann describes, "She shows herself as a femme fatale, a good little girl, as a woman of the world, as an Asian woman, as a childish brat, as a respectable creature, and as a widow." Various moods, from grief, naïveté, lust, and craziness to barefaced joy, are simultaneously explored. Gertrud Arndt's photographic dialogs demonstrate

• *Gertrud Arndt, Photographs from the series* Masken-Selbstporträts (Mask Portraits) 13, 19, *and* 38, *1930.*

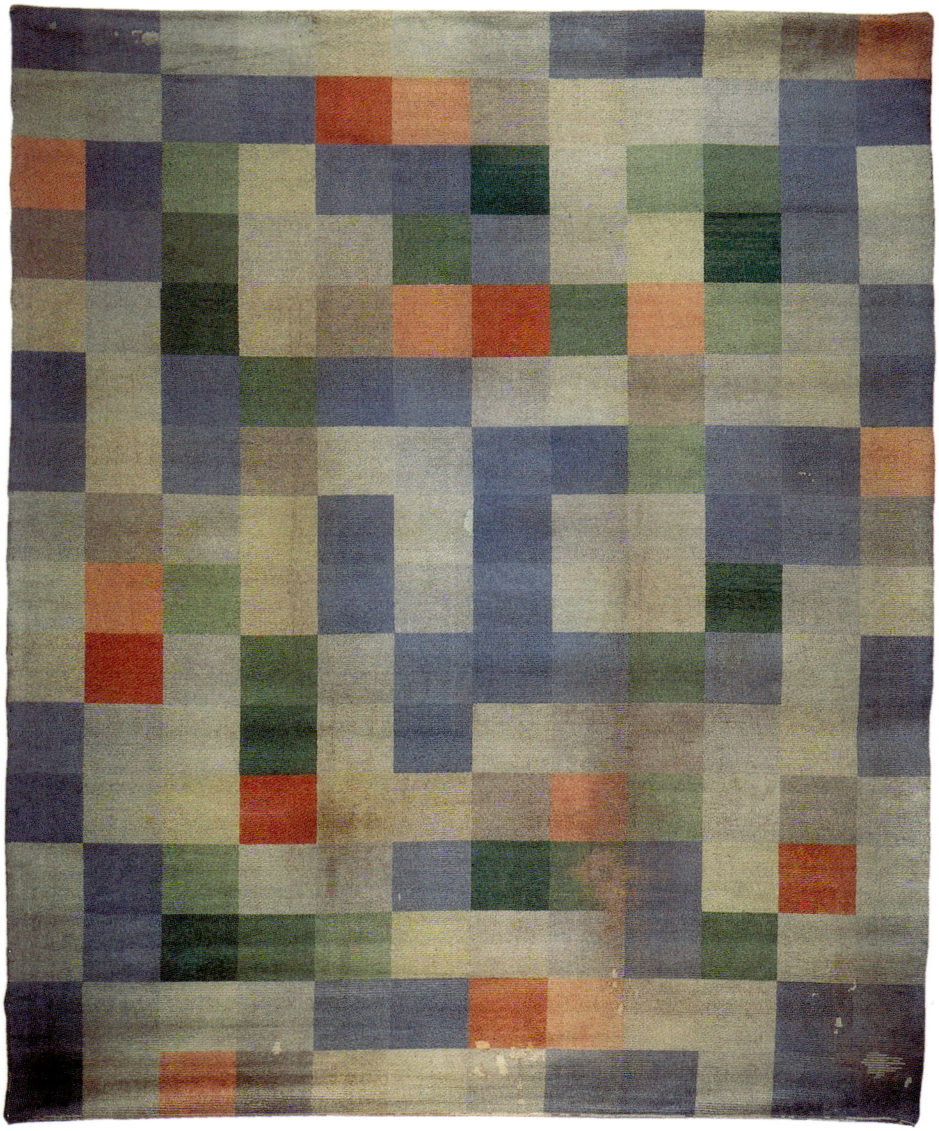

imagination, wit, and dauntlessness in the playful balance between self-preservation and boundary-crossing in a free, life-affirming personality which is at one with itself—and also an artist who is proficient at her job. The ninety-year-old described one of the sources of her unbridled curiosity in an interview with Sabina Leßmann: "I am simply interested in the face, what does one make from a face? There you only need to open your eyes wide and already you are someone else. Isn't that true?"

During her Dessau years Gertrud Arndt was friends with Gunta Stölzl. They traveled together, and Gunta Stölzl wrote about a trip to Brittany in 1927 that they were "lazy as shells in the sand and always very cheery."

Following their marriage in 1929, a close friendship developed with the Stölzl-Sharon couple. As architects, Arndt and Sharon had very many interests in common. The women improvised the household. They met in the canteen, as they lived in single rooms on one floor. Gunta Stölzl shared one room with her husband and child. She cooked in a "small galley kitchen." "We were always together ... we would not have been able to exist without mutual help," Gertrud Arndt remembered.

In 1930 despite all their economic difficulties the two couples traveled to Varazze, Genoa, and Lake Maggiore. The year 1931 brought profound changes: Gunta Stölzl had to leave the Bauhaus; Sharon traveled to Palestine to extend his visa, and remained there. In many empathetic letters Gertrud Arndt discussed her friend's fate, until her work in Dessau also had to end in 1932 and the Bauhaus was shut down. She wrote to Gunta in February 1932: "We are completely adjusted to travel, separation, and a new world. Do you have any connections? Dear little Gunta! Should we really find work, you will join us.... You see, in the end one always relies on old friends. Are we simply no longer welcoming?" In the same year, the Arndts moved to Probstzella, where Alfred firstly worked in advertising and from 1935 as an architect once more. During the war, and above all in the period following the war, there was great need and

• *Gertrud Arndt,* Thost, *knotted carpet, 1927.*

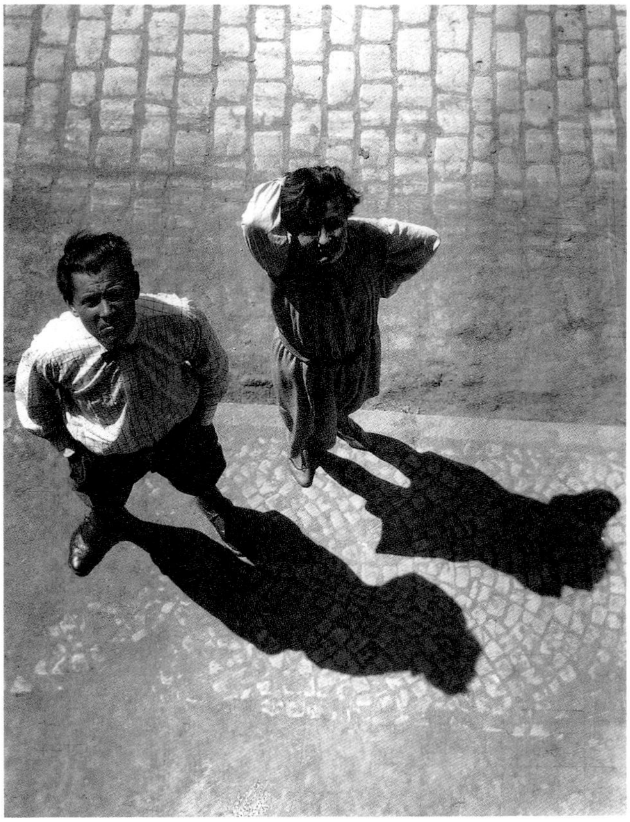

Gunta Stölzl's packages from Switzerland were very welcome. When the Arndts moved from the Soviet zone to Darmstadt in great difficulty in 1948, they were forced to leave very many of their possessions behind. Gertrud wrote to Gunta on August 2: "Everyone is afraid and everyone is hoping in God's name that the iron curtain does not finally fall. . . . How can everything be so sad. . . . The Russians won't let any furniture through. One has to chop up and break everything so that it doesn't look like furniture." Gertrud Arndt visited Gunta Stölzl in the summer of 1949 in her Swiss "paradise" and repeated the trip the following year.

After the war they resumed contact with the old Bauhaus members. The first meeting of Bauhaus members took place in Stuttgart in 1950, about which Gertrud Arndt later wrote to Gunta Stölzl: "The very real joy at seeing one another again did us all good. Short get-togethers have something very intensive about them. The differences don't hit you immediately and one is so taken by the simple fact that the other is there. And so is he or she. Without hair-splitting or chipping anything away. This chipping away is not really bearable. One presents oneself far more beautifully when polished to a shining finish."

Interest in Bauhaus products grew again in this period as did the number of publications. Gertrud Arndt said: "Whatever I have to say to the world would be so futile. I have often wondered about how some people find every little piece of fabric so important as if it were a revelation. For whom? For what? To earn money, yes that is necessary."

In 1994 Gertrud Arndt returned to Dessau once more, where the Vorwerk company was introducing a new carpet collection, Classic, which was the first to be designed exclusively by women. The Vorwerk brochure reads: "We had the unique, historic possibility to discuss the original designs with three Bauhaus women themselves, Gertrud Arndt, Monika Bella-Bronner, and Kitty Fischer, and to realize the production using the most modern manufacturing methods." On the occasion of the Vorwerk celebrations, Gertrud Arndt found out that Grete Reichert had been involved in one of the intrigues that had led to Gunta Stölzl's dismissal. Shattered, she burst into tears. Gertrud Arndt died in Darmstadt at the age of ninety-seven. In keeping with her good-hearted, warm character, she invited her friends and family to celebrate a joyful Bauhaus party after her death.

INGRID RADEWALDT, ULRIKE MÜLLER

• *Portrait of Alfred and Gertrud Arndt (with automatic release), Probstzella, 1927.*

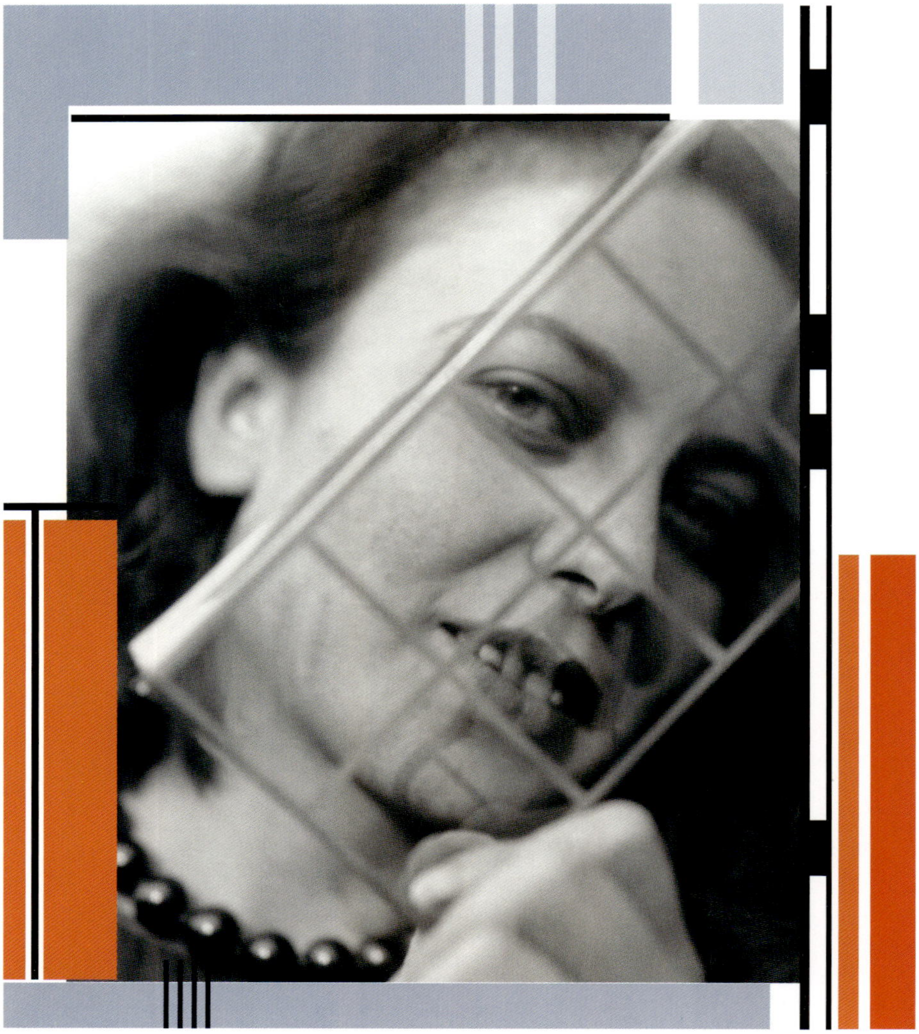

OTTI BERGER 1898–1944

"To become an artist, one has to be an artist and to become one when one already is an artist, then one comes to the Bauhaus, and the task of the Bauhaus is to make a human being of this 'artist' again."

Otti Berger

The new Bauhaus building designed by Walter Gropius had just been inaugurated when Otilija Ester Berger arrived in Dessau in December 1926. Like so many other Bauhaus members, she too had already completed a course of artistic training. Born in 1898 in Zmajevac, which was part of the Austro-Hungarian Empire until World War I, she became a Yugoslavian citizen in 1919 and attended the art academy in Zagreb from 1921 to 1926. She later described this as a "soulless place of tradition." She registered as Otti Berger under the matriculation number 131 at the Bauhaus in Dessau on January 1, 1927, and began the preliminary course with László Moholy-Nagy. In charge of the preliminary course since 1923, Moholy-Nagy oriented his lessons toward functional workshop activity, geared to industrial production. One of his focal points was training the sense of touch, which he practised on touching-boards with the students. Moholy-Nagy published Otti Berger's touching-board in his book *Von Material zur Architektur*. Many different thread triangles are stretched on a diagonal metal mesh strip, into which different, colored paper squares can be inserted. The board can be felt and read like a line in a book, creating a material alphabet, which demonstrated Otti Berger's great sensitivity for fabric. In October 1927 she began weaving classes under Gunta Stölzl, who had taken over the complete running of the workshop as young master that April. The focus was no longer on accentuating artistic expression and production of individual, one-off pieces, but rather on the development of prototypes for industry. Otti Berger tried out various loom systems in the training workshop and her design work often took place directly at the loom.

Technically experimental works were one side of the study program and were complemented by Paul Klee's

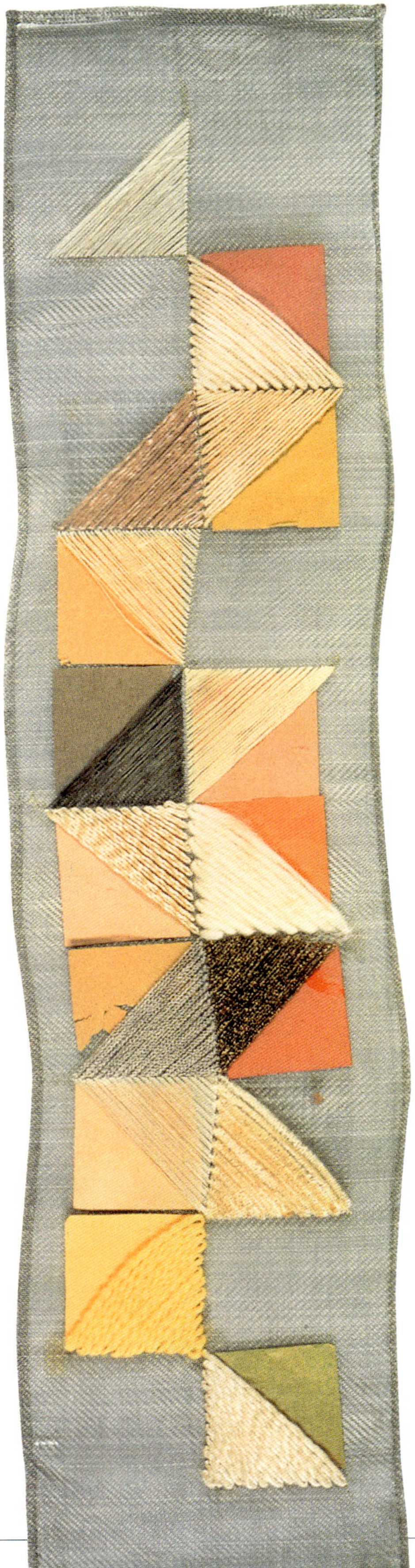

- *Facing page: Portrait of Otti Berger, from a series of ten portrait photos by Lucia Moholy, 1927/28.*
- *Right: Otti Berger, Moholy-Nagy's preliminary course, Touching-board with threads, 1928.*

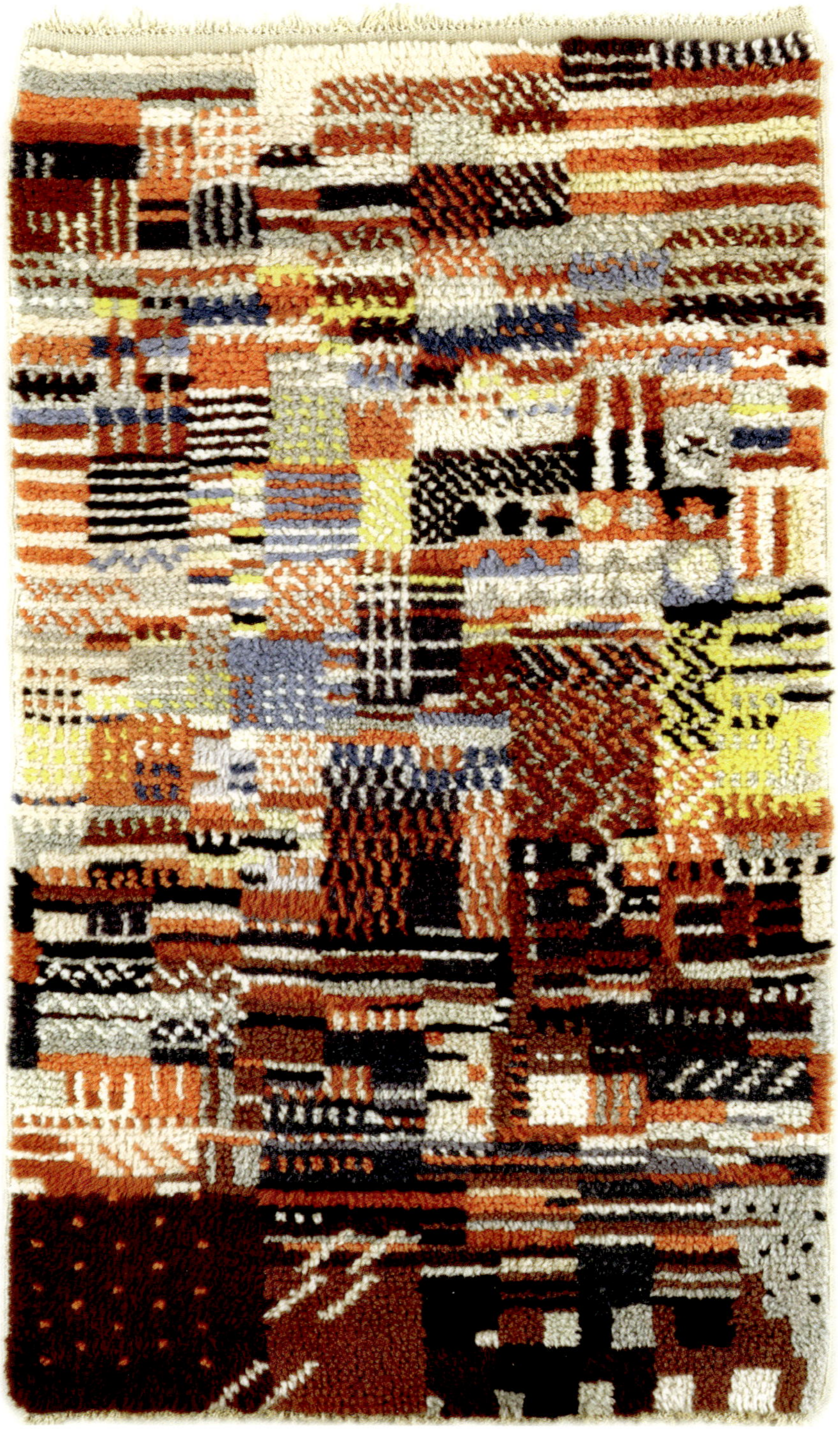

1928–29, which the Cassina company recreated in 1973 and which still radiates a classic elegance as a furniture fabric today.

Otti Berger's fabrics complied with Klee's call for economy of resources and restriction to few design elements. Klee's exercises with color gradients and color mixes, which she carried out in watercolor, were very influential for her work. Her very sensitive use of color gradations is evident in her curtain material from 1930, in which a complex textile composition is created from fine strips of different threads in varying yellow tones.

The harmony between various visual components to form a complex, transparent composition, called "polyphony" by Klee, was implemented by Otti Berger for a grand piano cover, of which she wrote in her seminal article *Stoffe im Raum* (Materials in Space) in 1930: "A grand piano cover, for example, can be music in itself, flowing, harmonious full of melodies and oscillations."

This free artistic training contributed to a rejection of outdated ways of seeing and addressed all the senses—even more important for Otti Berger as an illness had left her almost deaf. Her sense of touch was, therefore, very well defined. She had the ability to put herself in the position of the fabric in order

form classes, where Otti Berger created many sketches and color studies from fall 1927. She apparently found it easy to convert his color and form rules directly onto fabric, without forgetting functionality and technical precision. One example of this is the fabric Carré, from

• *Otti Berger, Knotted carpet, c. 1929.*

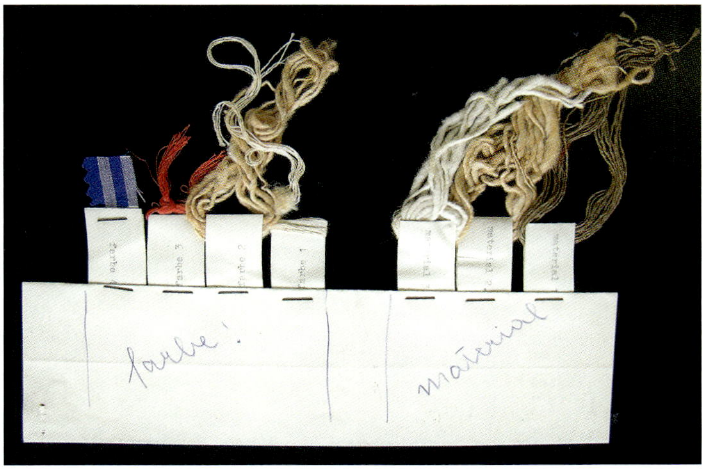

to experience its character, as Stanislav Vinaver remarked following a visit to Dessau in 1931.

She herself quoted Klee as she wrote in 1930: "Intuition is still a good thing! Because one has to eavesdrop on the fabric's secrets, feel the sounds of the materials, one must grasp the structure, not only in the brain but one has to feel it with the subconscious. Then one knows of the individuality of silk which is warmth, or of synthetic silk, which is cold." The horizon of experiences in hearing and seeing was widened "as the sound of color in fabric is richer than any other color sound." Otti Berger's sensitivity, alongside her technical perfection, very quickly led to excellent results in her work. Moreover, she had the ability to express theories verbally.

On November 1, 1929, following six month's work experience in a weaving school in Stockholm, Otti Berger became an employee of the weaving workshop, albeit at a reduced rate of fifty reichsmarks. Together with Anni Albers, she stood in for Gunta Stölzl who had given birth in October. Alongside developing new fabrics, Otti Berger had to ensure the production of new fabrics designed by herself in the workshop for the Bundesgewerkschaftsschule (National Trade Union School) designed by director Hannes Meyer, among them 120 bed covers in synthetic silk. In the summer vacation of 1930—Hannes Meyer had been fired without notice on August 1—Otti Berger took over in the weaving workshop. She published an article, "Stoffe im Raum," in the Bauhaus special edition *Red* of the same year, in which she very cleverly and sophisticatedly examined the transformed functions of fabrics and defined their role in home decoration. Similarly to architect Hannes Meyer's requirements of modern construction, she saw the meaning of textiles in practical, functional use which excludes any superfluity. The textiles, however, had to be very sensitively and sophisticatedly designed: a harmony must be created between material, structure, and color. "The fabric becomes expression. Why then do we need flowers, climbing plants, ornaments? The fabric itself lives."

The change from individual handweaving to what is called textile design today, was successfully carried out in Dessau, not without some conflict, during those years. Anni Albers and Otti Berger were among the students who represented the industrial designer type early on.

Gunta Stölzl, who was only one year older than Otti Berger, valued her talent and suggested her and Anni Albers as her substitutes. She confirms her artistic capabilities and talent as an educator, which she proved as an employee, in a letter of recommendation of September 9, 1930. According to Stölzl: "Her work was always very intense and belongs among the best which the department ever produced. . . . I imagine that her works speak most convincingly for her ability."

Otti Berger passed her journeyman's examination in Glauchau, Saxony, on October 5, 1930. On November 22, she received her Bauhaus diploma number 31 and as of November 1930 she was employed at various textile factories in eastern Germany. In the beginning, as a novice in her field, she adapted her designs to the companies' clientele, and was nevertheless able to create interest in Bauhaus fabrics, with the result that a licensing contract was signed with a company in 1932. Otti Berger was also a member of the Bauhaus jury, which

• *Otti Berger, Schriever cartridges, fabric sample, sample weave on graph paper, 1936–38.*

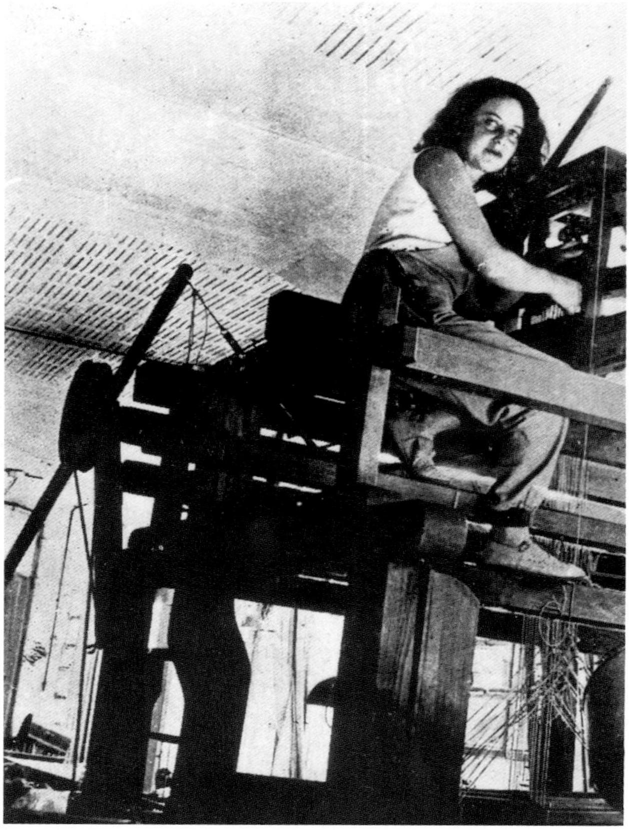

chose the fabrics to be produced industrially. She self-confidently named one of her own designs *Otti Berger Stoff*.

Great changes were afoot in the Bauhaus workshop, partially initiated by a change in directorship and various intrigues. Gunta Stölzl resigned in September 1931. In October, Otti Berger was given the task, for 200 reichsmarks, of teaching a four-week introductory course in the organization of work for a production company with mechanical looms. At the same time she took over the artistic and technical directorship of the weaving workshop.

Along with the new Bauhaus director, Ludwig Mies van der Rohe, came his colleague and girlfriend Lilly Reich, upon whom Mies then conferred the position of overall supervisor of the workshop. Otti Berger was now employed with half a week's teaching and her contract was extended until August 1932. Lilly Reich, who had made her name as a designer, now defined the style and direction to be taken by the workshop but was dependent on Otti Berger's support, as she herself had no knowledge of weaving technique. Otti Berger completed many weaving designs with her now small group of students in the ensuing months, which often appeared under the Bauhaus name. Some joint efforts were named Reich/Berger. The published books of samples show fabrics of restrained elegance and good quality, which surely fitted the style of both women. According to a private account, there also appears to have often been some conflict, as in it Otti Berger speaks of "complete dependence."

Following the dissolution of the Dessau Bauhaus in October 1932 by the local council, Otti Berger purchased looms and materials from the workshop and set up her own studio in Berlin. She viewed it as a kind of laboratory in which she developed fabrics for architects and textile companies on the one hand, and on the other hand, developed individual material mixes some of which she patented. Many of these sample swatches can be viewed at the Busch-Reisinger Museum at Harvard. In 1933 she designed fabrics for the house of a factory owner which was built by Hans Scharoun. At the same time, she began a cooperation with the Wohn-bedarf AG in Zurich as well as the De Ploeg company in the Netherlands. The fabric collections were of high technical quality and influenced textile design in the 1930s with their sophisticated flair.

Otti Berger's situation became increasingly difficult following the Nazi seizure of power. As a Jew, a declared "non-Aryan foreigner," she was obliged to apply for a new residence permit every year. While she was accepted into the Bund deutscher Kunsthandwerker (Union of German Craft Workers) in 1934, her application to the Reichskammer der bildenden Künste (Imperial Council for the Visual Arts) was definitively

• *Otti Berger at the high loom.*

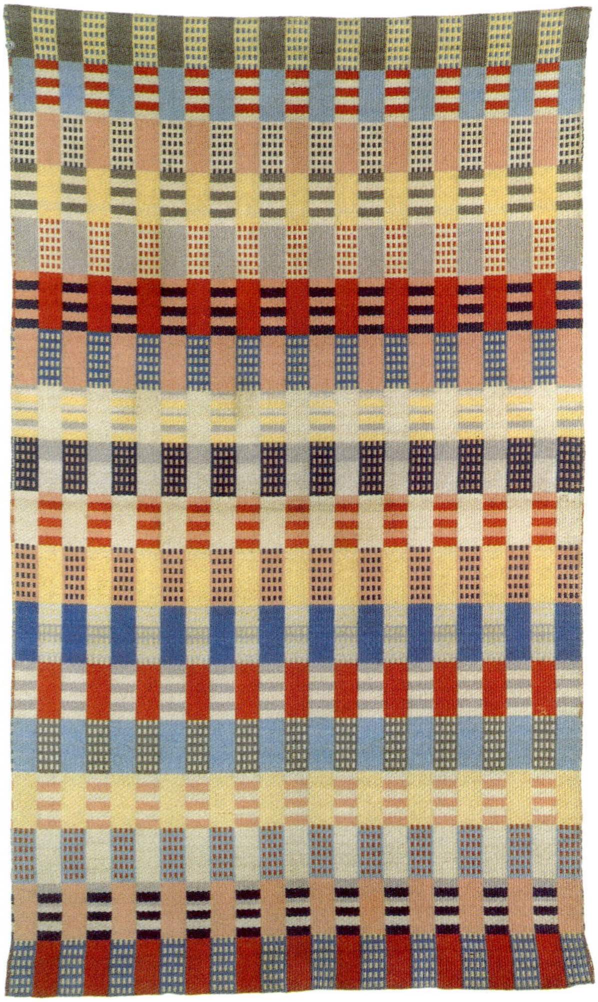

denied in 1936. This was tantamount to professional disqualification and so her financial situation became more and more problematic. Even the Bauhaus still owed her 800 reichsmarks in design fees. She was forced again and again to prove her income in order to acquire a residence permit.

In February 1937, at Walter Gropius's suggestion, she made contact with the English textile industry and emigrated to England in September. Despite all efforts, for example ten weeks working in a textile factory without pay, success was nowhere to be seen. It was not until June 1938, when she worked for five weeks as a substitute, that she found her first and only job in England with the company Helios. She made very little contact with people, not least because of her hearing problem. She wrote to an acquaintance in 1938: "I can't reach the people, sit day in day out evening upon evening alone, sad and without courage. Hilb writes consoling letters." "Hilb" is the architect Ludwig Hilberseimer with whom Otti Berger had been friends since Dessau and with whom she had planned a new life in the United States. Her great hope was Moholy-Nagy, who had offered her a leading position at the weaving workshop at the New Bauhaus in Chicago. Her start there was delayed, however, while Hilberseimer had already followed Mies van der Rohe to Chicago in August.

Before he left he met Otti Berger in London. She had been planning to visit her family in Yugoslavia. Hilberseimer warned her against this journey because of the political situation, but Otti Berger's mother was seriously ill. So, she travelled nevertheless.

By the time her mother had recovered one year later, war had broken out and Otti Berger was unable to acquire a visa for the United States. She reported to a friend in 1941 of her cramped, isolated life with her family, of her work on a carpet, and the hope of being able to leave. After this, there was almost no further sign of life. Waldemar Adler wrote to Hans Meyer in 1947: "We know nothing of Otti Berger apart from Hilberseimer's assumption that she was gassed by the Nazis. But we cannot believe it."

In December 2005 information from Russia was published in Yad Vashem, Israel. Along with details about her family, her location during the war years is given as Vorosmart; then, her place of death: Auschwitz, and her date of death: April 27, 1944.

INGRID RADEWALDT

• *Otti Berger, Nursery carpet, 1929.*

Creations, Circles, and Crockery

Ceramic Artists

The two women ceramic artists in this chapter had already made their names in industrial design in Germany before they were forced to emigrate after the National Socialists' seizure of power and build new lives in exile. Marguerite Friedlaender-Wildenhain successfully exported the craft ideas of Bauhaus pottery to the United States, while Margarete Heymann-Loebenstein-Marks gradually made her home in Great Britain, with painting as a second means of support.

As young women both had studied at the early Bauhaus but under very different circumstances.

A ceramics department only existed in the Weimar period of the Bauhaus, from 1920 to 1925. This training was discontinued in Berlin and Dessau. Even in this short period, the Bauhaus pottery developed an individual, recognizable style, which impacted on industrial stoneware and porcelain production in the 1920s and 1930s. The fundamental characteristics were high technical quality and a clear and simple shape with a functional orientation, which was subordinate to the external design. Marguerite Friedlaender was one of the most important representatives of this style. In the case of Grete Heymann-Loebenstein, on the other hand, she can be incorporated into this style when her work is placed clearly alongside Bauhaus ceramics. In the first place, she only studied at the Bauhaus for a short time; and in the second place, she developed a style which demonstrates the experimental influences of early Bauhaus artists more than the Dornburg style.

At the beginning in Weimar, when the cockle-stove factory J. F. Schmidt in Weimar ended a short period of cooperation with the Bauhaus, the Bauhaus directors turned to master potter Max Krehan to set up a ceramics department in his traditional workshop in Thuringia. Krehan was hired as workshop master in September 1920. The sculptor Gerhard Marcks was form master at this time. In May 1920 Marcks's living and working space was in the stables of Schloß Dornburg. Added to this were a communal kitchen and simple living quarters for students. The first five apprentices received training in Krehan's workshop. Production of conventional "peasant pottery" served not only to teach clay preparation, throwing, glazing, and firing, but also gave the workshop its financial basis. In Marcks's classes, however, the main focus was on making forms and free experimentation with vessel shapes and the appropriate surface design. Marcks also gave drawing classes and offered insights into the ceramics traditions of other eras and cultures.

For all the romanticism, life in Dornburg was very hard. Eva Deutschbein-Oberdieck, who studied from fall 1923 to spring 1925, and was later a faience painter in

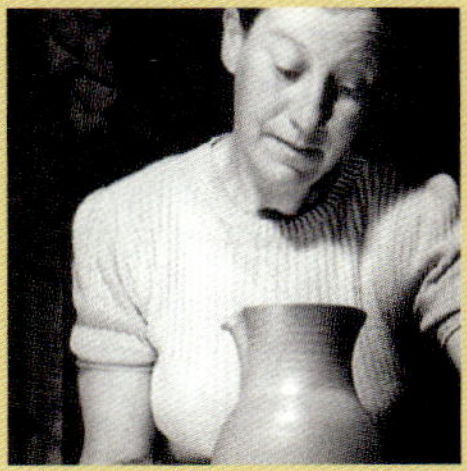

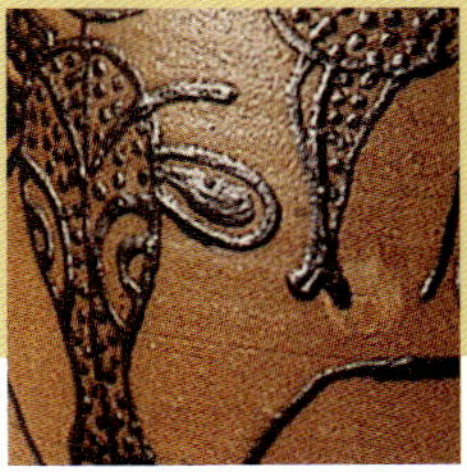

Hirschau as well as a ceramic artist in Gosslar and Graz, described the situation in her *Erinnerungen einer "alten Dame" an Dornburg* (Memoirs of an Old Lady at Dornburg, 1966): "As far as our money was concerned, we received 5.76 marks and in the winter, coal. . . . We were really on the edge when the money did not stretch to the weekly loaf of bread. Sometimes it was awful. One had to go to the wild damson trees . . . run off, or exchange a few drinks for potatoes. . . . This poverty didn't bother us at all, but rather strengthened the feeling in us that we were a little group of chosen ones, free of all of the restrictions of humanity, as far as the luxuries of the table or elegant robes were concerned, but subordinate to the strictest rules of art."

Up until 1925 there were a total of seven male and eight female students at the Dornburg pottery. Any woman training here had to have a lot of persistence. By spring 1921 three of the four women who originally went to Dornburg to start up the pottery workshop had dropped out—Else Mögelin, Gertrud Coja, and Lydia Foucar. Foucar married her fellow student Johannes Driesch in May 1921 and ended her training prematurely. She set up a "workshop for artistic gingerbread" in 1934 in Friedrichsdorf. Greta Heymann was given a "trial" at the pottery in April 1921 at a time when the input of women was being questioned. She was gone again in the winter of 1921. In 1923 Marcks spoke out against the acceptance of women in the pottery. Marguerite Friedlaender was still there, however—and had been for over a year as the only woman—and proved herself in a talented trio alongside Otto Lindig and Theodor Bogler. As there were not enough students, Renate Riedel, Eva Deutschbein-Oberdieck, and Thoma, Countess Grote were accepted in the same year. All three remained until 1925. The countess took her masters' exam in 1931 and in 1945 was employed in the HB-Werkstätten by Hedwig Bollhagen.

The development of prototypes for industrial ceramic production, which began at the Weimar Bauhaus, continued after 1925 by former students at various locations: Marguerite Friedlaender-Wildenhain ran the ceramics department of the Kunstgewerbeschule Halle in Schloß Giebichenstein and developed models for the KPM (Imperial Porcelain Manufacture). Theodor Bogler and Werner Burri consecutively ran the stoneware factory in Velten, which had been founded in 1913 by Hermann Harkort. Greta Heymann-Loebenstein successfully produced her idiosyncratic art in her own workshops.

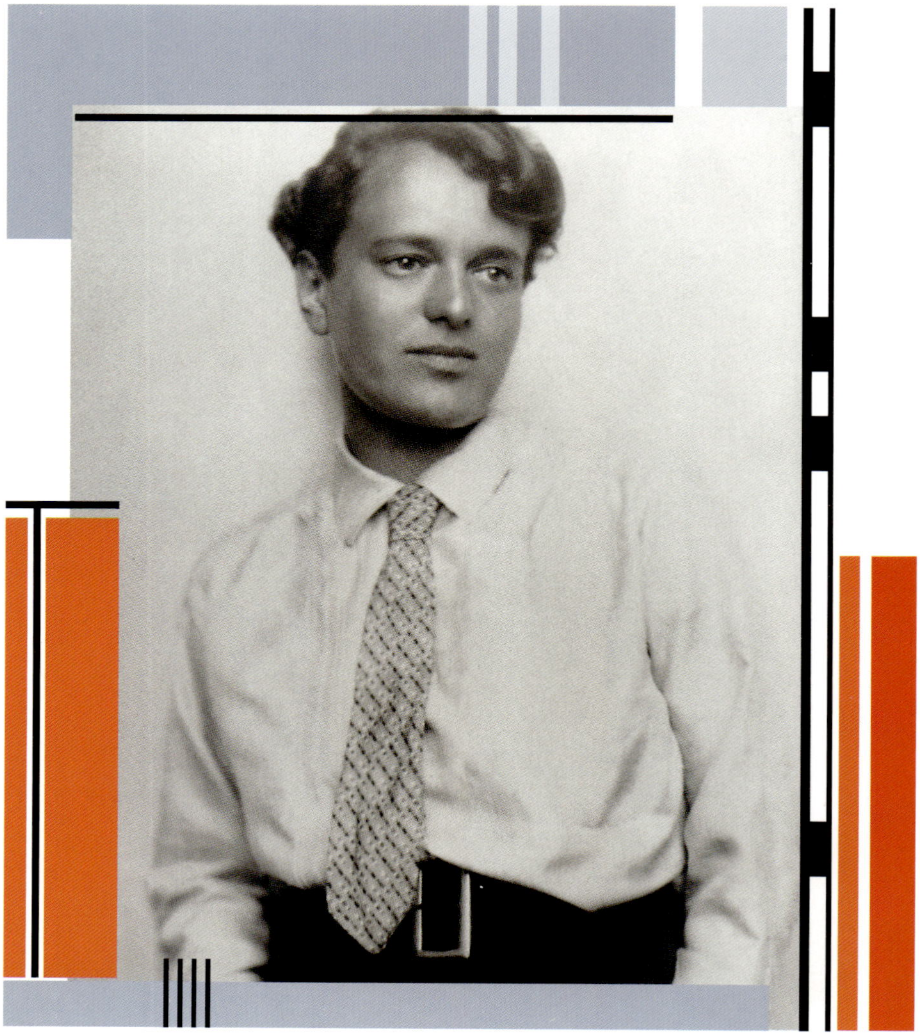

MARGARETE HEYMANN-LOEBENSTEIN-MARKS

1899–1990

"The Haël Workshops in Marwitz are making positive advances in the decoration of faience surfaces.... They cover the fragments with a matte zinc glaze of grand beauty. This glaze brings out pastel colors, a particular blue, a sonorous, warm browny-yellow.... This is not decoration in the normal sense but a modern adornment of fine stature, developed from and subsequently chiming with the form itself."

Kunst und Kunstgewerbe, *1927*

Ever since an exhibition on the Haël Workshops for Art Ceramics in Marwitz at the Ofen- und Keramikmuseum (Kiln and Ceramics Museum) in Velten in 2006, initiated by Monika Dittmar, numerous works by ceramic artist, Margarete "Grete" Heymann-Loebenstein have been constantly on show north of Berlin in this town rich in tradition. Hedwig Bollhagen, who had already become a legend in her own lifetime, returned to the public's notice one year later, with the exhibition *Werk und Wirken* (Work and Influence) in Potsdam, in the summer of 2007. The factory, which began work under the artistic direction of Hedwig Bollhagen at the end of April 1934 in Marwitz near Velten, had, only days before belonged to the German Jew Grete Heymann-Loebenstein. The success story of the new HB-Werkstätten had, up to then, been that of the Haël Workshops in Marwitz. Thus the beginning of one artist's career was historically connected with the exile of another.

Margarete Heymann's mother came from a family whose ancestors numbered poet Heinrich Heine among them. Her father was a wealthy drapery manufacturer and Margarete was born in Cologne in 1899. Her versatile artistic talent was already apparent in her childhood and as a young woman she was for a long time unable to decide to which muse she should devote herself. In the end she decided on fine arts rather than music. She first attended the Kunstgewerbeschule in Cologne in 1916 and then the Akademie der bildenden Künste (Academy of Fine Arts) in Düsseldorf, where she studied painting.

The first of her works were seen in 1920 at the Kunstverein (Art Association) in Cologne. Grete Heymann was accepted at the Bauhaus, Weimar in November 1920 and initially visited Itten's preliminary course. She took part in Gertrud Grunow's harmonizing classes from March 1921 as well as classes with Georg Muche and Paul Klee. A Bauhaus study by Grete, a watercolor on Japanese paper from 1921, is now in the Berlin Bauhaus Archives. No ceramic works from the Bauhaus workshop are traceable, however, and only her signature emblem remains. Part of her later works shows clear Bauhaus influences, in the playfully exhaustive reduction to basic forms and in the light, abstract painting. Nevertheless joyful, avant-garde experimentation, as in Itten's rhythmic preliminary course studies, like Klee, or in later Kandinsky are more evident than the earthen heaviness of the "peasant ceramics" from the Dornburg pottery. Grete Heymann's ceramics also show traces of her engagement with Japanese and Chinese art, which she had got to know early on in the East Asian collection in Cologne.

Grete Heymann-Loebenstein's success with the Haël ceramics, which she developed in the 1920s, was first

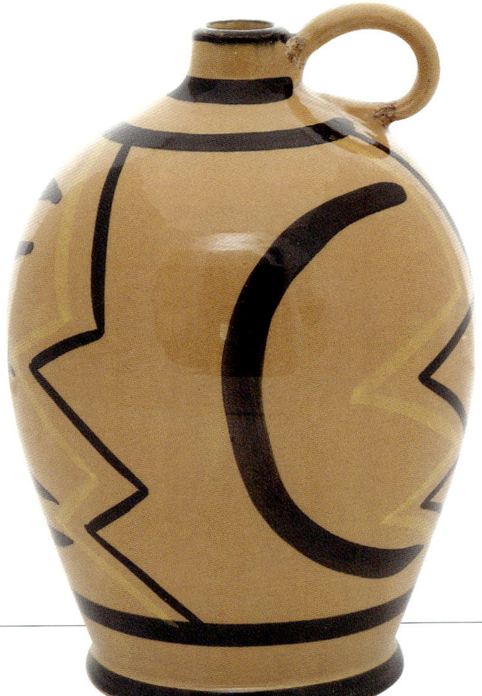

• Facing page: Margarete Heymann-Loebenstein-Marks, portrait from the 1920s.
• Right: Margarete Heymann-Loebenstein-Marks, Jar from the Haël ceramics sample book, 1924.

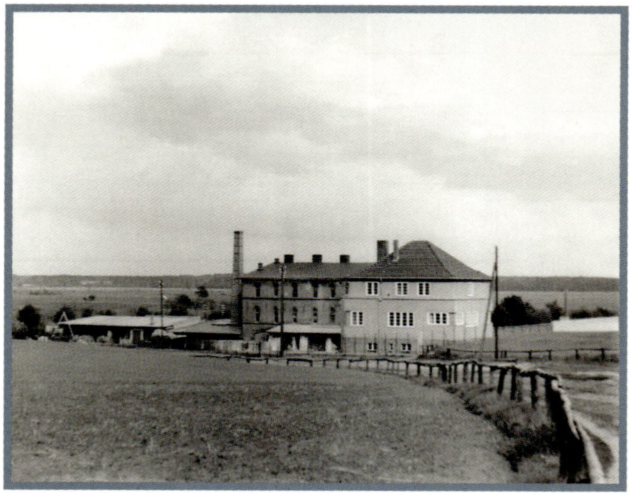

and foremost due to her great talent and drive. She did take important artistic inspiration from the Bauhaus, but the way in which she was treated there was hardly glorious. She was one of those female students for whom access to the workshop of their choice was made extremely difficult. She clearly applied just at precisely the "wrong" moment to be accepted into the ceramics department, and at the end of 1921 there was only one woman left out of the four original female students. A note in the minutes of the Masters' Council, published in 2001, reads: "Grete Heymann's request to be accepted in the Ceramics Department is rejected on the grounds that for the present, women will no longer be admitted to the pottery." In these minutes it is evident how form master Marcks and director Gropius both attempted to delay Heymann's acceptance in order to prevent it altogether, in the long term. In the minutes of April 6, 1921, we read: "The Masters' Council resolves to allow Fräulein Heymann a trial period in the Ceramics Department." On June 24, 1921: "Fräulein Heymann will not ultimately be informed until the end of the semester, as no fundamental judgment can as yet be made regarding her suitability for craft [pottery]." October 1, 1921: "It has been decided to wait before making a decision about Grete Heymann, who has not yet been officially accepted in the pottery, as [according to Marcks] she is being put under pressure by her parents to drop out." And on October 12, 1921: "In his acceptance of Grete Heymann, Marcks explains that he considers her to be talented, as does Krehan, but not suitable for the workshop. Decision postponed till next meeting." Grete Heymann left the Bauhaus not long after. In Dornburg she is said, along with others, to have indulged in a dramatic departure scene—a huge row with form master Marks.

The photograph of Grete Heymann from the 1920s shows a "New Woman" par excellence in the urban Berlin style—a boyishly androgynous lesbian, or even a confident young entrepreneur. Dressed in this way, she probably did not stand out in Itten's alternative classes but one can imagine that she clashed with the conservative Marcks who was strict in his ways, and that she did not blend in with the frugal life of a Thuringian village.

Following her Bauhaus intermezzo, Grete Heymann gave a course in ceramics for children at the Kunstgewerbeschule in Cologne, in which she included elements of Bauhaus teaching in the same way as Alma Buscher and Friedl Dicker. She also worked in a ceramics workshop in Frechen and later in a stoneware factory in Velten, in which Hedwig Bollhagen, among others, spent important training years. There were strong artistic contacts

• *Haël ceramics factory in Marwitz near Velten, c. 1929.*

• *Häel ceramics logo.*

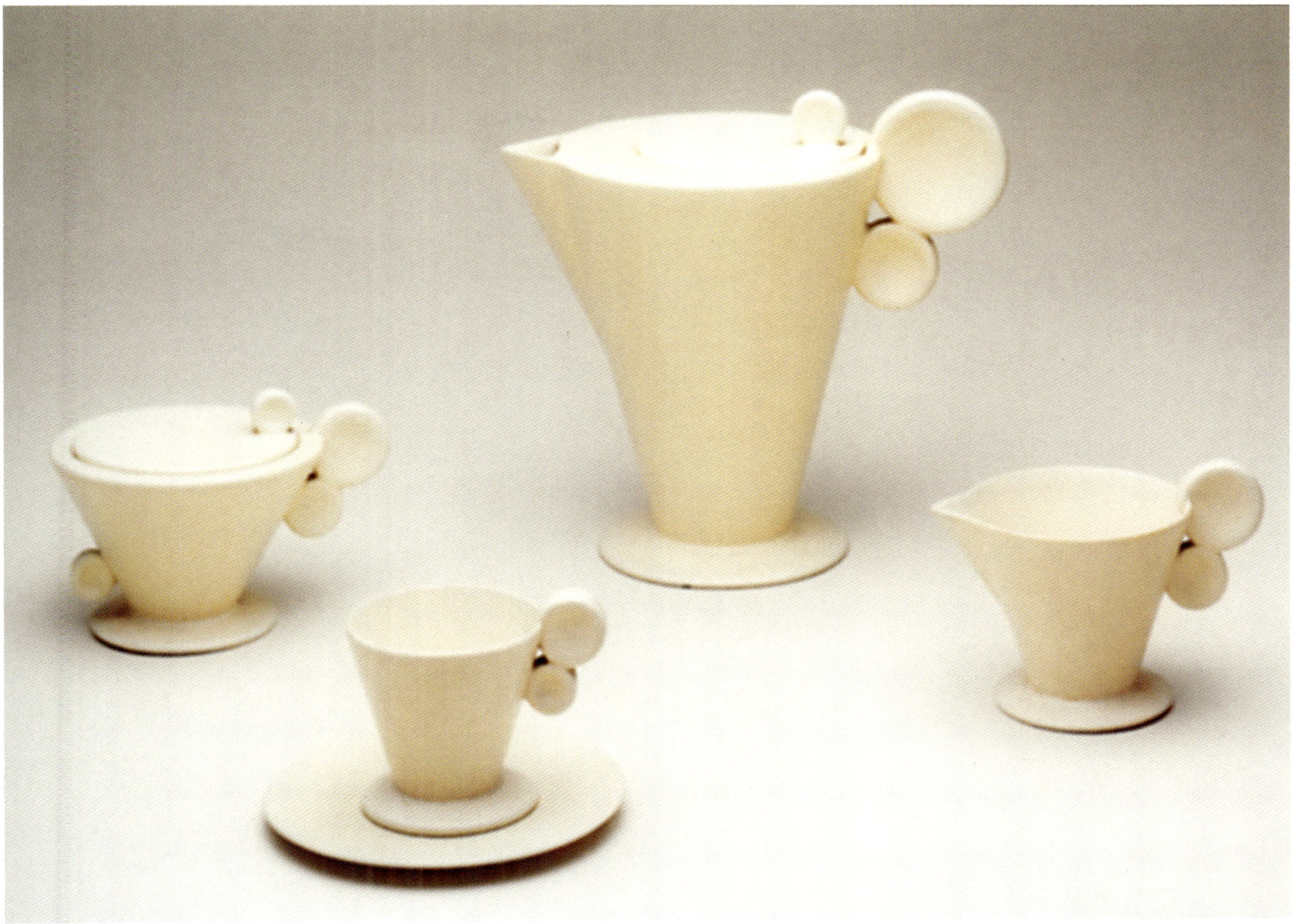

between the Bauhaus and Harkorts Stoneware Factories in Velten-Vordamm. In 1923 a new factory in neighboring Marwitz competed with the successful Velten plant. Grete Heymann married the economist Gustav Loebenstein in August of that year and together with him and his brother Daniel, founded the Haël Workshops for Art Ceramics (*Haël* deriving from the initials of Heymann and Loebenstein) in a disused cockle-stove factory in Marwitz. In a few years the workshops developed into a much sought-after company in both Germany and abroad as far as Africa and Australia. Approximately 120 people were employed there in 1930. Comparing the catalogs from 1924 and 1929–30, we can see changes in the range and development of products. If the early products, from sets of dishes, vases, and lamp stands to cactus pots, were made of brightly painted clay or unpainted stoneware, later on the range of stoneware expanded noticeably using colored, shiny, or matte glazing effects. All pieces were of the best quality.

The focal point of the range were avant-garde creations in the art deco style but also classically plain vases and bowls, aimed at the discerning, modern buyer. At the same time there was a wide product range which suited very different tastes. The Loebenstein brothers' successful management and Grete Heymann's talent for recognizing the signs of fashion, and adapting her own avant-garde style accordingly, guaranteed the company's success, as well as a comfortable life for the family in the city of Berlin.

When Gustav and Daniel Loebenstein both died in a car accident in 1928, Grete Loebenstein continued to run the company as the single owner, and no less successfully than before. The company continued to attend fairs and exhibitions. The Haël Workshops even survived

• *Margarete Heymann-Loebenstein-Marks, Tea service with double handle, c. 1930.*

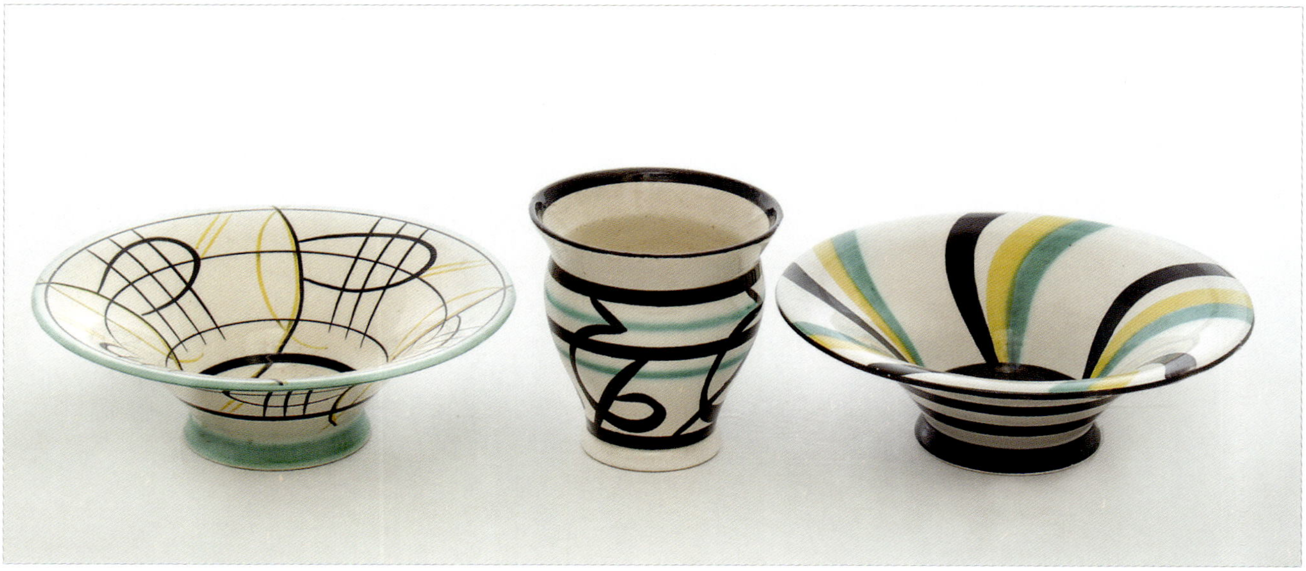

the economic crisis, albeit with great losses. However, with the seizure of power by the Nazis, Jewish factories came under increasing pressure, through boycotts, agitation, and restrictive legislation.

Grete Loebenstein, too, finally felt forced to shut down her factory on July 1, 1933, and to sell it ten months later for the giveaway price of 45,000 reichsmarks. As Ursula Hudson Wiedenmann, who devoted much research to Grete Heymann Loebenstein proves, the sale did not take place on economic grounds. In the summer of 1933, Grete Loebenstein was denounced for allegedly "deriding and undermining the authority of the German state as well as poor treatment of her employees to date." Shortly before her threatened imprisonment by the Gestapo she fled to Bornholm. At the same time her total goods inventory of around 10,000 reichsmarks was confiscated. The owners of the company Velten-Vordamm, which had been shut down due to the economic crisis, had already expressed an interest in buying the firm in September 1933, giving as their reason: "The Marwitz plant must become a German company without the influence of non-Aryan persons." In April 1934, Dr. Heinrich Schild, National Socialist German Worker's Party (NSDAP, or Nazi Party) member and general secretary and officer for the Consolidation of Institutional Powers of German Craft received the tender and his choice of artistic director, Hedwig Bollhagen, took over the company. Schild had camouflaged the agreement as a land sale contract in order to conceal the fact that a company, with house, office, machines, casting molds, all plant documents, and customer indexes, had been "taken over" at far too low a price.

While Grete Loebenstein's Norma table service remained part of the HB-Werkstätten product range, at the same time pieces from the designer were exhibited as "degenerate art" in a sort of "chamber of horrors" in a room specially set up for this purpose in the HB-Werkstätten by the Nazis. "They fill the observer with horror," warns the author of an inflammatory article titled "Jewish Ceramics in the Chamber of Horrors," in the Nazi propaganda newsletter *Der Angriff* of May 20, 1935. One of the photos shows a Loebenstein piece next to a Bollhagen piece. The caption "Two races find different forms for the same purpose. Which is more beautiful?" points the German housewife to the educational intent behind the comparison: Your Aryanized pantry should finally be freed from the "legacy of a raped ceramic art."

Grete Loebenstein lived another for two years in Berlin following the loss of her factory. She set up a studio for children in her apartment, taught at a Jewish school, and exhibited. Above all, she was looking for a

• *Margarete Heymann-Loebenstein-Marks, Bowls, form 85; vase, form 107 from the Haël production.*

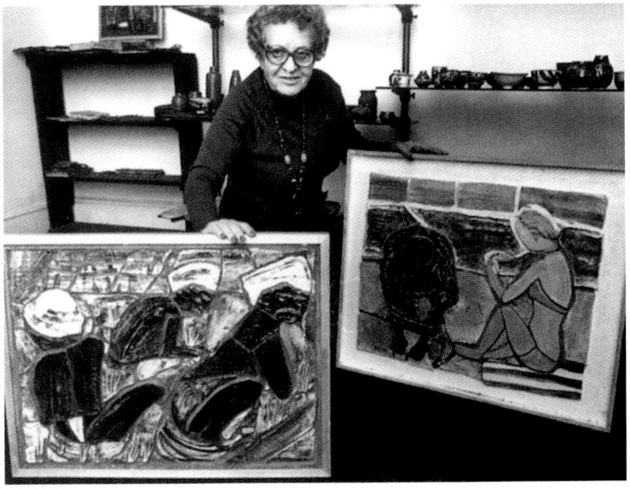

suitable country to which she could travel, and in the end decided to go to England. Her exile began.

With the help of a recommendation she began in 1937 to design prototypes for tableware for the Minton factory in the traditional English pottery center, Stoke-on-Trent. She also took on a short-term teaching position at the Burslem School of Art. She put on a large exhibition of drawings, paintings, and ceramics in the same year. In 1938 she married Harold Marks, with whom she began a small business, the Greta Pottery. A range of her Haël tableware designs was produced under this name at the Ridgway stoneware factory in Shelton until 1939. Despite active support from progressive London designers and business people, Grete Marks would never be able to recreate her German success in England. This was due to the fact that English ceramic design was, at that time, in a state of change and Grete Marks's works were generally perceived to be too "excessive and wild," despite her efforts to adapt. Also the production and sales processes in Stoke were far more traditional than she had been used to in Berlin. A woman who literally wore the pants in a business and at the same time took her products to the shops herself failed every job description in a gender-specific division of labor.

During the war Grete Marks lived with her daughter in a village in Derbyshire. In 1945 she was able to continue in her own workshop in London with ceramic wall hangings as well as the ceramic receptacles inspired by studio pottery. She also worked as a teacher at the Camberwell School of Art.

In the 1950s she turned to painting. While in Germany her focus had been on watercolor, she now began to use oils. She was given solo exhibitions time and again, especially in London. She also taught experimental painting and gave courses in a clinic. Many paintings resulted from her journeys to India and West and South Africa. Her favorite motifs were harbors and ships. Grete Heymann-Loebenstein-Marks died in London in 1990.

She was only rediscovered as an important exiled artist after her death. She was officially recognized as a victim of Nazi persecution in 1961 and was compensated for the loss of her business. She is said to have kept the drama of dispossession from her daughter until the very end. She never returned to Marwitz and never met Hedwig Bollhagen.

ULRIKE MÜLLER

• *Margarete Heymann-Loebenstein-Marks in her studio in London, 1977.*

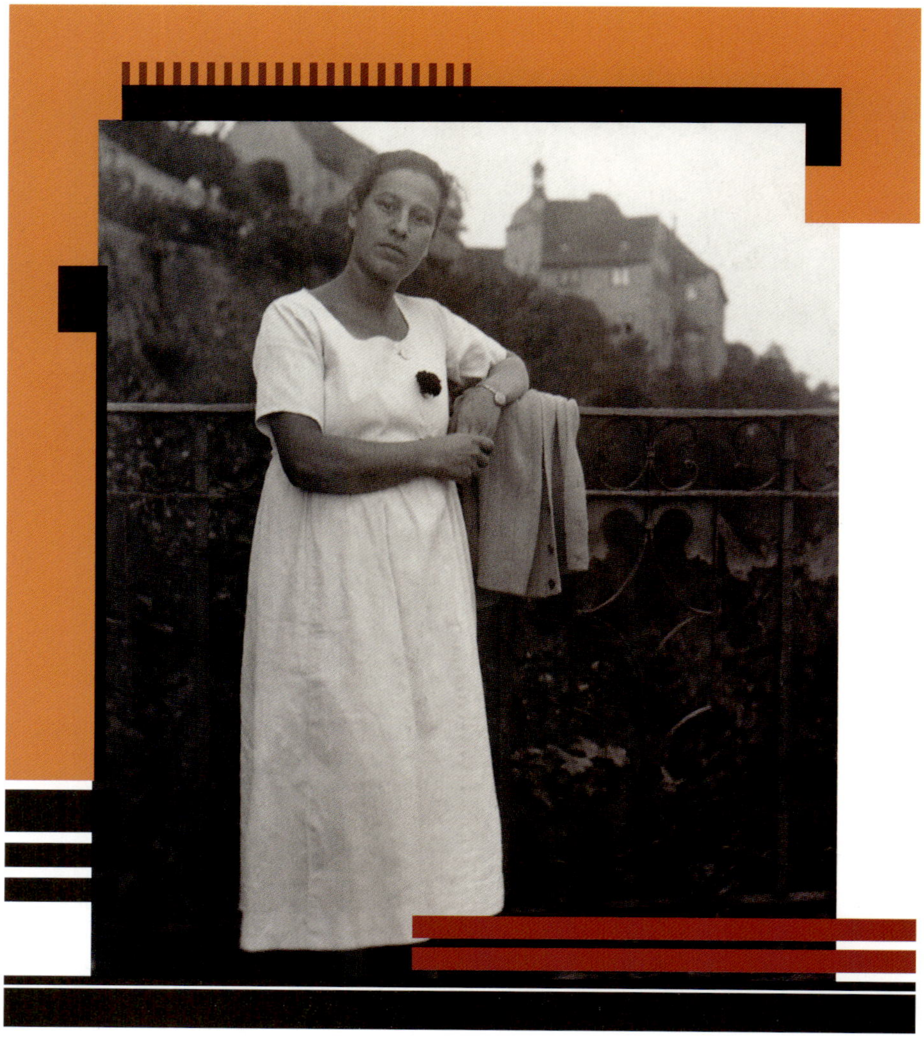

MARGUERITE FRIEDLAENDER-WILDENHAIN

1896–1985

"I would like my pots to be good not only now but in ten or a hundred or a thousand years and to be able to stand next to the good pottery of Greece, China, or Peru and have as timeless, distinct and independent a character as they have. To reach this point, even if only with a few pots, would be worth a whole life of intense effort."

Marguerite Friedlaender-Wildenhain in The Invisible Core: A Potter's Life and Thoughts, *1973*

The ceramic artist Marguerite Friedlaender-Wildenhain is one of those Bauhaus artists who emigrated to the United States, experienced great success, and made a name for themselves. Her path from the "bright beach" of the Saale landscape in Thuringia to the Pacific shores of California was a difficult, important, and very labor-intensive one.

Marguerite Friedlaender-Wildenhain always connected her artistic practice with the same ethical purpose which also determined her educational style: to harmonize one's personality, mind, feelings, and conscience in artistic activity with nature, and with one's own life so that they form a complex unit—a philosophy, which influenced many intellectual changes in modernism, including those of the Bauhaus. Marguerite Friedlaender would probably not have gotten very far at the Weimar Bauhaus without her personal strength and 150-percent dedication, given that there was considerable resistance in the Dornburg ceramics workshop against accepting women. Yet Marguerite Friedlaender counted among the best students, along with Otto Lindig and Theodor Bogler, soon after she entered the pottery in 1921.

She began her studies at the Bauhaus in the winter semester of 1921 with Johannes Itten and Gertud Grunow's preliminary course. Thereafter, she took classes by Gerhard Marcks, Lyonel Feininger, and Paul Klee, all of whom were artistically close to her. But what enticed this young cosmopolitan, who had been born into comfortable surroundings in France, did her school-leaving examination at an English boarding school in Folkestone, and had already studied in Berlin, to a gnarled pottery master in a sleepy village in Thuringia? First, she had the possibility in Dornburg to learn a literally solid traditional, peasant craft far removed from

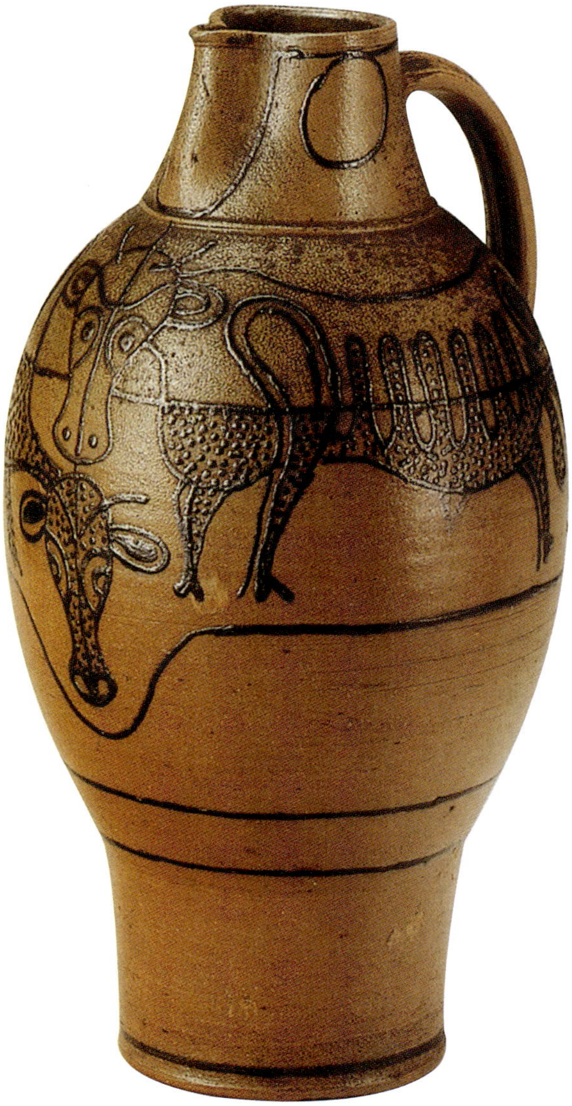

• *Facing page: Marguerite Friedlaender-Wildenhain in front of Schloß Dornburg , portrait photograph, 1925.*

• *Marguerite Friedlaender-Wildenhain, Handled jug with slip-glaze painting, 1922–23.*

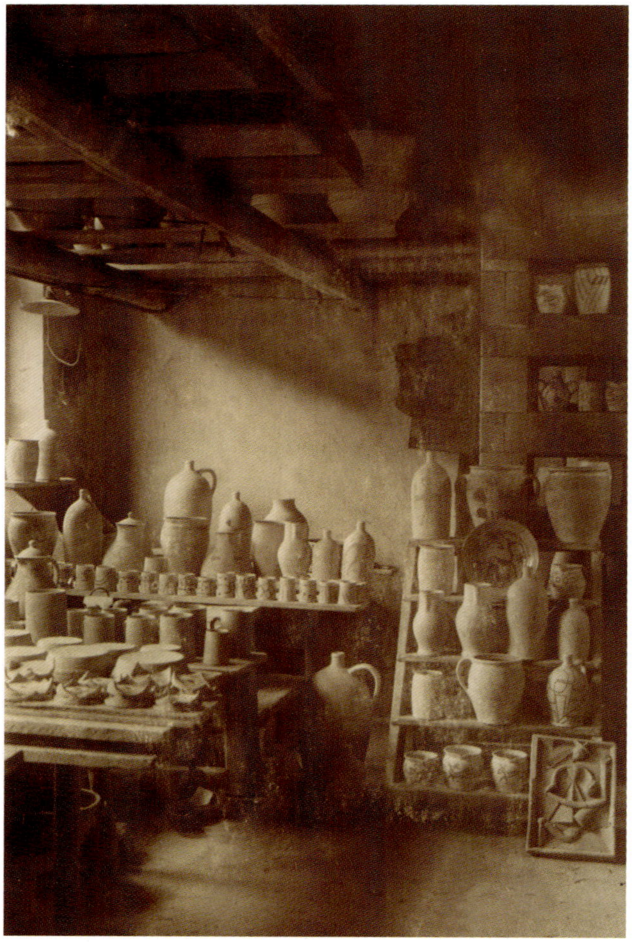

abstract theoretical debate, which she had always detested. Then there was the fact that her mother's ancestors had come from Thuringia. Perhaps this is also why she designed patterns for a porcelain manufacturer in Rudoldstadt in Thuringia following her studies at the Berlin Hochschule für angewandte Kunst from 1914 to 1916, where she studied drawing and wood sculpting. She felt at home in central Germany, hiked a lot, and drew. Since her childhood a love of nature and enthusiasm for art went together. Her mother had awakened in her an early passion for both.

Lydia Driesch-Foucar, then one of Max Krehan's five apprentices, described the pottery in her memoirs as the rotating, "earthy" transfer point from nature to culture. "The six turning tables stood one behind the other along the length of the workshop, before the windows. At the top of the workshop sat master Krehan, so that he could see each of us in a row before him, from the perspective of his table. It was important to him that one work process after the other was learned thoroughly, and that every movement became second nature, before moving on to the next. We often believed we had created a board full of 'beautiful' little pots which would then be thrown in the clay hole by Krehan while he mumbled a merciless, 'botched.'" Max Krehan must have been an absolute master in clay throwing. Marguerite admired him greatly and continued in his workshop after her journeyman's examination in 1922. Her work was, therefore, very strongly influenced by Krehan and Thuringian peasant pottery. Fifty years later she was teaching her American students that practice at the potter's wheel was much more important in working with clay than the creation of abstract artistic pictures.

Eva Deutschbein-Oberdieck, fellow student of Marguerite Friedlaender in 1923, establishes in her memoirs that she learnt nothing about glazes and firing in Dornburg but "I believe and hope that I learnt to distinguish a good shape from a misformed one." The specialist in thin-walled receptacles, Otto Lindig, expressed himself a little more precisely: "Pottery for me is always and above all a three-dimensional affair."

When Gropius called on the pottery for the production of industrial models in 1923, he was not exactly met with cries of delight. Marcks warned against such an appropriation. With some success Bogler and Lindig had been testing the production of such models in the plaster-casting workshop in Dornburg. Initial contacts to industry had also been made. A fundamental problem could, however, not be solved: forms which had been designed for a specific material, such as clay, to be thrown on the potter's wheel, could not be easily transferred to another material, such as porcelain. Few

• *Krehan ceramics workshop in Dornburg, c. 1920.*

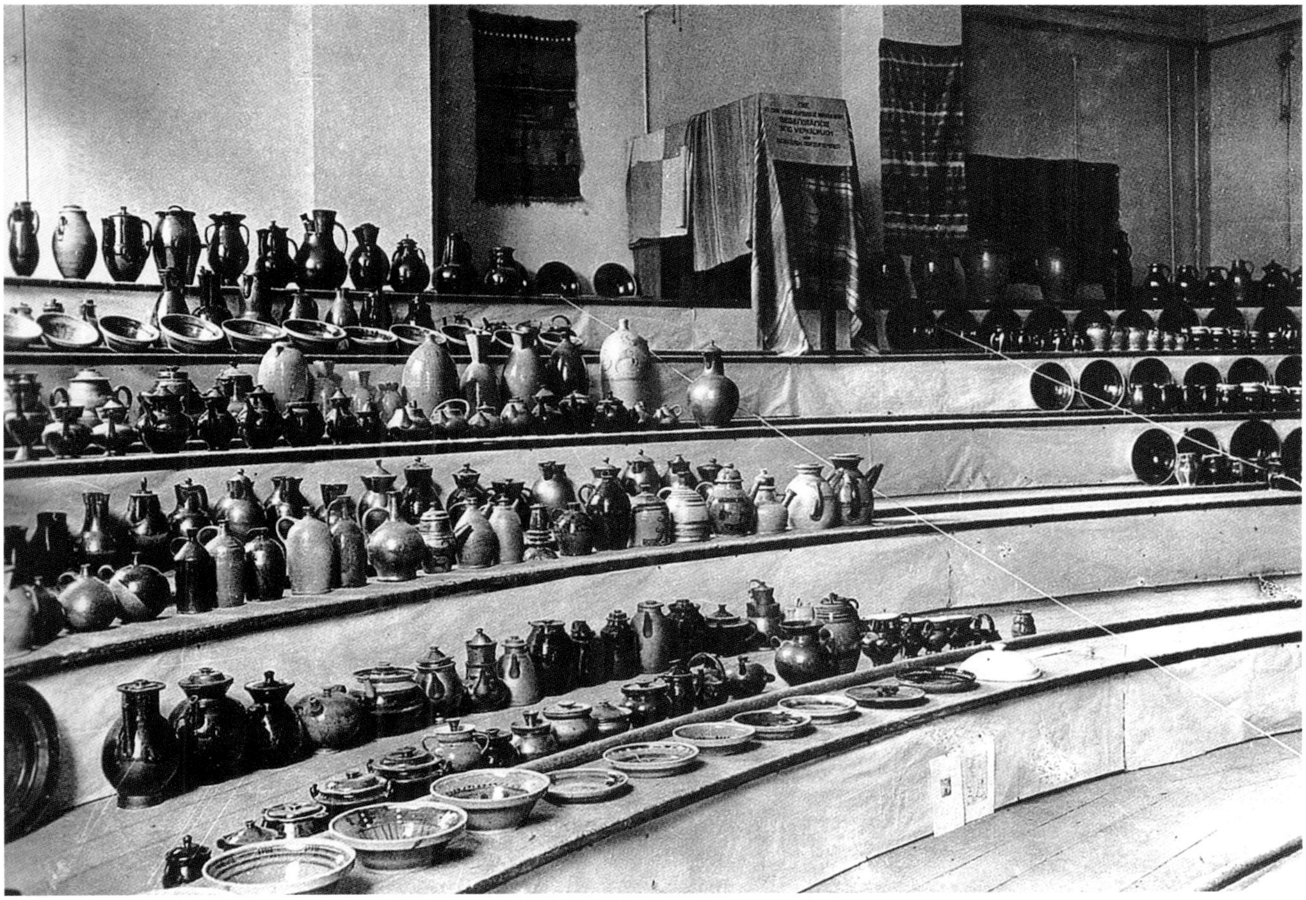

pieces remain from Marguerite Friedlaender's time in Dornburg, among them a simple handled mug and handled jugs decorated with plain painting, all markedly unembellished, reduced to basic forms but with soft intersections. Her learning curve can be traced in pieces such as these handled jugs. In her book *The Invisible Core* (1973) she describes the importance of, for example, decoration in the re-finishing of a receptacle: "It was . . . very, very educational! Only when one tries in earnest to copy a beautiful, lively line does one come to know its specific characteristic, to perceive the fine differences in pressure and strength in a lively movement or a relaxed gliding." Designing the shape and designing the surface, three-dimensional thinking and linear thinking were always tightly bound together for Marcks, a principle to which Friedlaender also felt obliged. The life-long friendship between the two, which had already developed in Dornburg, was based above all on artistic agreement. In his relationship to Friedlaender at least, Marcks's prejudices against women in the Bauhaus pottery had dissolved. Each had confidence in the other in an unusually liberated way.

When the Bauhaus moved to Dessau, the Dornburg workshop remained with the Weimar architecture school. There was no longer a ceramics department at the Dessau Bauhaus. Whoever did not wish to take part in the new call of "Models for Industry!" went to the Kunstgewebeschule Halle at Schloß Giebichenstein, which was seen as one of the most progressive schools of its type along with the Bauhaus. Marguerite Friedlaender remembered in 1935: "I tried to create the first three years of Bauhaus thought for myself (all creative forces into craft and not into bad art). . . . Bauhaus thought as it appeared to me later in Dessau is for me hostile to life and art because it continuously elevated theories to artistic ideals."

• *Ceramics exhibition room at the State Bauhaus, Weimar, 1919–23.*

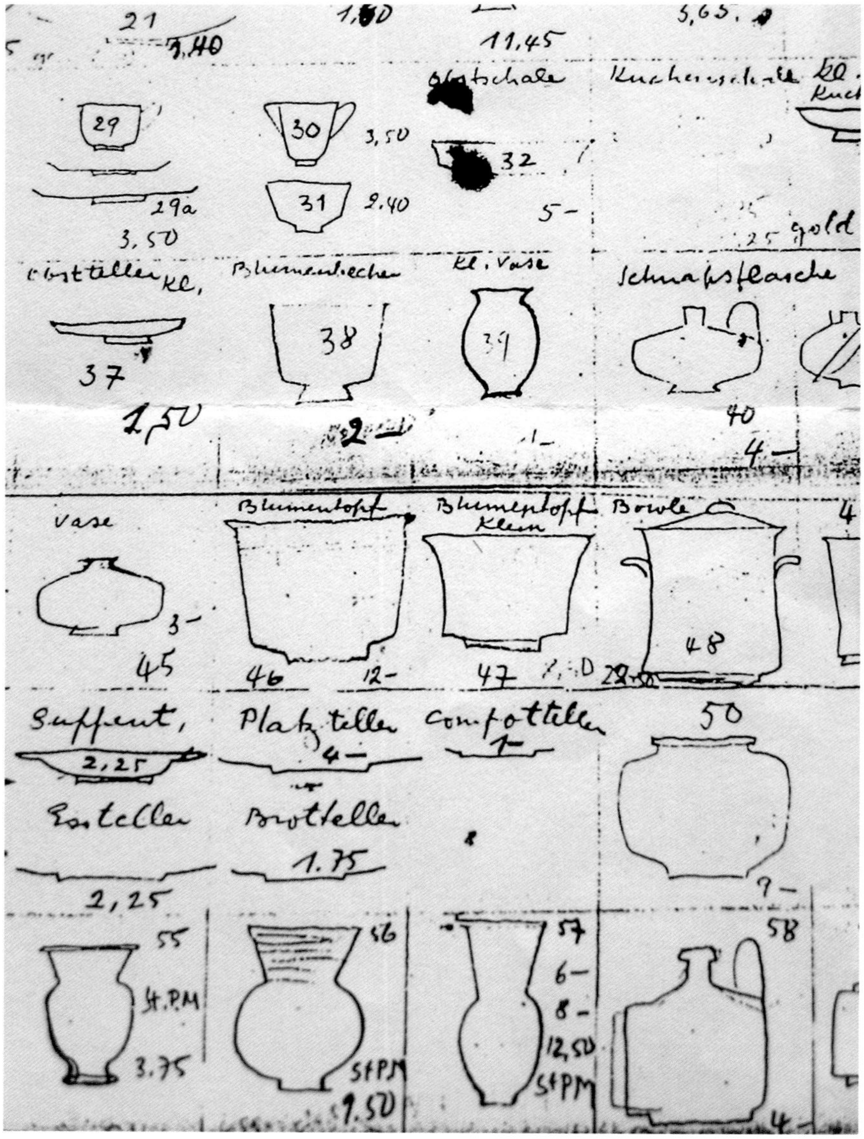

From November 1, 1925, Marguerite Friedlaender ran the ceramics workshop in Schloß Giebichenstein; Gerhard Marcks had already taken over the sculpting class the same year.

After she had completed her journeyman's examination in 1926, she was the first female pottery master in Germany to hold such a leading position. From then on, she worked as a self-employed ceramicist on the basis of her Dornburg experience, testing material mixes, firing techniques, glazes, and color combinations in endless experiments. Form still played the leading role in design. At Gebiechenstein, Friedlaender managed to create a synthesis between the two Dornburg components of manual work and prototype design for mass production. Her successful cooperation with the traditional KPM (Imperial Porcelain Manufacture) or StPM (State Porcelain Manufacture, Berlin, from 1918 to 1988) began in 1929. The director, Günter von Pechmann, founder of the Neue Sammlung in Munich, aspired to a unity between tradition and innovation, as represented also by Marguerite Friedlaender. While her student, friend, and, as of 1930, husband, Franz Rudolf Wildenhain, nine years her junior, took over the running of the ceramics workshop in Giebichenstein, she designed a total of fifty-nine single pieces and five tableware sets for StPM in 1933 in the "manufacturing test lab" belonging to the porcelain workshop which she ran. Among them were the tea and coffee sets Hallesche Form, the hotelware Hermes, and the dinnerware Burg Giebichenstein. Her pointedly simple shapes developed from craft ceramics for porcelain production, which was until then connected with the fashions of Frederick the Great and Jugendstil, established German porcelain design decisively on the road to modernity. The special thing about Friedlaender's KPM porcelain was the undecorated, white surface—this was previously only known from industrial porcelain—through which the "three-dimensional quality and strict elegance" (Klaus Weber) of the simple forms were accentuated most effectively.

• *Marguerite Friedlaender-Wildenhain, Drawing samples for Hallesche Form, personally inscribed, "models made by me for State Porcelain Manufacture, Berlin, 1929–33."*

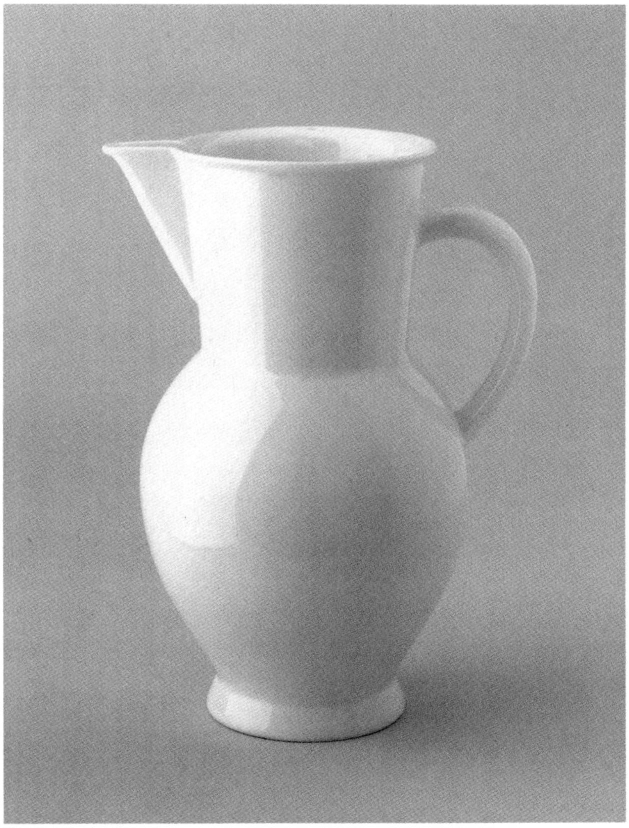

This hopeful development stopped abruptly when the Nazis took power in 1933. In her book *Ein Leben für die Keramik* (1973) Marguerite Friedlaender describes her departure: "One day the mayor (came) to me and asked me, with tears in his eyes, if I could do him the sad favor of quitting of my own volition. I was the only Jewish teacher at Schloß Giebichenstein and he hoped that he could save the school if I left. I did not hesitate for a moment and left the next day." Her resignation had absolutely no positive effect for the school. Four other employees, among them Wildenhain, had to leave. Marcks who had been director of the school since 1928 and fought vehemently for Marguerite to stay, was forced to leave in 1938. During Nazi rule, the StPM continued to produce the Burg Gebiechenstein collection by the "degenerate" Jew, Marguerite Friedlaender. They simply blocked out the artist's name. Her airplane cup from 1932 was, however, no longer produced.

Marguerite Friedlaender drove to her parents in Versoix, Switzerland. Since the eighteenth century the family had belonged to the emancipated European Jewry. Moses Mendelsohn's friend David Friedlaender was an ancestor of Marguerite. Her father, a worldly-wise businessman, ran a branch of the family's silk production company in Lyon. Marguerite was born in Ecully, near Lyon, in 1896. She and her four siblings grew up in a free-spirited, enlightened environment. "Even though French was our native tongue, we were encouraged to speak three languages from an early age, as our father wanted us to be citizens of the world, not just of one nation," she said in her memoirs. She expressed the following perception of Jewish oppression in a letter to Marcks from Holland, her next country of exile in fall 1933: " I am neither Jew nor Christian nor heathen. I am what can be. I am as good and as honest, as truthful and as open, as I can be." Her reaction to the deep emotional injury and threatening hatred of Jews in Germany was to withdraw—withdraw into work. She did the work of three people in order to build up a new workshop, Het Kruikje, in Putten, near Amsterdam. She also withdrew into country life. "I have a real fear of people at present," she wrote to Marcks who had asked her, following a visit in 1934, "How can one live when one believes in any kind of earthly justice?"

Marguerite resumed mass production and worked with the Maastricht stoneware factory De Sphinx. Franz followed her from Germany. She visited the American architect Gordon Herr in 1939. He was delighted by both of them and invited them to work in California in a communal workshop, which he and his wife were planning. In 1940 the Germans occupied Holland. While Franz had to remain, Marguerite, as a French citizen, obtained a visa and traveled on board one of the last ships to New York, where most of the family gathered at her brother George's house.

• *Marguerite Friedlaender-Wildenhain, Jug (Hallesche Form), 1931.*

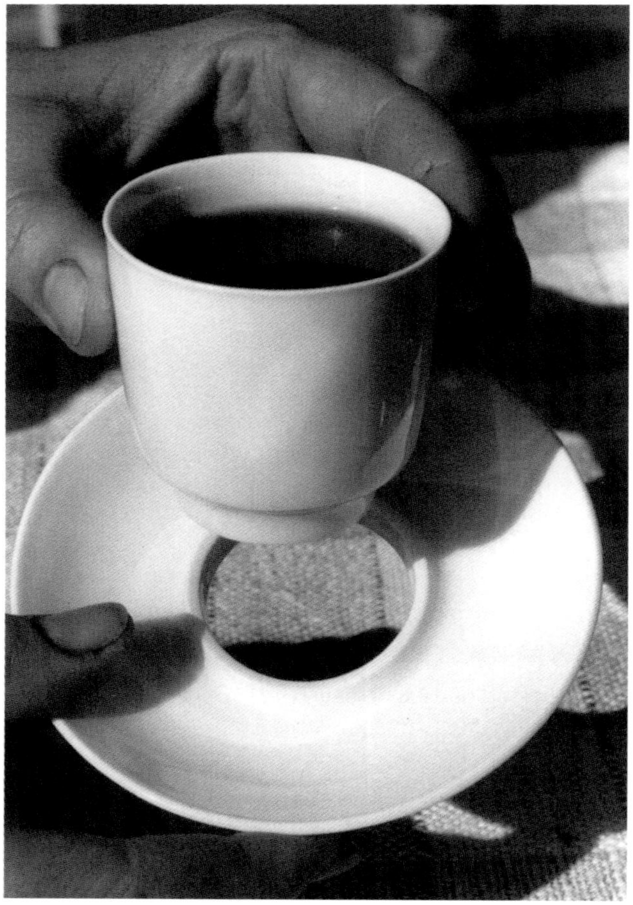

Marguerite's KPM design was well known to specialists in the United States. Drawing on her own strengths she now began to build a new life for herself, for the third time. Having been unable to find employment in New York and finding life in the metropolis oppressive, she moved to San Francisco. In the broad city by the sea and the beautiful landscape in California she was able to breathe and so she stayed. She worked for two years as director of the ceramics workshop of the California College of Arts and Crafts in Oakland. She organized an exhibition in San Francisco and showed her art there for the first time as *Art in Action*.

She moved to the country in 1942 where Jane and Gordon Herr were working on their project.

Immigrant artists met at Pond Farm, a former ranch near Guerneville, north of San Francisco. Metal and textile workshops were built up and Marguerite set up a pottery. She described the beginnings of Pond Farm in an American magazine in 1948: "The house was just a little ship's cabin. I was alone and I filled my mind completely with my work in pottery. That way I did not suffer so much—art can involve the mind, you know; it can become an anodyne for pain." Franz came to America in 1947 after seven long years—contact had been completely broken off—and so the "ship's cabin" was extended by two rooms. There was neither electricity nor telephone but in Marguerite's room there was a Picasso, a sculpture by Marcks, and some Chinese art treasures.

The joy of seeing each other again did not last long. There were fights. Franz became jealous of Marguerite's success in the United States and claimed that she had built up her career at his expense. For her part Marguerite, who had grown up in a privileged environment, envied him, the simple laborer's son, his undisguised creative inspiration. Franz left Pond Farm for good in 1949. Their divorce followed one year later. The artist's colony disbanded in 1949 following the death of Jane Herr. Everyone left, only Marguerite stayed. She lived alone on Pond Farm from 1969 onwards. Her partners were the potter's wheel and nature. She continued to carry water, grew vegetables and remained a "minimalist in her lifestyle," although her Pond Farm pottery became increasingly well known. She was a woman of unbelieveable energy with a passionate leaning toward the absolute, who appeared silent even when she gave lectures and wrote books. She was now a recognized talent in the United States. In 1959, her book, *Pottery: Form and Expression* was published which described her commitment to craft the way that Krehan also understood it: "For whatever the brain conceives, the hand has to make to give it life and force; without the skilled hand the most imaginative craftsman is impotent. Abstractions often help to clarify, but they can for me

• *Marguerite Friedlaender-Wildenhain, Model of airplane cup, 1932.*

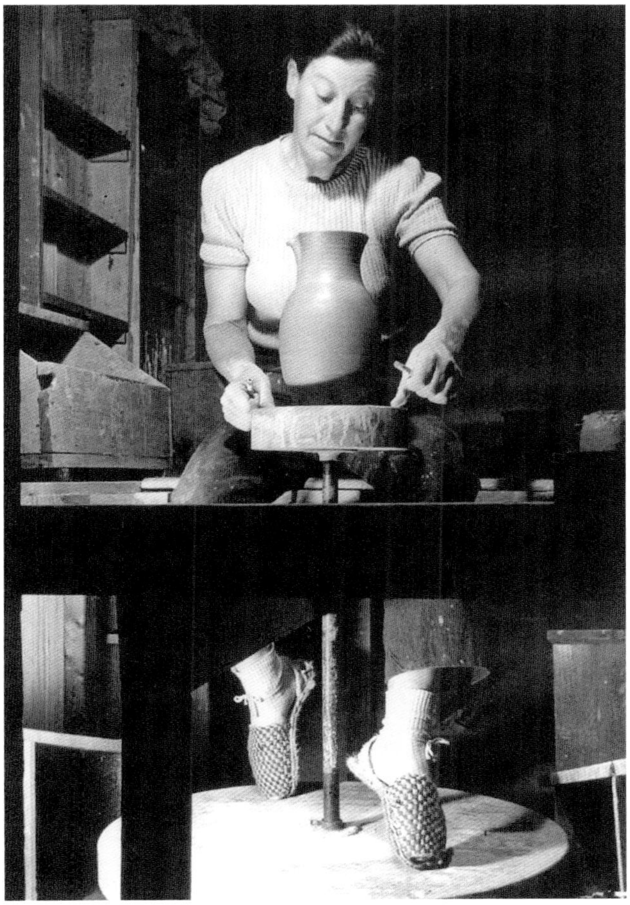

never be either the source nor the aim of a craft." She was showered with honors and prizes, held lectures at congresses, gave courses at universities, traveled the land, demonstrated throwing at the potter's wheel, as American ceramics had no such craft tradition. The students, her "children," as she referred to them, who attended her summer school at Pond Farm and gathered around her, learned not only craft from her, but at the same time a way of life which offered an intellectual alternative to the "more-faster-nicer-bigger" philosophy of aspirational white America: quality and authenticity, immersion and concentration, respect for others, and harmony between oneself and nature. Marguerite Friedlaender was, for many, a role model, even a moral guide.

Marguerite never went back to designing for the porcelain industry. She stayed with pottery and with individual pieces. Further influences now joined the Dornburg craft and Giebichenstein design canon such as Japanese and Indian ceramic traditions. She undertook regular, long winter trips, from 1965, to South and Central America and allowed herself, like Anni Albers at loom, to be inspired by old Indian cultures. Proportions and surface treatments in her work gradually changed. The exteriors were decorated with rich engraving, cutouts, or paintings. For these, she used abstract ornament as well as representational scenes and figures. By the end she was creating free three-dimensional designs, with no functional connection on her wheel.

Her autobiographical work, *The Invisible Core: A Potter's Life and Thoughts*, was published in 1973. Exhausted from the marathon that was her life, Marguerite Friedlaender suffered from a weak heart but lived twelve more full years with a pacemaker. She died in 1985 at almost ninety, in Guerneville. Her works can still be seen today in many museums in Europe, America, and South Africa.

ULRIKE MÜLLER

• *Marguerite Friedlaender-Wildenhain at the potter's wheel in her workshop at Pond Farm, c. 1950.*

Hammer and Chisel, Drawing Board and Paintbrush, Costume and Patent

Multitalents in Painting, Graphics, Sculpture, and Theater Design

On September 2, 1920, director Walter Gropius wrote to the masters of the council who represented the Bauhaus teachers: "The ratio of male to female students is such that the acceptance of women should, without question, be restricted . . . therefore, I suggest that for the foreseeble future, only women of extraordinary talent be accepted at the school."

The women in this chapter—Friedl Dicker, Ilse Fehling, and Lou Scheper—were of extraordinary talent. And they were accepted. Drawing played a central role for all three. They each worked on the Bauhaus stage at different times. They studied in Weimar between 1920 and 1923 in the early ideological phase of the Bauhaus, and wanted to work in workshops, which Gropius would have preferred to reserve for male students. He had envisaged at most one-third female and two-thirds female applicants. The numbers were now, to his surprise, almost one to one. The fact that the women often applied more pressure to gain access to the workshops than the men made his situation all the more difficult.

Crafts courses had been open to women since the end of the nineteenth century, but to study painting or even sculpture at an academy was almost impossible. Nevertheless, a few more women in Germany dared approach this terrain. Among them were Clara Westhoff, Milly Steger, Käthe Kollwitz, and Renée Sintenis, the Berlin animal sculptor whose bears are still awarded annually at the Berlinale today.

Ilse Fehling wanted to be a sculptor from the very beginning and chose this as her main subject at the Weimar Bauhaus. She was also allowed to study in the theater workshop. As far as can be ascertained, Ilse Fehling was the only sculptor among the Bauhaus women. Sculpting, whether from wood or stone, presented a problem at the Bauhaus as the necessary practical relevance and contracts from outside were only attainable in exceptional circumstances. Within the school, the only possibilities were in mural design, e.g., Oskar Schlemmer's reliefs and murals in the staircase of the workshop building, and on the Bauhaus stage. Friedl Dicker was sometimes to be found on the Bauhaus stage. She had it easier than other women in the workshops in fulfilling her wish because she was one of the "Vienna Group," who had come to Weimar in 1919 with the teacher and painter Johannes Itten, and was very strongly mentored by him. She attended the weaving studio for a time, worked later in the print graphic workshop, in the theater, and also in the carpentry shop.

Lou Scheper decided to study in the mural workshop which was an unusual choice for a young woman. Dörte Helm also took this step in Weimar. Central to the architectural debate of early modernism was the challenge of

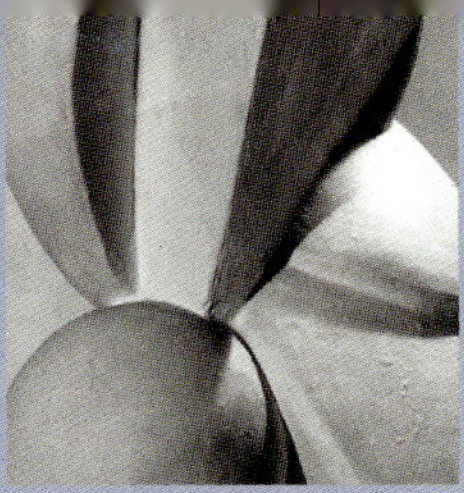

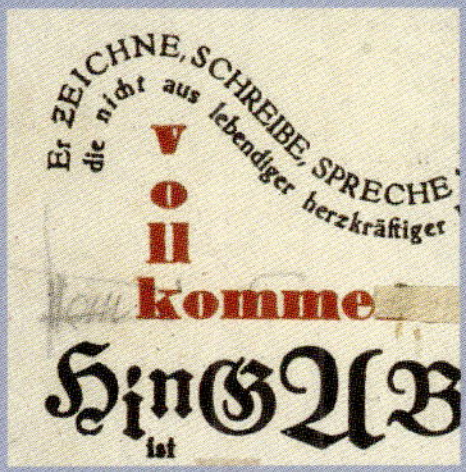

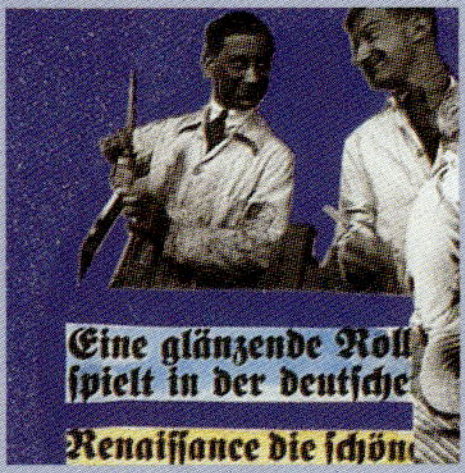

a new color method as an alternative to the gray-on-gray of stone and plaster elevations in the cities. In many suburban areas of the larger cities, so-called paintbox housing estates were created as alternative experiments—intensely colored new prototype buildings. The leading "color propagandist," the architect Bruno Taut, saw a possibility in this color design, despite the limited resources in public housing, not only to prevent monotony, but to create the appearance of connectedness. This also gave a feeling of homeliness and would improve the quality of living. The numerous different design approaches for colorful architecture were strongly influenced by the Dutch De Stijl movement whose concept included the use of primary colors only. The Bauhaus went its own way in 1925, using color as a subordinate result of the architecture. Pastel tones, whose effect was intensified by varying gray tones, were predominant. The designs for the famous Bauhaus wallpapers were also born of this concept.

Free painting and murals remained the focal points of Lou Scheper's artistic work. Painting was also at the forefront for Friedl Dicker, who created important graphics at the Bauhaus in parallel with her teaching. There was, however, no class for free painting at the Weimar Bauhaus. Art was to be taught in connection with craft and technology. But the formative masters themselves, such as Johannes Itten, Lyonel Feininger, Paul Klee, and Wassily Kandinsky, were free painters, even though they ran different workshops. When Gropius pronounced in 1923: "Art and technology—a new unity," this was potentially inflammatory as not everybody at the Bauhaus agreed to sacrificing the freedom of art for industry. This was about ideological standpoints. "Art and technology . . . remain fundamentally different in their creative value," said Georg Muche, "art can do nothing else but achieve its value in an idealized objective." The tension between art and technology gave rise to important discussions in the Weimar period, but also led to the departure of important artists such as Itten.

Friedl Dicker also left the Bauhaus in 1923, as did Ilse Fehling, albeit because she had been given a job as a theater designer and was attracted by the work experience. Lou Scheper married for the first time—a Bauhaus member, of course.

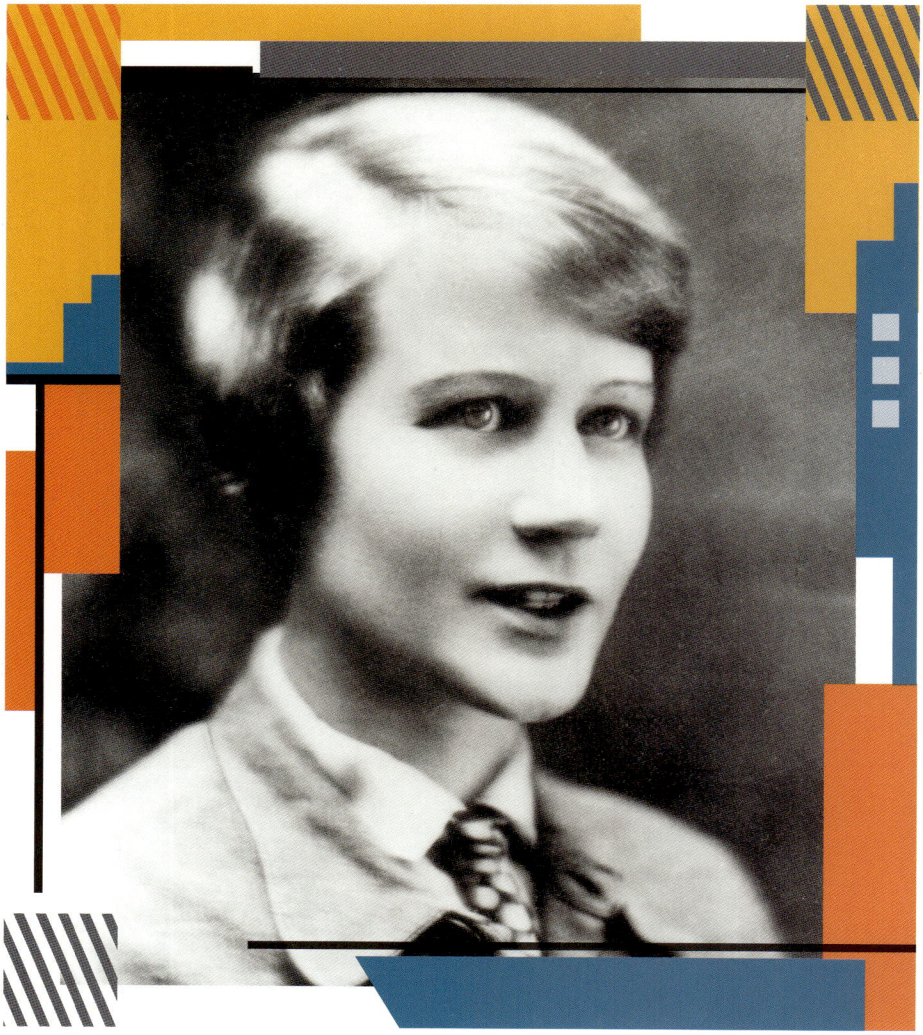

ILSE FEHLING 1896–1982

"I would like to see anyone try to imitate what we went through in terms of the misery of life. The atmosphere in the school did not only affect us creatively, it made us believe in something unprecedented, an artistic event that was handed to us on a plate."

Ilse Fehling in a letter to E. Stenenberg, March 11, 1968

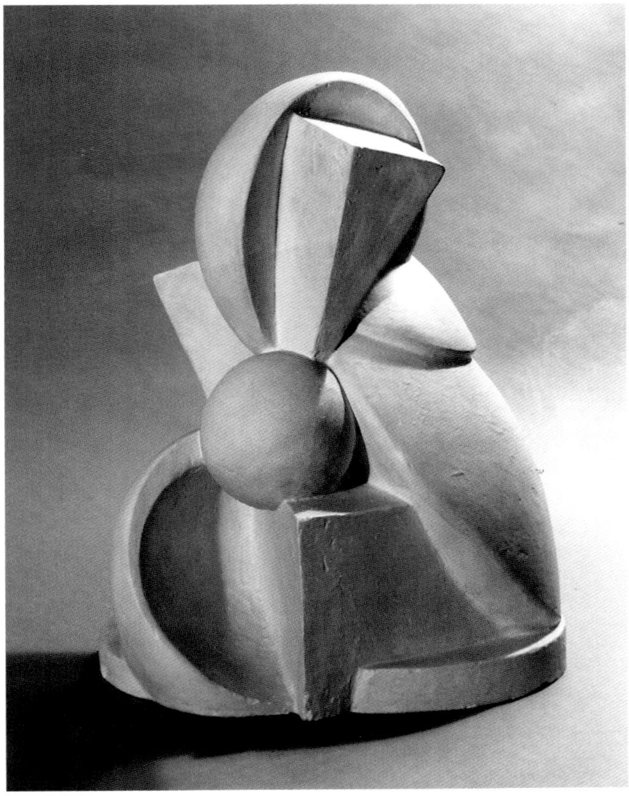

Ilse Fehling. bauhaus bühne akt skulptur 1922–1967 was the name of an exhibition presented by the Munich gallery owner Bernd Durr in 1990. Even the title of the exhibition demonstrates the versatility of the artist, who is one of the lesser known in the group of Bauhaus women, and whose wide-ranging work is still little known by the public today. The exhibition showed life drawings and designs for stick puppets, construction plans for a round stage for the puppet theater, terracotta sculptural objects, fired clay, plaster, and bronze; curtain, stage, and costume designs for plays and films.

Although her designs from the Weimar Bauhaus period were indeed spectacular, she was unable to make her mark with her sculptural objects and drawings in the 1920s and 1930s. She was not different enough for her time in either decade. She achieved great public fame through her work for theater and film. She created stage and costume designs for around forty plays. Ilse Fehling's filmography comprises some fifty films, mainly from the 1930s, for which she had created the costumes, including: *Viktor, Viktoria* (1933), *Kreutzersonate* (1937), and *Falstaff in Wien* (1940). In 1935 Ilse Fehling created the design for the first sleeveless, waisted shirtdress in German film for Renate Müller, the female lead in *Liselotte von der Pfalz*. The Berlin magazine *Ausschnitt* (2,90) described not only her costumes, but also her way of life as extravagant.

As a single mother and independent artist, she was viewed as a "femme fatale of her time."

Apart from such broad judgments information about her private life is scarce. One thing is known, however: the young Ilse Fehling's ambition was to become a sculptor, although, as she said in an interview for the magazine *Die Deutsche Frau* in 1935, she did not wish to make a living from sculpting, considering sculpting too sacred for that.

Ilse Fehling was born on April 25, 1896, in Danzig, but her family soon had to move to northern Germany as her father was a professional soldier. She attended the girls' school in Verden/Aller and, following her parents' divorce in 1913, the Roquette "ladies' college" in Lübeck. In 1918 she began studying in one of the most progressive institutes in the new republic, Albert Reimann's Kunstgewerbeschule in Berlin. She took classes in costume design, history of costume design, sculpture, lettering, graphics, and tailoring. She also studied sculpture under Professor Schmarje at the Berlin Kunstgewerbeschule in 1919–20.

In 1920 she moved to the Weimar Bauhaus in 1920 and took courses with Johannes Itten and Georg Muche as well as the obligatory second semester course with Paul Klee. Ilse Fehling remembered her beginnings at the Bauhaus in a letter of 1968: " we collected tin, threads, cardboard, and paints, we invented costumes free from any of life's worries—there was nothing to eat anyway! We took Klee's courses with eagerness, admired Schlemmer's 'triadic experiments.' As the most talented

• *Facing page: Portrait of Ilse Fehling, 1928.*

• *Above: Ilse Fehling, Abstract sculpture* Bühnenkubus (*Stage Cube*) *(work for the preliminary course), 1922.*

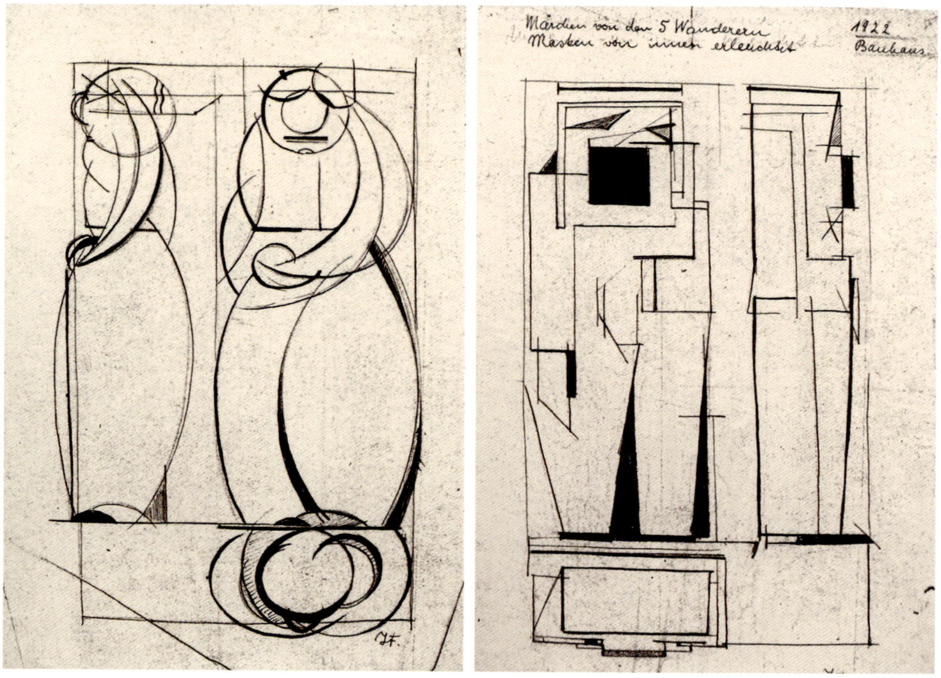

of our student days we admired the creative possibilities open to us and lived uninhibited by the despair the residents of Weimar felt (regarding us!)." She did not allow herself to be pushed into the women's class following foundation training, but attended Lothar Schreyer's stage class and Oskar Schlemmer's sculpting class. Schreyer's teaching was, like Itten's, strongly influenced by the Utopian idea of the "new man." He studied dance and movement with his Bauhaus students while wearing masks. Ilse Fehling was not officially permitted to attend the stage workshop until a year later, according to the minutes of the Masters' Council meeting of October 2, 1922: "It has been decided, according to Schreyer's wish, to admit her on condition that she actually works."

Despite her laziness, which is documented in numerous written warnings, she presented a great range of work in her four Bauhaus years, especially designs for the puppet stage. These were based on themes from theater work. Among her works are the designs in pencil and fountain pen for the marionettes, Rüdiger, Uhlhorst, Effi and Leonore for Frank Wedekind's *Schloß Wetterstein*. The figures, ranging in size from 20 to 30 centimeters, and made from fabric and metal, appear to have been inspired by Schlemmer's figurines for the "triadic" ballet. Their bodies are reduced to basic geometric forms, from which their mechanical movements are derived. For all their reduction, they do demonstrate distinctive characters for the stage, stronger than Schlemmer's figurines which were derived from each construction plan. In 1922, Ilse Fehling developed a round stage for the puppet theater, also for *Schloß Wetterstein*, and "a moving backdrop for puppet stages, which is unwrapped from one roller and re-wrapped around another, forming a spiral-like track in plan around the stage. The moving backdrop should be made of translucent material so that the audience would see numerous backdrop changes one behind the other." The twenty-six-year-old student received the German *Reichspatent* (imperial patent no. 387 832) for her circular stage design in 1922. Apart from the exact construction plans, a 34-centimeter high model of the open round stage still exists, made during the preliminary course in 1921, a material composition built compactly of geometric elements.

She brought her work for the stage and in sculpture closer together in her stick puppet designs for the play *Fünf Wanderer zwischen den Welten* (Tale of the Five Wanderers)*, Märchen aus 1001 Nacht* (Tales from the Arabian Nights). There is a drawing and plaster cast, about '25 centimeters' high, of each of the five figures. All plaster models are labelled, "mask to be lit from inside." The term "mask" fits the construction method of the figurines: they are constructed in relief on the face side, the elementary right-angled basic shape, the high level of abstraction, the play on geometric lines, the

• *Ilse Fehling, Figures for the puppet theater* Märchen von den 5 Wanderern *(Tale of the Five Wanderers), 1922.*

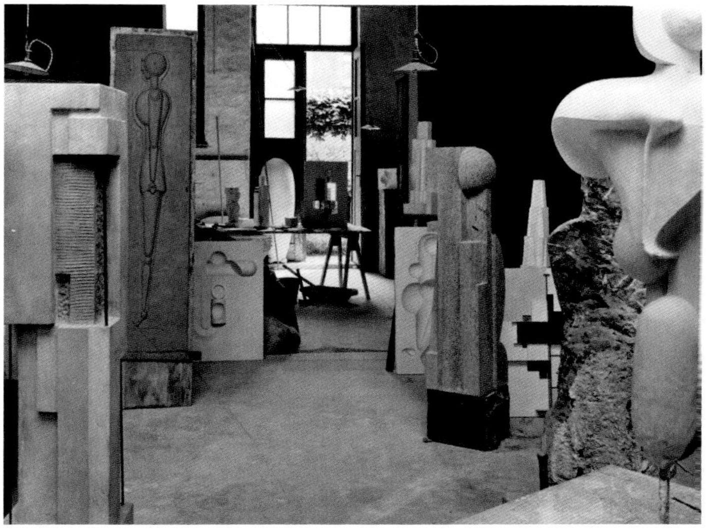

dehumanizing of the human form, and the simultaneous humanizing of abstract geometric form. In this work, Ilse Fehling pictorially implemented the new unity of art and technology proclaimed by Gropius and Schlemmer.

In 1923 Ilse Fehling married Klaus Henry S. Witting and became Ilse Fehling-Witting. Her biography reveals little more. The marriage did not last. They divorced after the birth of their daughter, Gaby, in 1928. Other relationships lasted longer. During her studies at the Bauhaus, Ilse became close to the Russian student Nicol Wassilieff. They immortalized themselves in a photograph, *Doppelbild in Spiegelung* (Reflected Double Image), one of the first photographic experiments of the early Bauhaus. She continued to create sculptures of Nicol, and a range of life drawings into the 1930s. They remained in contact even after World War II.

At the eighty-nineth collective exhibition of the Overbeck Society in 1922 in Lübeck, Ilse Fehling's work was shown for the first time. She got her first job as stage designer in 1923 for *Chrysanthus and Daria* by Calderón, at the Berliner Theater on the Kurfürstendamm. The etched designs, especially for the doctor's costume, are influenced by the Bauhaus stage style. The robe is made of connected squares and triangles, and the body appears architecturally built rather than flexible. The following year Ilse Fehling became solo costumier to the Schauspieltheater in Berlin. The contours of her costumes became softer over the years, the basic forms were no longer as geometric. Body and robe appeared more flexible, even buoyant. The Bauhaus influence remained undeniable, but it shifted from a strictly formed main body to a lighter, more flexible symbolism: characters could, for example, take on the form of numbers or letters.

However, sculpture remained for Isle Fehling at the heart of her creativity. She had her own studio in Berlin from 1923. Her sculptures, such as the head of Maximilian Harden from plaster and galvano (1927), or the torso figure *Maria, lebensgroß* (Maria, Life-size) from plaster and firing clay in English red (1929-30), hardly appear to be influenced by the Bauhaus. They are stylistically uniform, above all in the surface design. The strong Mary does not hold a Baby Jesus, and is not wearing a blue robe, but is naked. And she is neither "Queen of Heaven" nor "pure maiden" but a resplendent "new woman" of early Modernism, both emancipated with short hair and sexual with bushy pubic hair.

From 1927 onwards stage work and sculpture formed a new alliance in Ilse Fehling's work. She designed costumes for her first movie *Liebe*, and for her first love at the movies, the leading lady Elisabeth Bergmann. She later created a portrait bust of the actress who embodied the boyish "New Woman." Thereafter, she made portraits of theater people who specially impressed her, among them Victor de Kowa before the war, and after 1945, Karl Böhm and her relative, the director, Jürgen Fehling.

After her work had been shown in numerous exhibitions, for example in the first show of the Deutscher Staatsbürgerinnenverband (German Union of Women Citizens), Die gestaltende Frau, and in the spring exhibition of the Verein der Berliner Künstlerinnen (Union of Berlin Women Artists) in 1930, she received in 1931 a

• *Workshop stone sculpture, 1923.*

one-year scholarship to the Villa Massimo in Rome, from the Prussian Akademie der Künste (Academy of Art), for her achievements in sculpture. Ilse Fehling's work with the female form produced numerous life drawings, impressive in her accurate, economic, line. When Fehling returned from Italy, she had changed her style. She had acquired new insight into the nature of three-dimensional design, which she formulated thus in 1935: "The means of expression is to find the character of the material as felt from within." She also created many large sculptures such as *Die Singende* (Singing,1933).

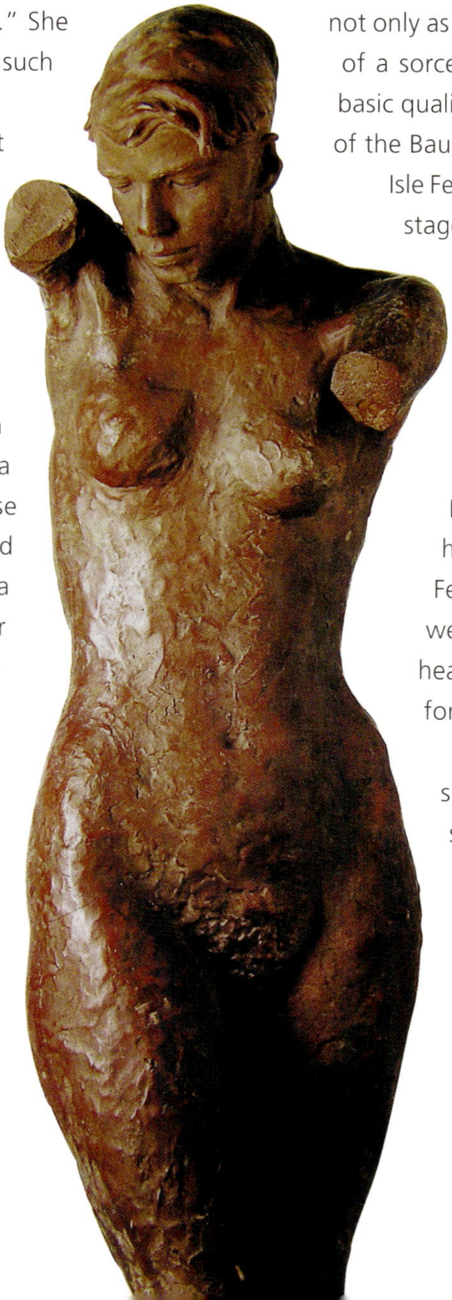

In 1933 the same academy that had supported Isle Fehling, rejected her work as "degenerate." This ostracism created a change in her artistic development. She still created some isolated sculptural works, but the corresponding duality between visual and applied arts, between a serious and a more frivolous muse had broken down. Ilse Fehling could still continue to earn her living as a successful costume designer for movies. At the *Reichsausstellung der deutschen Textil und Bekleidungswirtschaft* (Imperial Exhibition of the German Textile and Clothing Society) in Berlin in 1937, she exhibited the collage *Zusammen mit Mies van der Rohe,* which clearly shows Bauhaus design elements, as well as stage designs and theater curtains. She became chief outfitter for Tobis Europe in 1940, rebuilding and expanding the entire wardrobe department, setting up a new department for the recycling of artistic costumes, and developing a method for re-using old costumes. In an undate newspaper article titled *Wunder des Fundus* she explains why it was so easy: "Because every woman with imagination (and which woman has none?) has always been used to creating new from old, and to seeing this inventing game not only as a practical talent but feels in it the desire of a sorceress." Ultimately, she is describing the basic quality which was responsible for the success of the Bauhaus and its students in the early years.

Isle Fehling still designed theater costumes and stage sets from time to time, including for the Kammerspiele in Munich and the Thalia Theater in Hamburg. The Nazis confiscated her apartment with its sculpture studio in Berlin in 1943 and all her sculptures and work materials were destroyed by bombing. Demoralized by increasing restrictions on her work and the postwar shortages. Isle Fehling suffered a breakdown in 1947. She went to Geneva and was able to keep her head above water principally with sketches for the press.

She moved to Munich in 1952, where she stayed and worked again on f lms such as *Der große Zapfenstreich* (1952) and *Gestatten, mein Name ist Cox* (1955). She was also able to gain a foothold in the theater: she created all the sets for two Ionesco plays in Cologne (1959). Her work was exhibited

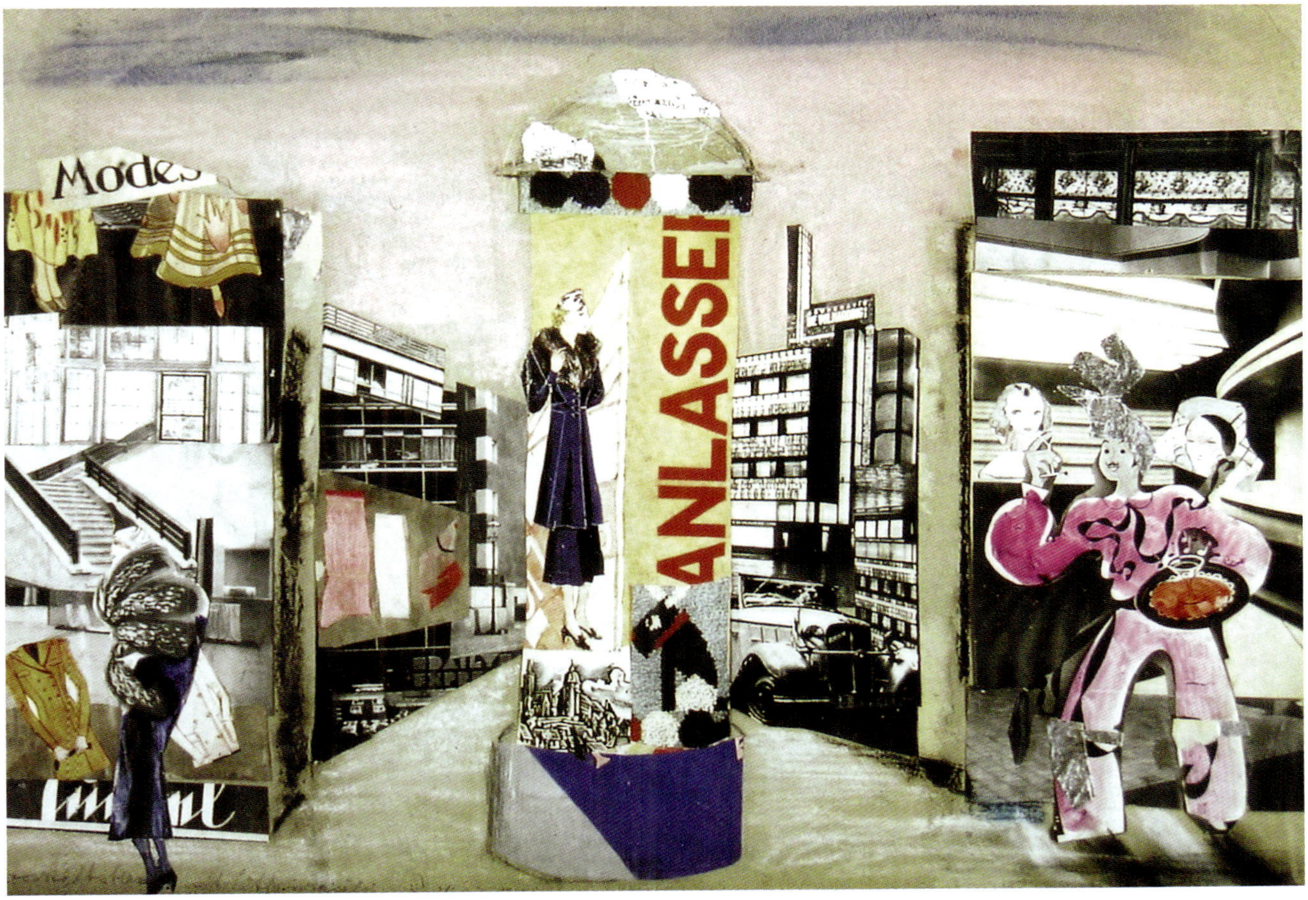

from time to time: in 1963 the Wolfgang Gurlitt Gallery in Munich dedicated a solo exhibition to her and larger collective shows followed.

She tried in vain to reconstruct her artistic career from the period before the Third Reich. After she had apparently heard a broadcast about the further development of the Bauhaus in the United States, she asked Gropius for documents relating to early Bauhaus history. Three letters from Walter Gropius in the United States, to Ilse Fehling remain from the years 1957–59. In his reply, he referred to the early students such as Helene Schmidt-Nonne, Lou Scheper, and Josef Albers, who would be able to give her information, and also to the book written by Wolfgang Wangler, *bauhaus – 2. generation*. The Bauhaus Archive contains letters from 1980 from Ilse Fehling to Wangler. The content is mostly about a book contribution which he asked of her, about which there were apparently differences regarding content in the end. The eighty-four-year-old politely but assertively and critically pointed out that she did not agree with Herr Wangler's portrayal of the Bauhaus generation and wished, therefore, to withdraw her manuscript. She was, however, finally included in the book.

Ilse Fehling died in Munich on February 25, 1982. Following a major solo exhibition in Munich in 1990, her pieces were once again shown at the Bauhaus Dessau exhibition of 1992.

ULRIKE MÜLLER

• *Facing page: Ilse Fehling,* Maria, *1929–30.*

• *Above: Ilse Fehling,* Großstadtstraße mit Litfaßsäule *(City Street with Advertising Pillar), collage, 1935.*

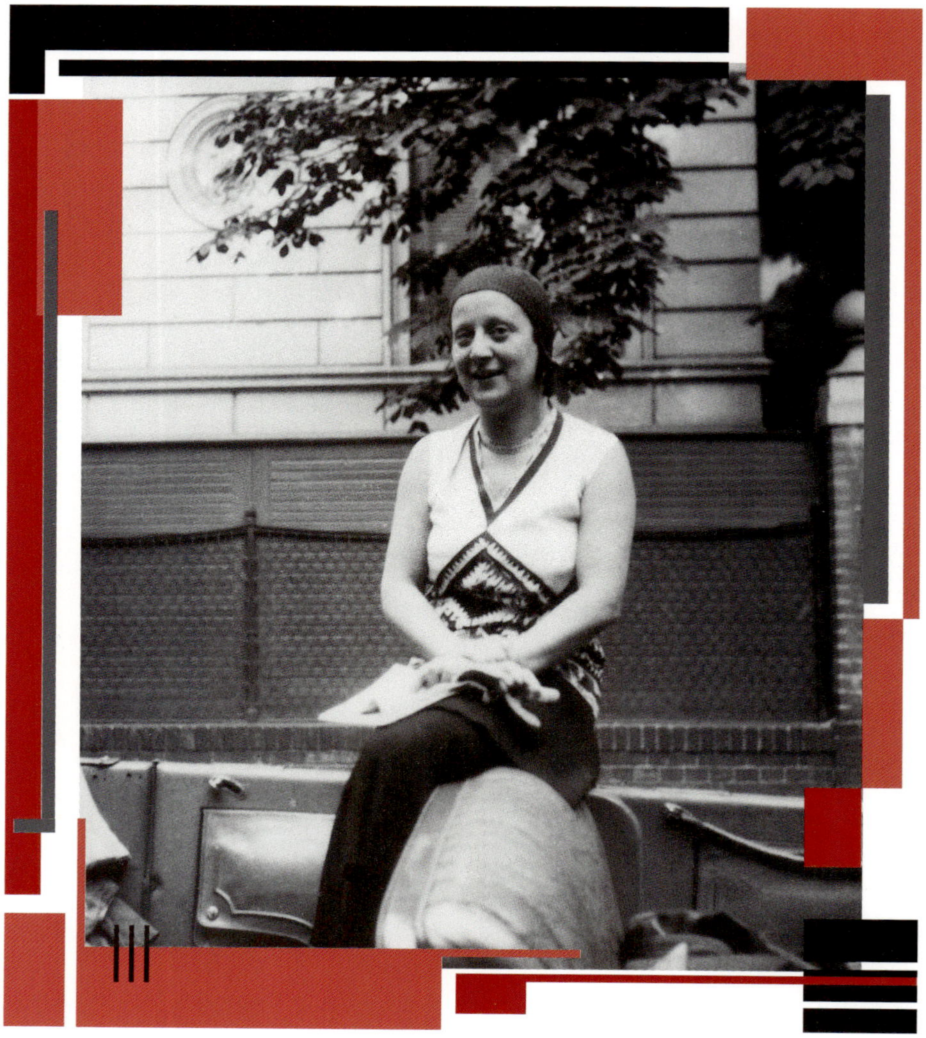

FRIEDL DICKER 1898–1944

"Dear Anny, . . . big costume festival at the Bauhaus. . . . Weimar is totally penniless. . . . We are not destined to be rich, and that is good, we do not need it. And just think, as often as we lost our patience, and it seemed as if this were because of money, it was always an internal cause. I believe the worries that people have are only there to cover up the real cause of their inner restlessness. Let us make sure that this is obliterated and that all is well."

Friedl Dicker to her friend and fellow student Anny Wottiz, c. 1921

Friedl Dicker was a talented person with a versatile, creative personality, and was one of the most important representatives of the early Weimar Bauhaus. She made her mark there, and in her workshops in Berlin, Vienna, and Prague with graphics, three-dimensional figures, book covers, leatherwork, and jewelry, but also with theater costumes, designs for houses, living and work rooms with modern convertible furniture and toys. One of her best-known graphic designs is an invitation poster to a Bauhaus evening with Else Lasker-Schüler. She then proved her extraordinary talent in education and therapy, under terrible conditions, in the Theresienstadt ghetto where she gave painting and drawing classes to the imprisoned children from the time of her own internment in 1942 until her murder in Auschwitz in October 1944. Around six hundred of the five thousand remaining children's drawings from the ghetto show a clear link with the Bauhaus educational methods of the Weimar period. The children's pictures from Theresienstadt and her own works, as well as Friedl Dicker's works which are scattered throughout the world, have been shown at various locations throughout the world and have allowed the name, work, and importance of this artist to live on.

Friedl Dicker was born in Vienna in 1898. She grew up in a bourgeois Jewish home. Her mother Karoline née Fanta died when her only child was just four years old. Friedl had her first creative experiences at pre-school age in the paper business in which her father, Simon Dicker, was a salesman. That precious paper was not for children was something she noted for life. Many of her sketches were later irretrievably lost because they had been made on newspaper. She attended the Vienna state school for girls from 1909 to 1912. Even as a young girl she had a passion for beautifully designed

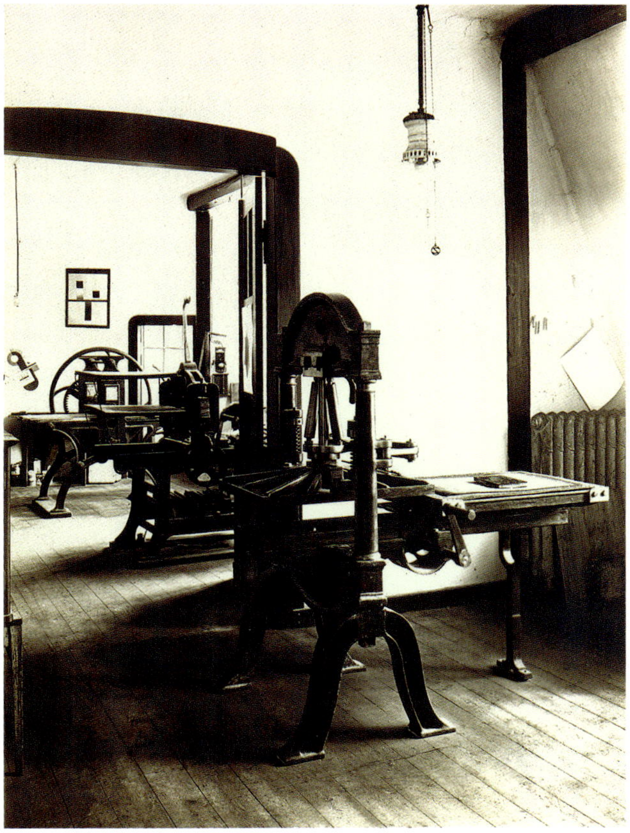

books. She earned her first wage by producing puppets and putting on puppet shows. Friedl Dicker took an apprenticeship in photography and reproduction techniques from 1912 to 1914 at the Graphischer Lehr- und Versuchsanstalt (Institute for Graphic Design and Experiment) in Vienna—quite an unusual career path for a young girl at that time.

She then attended textile class at the Kunstgewerbeschule from 1914 to 1916. The artist and education reformist Franz Cizek was one of her teachers and the one who introduced her to the artistic possibilities of free creativity. So Friedl cut her hair short, gleefully played truant from evening classes at the Freie Lyzeum, for which she was also registered, abandoned herself to the adoration of Rembrandt and Beethoven, and threw herself into the arms of the theater. She studied at Johannes Itten's private art school from 1916 to 1919. There was war in the ice-cold classroom (fuel was scarce), and with the most unorthodox teaching methods the young charismatic teacher fired up the hungry pupils with

• *Facing page: Friedl Dicker in a car by Hans Hildebrandt, late 1920.*

• *Above: Print workshop, c. 1923.*

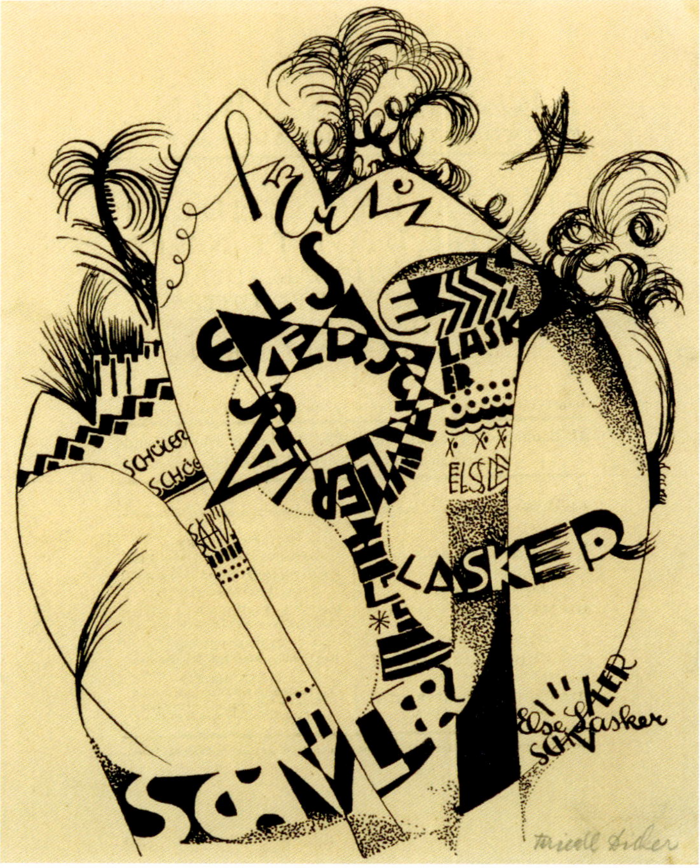

enthusiasm for his mystical ideas and practical exercises to achieve intellectual advances through art. Following his educational studies in Bern and art studies with Adolf Hoelzel in Stuttgart, whose teachings in color theory went back to Goethe, Johannes Itten had exhibited abstract paintings at Berlin's Sturm gallery and had become absorbed in questions of art theory, therapy, and education. From 1916 he had engaged with Middle and Far Eastern mythical traditions. In 1919 he joined the Zoroastrian religious movement, Mazdaznan, which had recently been founded in Los Angeles. He developed an individual art-educational concept for his students according to which the analyses of Old Masters had been incorporated into the syllabus since 1917, and which he had first come to know through Hoelzel.

When Itten took up his post at the Bauhaus in October 1919, around twenty of his students from Vienna awaited him, among them Friedl Dicker, Franz Singer, Margit Téry, and Anni Wottiz. Itten's preliminary course became compulsory as of 1920, and thereby formed the basis of Bauhaus work. With his shaved bald head and Mazdaznan outfit, the master met with derision from many students, but many more were fascinated. His way of life, which included meditation and a vegetarian diet, was contagious for students and colleagues but met with rejection outside the Bauhaus. Itten's cloisterish renunciation of "worldly things" finally brought him into conflict with Gropius, who aspired to a stronger relationship between art and industry. And his colleague's sectarian behavior unfortunately contributed greatly to the Bauhaus's negative reputation among conservative politicians and the public.

During her entire time in Weimar, Friedl Dicker belonged to the circle of Itten's followers. She collaborated on the design of the magazine *Utopia*, a programmatic key work of the early Bauhaus period. She demonstrated her well-honed graphic talent above all in Itten's preliminary classes, which encompassed the analysis of Grünewald's *Isenheim Altarpiece* as part of the studies of Old Masters. Dicker's resulting "expressive Phantastik" is reproduced again and again in the artist's prints and paintings, according to Hans M. Wingler at the Dicker-Singer-Exhibition in 1970 in the Bauhaus Archive, Darmstadt: "Friedl Dicker obviously created from an enormously powerful imagination." Winger asserts that from the melancholic, visionary composure of her works, no immediate inference can be made about the artist's mood. A long-standing friend of Dicker, Lily Hildebrandt described her as a happy person, "inspiring, full of ideas," and equipped with levity and a talent for improvization. The art therapist, Dicker researcher and former student, Elena Makarova remarked that Friedl Dicker's great passion for music and theater was of major importance in her work. She speaks of Dicker's "great

• *Poster for first Bauhaus evening with a reading by Else Lasker-Schüler, lithograph by Friedl Dicker, 1920.*

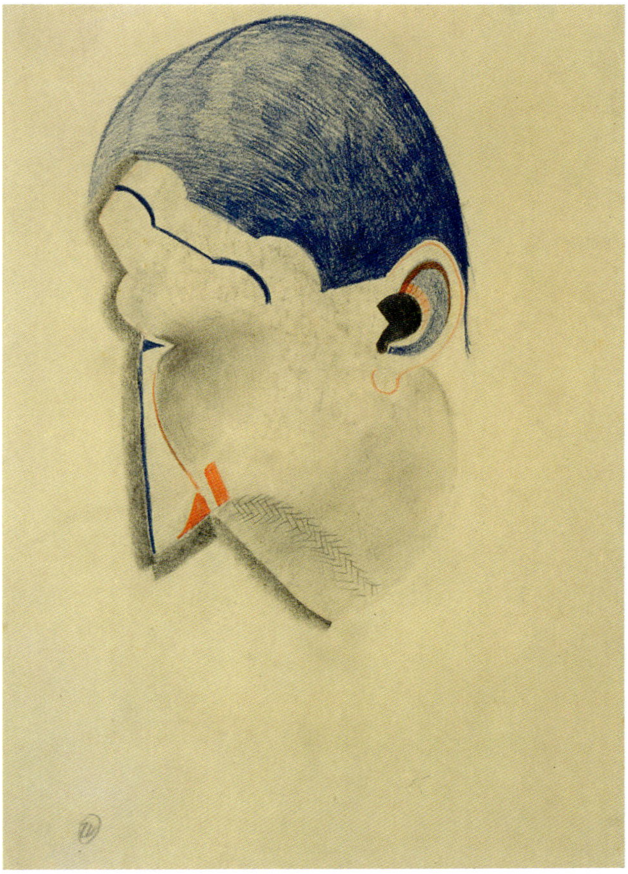

talent to absorb herself in a world beyond the mirror of representation."

Besides Itten, Paul Klee was especially close to Dicker as an artist and as a person. She possessed the ability to see things from the inside and from all sides and thereby open herself up to the inner world of children beyond the experience of Theresienstadt. On the other hand, she lived out her spirited, exhibitionist side in Oskar Schlemmer's scuplture workshop. Schlemmer's "triadic" ballet figures, which had been created for the stage, fired her design and production ideas for the theater. In the spring of 1921 Friedl Dicker was the only student to receive a scholarship. There is evidence in the Masters' Council meeting minutes to suggest that, due to her extraordinary performance, she was sometimes entrusted with teaching assignments during her studies. The references she received from Itten and Gropius in 1931 confirm this. Itten wrote: "Fräulein Friedl Dicker was my student in the years 1918–23 in Vienna and at the State Bauhaus in Weimar. Artistically, she is an extraordinary person whom I hold in highest esteem. I have no hesitation in recommending her to the education authorities." The Masters' Council decided at its meeting on October 12, 1921, that Friedl Dicker, as one of twelve students, would be relieved of tuition fee payments from Easter 1922: most of the Bauhaus students lived under pressured financial circumstances. Between 1920 and 1924, Friedl Dicker and Franz Singer designed and created stage sets and costumes for theaters in Dresden and Berlin. They worked with Berthold Viertel and later with Bert Brecht. Dicker appears to have been an exception among "Itten fans" in her creative independence. She reflected on this phase of her development in a letter to her friend, Hilde Kothny in 1940. She wrote that Itten had "helped [her] to crawl out from a used-up form—it was a very hard eggshell. . . . The things I learnt back then seem to have been fully absorbed—a sign of how good they were."

In 1923 the early Bauhaus period was moving to a close. There were strong arguments among the teachers regarding content. In June 1922 Schlemmer had already seen that the "machine for living" would replace cathedrals; Itten left the Bauhaus at Easter 1923; the music teacher Gertrud Grunow left in 1924. Her classes in "harmonizing theory" were certainly important for Friedl Dicker's educational and therapeutic work. Dicker's studies at the Weimar Bauhaus ended, according to her certificate, in September 1923. The Vienna group did not comply with the new direction. They did, however, remain in contact with each other following their departure from the Bauhaus. Friedl Dicker and Franz Singer had already had an intensive work and personal relationship for many years. Her private life had been very complicated since 1921 when Singer married Emmy Heim and

• *Friedl Dicker,* Stilisierter männlicher Kopf *(Stylized Male Head), 1920.*

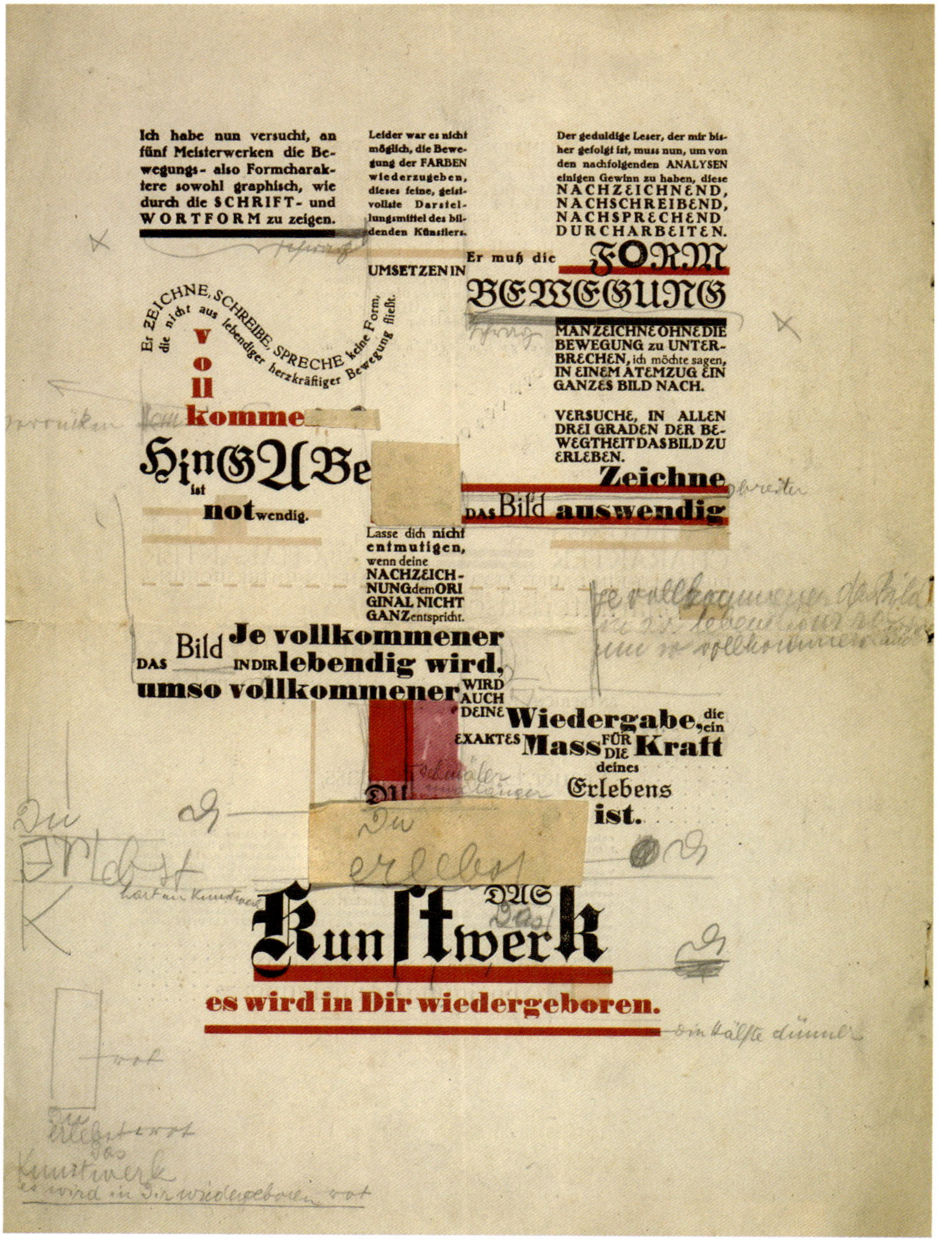

• Analysis of Old Masters, *lithograph by Friedl Dicker and Johannes Itten, no. 10 from Bruno Adler, ed.,* Utopia. Dokumente der Wirklichkeit *(Utopia: Documents of Reality) (Weimar 1921).*

had a son with her. Friedl, who eagerly wished to have children, became pregnant by Singer several times but because he did not want to have children with her, she felt forced to terminate each of the pregnancies. Although this was a cause of great turmoil for both of them, their stormy emotional and professional relationship continued. With Singer she founded the Werkstätten Bildender Kunst (Fine Arts Workshops) in Friedenau in Berlin in 1923, and 1926 saw the opening of their shared studio, "Singer-Dicker," in Vienna, which was highly successful. Their pieces won numerous awards and were shown in exhibitions, including at the *Moderne Inneneinrichtungen* of 1930 at the Österreichisches Museum in Vienna. Both were involved in numerous projects; Dicker primarily in interior design, where she achieved prominence with her unorthodox principles of form, distinctive colors, and "sensual materials." Bauhaus origins were clear in the work of both artists. The modern spatial concept of convertible practicality embodied the principles of freedom, openness, and tolerance in the smallest area.

In 1931 Friedl Dicker separated from Franz Singer and opened her own studio in Vienna. But the political and social situation had begun to change, not only in Germany. Red Vienna was slowly turning brown. Dicker, who had become politically active, and in 1931 had become a member of the Communist Party, was arrested in 1934. Following her release she managed to emigrate to Czechoslovakia. She settled in Prague and began to build up a new life as an interior designer and drawing teacher working for the cause of Communist emigrants against Fascism. Friedl Dicker was among the artists of the twentieth century whose existence was threatened in three ways by the National Socialists' totalitarian ideology and despotism: as a Jew, as a communist, and as a artist creating what was soon to be condemned as "degenerate art."

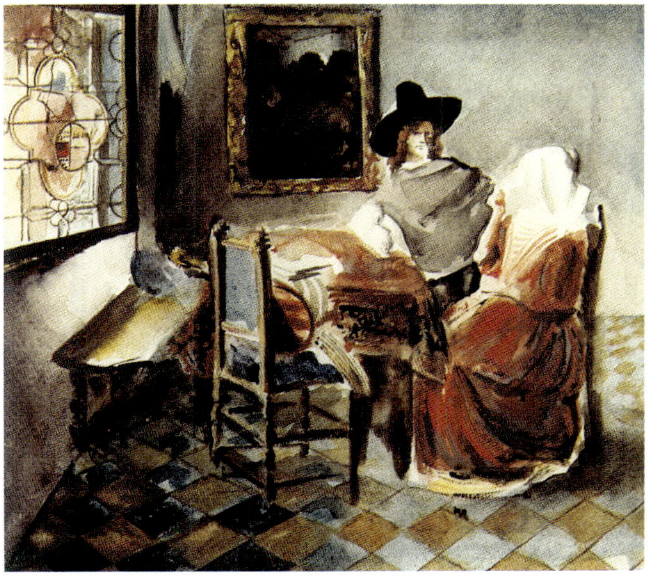

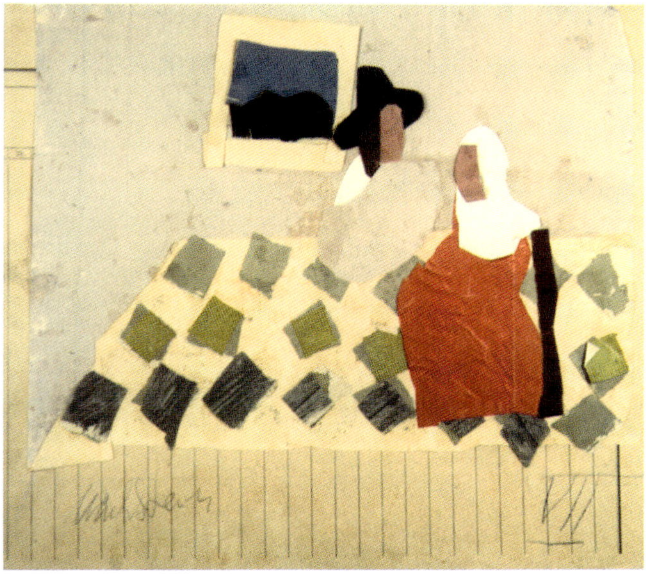

In 1936 she married her cousin Pavel Brandeis and became a Czechoslovakian citizen. But this period of personal happiness was to be short-lived. Her situation was already threatened before Hitler marched into Prague. Nevertheless, she rejected a visa for entry into Palestine and moved with Pavel to the Bohemian city of Hronov. She won the gold medal and received an honorary diploma at the exhibition, *Ausstellung 38 Nachod* at the Spiegler & Söhne textile factory in Hronov. In 1949, twelve of her pictures were shown at the Royal Academy in London.

In September 1942, Dicker and Pavel Brandeis were deported to Theresienstadt. Her paintings, designs, sketches, and the children's pictures from Theresienstadt were found in two suitcases after the Liberation in 1945. The fact that they show hardly anything of the horrors of day-to-day life in the camp demonstrated that Friedl Dicker, although her own life was threatened, managed to transport the children for a few hours a day to another, healing world far away from trauma and the fear of death. In this deeply inhuman environment she followed the goals of her holistic, humanistic upbringing, through art. Wingler wrote: "As with Itten, Old Master works—that is to say reproductions—were looked at for their content, and as structural analysis is not possible for children, an attempt was made at doing so by copying. So the same Cranach, which had once so absorbed the students in Weimar, appears in the Theresienstadt drawings." Elena Makarowa also rediscovered the central meaning of Bauhaus teaching and the Itten's methodology in the children's drawings: "Collective artistic work is part of the Bauhaus tradition and Friedl used this custom in her teaching. Just like at the Bauhaus, every work was discussed in the group once it was finished. This alone was educational for the children—it taught both precision and tolerance."

Apart from her practical work with the children, Friedl Dicker also found the strength for art-educational, theoretical thoughts which she put to paper in her essay "Kinderzeichnen" in 1943. "So should the child be trusted unconditionally? If we wish to do the best for the child, we give him material and encourage him to begin work. At this stage all our 'aesthetic evaluations' are meaningless."

ULRIKE MÜLLER

• Above, left: *Drawing alluding to Vermeer's* Girl with a Wine Glass, *watercolor, 1943–44.*

• *Above, right: Collage after Vermeer, 1943–44, by Dicker student Marie Mühlsteinová (March 31, 1932 to October 16, 1944).*

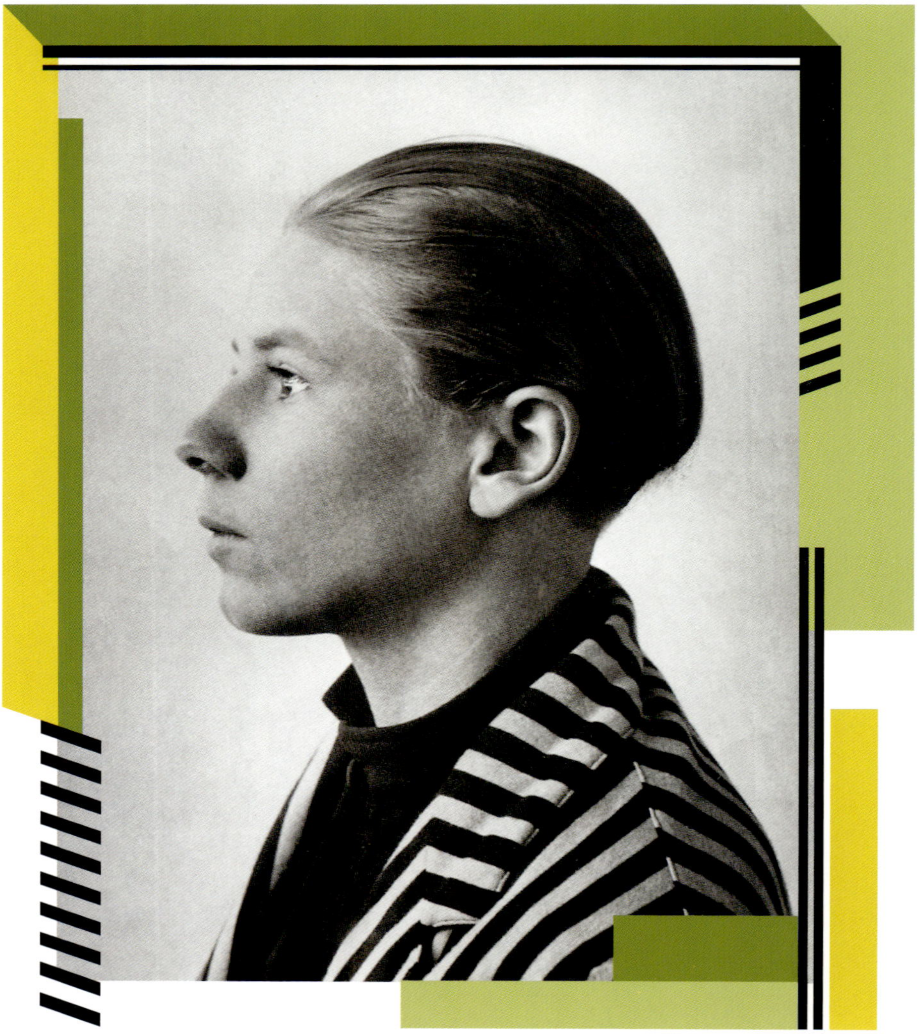

LOU SCHEPER-BERKENKAMP 1901–1976

"A fragment, without doubt, our now legendary Bauhaus transfigured by the allure of the incomplete. But even today more moving than some which were completed and paralyzed."

Lou Scheper in Rückschau, *1971*

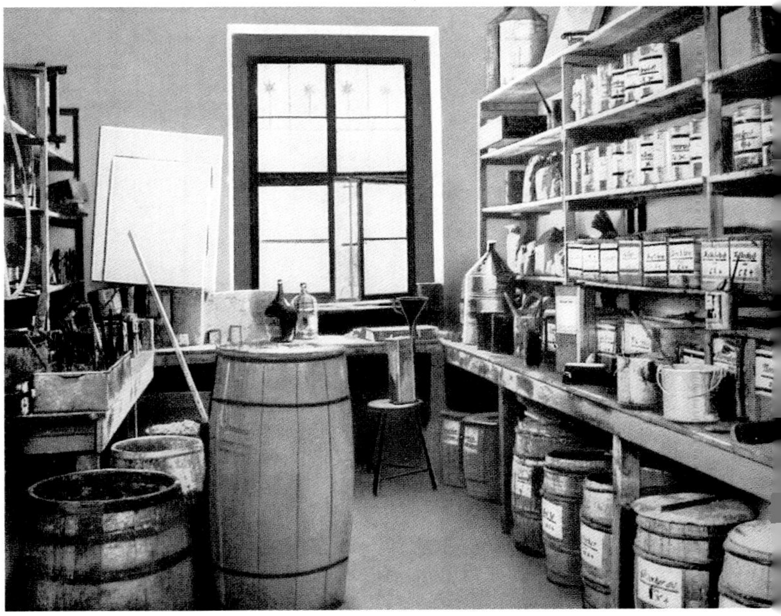

Not many female artists left the Bauhaus as free painters. Among the few who did was Lou Scheper-Berkenkamp. Since the Bauhaus program promoted a new balance between art, craft, and technology, painting could never develop unchallenged as a free artistic activity at the Bauhaus. There were no painting classes before those given by Paul Klee and Wassily Kandinsky from 1927–28 at the Bauhaus in Dessau. The young Lou Scheper chose mural painting for her studies in 1920 at the Weimar Bauhaus, to which women were not actually admitted because it was closely connected with the king of disciplines, architecture, which was claimed by the men. After her studies, Lou Scheper-Berkenkamp worked for many years as a painter and illustrator. However, in her last two decades she returned to mural painting.

She was responsible for color design on many great German architectural projects, often cooperating with Walter Gropius. She maintained a conceptual and personal relationship with the Bauhaus throughout her life.

Luise Berkenkamp, known as as Lou, was born on May 15, 1901, in Wesel in the Lower Rhine area. She came from a wealthy background. Her father Adalbert Berkenkamp was a factory owner. Her parents must have been quite progressive as Lou, most unusually for a young girl of that time, was able to take her school-leaving examination at the high school in Essen after four years at the Lyzeum in Wesel. She immediately applied to the Bauhaus even though she could not demonstrate a comprehensive artistic education up to that point: "My work was created in drawing class in school and during my few spare hours." The reply from the Bauhaus directorship on April 22, 1920, read: "The Masters' Council has decided to accept you to the Bauhaus based on your submitted works" (the important word *probeweise*—"for a trial period" is inserted handwritten into the sentence). On May 1, 1920, she signed a contract for a three-year study period in "Decorative Painting". Despite Gropius's reservations that the many female students would take away valuable workshop places from the men, the final acceptance of five young women (and five young men), following successful completion of the trial period, was decided upon in the Masters' Council of October 9, 1920. Among them was Lou Berkenkamp.

She attended the preliminary course given by Itten, design courses with Klee and Kandinsky, and learnt mural painting in the workshop. In her book *Farbenfroh! Die Geschichte der Wandmalerei*, Renate Scheper, who is married to Dirk Scheper, Lou Scheper's youngest son, explains that there were major teething problems to be overcome in this department of the Bauhaus. The Weimar decorative painter, Ranz Heidelmann, was appointed in the winter semester of 1919–20 to give daily lectures in order to "impart knowledge about pigments, additives, and binding agents as well as craft techniques." He withdrew from the Bauhaus again, however, in September 1920 because he feared competition from his Weimar colleagues. Leadership of the craft workshops was provisionally conferred on three

• *Facing page: Photo-portrait of Lou Scheper-Berkenkamp by Florence Henri, c. 1929.*

• *Above: Mural painting workshop in Weimar, 1923, photo by Lucia Moholy, 1923.*

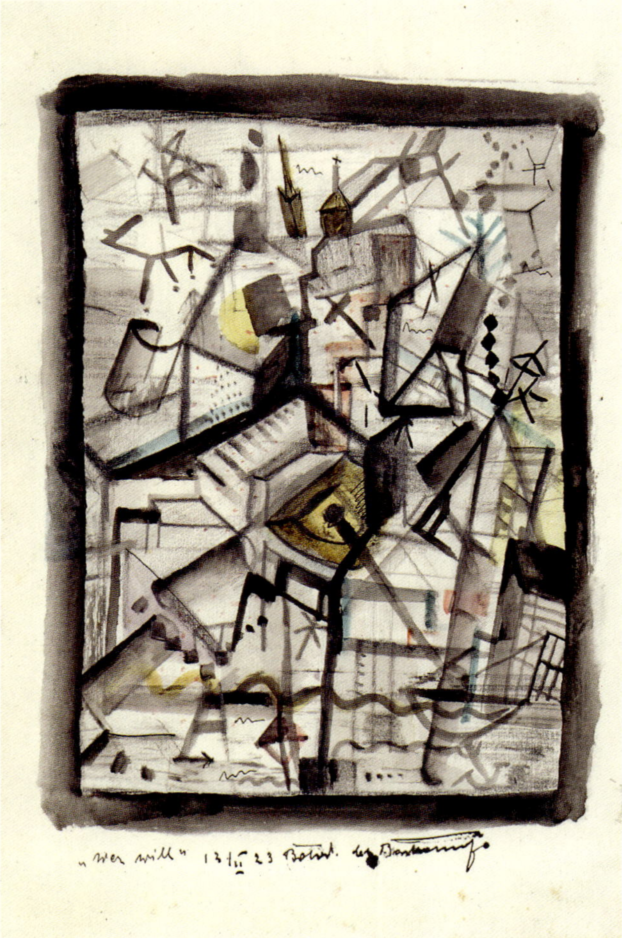

students, one of whom was a certain Hinnerk Scheper. Gropius handed over the artistic directorship of all workshops to Johannes Itten and Georg Muche. The mural-painting students, one of whom was Lou Berkenkamp, were carrying out their first independent projects such as decoration for the Bauhaus parties, the new canteen, and the corridors of the college. "We painted and sprayed together ... with enthusiasm and a bad conscience, as it was apparent to us that our activity was completely non-functional," recalls Lou Berkenkamp in her *Rückblick*. The color combinations must have been cheerful and chaotic. The Berlin newspaper *Tägliche Rundschau* described them in detail on December 2, 1920: "They have painted the corridors according to their own taste, every wall, every pilaster is different ... red ocher and black frieze hieroglyphics, arrows, spirals, eyes, parts of steam ships, and letters run meters high across ocher-yellow walls." A further contribution followed in the new Bauhaus pottery studios at Dornburg in 1920. The color coordination of the top-lit hall in the main building was carried out for the first time according to an exact concept under Itten's direction using muted colors. He had the anarchic resplendance of the canteen painted over under protest from the students. Lou Scheper remembers: "Itten, the law-maker, separating us from our expressive ardor, expected a joyless, contemplative gray-green as background for a Far Eastern motto that was supposed to edify us at mealtimes. But this was the swansong of his influence on mural painting at the Bauhaus."

Itten was now no longer of interest for her as a teacher of interior color design although he had introduced a muted color system, as she later defined the Bauhaus wall design. He found her too esoteric, not space or material oriented, not "architectural" enough. The fact that Oskar Schlemmer took over the artistic direction of the workshops in the middle of 1921 and his brother Carl became workshop master appeared to have little importance for her relationship to mural painting in this phase. Gropius's architecture and Hinnerk Scheper's experiments in architectural color design were much more significant: "Space opens up to the outside sequentially. The architectural arrangement in the interior spaces is transformed into a division of surfaces in harmonious color ... a stronger differentiation of the walls using materials. They were highly polished or matt, roughened or structured. Layered glazing of various colors gave an effect of diffused color." This was Lou's description of the new beginnings in *Rückschau* (1971). From 1921 Gropius involved the Bauhaus workshops in contract work for his architect's office in Berlin. Among the properties were the Villa

• *Lou Scheper,* Wer will, *watercolor, 1923.*

Sommerfeld with color design by Hinnerk Scheper (1921) and the Otte House color-designed by Dörte Helm (1922). Lou Berkenkamp worked with Scheper on the Sommerfeld wall designs. Alongside her craft work she worked freelance, developing her imaginative, ironic style in illustrated letters, greeting cards, and "alternative" city maps such as the one of Weimar, on which the "places of amusement" of the Bauhaus members are marked.

Lou Berkenkamp and Hinnerk Scheper were not only brought together by wall decoration, but had also fallen into the dynamics of Bauhaus love life, which according to statistics, gave rise to seventy-one marriages over the entire history of the institutes. They did not wait long to marry on Christmas Eve 1922, and in November 1923 Lou Scheper gave birth to her first son, Jan. She announced her departure from the State Bauhaus on July 28, 1922. As a mother she now worked as a freelance artist. There is an abstract ink drawing by Lou from the economic crisis year of 1923 in the Weimar archive entitled *Wer will*. In 1925 the Bauhaus moved to Dessau and Hinnerk Scheper, young master since 1922, became director of the mural painting workshop. In the following years he greatly influenced the new Bauhaus style with a color design which appropriately served architectural purposes: light pastel tones, accentuation of architectural elements, variability of materials and surfaces in order to increase the impact of the room. Lou was now no longer a mere student but a "master's wife" and lived with her family in a master's house. She worked in the Bauhaus theater, which was led by Schlemmer until his departure in 1929, and continued to work as an independent painter. Many different references to the Bauhaus are to be found in her work. She comments on the Dessau residents' hostile relationship with the Bauhaus through a fictional newspaper page in which she wrote: "What Germany is to the shameful treaty of Versailles, so is Dessau to the shameful treaty with the Bauhaus." Her second child, daughter Britta, was born in March 1926. Over the next few years, during her travels through Holland, Italy, Yugoslavia, and Switzerland, where she was a guest in Ascona of Marianne von Werefkin, some imaginatively illustrated letters were sent to Bauhaus friends. The Bauhaus Archive contains numerous illustrated letters from Lou, or Lou and Hinnerk Scheper, to Günta Stölzl.

The term, "young Bauhaus painter" first appeared in the Bauhaus magazine in 1928, referring to young Bauhaus artists who had come together at this time and put on collective exhibitions, for example, in Halle and at the *Juryfreie Kunstschau* (Juryless Art Show) in 1929 in Berlin. Lou Scheper-Berkenkamp was a member of this group.

In 1929 Hinnerk Scheper was called to Moscow to set up a consultancy center for color in architecture and the cityscape, for which he was furloughed from the Bauhaus. Lou visited him many times, wrote contributions

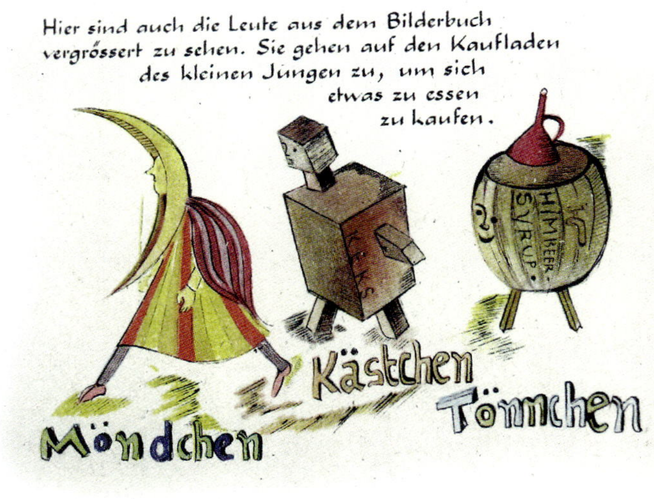

• *Lou Scheper, illustrated page from the children's book* Tönnchen, Knöpfchen and andere, *Leipzig, 1948.*

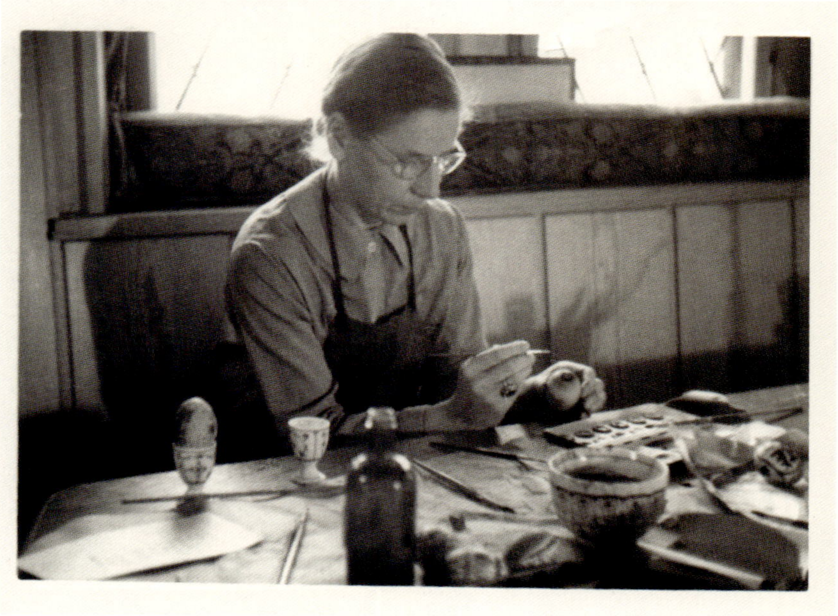

for the weekly, German-language magazine *Moskauer Rundschau* and captured scenes of everyday Russian misery with an expressive brushstroke and critical eye. Scheper resumed his work at the Bauhaus in 1931, and in 1932 they moved to Berlin. When the school closed under Nazi pressure in 1933 both were dependent on freelance work. Lou wrote texts for her husband's photo series, but at the same time pursued her own artistic plans. She had developed a symbolic language in her work for poetry and satire, fairy tales and social criticism, often with ironic reference to the picture titles, and using figures which could have come from "triadic" productions on the Bauhaus stage. With the help of the "unitary building blocks," the square, triangle and circle, she caricatured and criticized the modern masses and equally derided the Bauhaus's "new line," which systematized and standardized works into products. A good example of this is her drawing *Normen-Menschen Menschen-Normen Weiblichen Geschlechts Zusammenklappbar* and the male version *Zusammenlegbarer Typ*.

In August 1938 their son Dirk was born under a bleak omen. "Light and dark tones, pure white and pure black, varying shades of gray without staining, that was the color-world into which the awful brown and the burnt red of the Third Reich broke." This was Lou Scheper's description in *Rückblick* of the devastating effect of National Socialism on art and culture. The family survived the war years in quiet seclusion. Easter-egg painting, which was not only traditional in their family, but also in the Bauhaus, was one of the special highlights of their happy time together. They resumed artistic activities after the war. In 1945 Hinnerk Scheper took over directorship of the Amt für Denkmalpflege (Department for the Preservation of Historic Monuments) in Berlin. Lou Scheper published her first illustrated stories for children in the same year. The messengers from her better world, her parallel world were always birds, prehistoric birds, birds of paradise, "ghost birds at the end of the world or heavenly birds and fowl whose existence has been witnessed" as she commented on her pictures in the story. Her magical book, *Tönnchen, Knöpfchen und andere*, with texts and color lithographs was published in Leipzig in 1948. The protagonists in the story are three everyday objects, in the best Bauhaus style—a cube, a pyramid, Berufsverband Bildender Künstler (Association of Visual Artists) and was involved in the organization of the annual Berlin Art Exhibition.

Hinnerk Scheper died in 1957, and it came as a heavy blow to his long-time partner. In heartfelt accordance with her husband's life's work, she returned to the problem of color in architecture and so to her own original Bauhaus work in 1959. She published articles on architecture, the nature of exhibitions and preservation of historical monuments, and took part in large projects such as new buildings and restorations as well as the color design of a daycare facility for children, a school

• *Lou Scheper at Veste Heldburg in Thuringia, painting Easter eggs, 1942.*

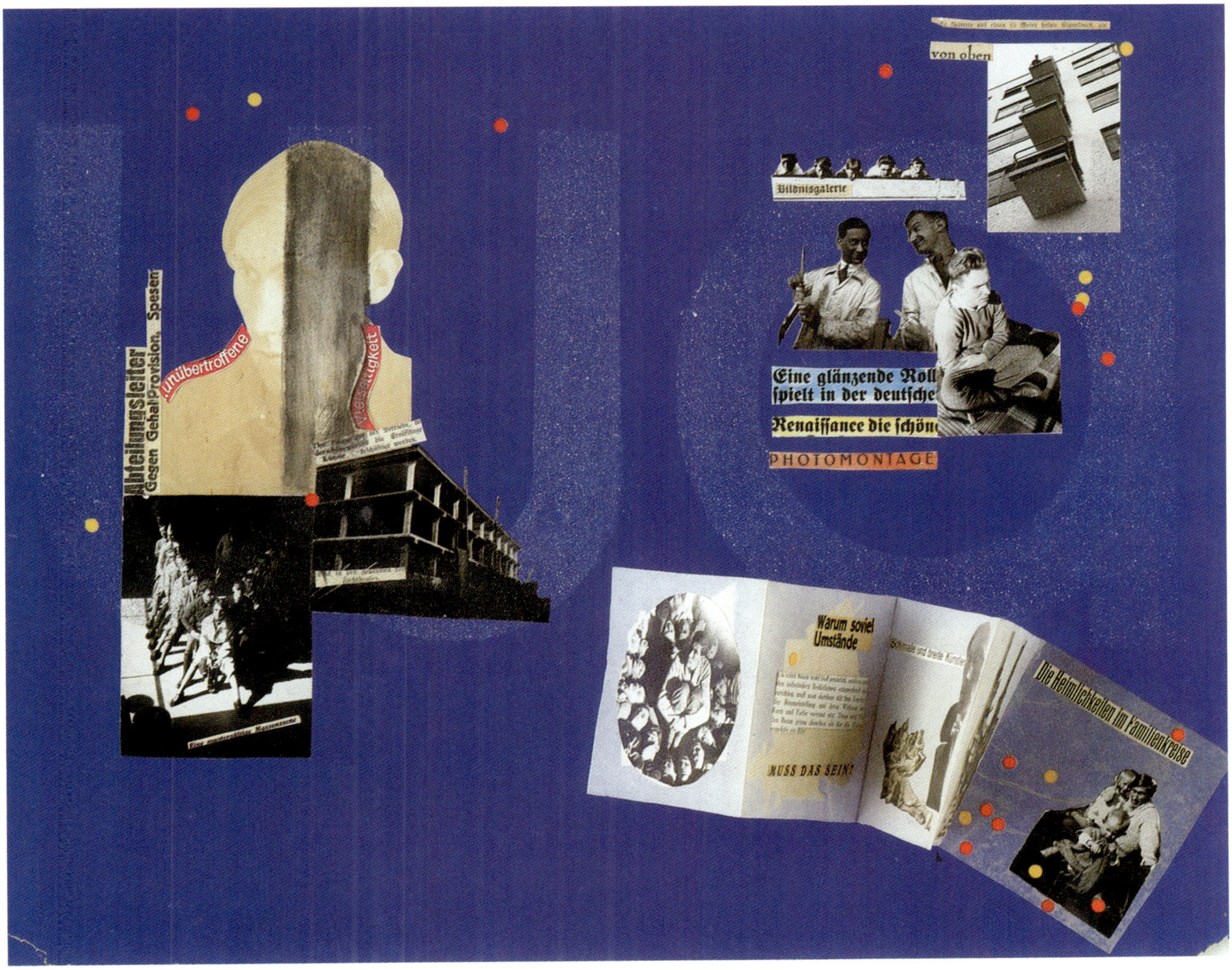

and a high-rise in Berlin's Gropiusstadt, the airport building at Berlin Tegel and the TU (Technical University) Berlin. and the restoration of the Germanisches Nationalmuseum in Nuremberg, and the Ägyptisches Museum in Berlin. Her pictures were shown in exhibitions, for example in Lugano and also in the United States.

She was responsible for the color design of the new Berliner Philharmonie as part of architect Hans Scharoun's team in 1962–63 and she worked on the design of the Berlin State Library until her death.

Lou Scheper-Berkenkamp and Hinnerk Scheper are among those who further developed and realized important Bauhaus initiatives in the German architectural landscape following World War II, accompanied by the understanding which Lou formulated clearly in her *Rückblick*: "There is little in architecture or in art today which was not already felt, formulated, or presupposed in the Bauhaus." Lou Scheper-Berkenlamp died in Berlin on April 11, 1976. There is a Scharoun Straße quite close to the Berliner Philharmonie; perhaps a Lou-Scheper-Straße could follow.

ULRIKE MÜLLER

• *Lou Scheper, Collage* wa *(mural painting workshop), c. 1928.*

Housewives in Construction or Constructive Women in the House?

Interior Designers; Furniture, Toy, and Metal Designers

Heimkultur—"homemaking"—the bourgeois cliché of the modest housewife, who rules the home and never rests, had been maintained for a long time, too long. But before this cliché was turned into a racist propaganda weapon by the National Socialists in a huge historical step backwards, history had indeed moved things forwards. Women had begun to rearrange things, to let light and air into the house, to look critically at lamps, furniture, dishes, all the furnishings, and all the rooms. They stepped outside, looked at the house from this perspective and thought: "I'd do it differently." Others announced: "I could do it just as well"; a few said: "I could do it better." And they dared to try. Of course, they did not change everything in one fell swoop. Men also set themselves up as master builders of the world in the Weimar Republic. Bauhaus architects were also to build the cathedrals of the future (albeit without an architecture department in Weimar). Female architects were still a rare breed. One of them was Margarete Schütte-Lihotsky (1897–1997), a pioneer of social building in Red Vienna. In her *Erinnerungen aus dem Widerstand* (1994) she says: "Everybody wanted to dissuade me from becoming an architect . . . my teacher, my father, and my grandfather. Not because they were so reactionary but because they believed I would starve. Nobody would have a woman build them a house." But many more wanted this than was assumed. Margarete Schütte-Lihotsky designed modern, functional housing developments, created the "Apartment for the Career Woman," and invented the famous Frankfurt Kitchen.

In 1920s Germany, two women in particular made names for themselves in the realm of interior design. Ruth Hildegard Geyer-Raack had studied at the Weimar Bauhaus for a short period, creating intimate rooms to withdraw into, with beautiful flowered wallpapers for the discerning lady—"boudoirs for female souls" as art historian Sonja Günther called them. Lilly Reich, one of the candidates in this chapter, achieved a unified aesthetic between people and culture with her functional furniture and trendy textiles in generous, bright rooms.

Already at the beginning of the twentieth century some glass, ceramic, metal, and furniture designers were getting involved in modernizing domestic culture, in Vienna more than anywhere, where the Wiener Werkstätte, founded in 1903 as a visual artists collective and the Kunstgewerbeschule produced such important artists as Else Unger. Dresden was another center. Around 1900 the Werkstätten für Deutschen Hausrat, Theophil Müller, Dresden-Striesen built furniture designed by Margarete Junge and Gertrud Kleinhempel. Eileen Gray came to the fore in Paris after World War I. Her eccentric silver-coated, varnished furniture, and

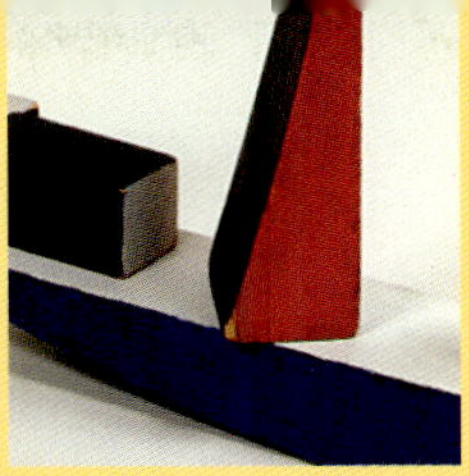

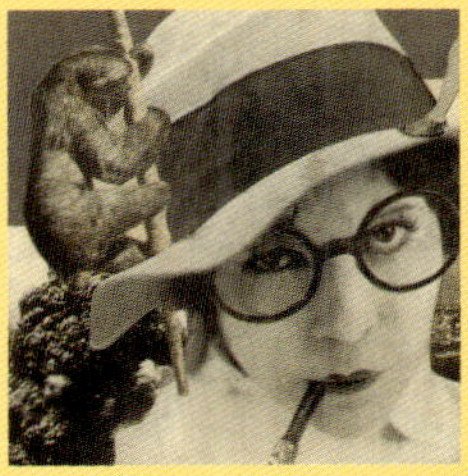

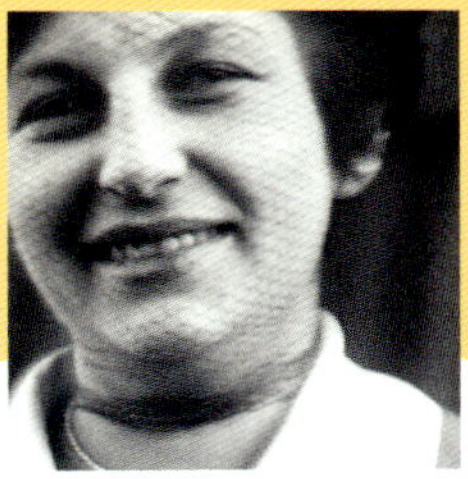

objects in glass and celluloid brought her the admiration of architects from Le Corbusier to Gropius, while her contemporaries are said to have been taken aback by such works. Bauhaus woman, Friedl Dicker was also successful in 1920s Vienna with her friendly, convertible furniture (see pp. 92–97).

The second artist in this chapter is the metal designer and photographer Marianne Brandt, who came to the Weimar Bauhaus at the end of 1923. László Moholy-Nagy was in the process of transforming the metal workshop, of which he had just taken over directorship, from gold-, silver-, and-copper smithing based on traditional craft, to an experiment laboratory for industrial design, and he became Brandt's great mentor. The year 1923 was also an important one for Alma Büscher, who designed multipurpose furniture for women and children as well as toys and children's books. She began her studies in the wood-carving workshop and continued into carpentry and woodturning. After 1921 when Walter Gropius was form master in the carpentry workshop, models which were a departure from the old craft tradition were already being developed. Alma Büscher was one of the students, along with Marcel Breuer, Josef Albers, and Erich Dieckmann, whom the Bauhaus carpentry workshop has to thank for its "golden age" in the years 1923 to 1925, because of their many ideas about form which shaped the typical Bauhaus style.

All three women came into contact with new developments in art and crafts during World War I. Lilly Reich had trained in the Wiener Werkstätte in 1908; Marianne Brandt was from 1912 at the Grand Ducal Saxon School of Arts and Crafts in Weimar, and Alma Buscher had imbibed important ideas during her training at the Reimann School in Berlin in 1917.

Alma Buscher and Marianne Brandt continued their training at the Bauhaus in Dessau. Fewer women studied here than in Weimar; some individuals, however, dared to enter the male domain, such as Wera Meyer-Waldeck (1906–1964) from Dresden. She chose carpentry as her main subject when she began in 1927 and received her Bauhaus diploma in it in 1932. The multitalented Katt Both (1905–1985) from Hesse came to the Bauhaus from the Kunstgewerbeschule in Giebichenstein. She attended art classes, learned carpentry, and also studied architecture and photography. She later worked for many years as an architect.

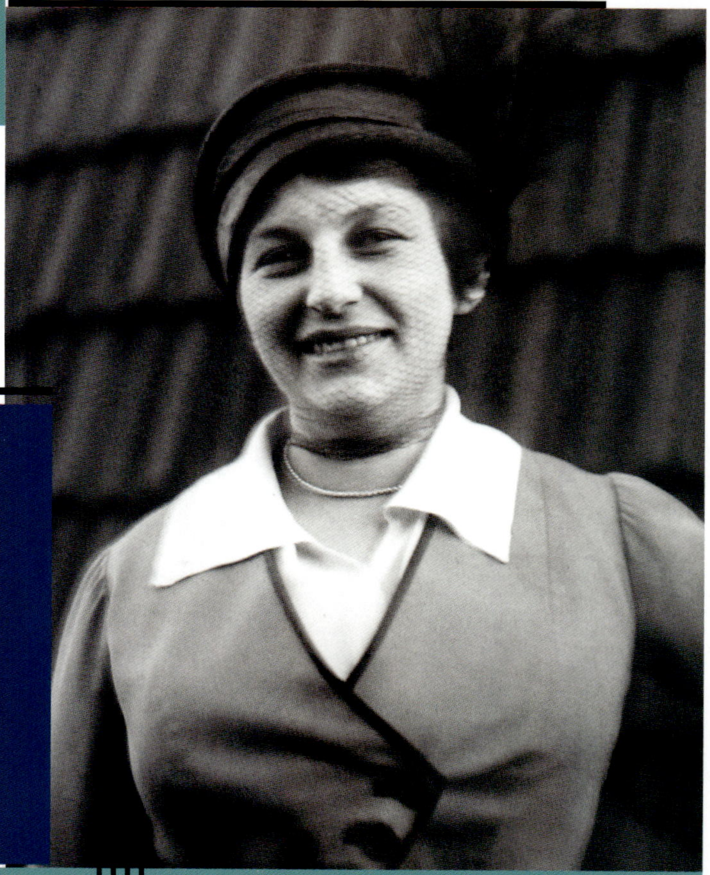

LILLY REICH 1885–1947

"Who would know how the way will be found in the new form? Not in the footsteps of today's defining circles. Haste makes waste, and expression of the female intellect, which wants to be what it is, and not appear to be what it is not, will be fundamental here."

Lilly Reich in Die Form, *1922*

Lilly Reich was forty-seven years old when she assumed a leading position at the Bauhaus in Dessau in 1932: she was an independent woman who already had a long-standing, self-contained, and successful career as interior designer, exhibition and furniture designer, and, as we would say today, fashion designer, behind her. Born on June 16, 1885, she grew up in a sheltered family home in Berlin. Her mother Ottilie, née Dix, came from Thuringia. Her father, Alwin Reich, worked for Siemens and later owned a small electronics factory. A good education for their children was part of her parents' generous lifestyle. While Lilly's sister Emmi, two years her senior, was later to be awarded a doctorate—most unusual for a young woman of the time—Lilly's career path, following her school-graduation examination, was more conventional. At first she trained in Berlin as a crank embroiderer. Her teacher was Else Oppler-Legeband, a student of van de Velde, who later ran the *Höhere* Fachschule für Dekorationskunst (Technical School for Decorative Art) in Berlin. The Wiener Werkstätte put on an exhibition in Berlin in 1904, which contained a new collection of straight-edged furnishings. The idea for this had come from Scotland. Lilly Reich obviously derived important inspiration from this for her consistently unembellished design. She went to Vienna in 1908 to work for Josef Hoffmann, an artist at the Wiener Werkstätte. A second important direction for Lilly Reich was the outlook which prevailed that textiles, whether dress, carpet, or curtain material are basic components in the domestic environment. On her return from Vienna in 1911, she opened a studio for interior design, decorative art, and fashion in Berlin, and received her first contracts for window dressing. She became friends with Anna and Hermann Muthesius, who had brought important ideas about architecture, interior design, and clothing from the English Arts and Crafts movement to Germany. While Anna Muthesius made a name for herself as a pioneer in the Reform Clothing Movement (healthy, comfortable, functional, and individual), Lilly Reich designed the "living room" for a youth center in Berlin's Charlottenburg district and a worker's apartment for the Berlin exhibition *Die Frau in Haus und Beruf* in 1912. The exhibition catalog reads: "The interior of the worker's

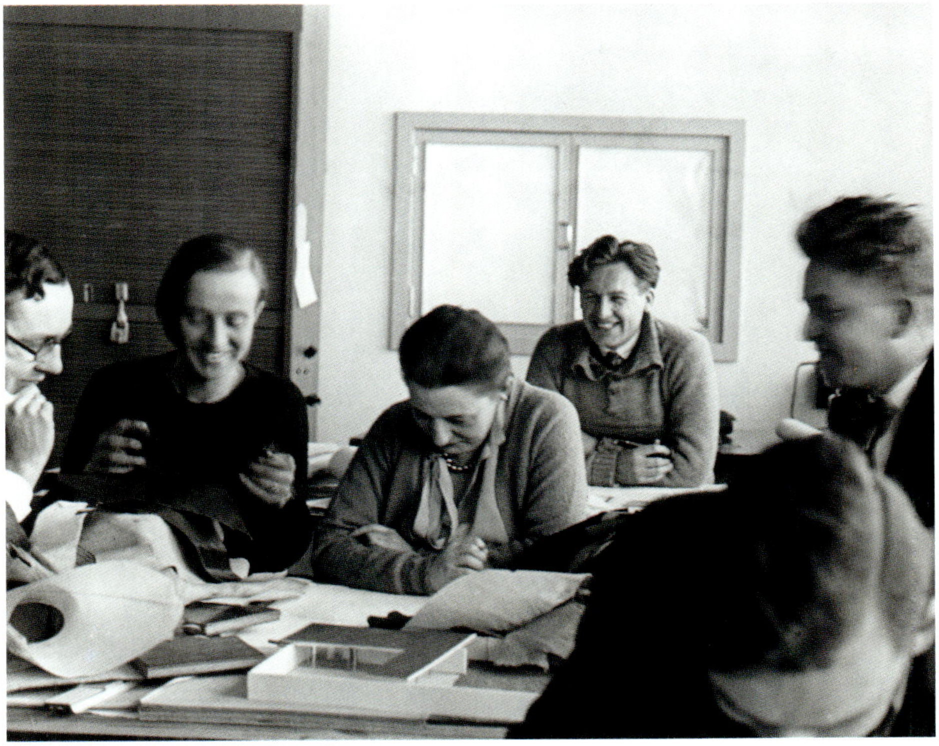

• *Facing page: Lilly Reich, portrait, c. 1914.*

• *Lilly Reich teaching in Dessau, 1932.*

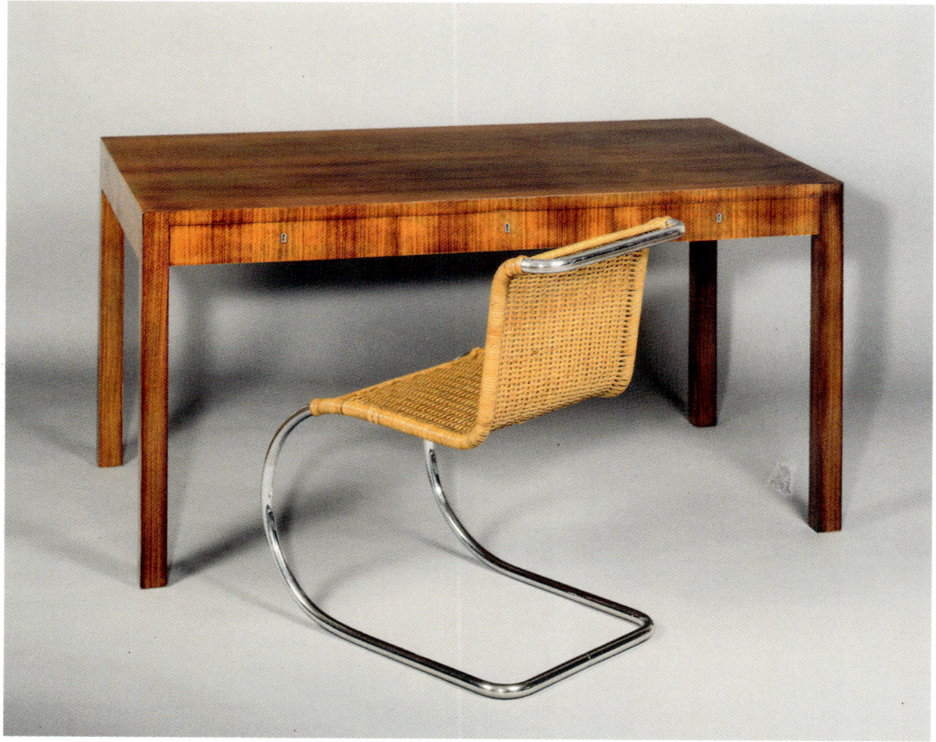

apartment is governed by simplicity, cheapness, and function." Lilly was accepted into the Werkbund in the same year. At the Cologne Werkbund exhibition in 1914 she presented a store front and a living room in the Women's House. During World War I she deftly secured her survival by temporarily transforming her studio into a tailoring shop. She single-mindedly resumed her career after the war. In 1920 she became the first woman member of the board of the Deutscher Werkbund. In an article in the magazine *Die Form. Monatsschrift für gestaltende Arbeit* she criticized the fashion addiction of her time: "The fashions of the old days had style, because they originated from stable ways of life and social requirements. . . . They developed slowly and organically. Today's fashion has no style, it is always only fashionable." She herself had an assured feel for her time and developed her own modern style with her characteristic mix of functionality, charm, generous elegance, and an eye for the overall look.

In 1924 she met the architect Ferdinand Kramer, an exponent the New Objectivity. She traveled with him to England and Holland to view housing developments. She moved to Frankfurt the same year, where she opened a studio and worked as an exhibition designer for the Trade Fairs' Organization Office. She encountered Mies van der Rohe two years later. The Werkbund, then under Mies's direction, exhibited the first great international demonstration of New Building, with architects such as Peter Behrens, Walter Gropius, and Bruno Taut in Stuttgart in 1927. For this exhibition, *Die Wohnung,* Lilly designed the interior of an apartment in a high-rise in Mies's housing development on the Weissenhof. Here is where she "first found her own voice," as Reich's biographer Sonja Günther puts it. She became well known, however, for the design of six exhibition halls. She received a number of follow-up contracts and returned to Berlin Her relationship to Mies deepened, personally as well as artistically, though Lilly always kept her own studio separate from their shared apartment. She assumed complete artistic direction for the German building department at the International Exhibition in Barcelona in 1929, thereby acquiring great recognition for Germany with her presentation.

The highlight of Lilly Reich's career was to be her contribution to the exhibition *Die Wohnung unserer Zeit* as part of the 1931 German Building Exhibition in Berlin, which Mies organized and in which the Bauhaus also took part. She was now among the top names of international interior designers. The exhibition program reads: "We seem to have a need for free, bright surfaces, projection screens for rays of a richer attitude to life." Indeed her two small apartments for the

• *Ludwig Mies van der Rohe and Lilly Reich, Desk with stool, design of 1927, palisander wood, chrome-plated steel tubing, caning.*

Boardinghaus conveyed this mood. In a living space of only fifty-three square meters for one person, Lilly Reich managed to create elegance, capaciousness, and comfort with the most economic, functional furniture. Sonja Günther wrote: "Both apartments had simple white walls, soft floor-length muslin curtains at the windows, and rice-straw mats as floor coverings." Some special elements included the movable "cooking closet," the divan sofa, and a small round table, as well as the bright "lady's bedroom" from her "Groundfloor House." The latter was situated directly next to Mies's pavilion and was—a rare personal sign—visibly connected to it by a walkway.

From today's perspective, the abundance of Lilly's achievements would appear to have been more than sufficient for a call to lead the construction department and weaving workshop.

Mies van der Rohe, who had been director of the Bauhaus in Dessau since 1930, proposed her to the Masters' Council. Lilly Reich also brought a new innovation to the Bauhaus whereby she "understood fashion to be an integral component of design and so extended the meaning of the term *Gesamtkunstwerk*, as the art historian Sigrid Wortmann Weltge explained in 1993. Yet, when Lilly Reich took up her position at the Bauhaus on January 5, 1932, she was at first met with criticism. She was a very highly qualified designer but was unable to weave. Her teaching was also part of the dramatic restructuring undertaken by Mies van der Rohe towards purely architectural training at the Bauhaus. The new concept was not welcomed by everyone. Ultimately the impression was formed, due to the fact that Mies had a personal relationship with Lilly, and in combination with Mies's authoritarian leadership style, that she had been given this position thanks to his patronage. She was viewed by many as his assistant and not as the independent, successful designer that she unquestionably was.

The carpentry workshop now only designed samples for industry. The school no longer had its own workshop. No systematic material research took place in the textile workshop under her leadership; instead, material print patterns were developed. The weaving faculty timetable was supplemented by "textile design . . . with regard to the requirements of new interior design," taught by Lilly. Weaving student Katja Rose, who came to the Bauhaus in the summer semester of 1931, remembers the difficulties: "Her classes comprised of having us create good combinations from the yarns at hand. It was fun but had little to do with weaving because the color harmony brought about in the weave gives rise to totally different tones from when they are simply placed side by side. She also liked to show us fabric samples for which she sporadically appeared in the weaving workshop to demonstrate one of her new collections. I found this to be a bothersome disturbance to our work and so was glad when Mies van der Rohe sometimes appeared in the doorway

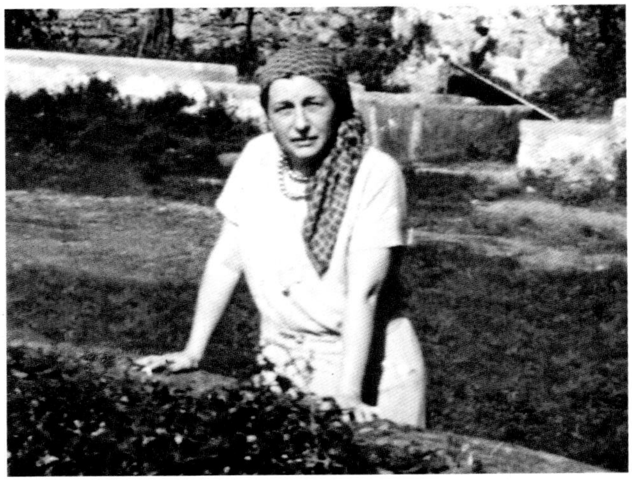

• *Lilly Reich, Pura, Ticino, Switzerland, October 1933 (detail).*

to call her away with the words 'are you coming now?'" (1984).

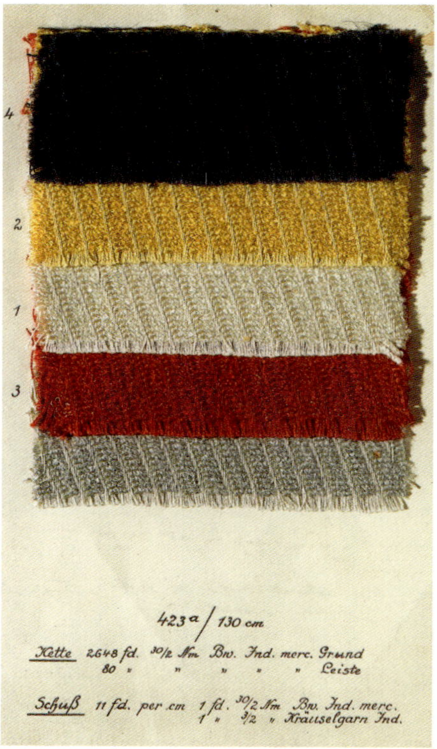

Lilly Reich, the only woman on the college faculty, surely did not fit the normal picture of an artist. She was neither an exotic flower nor a shrinking violet, but a life-affirming, dynamic, and somewhat sharp character. As a designer she was not only charming and innovative, but also assertive and moreover—to Mies van der Rohe's delight, who detested organization and bureaucracy—a resourceful manager upon whom he was glad to depend.

Hinnerk Scheper, director of mural painting, which belonged to the construction workshop together with carpentry and the metal workshop, now also under Lilly Reich's administration, wrote in a letter to his wife, Lou: "Frau Reich feels threatened by my work, jealousy and envy. . . . She is a cold, enterprising woman, it is of no consequence to her how other people get through. However, I would not dream of leaving the Bauhaus because of this woman." Reich not only demonstrated her power as the new boss, but also her work areas—samples for fabric print, interior design—were in direct competition with his. Scheper was responsible for the Bauhaus wallpapers and was, not unwarrantedly, afraid of being displaced by Reich. During the Bauhaus move to Berlin in 1932, it was Alfred Arndt and not Scheper who was forced to go, apparently because he was too leftist for the expressly apolitical Mies.

From time to time the students boycotted Lilly's classes in the weaving workshop. Otti Berger, who was well-loved and very talented as a weaver and educator, had provisionally taken over the running of the weaving workshop following Anni Albers's departure in the fall of 1931 and, in effect, retained this position when Lilly Reich arrived. Free experimentation, intelligent self-awareness, the freedom to try out anything were the fundamental components of teaching for her. This is why she gave the students free reign in designing. Lilly Reich, on the other hand, had no understanding of experimentation in the weaving workshop. Perhaps she viewed this craft as antiquated in the context of modern industrial design. Her interest was first and foremost in designs for fabric prints for clothing, curtains, and furniture. Katja Rose reported: "When Lilly Reich came to the Bauhaus, everybody in the weaving workshop did what they felt like doing. This is why it was not possible for her, in a short year, to fulfil her chosen direction. It also failed because a weaving pattern cannot be created as quickly as a drawing. A requirement for developing particular fabrics is experience at the loom. In order to gain experience, however, one must experiment. That is what Lilly Reich referred to as 'playing around.' But this was the way that the first Bauhaus weaving women chose and I followed them without realizing it." Otti Berger left the Bauhaus in the fall of 1933 and worked freelance. She nevertheless designed a collection of curtain fabrics with Lilly Reich for the company C. E. Baumgärtel & Sohn in Lengenfeld. The company

• *Above: Otti Berger, fabric samples for the Bauhaus sample book 1932–33 in five different colors.*

• *Facing page: Lilly Reich, small Thonet chair, 1936.*

van Delden in Gronau also bought patterns for curtain fabrics from the Bauhaus at this time. These could be seen at the Spring Show in Leipzig in 1933. A collection of three textile albums was published under Lilly Reich—the first and the last at the Bauhaus.

All further developments in the textile department were curtailed with the closure of the Bauhaus by the Nazis in 1933. Lilly Reich had already been dismissed by the Berlin magistrate as of December 31, 1932. She then made the dubious suggestion, together with Kandinsky, to attempt to have the Bauhaus assimilated into the Kampfbund (Fighting League for German Culture) as the "German Bauhaus." This salvage attempt proved useless. The Nazi view of the Bauhaus as an enemy was too profound, and the school remained closed. As far as is known, Lilly Reich was not associated with National Socialism but in order to stay on the ball professionally, she worked on many large Nazi propaganda projects. In 1934 she organized the special show *Glass, Porcelain, Ceramics* at the exhibition *Deutsches Volk und Deutsche Arbeit*. In 1937, she took part in the exhibition *Reichsausstellung der Deutschen Textil- und Bekleidungswirtschaft* together with Mies van der Rohe in Berlin. Both designed the textile section *Exposition Internationale des arts et techniques* in Paris. Mies, who clearly took much inspiration for his work from Lilly, emigrated to the United States in 1938 with the prospect of a great career. Lilly Reich visited him in Chicago in 1939 but returned to Germany due to a copyright case against the company Mauser involving the steel-tube furniture she had developed with Mies. She stayed for a time in Zittau during the war and was drafted by the Nazi civil engineering group Organisation Todt. Her studio in Berlin was destroyed by a bomb attack in 1943. After the war she opened a new studio for architecture, design, and fashion in Berlin on her own initiative. She also gave lectures on interior design at the Hochschule für Bildende Künste (College of Fine Arts) in Berlin. However, a serious illness ended her career. She died in Berlin on December 14, 1947.

ULRIKE MÜLLER

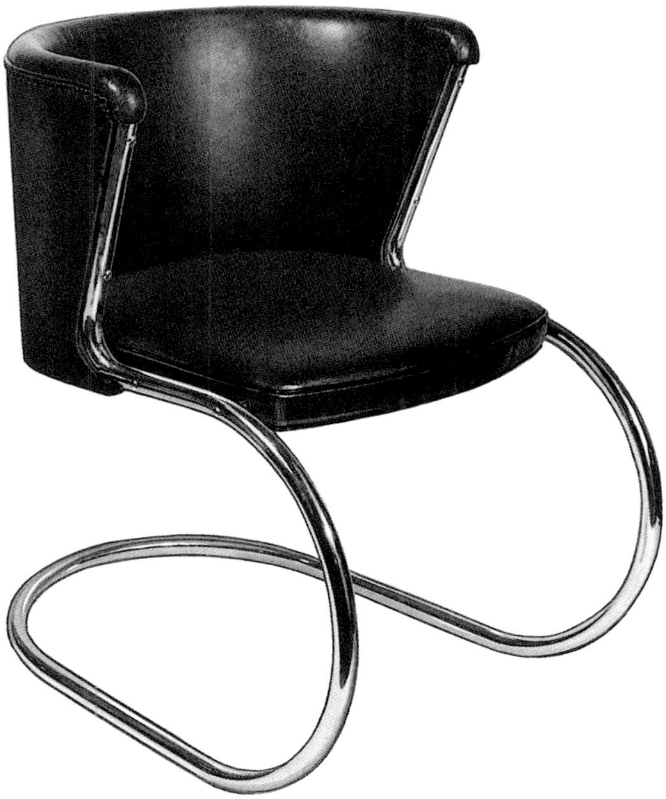

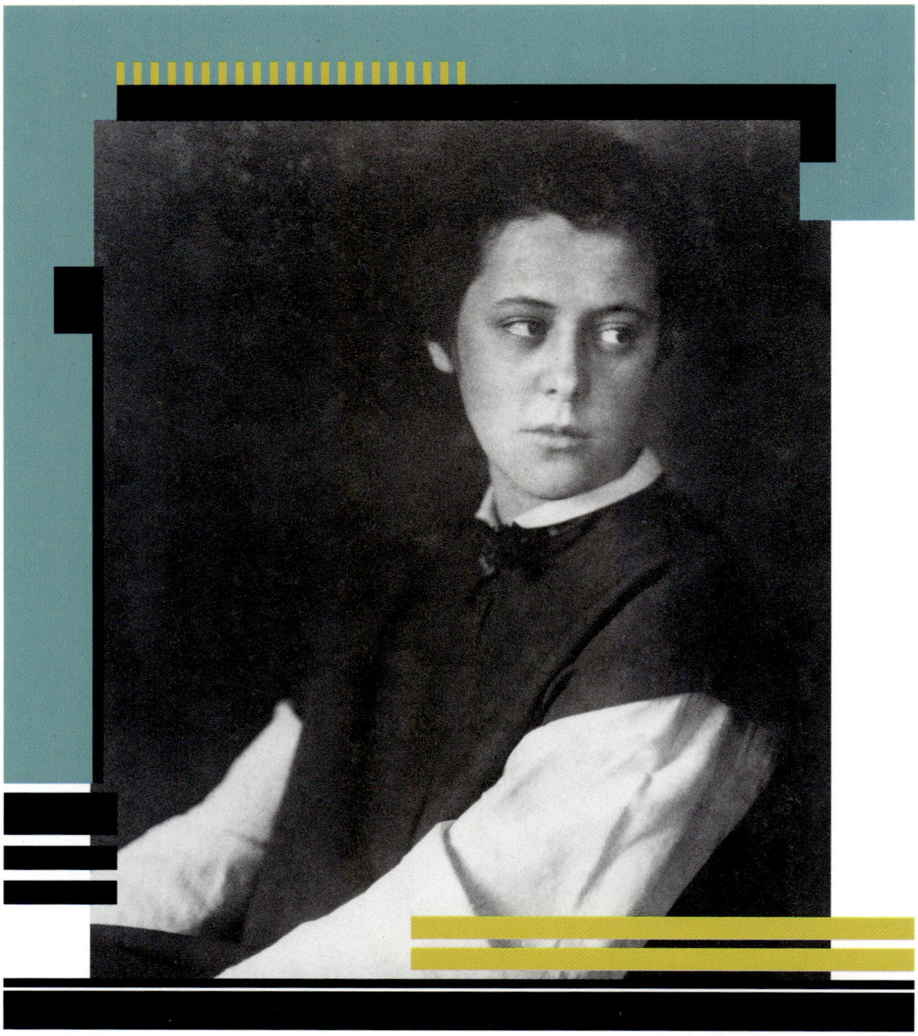

ALMA SIEDHOFF-BUSCHER 1899–1944

"If at all possible, children should have a space in which they can be what they want to be . . . everything in it belongs to them, their imagination forms it, no inhibition from the outside disturbs them, like the warning 'leave it alone'—everything accommodates them . . . practical goals should not hinder the opportunity to play."

Alma Siedhoff-Buscher in kindermöbel und kinderkleidung, *1926*

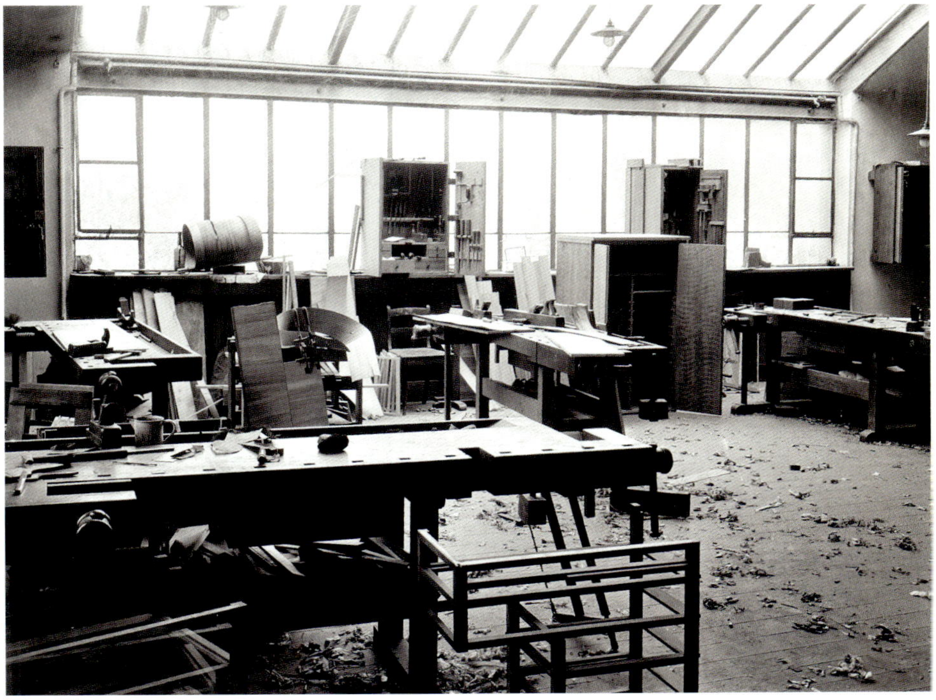

In the supplement to the *Thüringer Allgemeine Zeitung* of October 19, 1924, the Bauhaus master László Moholy-Nagy explained many important Bauhaus works, including those by Alma Büscher: "The educational axioms of the Bauhaus are clearly expressed through toys and the toy cupboard—creative self-affirmation as a basis for the elementary expression of life. The toy cupboard is arranged so that the large blocks are moveable in order to be used as benches, tables, houses, stables etc. . . . A cupboard door is . . . open at the top and fastened with a hook so that it serves as a hatch for a Punch-and-Judy show."

Alma Siedhoff-Buscher was among the students who most consistently implemented the educational ideas of the Bauhaus with great versatility and originality. As with the majority of the young women who registered at the State Bauhaus in Weimar, she had already received a sound artistic training. She finished her school education with a graduation certificate at the Margarethenlyzeum in Berlin and went on to complete a year of vocational training at the Elisabeth-Frauenschule, which indicates that her parents were open to new ways of schooling and vocational education for girls and women. In 1917 Alma Buscher began a three-year course of study at the Reimann Kunstschule. Klara and Albert Reimann, the founders of this leading, educational reformist institute for crafts in Berlin, worked toward a synthesis between art, craft, and industrial production, and were the first in Berlin to introduce the workshop system. Alma Buscher's second course of study took place in the vocational training institute of the Kunstgewerbemuseum (Craft Museum) in Berlin, which was one of the most important centers of the artistic avant-garde at that time. In 1912 the great exhibition of Herwarth Walden's Berlin Expressionist art group, *Sturm*, was shown there.

From 1922 to 1925, Alma Buscher studied at the State Bauhaus in Weimar and made her own unerring way from there. Her classes included Itten's preliminary course, as well as courses with Wassily Kandinsky and Paul Klee. As a female student, she was accepted into the weaving workshop in October 1922, but left of her own volition in 1923. She was almost humble in her request for a transfer: "I have never got on with thread but I wanted to try it because I believed that every material would bend to a serious will and to hard work." She continued her studies in the wood-carving workshop, under the direction of Georg Muche with Josef Hartwig as workshop master, a typical "men's department" at the Bauhaus. Her focal point was, however, one which conformed to the traditional women's role: children. Alma Buscher was thus one of the few female students at the Bauhaus who had artistic success outside of the normal women's classes.

• *Facing page: Alma Buscher, 1923.*

• *Above: Carpentry workshop, 1923.*

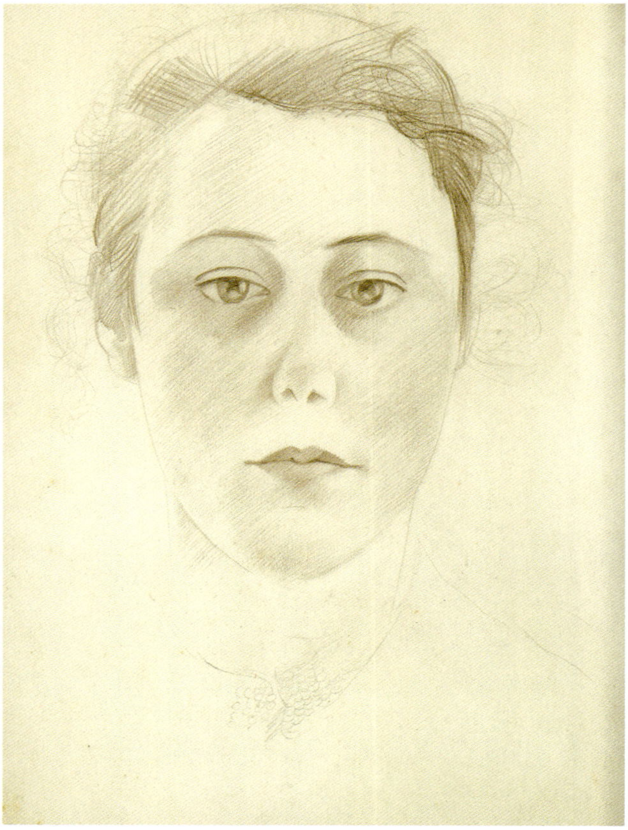

Alma Buscher's artistic development and varied ideas were impressively documented for the solo exhibition of her work shown in Weimar in 2004–05. A selection of the study papers and sketches left by her were displayed on two opposing walls, one showing her time in Berlin and one from Weimar. On the wall representing her time in Berlin appeared the comprehensive subject list from the Reimann School: nature studies, free painting, life drawing, and graphic techniques. There were also bookbinding sketches, for example, for an edition of E.T.A. Hoffmann's *Kater Murr*. On the Weimar wall were works from Buscher's classes with Itten which were exemplary of the teaching concept for the preliminary course. A self-portrait from 1923 was shown, many two-handed abstract lines and line-rhythm studies from 1922, a female nude and examples from the analyses of the Old Masters, each drawn with charcoal. Two-handed drawing and painting was part of the playful, free, yet thorough self-awareness desired in first-year students, as well as experimentation with different materials and techniques. This took place on Itten's courses but also on Gertrud Grunow's harmonizing courses. According to her holistic, educational concept, Grunow connected elements of music, visual arts, dance, and the practise of craft techniques, in order to activate her students' natural strengths in her subject which was a constant component of the preliminary course. In Grunow's critical evaluation for accepting students into the winter semester 1922–23 from the preliminary course of summer 1922, her comments about Alma Buscher are among the three most positive: "Fräulein Buscher is talented and intelligent. Following a few good work sessions, she wrestled greatly with releasing her natural strengths. She appears commendable." In a diary entry from March 13, 1923, Alma Buscher refers directly to Gertrud Grunow's teaching: "Grunow recently spoke to me about vision. Vision (to behold nature or art) should never be a single occurrence, there has to be a first, a second, a third, an assimilation, an empathy and a processing into its own shape if it is to endure and not be superficial." This connection was reflected later in Alma Buscher's concept and implementation of children's furnishings, toys, and children's books. They all encompassed these three steps of "assimilating, empathizing, processing" (i.e., processing creatively). Furniture and toys are conceptualized so that they invite children to use them according to this three-step logic.

A further important artistic correspondence is revealed in Alma Buscher's work with Paul Klee's form and color teaching—one thinks of her letter games, seating cubes, or her large sailing boat. "Alma Buscher took part in Paul Klee's form and color classes in 1922. Her notebook with study notes still exists, which can be compared to Klee's educational legacy," explains Michael

• *Alma Buscher,* Self-Portrait, *pen on paper, 1923.*

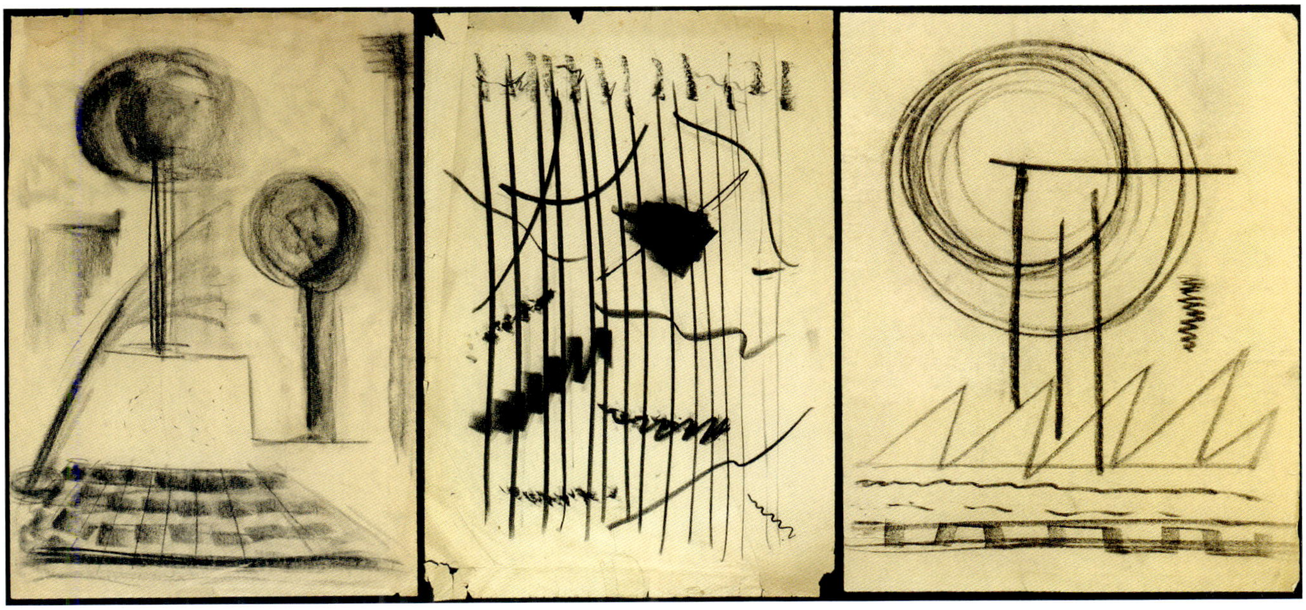

Sieberbrodt, director of the Weimar Bauhaus Museum, who organized the Alma Buscher exhibition there in 2004–05 in cooperation with Lore und Joost Siedhoff. The most consistent and, at the same time, self-contained implementation of Paul Klee's ideas at the Weimar Bauhaus are to be found in Alma Buscher's multidimensional, yet straightforwardly built toys as well as in works from the weaver Benita Otte with her cheerful, sensual communication between colors, shapes, rhythms, and the given context (surface, texture, space). A deep feeling for music, simultaneously connected with a social Utopia and a practical, art-educational concern are what connects Buscher, Grunow, and Klee, and connects them generally to the art of the early Weimar Bauhaus. In the center of this are the development of the personality, and playful, creative freedom. Alma Buscher wrote: "The games I have built for children I call free games, in contrast to the Fröbel and Pestalozzi games which were created out of purely educational ideas. I proceeded in the opposite direction almost without thinking, out of the joy of creating, from colorful shapes and with knowledge of my own desires, which I noticed in children and with which I empathized."

With Erich Brendel's support, Alma Buscher created the children's room in the show house Haus am Horn for the Bauhaus exhibition in the summer of 1923, and for which she first received international recognition. The *Kleine Schiffbauspiel* was one of her most important works during her time at the Bauhaus. It comprised of twenty-two colored wooden stones. She also created the *Große Schiffbauspiel* made up of thirty-nine pieces. Both games were produced in the wood-sculpting workshop at the Bauhaus in 1924 and painted in the mural painting workshop. Alma Büscher noted about the *Große Schiffbauspiel*: "It does not want to be anything, not Cubism, not Expressionism, just a fun game with color, made of smooth and angular shapes based on the principle of old building blocks." Other games created by Alma Buscher in her Bauhaus years are the *Bützelspiel* for small children and the *Kugelspiel* for children between three and five years. In her article *kindermöbel und kinderkleidung* (1926) she writes: "our toys [bauhaus]; the form—simple—unconfusing, clear and defined—variety and stimuli are created by the child himself by assembling, building. a constant development. the proportions: defined by feeling, as harmoniously as possible . . . color: only the primary colors yellow, red, blue, perhaps also green but above all white in order to increase colorfulness and thereby the child's joy, a powerful factor in educational games."

• *Preliminary course studies by Alma Buscher in charcoal.*
Left: Stadtpark *(City Park), undated; center:* Linienkompositionen *(Line Compositions), 1922; right: Untitled, 1922.*

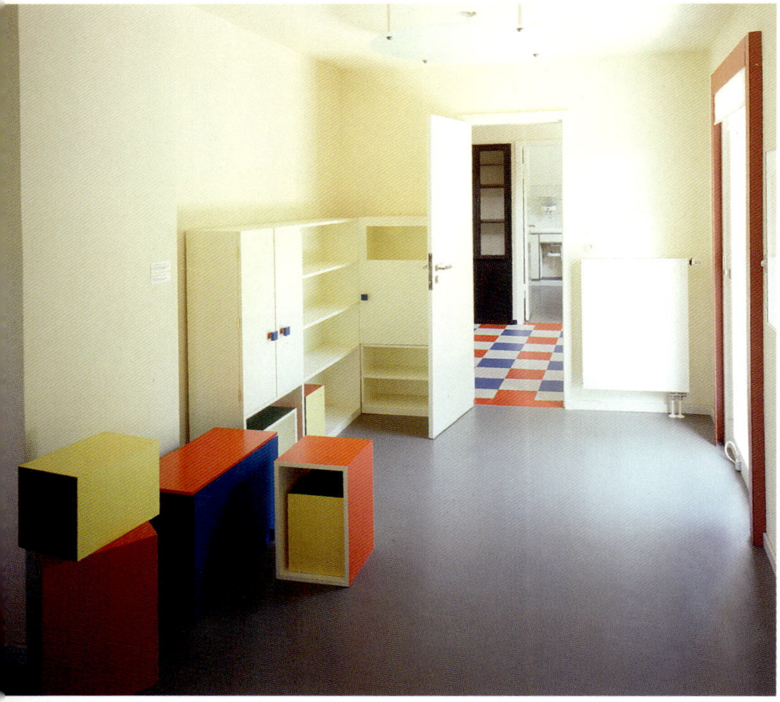

The idea of seeing childhood as a separate stage in human development, which requires a protected, free space, suitably equipped for children, was not very old. Industrial production of toys had begun in Germany in the second half of the nineteenth century, however the demand for simple toys which encouraged creativity in the child only began to prevail to any great degree with the advent of educational reform at the beginning of the twentieth century. Before World War I members of the Wiener Werkstätte, the Viennese Secession and the Berlin association Die Kunst im Leben des Kindes, founded in 1900, developed "alternative" children's toys using old craft techniques and materials. Later, Bauhaus artists designed experimental, visionary models for play figures, building blocks, play cities, puppet theaters, and children's furniture. Although the world of the child was never expressly made a central issue at the Bauhaus, play, as a space and medium for (purpose)-free development of the personality had its place as an interdisciplinary leitmotif in the educational ideas of the early Weimar Bauhaus. Encouraged by Itten, the students designed toys in the preliminary course. Nearly all of the artists active at the Bauhaus from 1919, such as Schlemmer, Muche, or Kandinsky, dealt with toys and toy-making. Artist couples like Julia and Lyonel Feininger or Lilly and Paul Klee made puppets and toys for their own children. Alma Buscher, with her raft of ideas, was in the best company and yet was the exception among these artists as she worked almost exclusively on designs for children. She published educational essays as part of her dealings with this subject. The company Paul Kohlhaas in Bad Berka took on production and sales of Alma Buscher's shipbuilding and Bützel games in 1924. Following their bankruptcy in 1925, they were produced and sold by the newly founded Bauhaus Dessau AG. Pestalozzi-Fröbel publishers in Dresden continued to produce the shipbuilding game. The artist received a patent, registered under number 441972, for her throwing doll in 1926. The official description was "doll with braid-like meshwork" and the patent said: "The new doll is distinguished by its flexibility and resilience." Alma Siedhoff-Buscher presented her work at the exhibition *Das Spielzeug* at the Städtischen Kunsthalle am Marientor in Nuremberg in 1926. For Otto Maier publishers in Ravensburg she designed the activity books *Kran* and *Segelboot* in 1927 and in 1930, two coloring books in which she developed a way of teaching children about form and color, based on Bauhaus educational and design concepts. While *Segelboot* was announced in the publisher's catalog, *Kran* only appeared in 1997 as a reprint from the publishing house of the bookshop Walter König. Alma Siedhoff-Buscher's stage-set, scene, and colored-lighting designs for children from 1923, which demonstrate a cooperation with the Bauhaus theater and Oskar Schlemmer and Ludwig Hirschfeldt-Mack, remain largely unknown. Her complete works still await cataloging.

• *Alma Buscher, Nursery in the Haus Am Horn, 1923; photo taken 1999.*

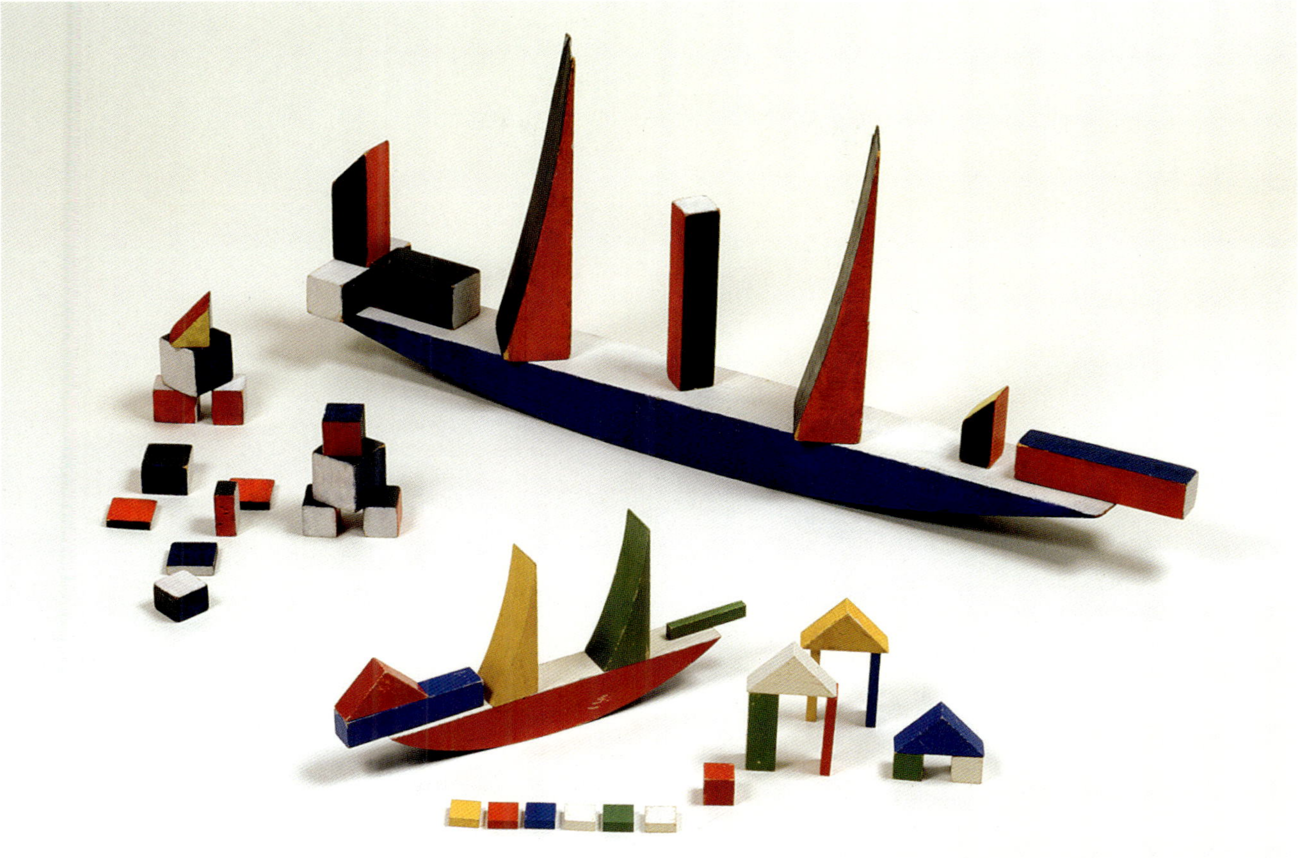

Alma Buscher studied at the Bauhaus Dessau from 1925 to 1927. She married the dancer and actor Walter Siedhoff in 1926. He worked with Oskar Schlemmer at the Bauhaus theater and gave lessons in physical education at the Bauhaus. Their daughter Lore was born in 1928. Because of Werner Siedhoff's career situation, with changing performance commitments, the family moved around frequently. They lived in Drewitz near Potsdam from 1933 and from 1942 in Frankfurt. On September 25, 1944, Alma Siedhoff-Buscher's life was ended abruptly. She died during bombing in Buschlag near Frankfurt.

It was not until the last third of the twentieth century that her work became gradually better known. Renowned toy companies and publishers produced and sold games and activity books based on the artist's prototypes. Her works have been shown in larger exhibitions in Japan, Spain, Italy, and the United States since 1993. The Deutsche Schloss- und Beschlägemuseum Velbert in Velbert, Saarbrücken, and Weimar showed the first one-woman exhibition on Alma Siedhoff-Buscher in 1997. Her works can be viewed in various museums today, many of them in the Bauhaus Museum in Weimar.

ULRIKE MÜLLER

• *Alma Buscher, Large and small shipbuilding game, wooden blocks, colorfully varnished, 1923.*

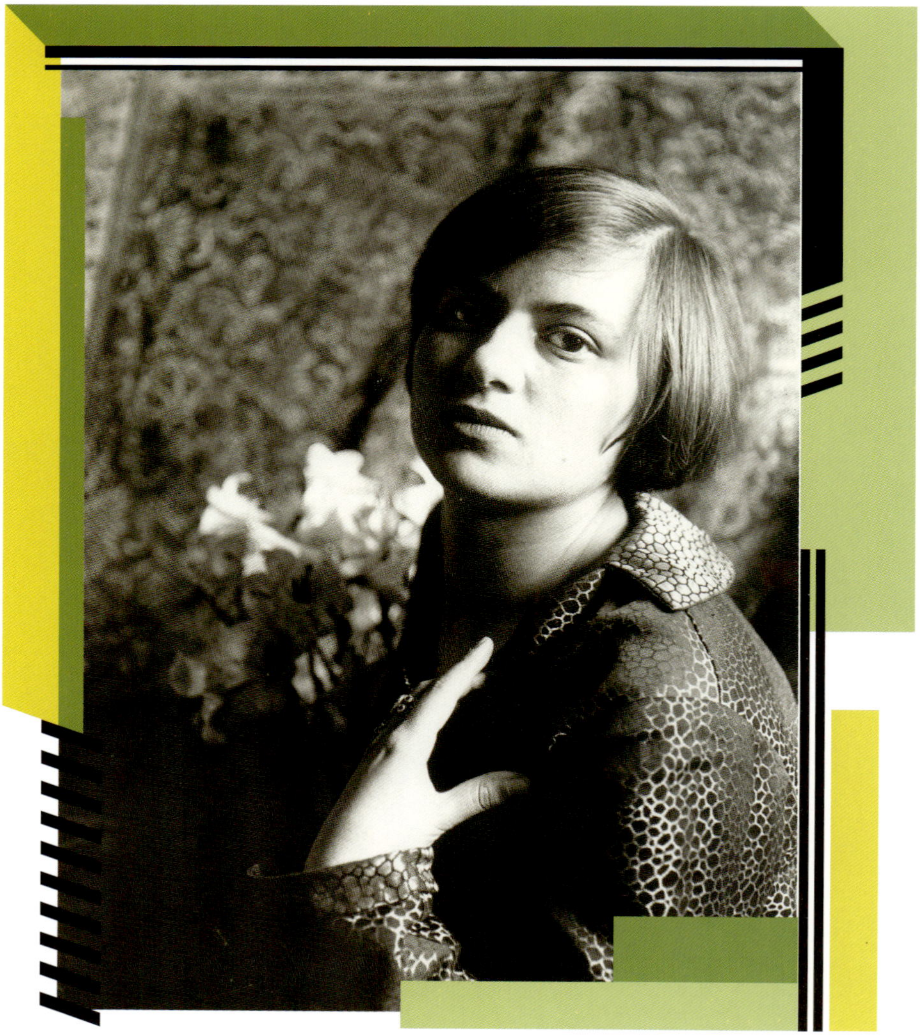

MARIANNE BRANDT 1893–1983

"At first, I was not accepted with pleasure—there was no place for a woman in a metal workshop, they felt. They admitted this to me later on and meanwhile expressed their displeasure by giving me all sorts of dull, dreary work. How many little hemispheres did I most patiently hammer out of brittle new silver, thinking that was the way it had to be and all beginnings are hard. Later things settled down, and we got along well together."

Marianne Brandt in Letter to the Younger Generation, *1970*

They are well known: the spherical teapots and the flat teapots, the sugar bowls, creamers, and ashtrays designed by Marianne Brandt, which we can still admire today at the Bauhaus Museum in Weimar. The shapes of the models she created in 1924, in their simple elegance and subliminal extravagance, are almost a matter of course in what we are used to seeing today, because the "conviction that a thing must be purposeful in its function and possess a beauty appropriate to the material used" as the artist expressed retrospectively, has influenced our tastes for a long time. It is also known that Marianne Brandt was one of the few female students who did not wish to study in the "women's department," the weaving workshop. She went instead to the metal workshop, where she set new standards for metal design in classical modernism, following only a short period of training. It is perhaps just as well known that despite her outstanding performance, Marianne Brandt only achieved the leading position of acting master of the metal workshop at the Bauhaus in Dessau in 1928. From her time at the Bauhaus in Dessau, her Kandem lamps, desk models, and a night-table lamp went down in design history. What was not so well known for many years is that apart from metal design, Marianne Brandt was also very accomplished in the new discipline of photography and up until the 1930s, created around fifty montages and a host of experimental photographs. Approximately thirty of them have been preserved. In these works, which she later referred to as "photomontages," she examined contemporary themes such as large cities and interpretive dance but also war, militarism, gender relationships, and the "New Women" among which she herself belonged. The montages *Helfen Sie mit! (Die Frauenbewegte)*, *Faultier und der Boxer auf dem Hut der androgynen Frau (geschminkt und mit Pfeife)*, and *Landschaften mit Gräberfeld und Explosion* (Landscape with Graveyard and Explosion) out of which she looms, all created in 1926, create a sense of unease. How much room for maneuver did this "liberated woman" really have in her own time? This is a question which also affects Marianne Brandt's personal fate.

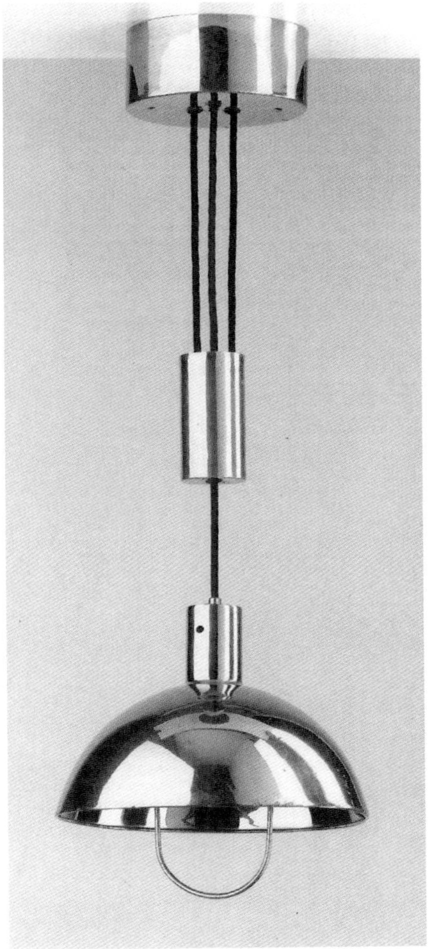

She was a presence among designers of the Bauhaus avant-garde in Europe between 1924 and 1933. She showed her work in exhibitions, exhibited herself in photos and at parties, sometimes provocatively staged, mostly with reference to her area, the metal workshop. Of all the workshop employees, she received the most commissions up to 1929. Her prototypes were produced by renowned companies. However, in 1933 she quit her career. As an artist she was forced to disappear from the radar, like so many others, from 1933 to 1945. As for her personal life, her marriage broke

• *Facing page: Marianne Brandt,* Selbstporträt mit Lilien *(Self-Portrait with Lilies), c. 1923.*

• *Above: Marianne Brandt and Hans Przyrembel, Hanging lamp with pulley, nickel-plated sheet brass, 1926.*

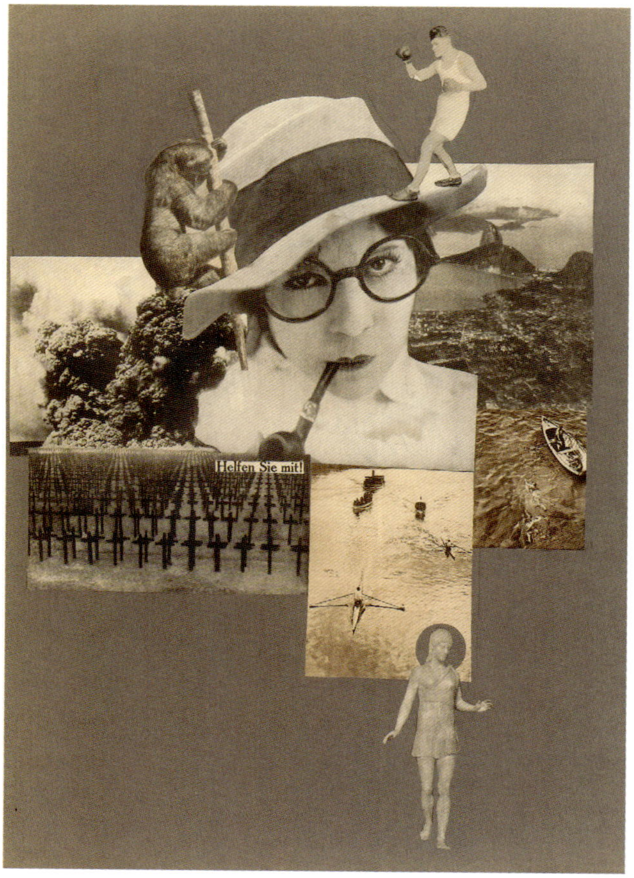

down. As a Bauhaus member she was pigeonholed as a "degenerate artist" by the Nazis. As the official wife of Erich Brandt, now an unwanted citizen of the enemy, Norway, she was also prevented from any kind of artistic development by the constant lack of materials, and so she emigrated inwardly. In the confines of her parents' house in Chemnitz, she took the paintbrush in her hand once more, and even created a tapestry in remembrance of the Bauhaus. She immediately returned to the public eye in 1946 with exhibitions, got involved in the Kulturbund (Cultural Association), the union, and the Künstlerbund (Artists Federation). She worked as a teacher from 1949 to 1951 at the Hochschule für Bildende Künste (College of Fine Arts) in Dresden, and at the Hochschule für angewandte Kunst (College of Applied Arts) in Weißensee near Berlin. She traveled to China on a state visit in 1953–54 at the age of sixty and spent many months there, organizing exhibitions. Chemnitz had become Karl-Marx-Stadt by the time she returned and she withdrew for the second time, this time until well into the 1970s. Who would know Marianne Brandt now?

The new up-and-coming German Democratic Republic (GDR) offered no place for experimental design and no recognition for individual artistic achievements. Brandt's avant-garde creations from the 1920s were of no interest and the heating and light fittings, pipes and bulbs, which she now designed for nationalized companies were lost in the uniform style of socialist industrial design. Isolation from countries in the west exacerbated Marianne Brandt's already claustrophobic situation in her parents' house. As interest in the Bauhaus, and in Brandt, slowly reawakened in the GDR at the end of the 1970s, it was too late for her to make a comeback. The Bauhaus exhibition in Leipzig in 1976, where her works were shown again for the first time, came too late for her. Marianne Brandt was over eighty years old, she was tired, worn down, and also ill. Yet in the last years of her life she returned to her camera in Kirchberg, Saxony, near Karl-Marx-Stadt, photographing from a highly isolated position, out of her window and thus, at least, bringing the outside world into her room: "I do nothing that could satisfy me. The only thing is photography . . . there is no way that I can design or paint, I am too depressed for that." And yet she lived to the age of ninety. In 1999, when Weimar was European Capital of Culture, sixteen years after her death, and eighty since the founding of the Bauhaus, her name and her tea infusers were printed on a German stamp. A weighty milestone for a woman on her way to taking her place next to the great masters.

But to return to her beginnings. Marianne Liebe, born in 1893, and her two sisters, Johanne and Susanna, came from a bourgeois family in Chemnitz, Saxony. Her

• *Marianne Brandt, Photo-montage* Helfen Sie mit! Die Frauenbewegte *(Help! Liberated Woman!), 1926.*

father, the lawyer Franz Bruno Lieber, was a local councillor and a supporter of theater and the arts. The girls grew up in the elegant legal district in an open house, in wh ch art, music, and literature were part of everyday life. Marianne first went to the upper level of the state school and then to the upper level of a private school for girls. At eighteen she went to Weimar, attended the Freie Zeichenschule (Free Drawing School) for one year, and was accepted to the Grand Ducal Saxon School of Arts and Crafts. Her painting teacher was the college's director, Fritz Mackensen, who was associated with Jugendstil. After Marianne Liebe returned to Weimar in 1916 following a year of training in Munich, she met the man who was later to become her husband, the Norwegian Erik Brandt, who, like her, had studied art in Weimar. The style of her paintings had a lot in common with German expressionism. They often depicted women, breast-feeding mothers and children. She completed her studies with a diploma in 1918. After their wedding in Oslo in 1919, Marianne and Erik Brandt remained in Norway for a year, and spent a further year in France to study art. They returned to Weimar in 1921. She began a second course of study, sculpture with Richard Engelmann, at the reopened Kunsthochschule (Art College).

The change came in the summer of 1923. At the great Bauhaus exhibition she saw a totally new type of art and design, which opened up a completely new view of artistic creativity to her. After twelve long years of learning and creative productivity, she fundamentally questioned everything she had previously done. Suddenly the thirty-year-old artist knew what she wanted and what she no longer wanted. It spelled the end of painting with which she could not earn money and of representational art. In 1926 she burnt all her previous old-style paintings.

In the winter semester of 1923–24, she moved to the State Bauhaus and in January 1924 began the preliminary course with Josef Albers and László Moholy-Nagy, as well as art classes with Wassily Kandinsky and Paul Klee. The Hungarian Moholy-Nagy, who succeeded Johannes Itten as preliminary course teacher, was to become her most important instructor, inspiration, and supporter. Over the years he came to wish for more, but Marianne wanted to leave the relationship as it was, because he meant so much to her artistically.

Moholy-Nagy marked the end of the romantic phase of the Weimar Bauhaus. The versatile artist and art theorist brought Constructivist design elements, strict abstraction, photographic experimentation, and a relationship with technology and industrial production for the first time into the teaching. In the production of

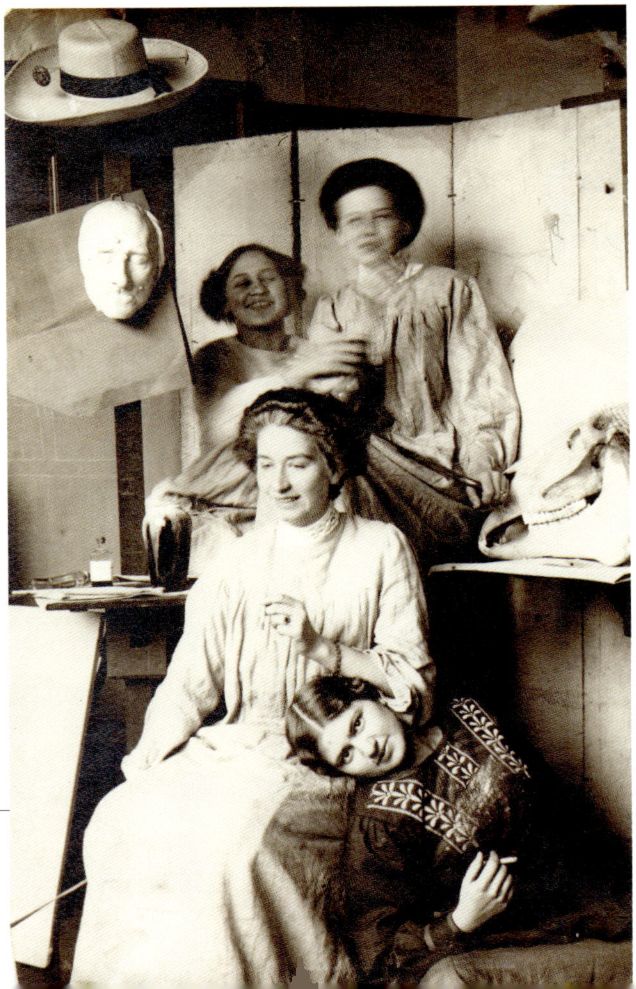

• *Marianne Brandt and fellow students in the painting class at the Grand Ducal Saxon School of Arts and Crafts, c. 1917–18.*

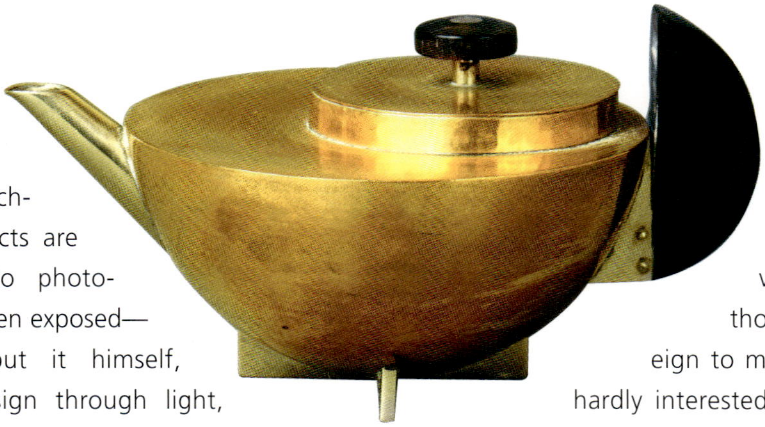

photograms—a technique whereby objects are placed directly onto photographic paper and then exposed—he saw, as he put it himself, "possibilities of design through light, whereby light is a new *design tool* in the way color is to painting or tone is to to music, and can be managed expertly." Moholy-Nagy was unflagging in his experimentation, and also in communicating theoretical approaches to the new medium of photography. Lucia Moholy, who was married to him at this time, was the first to photographically document Marianne Brandt's pieces. Marianne Brandt herself had been long captivated by a passion for photography. One of her first photographic works, Selbstporträt mit Lilien (Self-Portrait with Lilies), was created as early as 1923. She was later to become the female Bauhaus artist to most often include self-portrait and self-representation in photographic experiments. But at first she separated herself radically from representation. Her photograms, *Montage I* and *Montage II* of 1924 are consistently, abstractly designed like no other montage created in the years that followed.

Walter Gropius entrusted the innovator Moholy-Nagy with running the metal workshop, too, which he radically modernized in 1924. In the end, no more silver teapots were produced, but prototypes for electrical household appliances and lighting were developed. Convinced of her extraordinary talent, Moholy-Nagy encouraged Marianne Brandt, after only a few months of preliminary classes, to work in the metal workshop. She described the decision process to Eckhard Neumann around forty years later (in a letter of October 8, 1966): "The way painting was done in those days . . . was very foreign to me . . . and mural painting hardly interested me. The atmosphere in the weaving workshop didn't really suit me, and wood, which would have been more my thing, required a physical strength which I did not have. I discussed this with Moholy-Nagy and he encouraged me in the direction of metal. That is all." Of the new students who entered the workshop in October 1924, Marianne Brandt and Wilhelm Wagenfeld soon took on dominant roles. Over fifty percent of all models from the workshop are attributable to their designs. It is amazing, in hindsight, how quickly Marianne finished her apprenticeship. She herself said later: "We were not granted a long training period. From very early on we were told, 'design, execute, help, put yourself about'. . . ."

Her first models for production in the metal workshop were two ashtrays (1924), shaped from the elementary forms which belong to the Bauhaus Weimar

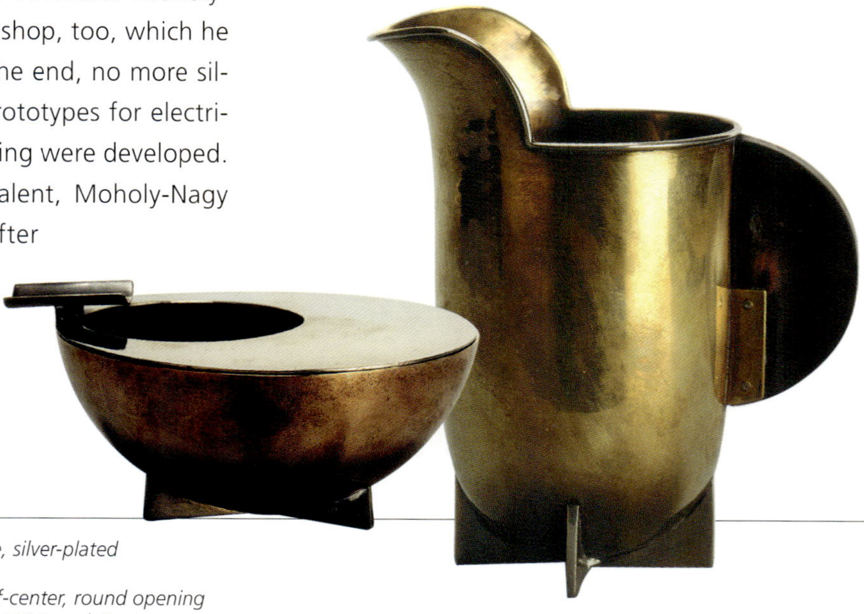

- *Above: Marianne Brandt, Teapot, bronze, silver-plated interior, new silver, ebony, 1924.*
- *Right: Marianne Brandt, Ashtray with off-center, round opening and cigarette holder, bronze, new silver, 1924; and Creamer, new silver, silver, 1924.*

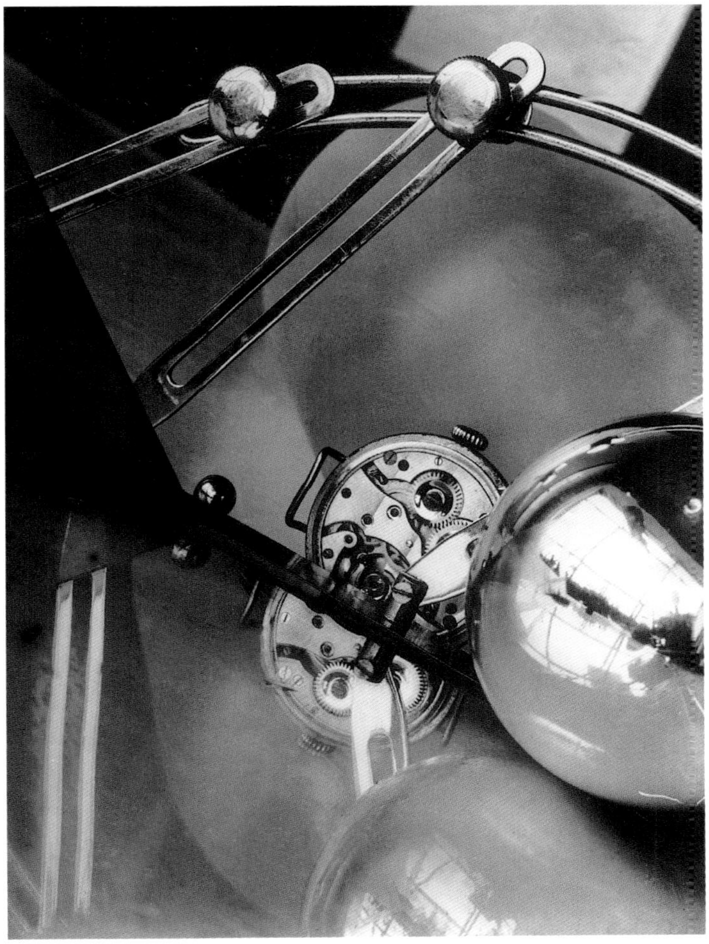

program, and which consciously question what had up to then been the normal design of such practical implements. In a conversation with Heinz Hirdina in 1979 she explained: "We were so obsessed by simple shapes that even the opening to the hemispherical ashtray was a triangle, but the eccentrically arranged oval was much better. We were also so obsessed because the kitsch of the *Gründerzeit*, and not only of that period, was still very present. All of that stuff still existed. I had a collection of it at home." Her famous teapot, made of silver and ebony, is still seen as one of the icons of Bauhaus design today. In her designs, Marianne Brandt meticulously followed the rule of reducing the object to the basic shapes of circle, square, and triangle. However, strict attention was also paid to functionality: "We wanted to revert to simple shapes, but the most important thing was that no pot left our factory that did not pour without dripping. We experimented using and especially pouring the pots . . . that was a matter of course for us" (1979).

Following the Bauhaus's forced move from Weimar to Dessau in April 1925, Erik and Marianne Brandt gave themselves nine months' break in Paris, during which Marianne created photo-montages including *Pariser Impressionen*. When she returned in 1927, she received her first paid job as an "employee" of the metal workshop. She now successfully negotiated industrial contracts for the production of light fittings. She also took an active role in art-theoretical debate in the magazine *Bauhaus* (1929). Besides metalwork she resumed her photography with renewed vigor. She created portraits, photographed architecture and materials, tried out many-sided reflection effects, for example in metal spheres and lamps, to illustrate the metal workshop and herself. Her self-portraiture for the *Metallisches Fest* (1929) is a good example of this. In her photo-montage with the dedication, *Me* (meaning metal workshop) for the portfolio, *9 Jahre Bauhaus* for Walter Gropius's departure in 1928, all the different aspects of the workshop—buildings, products, people—are captured from various perspectives as simultaneous events in one of two diagonally mastered compositions. Marianne herself, Moholy-Nagy, and the aluminum hanging lamps which she designed, take center stage.

In 1929, which was such a productive year for photography, Marianne Brandt decided to take her career in a new direction and to leave the Bauhaus. The design and construction of larger pieces of furniture brought a change of direction in the metal workshop. The fact that Marianne Brandt was at her physical limit was taken as an opportunity to question her leadership position. The sharpest attack came from, of all people, her younger colleague Hinnerk Bredendieck, whom she had

• *Marianne Brandt, Untitled (Still Life with Clock and Metal Ball), c. 1929.*

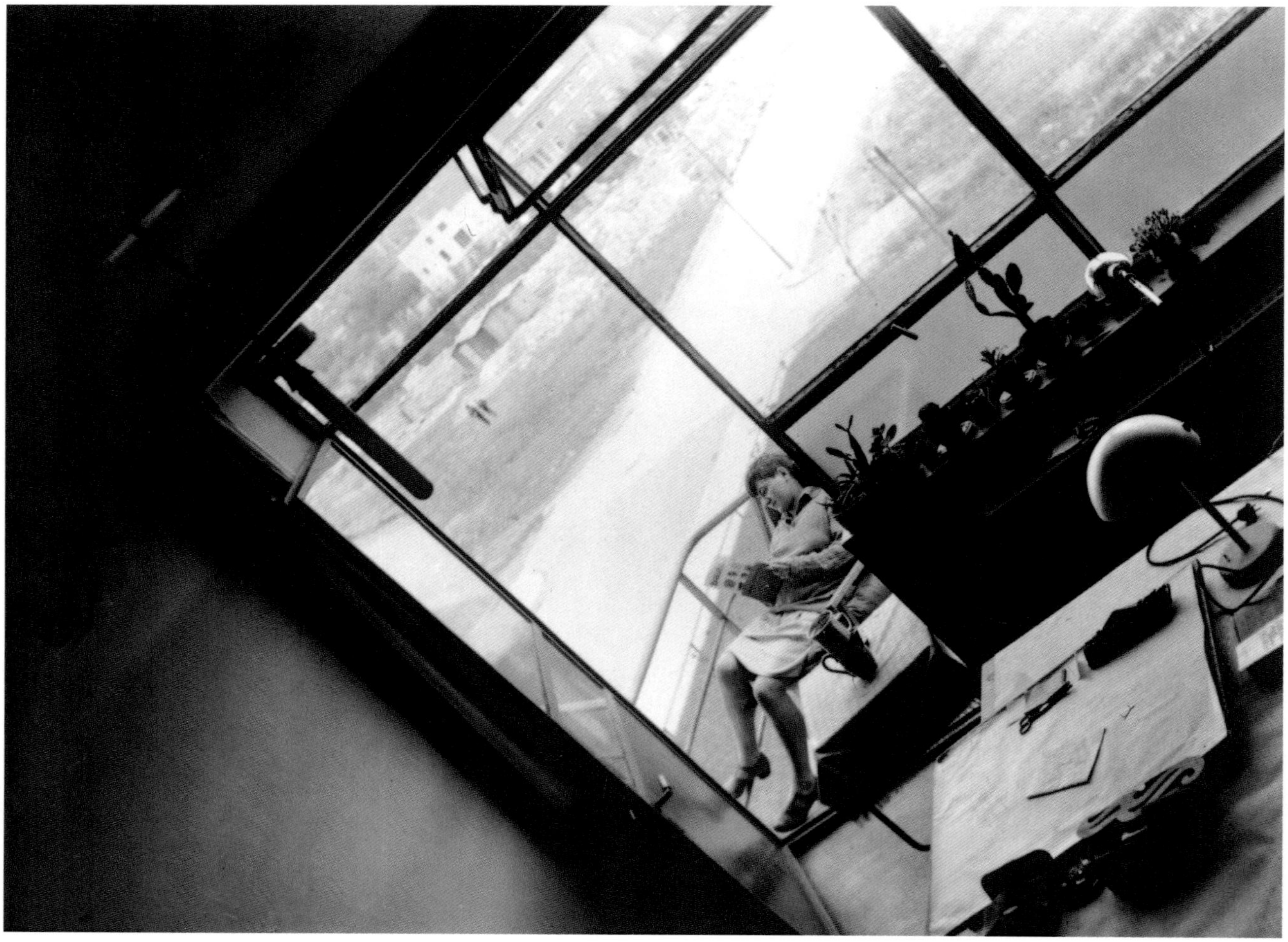

taken under her wing. He accused her of only being capable of making models on paper, as she was a woman. It is obvious that intense competitiveness played a great role in this situation. Marianne Brandt's riposte, in a letter to director Hannes Meyer from April 25, 1929, reads very nicely: "i myself am of another opinion regarding the nature of my work, as i am fairly comprehensively proficient in some particular areas and am capable of putting these skills to good use, which i believe i have proved during my employment here. as i am also trained in craft, albeit one-sidedly, and have gained an all-round insight into machinery and processes through observation, conversation, and experience, i must expressly insist on my right to create models."

These words sound like those of a woman who knows what she is capable of. However, Marianne Brandt was also described by those around her as "in no way robust, but sensitive, moody, and at times very depressed". Her friend Liselotte Lange is quoted as saying that Marianne said of herself later that she was a pessimist and life had proven her right in that.

In 1929 Marianne Brandt retrospectively received her Bauhaus diploma in metalworking. She took part in the Werkbund's international exhibition of film and photo in Stuttgart and worked with Gropius in his Berlin architectural office. She showed her metal pieces at the Werkbund's exhibition in Paris in 1930. Moholy-Nagy, who stood up for her with a passionate fervor time and again, was a great source of help and encouragement during this period. He wrote in a letter to Ernst Bruckmann on June 26, 1929: "my best and most gifted student (90% of all bauhaus models came from her) frau marianne brandt". Gropius also continued to support her and helped in her search for a new position when

• *Marianne Brandt on the balcony of her studio, 1928.*

he no longer had work for her. She then managed to make her living in the metal factory Ruppel in Gotha, where she designed prototypes for functional implements such as lights, tea trolleys, and letter openers. Her most beautiful work from this period is a spherical inkwell. In 1933 Marianne Brandt was made unemployed and she began to "disappear."

The task of seeking out former Bauhauser members in postwar Germany and rediscovering the avant-garde of the past was initially carried out by those Bauhaus artists who had emigrated, especially Ise and Walter Gropius. The latter had made written contact with Marianne Brandt from the United States and supported her for years with advice and care packages, which had little to do with artistic endeavor at first and more to do with rebuilding her parents' house, which had been severely damaged in a bomb attack. In the 1960s the Bauhaus researcher Eckhard Neumann made contact with Marianne Brandt from the United States. The result of their correspondence, which lasted many years was the essay, "Letter to the Younger Generation" in Neumann's book *Bauhaus and Bauhaus People* (1970). As an old woman, at least, she experienced the resurgence of interest in the Bauhaus in her own country. Today, her work and life in both East and West Germany are gradually being awarded the attention they deserve. As a metal designer, industrial designer, and photographer, the Bauhaus artist Marianne Brandt has long earned her place in the encyclopedia of the history of modernism in art. Production still continues, or has been resumed, of objects based on her prototypes.

ULRIKE MÜLLER

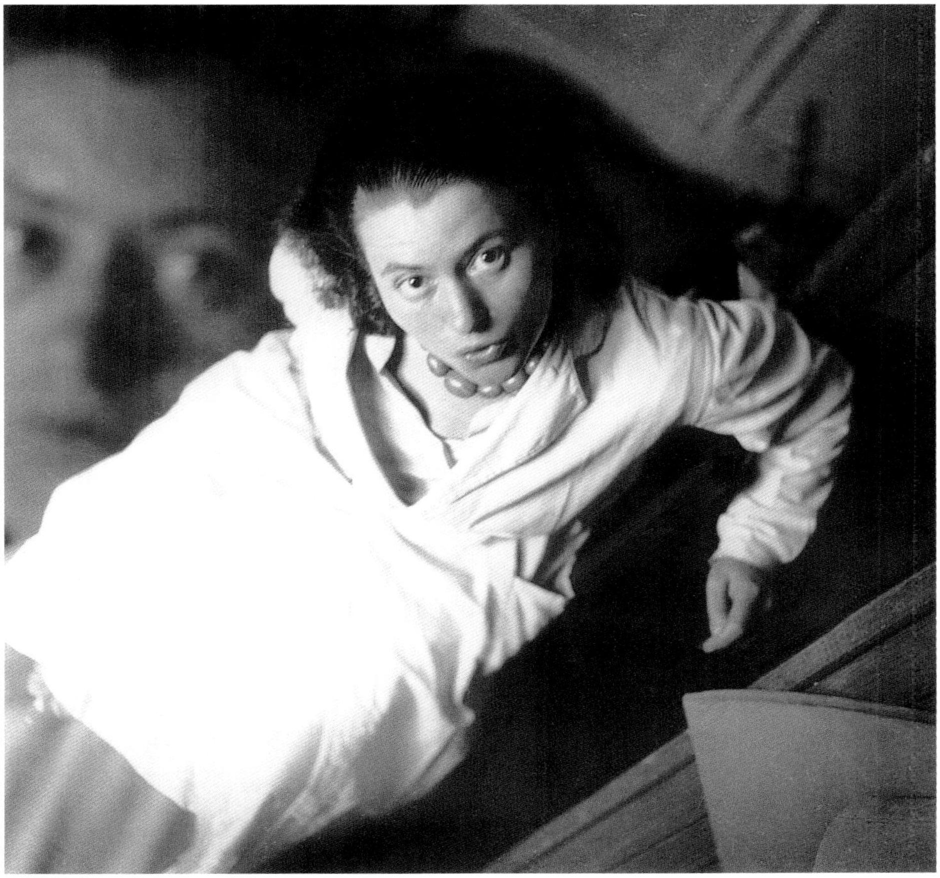

• *Marianne Brandt, Untitled (Simultaneous Self-Portrait), c. 1930–31.*

Between Experiment and Documentation

Masters of Photography and the Diary

The image of women in early Modernism underwent a decisive change when women left the private sphere and entered public life. Women were becoming secretaries or shop assistants, but also scientists, journalists, and photographers. Rigid male perspectives of the world changed through multifaceted female views, and nowhere did this take place more remarkably than in photography. Alongside many varied experiments, women now created many more portraits and self-portraits, from behind the camera, than had ever previously been seen in another pictorial medium. Aenne Biermann, Lotte Jacobi, Tina Modotti, Germaine Krull, Margaret Bourke-White, and Gisèle Freund were among the great women photographers of this era.

At the Bauhaus photography was the discipline in which most women could be found, apart from the weaving workshop. Some photographed for pleasure, others made a career of it. Three of the women in this chapter worked professionally with the camera, the fourth preferred her typewriter as a tool, but was still a good photographer. While Florence Henri and Grete Stern studied at the Bauhaus, Ise Gropius and Lucia Moholy were officially, merely "masters' wives." Ise Gropius was happy with her position at the side of the Bauhaus director and wrote her diary from this perspective. Lucia Moholy may have worked with her husband, however at the same time she was an independent photographer.

Although the medium of photography ideally corresponded with the Bauhaus maxim "Art and technology—a new unity," it was amazingly neglected at the school. Until the first photography class was introduced in Dessau in 1929, the students tended to work more casually in a playful manner with the camera. Yet many very original works emerged from precisely this carefree attitude. They can basically be grouped according to the various elements of the New Vision, but did not give rise to any specific Bauhaus style. In 1993 the weaver, Gertrud Arndt, who created her photographic *Maskenporträts* in Dessau in 1927 (see page 59), told her interviewer, Sabina Leßmann, of the beginnings of her studies: "Nobody could take a photograph when I arrived in Weimar, the only one who could use a camera was Lucia Moholy, she had learned it. She came to the Bauhaus as a photographer." She herself could also already take photographs. As Lucia Moholy began to photographically document the Bauhaus in 1923, Marianne Brandt appeared at the same time working on experimental self-portraits and on photograms one year later (see pp. 118–25).

Lucia Moholy and László Moholy-Nagy represent two different directions in early Modernist photography.

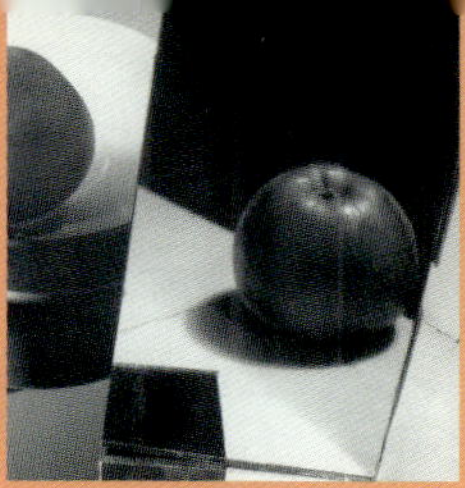

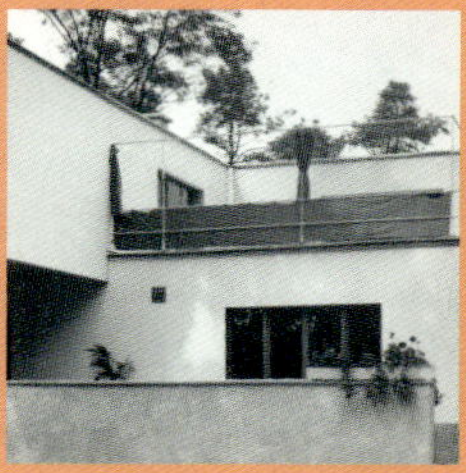

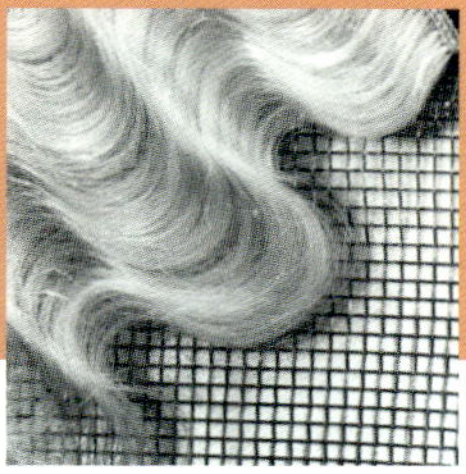

In their theoretical work, *Malerei, Photographie, Film* (1925), they differentiate between the experimental "productive" art photo and the "reproductive" photo, which is beholden to reality. "Productive" photography, as represented by Moholy-Nagy, involved the alienation of the motif through extreme visual angles, compressed details, optical distortion, or deliberate blurring through the use of glass, metal spheres, or mirrors, as well as the use of special photographic techniques like inversing negative and positive (the photogram), and double or multiple exposures. On the other hand, Lucia Moholy, who had discovered the photogram technique together with her husband, did not make use of these experimental photographic methods. She saw herself as a participating documentary maker, not as creator of an artistic scene, and devoted her art to reportage photography. Walter Peterhans who gave the first photography lessons at the Bauhaus from 1929, represented the New Objectivity much more extremely and dogmatically than Lucia Moholy. For him, son of the director of Zeiss-Ikon, who had studied mathematics, photo-optics, and laboratory techniques should be utilized and optimized on a scientific basis, which serves the precise reproduction of the object. Apart from theory and technique, Peterhans's classes were oriented toward practical use in advertising and photo-reportage. Many women, who later became professional photographers, took his courses: Irene Bayer, Katt Both, Irene Hoffmann, Elsa Thiemann, Hilde Hubbuch, who later made a name for herself with her children's portraits in New York, and Lotte Beese, who emigrated to Holland in 1935 where she became an architect of some renown. Some prominent students of Peterhans came from Eastern Europe, among them Irena Blühova from Slovakia, who was active in the anti-Fascist resistance in Bratislava in 1945 and who, after the war, founded the Slovakian Educational Library. Etel Mittag-Fodor from Zagreb emigrated to South Africa in 1938 and worked there as a photographer and weaver.

Literature specialist Elisabeth Lenk captured this phase of enthusiastic, experimental self-discovery among the early modernist women artists in her cultural history *Kritische Phantasie* (1986): "Woman becomes a live mirror for woman, in which she loses and then finds herself again." Women no longer allowed themselves be consigned to the clichés of femininity. With every masking, staging, discovery, or duplication of the ego, they claimed new territory for the female identity. For women photographers, the new self-defined look in the mirror, the look into, through and behind the camera was in their own hands, and indeed, many self-portraits took the form of mirror studies.

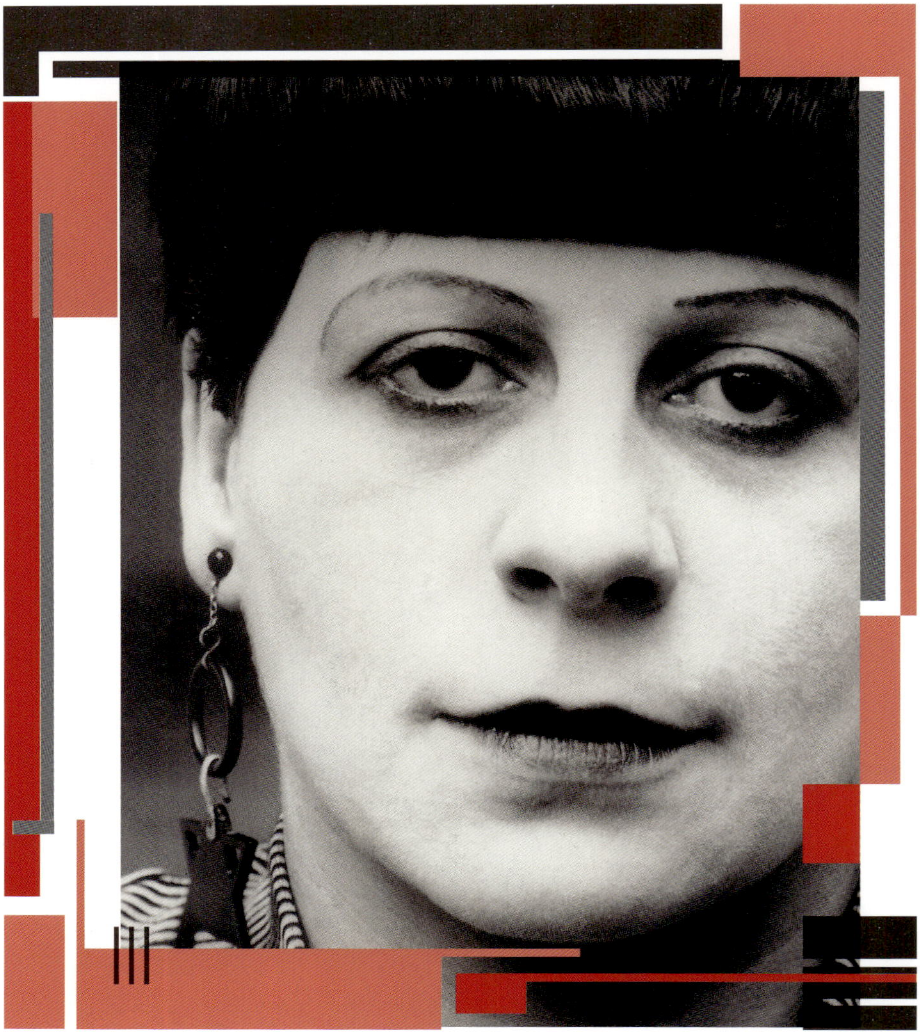

FLORENCE HENRI 1893–1982

"Now some news: I am taking photographs. If I enjoy it, I will stop painting (temporarily) and really do this as a career. I am so sick of this vague painting in a vacuum and have so many ideas for photos."

Florence Henri, February 11, 1928, in a letter from Paris to Lou Scheper in Dessau

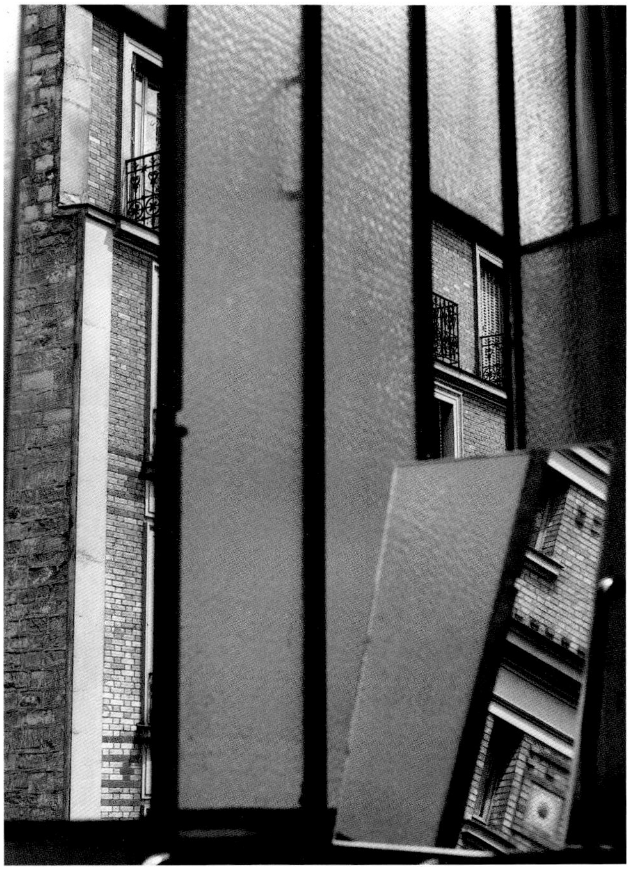

• *Above: Florence Henri,* Pariser Fenster *(Parisian Window), 1929.*

Florence Henri is one of those early modernist artists for whom photography became the medium, even the key, to female emancipation. She combined the possibilities of the "New Vision" with aspects of modern painting to create her own style with which she brought the "New Woman" and also herself into focus. In this, she used more the methods of painting than effects created by optics and photography. Reality was not blurred, made crooked or carried to extremes or exposed in close-ups but, because it cannot be avoided, was tricked, undercut, and relieved of its temporal and spatial limits with the use of mirrors. "Two shining spheres lie in the confusing mirror image, in front of them sits Florence Henri like a photographic fortune-teller.... She looks at herself ... reality has disappeared." This was a commentary which appeared in an article published by the *Frankfurter Rundschau* in 1928 on Florence Henri's first self-portrait.

In her more than fifteen years of development as a painter, Florence Henri had dealt with famous representatives of modernity before she herself became famous as a photographer in 1928. Although she returned to abstract painting during World War II and, with a few exceptions, stayed with this medium until the end of her life, she is still better known today for her photographs; portraits of women, nudes, still lifes, compositions with objects such as spools of thread, spheres, perfume bottles, and gramophone records (she later also took landscapes), in which she experimented with prisms and mirrors again and again. Florence Henri's works were published in art magazines such as *foto-auge*, *Der Querschnitt*, *L'Art Contemporain*, and *Arts et Métiers graphiques*, and shown at exhibitions such as *FiFo*, the international film and photo exhibition of the Werkbund in 1929 in Stuttgart. In 1931 she received an award in New York as part of the exhibition *Foreign Advertising Photography* on contemporary European advertising photography, for her *Komposition mit Zwirnrollen*. At that time Florence Henri was regarded on the photographic scene as the main representative of the French avant-garde. In this she was truly cosmopolitan.

Florence Henri was born in New York in 1893. Her mother, Anna Schindler, came from Silesia which then belonged to Germany; her father, François de Montague Henri, came from France. Following the early death of both parents, she spent her childhood in Silesia, attended a boarding school in Paris in her teens, and then went on to Rome where she discovered futurist painting. She then traveled to London to study music. She continued her music studies in Berlin in 1912 where she sometimes accompanied silent films. Two years later she changed to the Berliner Akademie to study painting and stayed for a further ten years, interrupted by visits to Düsseldorf and Munich. She met

• *Facing page: Portrait of Florence Henri, photograph by Lucia Moholy, 1927.*

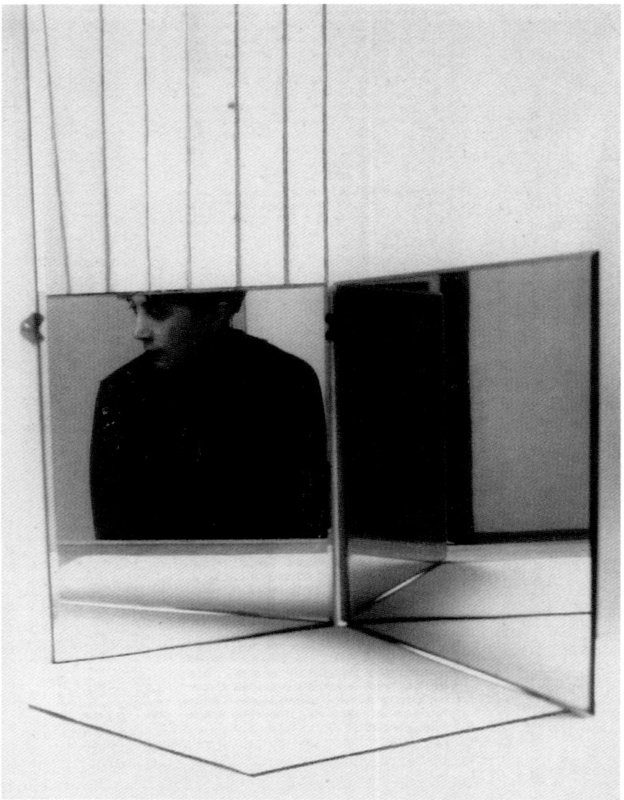

Hans Arp and John Heartfield, made contact with László Moholy-Nagy, and engaged with the Constructivism of El Lissitzky and Kazimir Malevich. She visited Paris for the second time in 1924 and initially studied at the Académie André Lhote—the sculptor Lhote was later to become a cubist painter—then went on to study abstract painting at the Académie Moderne with Fernand Léger. She had some artistic success as a street painter. After one semester at the Dessau Bauhaus she settled in France in August 1927.

"Please write me how things are and if you intend to stay on delightfully with your husband and Jan? I can hardly believe that such a thing can last so long, but perhaps it is possible for you, as there is so much of it. The delightful evenings with you. Everyone is waxing lyrical about them," wrote Florence Henri, who was referred to as "Monti" by close friends, on August 28, 1927 from Paris to Lou Scheper in Dessau. During her studies in 1927, she had become friends with Lou, who had studied at the Bauhaus in Weimar, and her husband Hinnerk, Bauhaus master since 1925. The letters she wrote to the painter following her departure give an insight into her Parisian life. Her time in Dessau had obviously changed her perception of the city: "Paris created an extremely unmodern impression after the Bauhaus. I am no longer overcome by its charms," she wrote in the same letter. Instead, she was overcome by the charms of photography, which she discovered accidentally one day, as she herself described it, when her roommate's camera fell into her hands. She shared her day-to-day life and a studio with the painter Margarete Schall, whom she had known since her time in Berlin, and often portrayed in photographs. (Margarete Schall was, according to the architect Renate Scheper, her mother-in-law, Lou Scheper's drawing teacher at the grammar school in Essen, and a good friend of the Schepers.) A black cat served as male companionship in the female artists' studio. Decades later, when Florence Henri had withdrawn to Bellival, Picardy, in 1963, she lived in the peace of country life surrounded by a family of cats headed by a red tomcat.

Renowned painters met at Florence Henri's Parisian studio: Sonia and Robert Delaunay, Piet Mondrian, Fernand Léger, and the artistic group Cercle et Carré to which Florence Henri herself belonged from 1930. Photographers such as Man Ray, André Kertész, and Germaine Krull were also visitors there. After Florence Henri had mastered the technical side of photography herself, she opened a photo studio offering portraits and advertising photographs. She also continued with her photographic experiments and taught. Her most famous student was Gisèle Freund, who later made her career with photographs of the Parisian Left Bank scene.

With her camera Florence Henri had a command of all formal methods but had no interest in technical excellence and no patience with darkroom perfection.

• *Florence Henri,* Portrait of Margarethe Schall, *1928.*

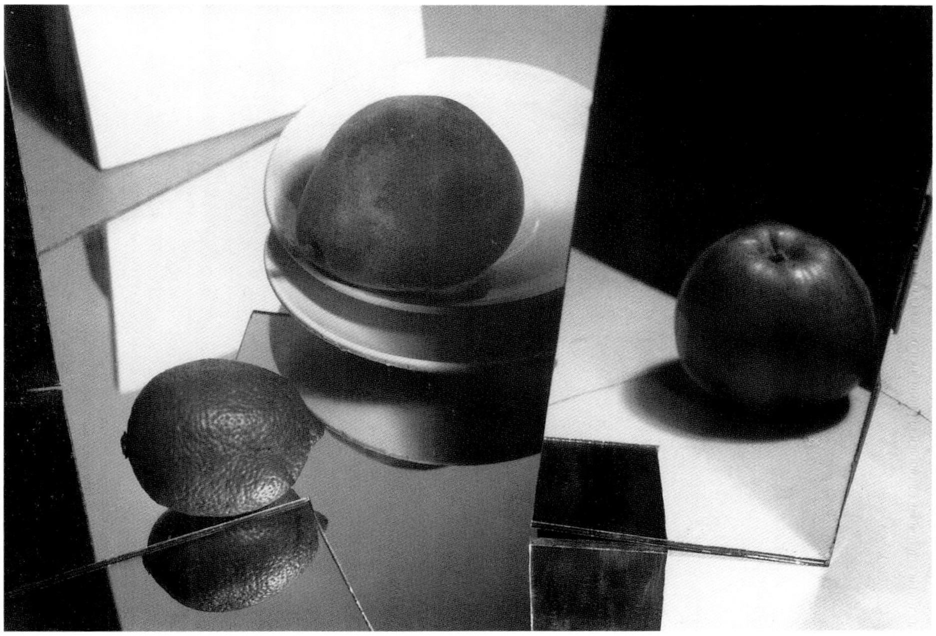

Lifelike representations of reality were not important to her. The extension of photography by the use of mirrors was, above all, a way of creating spatial perspective and the impression of depth which she could not achieve in painting. She is said to have happily and unscrupulously made changes to negatives, for example by intensifying weak lines with a soft pencil.

Just how did Florence Henri come to photography? While studying at the Bauhaus in Dessau from April to July 1927, she attended courses given by Paul Klee and Wassily Kandinsky, as well as the preliminary course under Josef Albers and László Moholy-Nagy, where her first photographic exercises were carried out. Her interest in photography was awakened at the Bauhaus, however painting was still then her main interest. Before an official photography course was established under Walter Peterhans in 1929, innovative directions for photography at the Bauhaus came principally from Moholy-Nagy. Florence Henri's photographs, which were published in the magazine *i-10* in Amsterdam in 1928, appeared with a commentary from him. Alongside elements of abstract painting, critics nevertheless see in her work correspondances with the ideas of Bauhaus master Georg Muche, who had already experimented with the effects of mirrors and metal spheres in 1920–21.

World War II interrupted Florence Henri's photographic activities. She received no commissions, even after 1945. The Swiss magazine *du* published Florence Henri's portrait series *Pariserinnen* in 1947. For a long time thereafter, none of her works was published. When the gallery owners Ann and Jürgen Wilde sought out the eighty-year-old one day in the pastoral peace of Bellival to prepare an exhibition of her work in Germany, Florence Henri was very surprised by the interest in her past as a photographer in Germany. But she made her old glass plates available for new prints and gave Ann Wilde a present of one of her cats as a parting gift. The exhibitions shown by the Wildes in 1974 in Cologne contributed greatly to Florence Henri's rediscovery. At her advanced age she witnessed the beginning of a renaissance of her photographic work. She died in 1982, aged eighty-nine, in Compiègne, near Bellival. She was honored with exhibitions in New York and Paris the same year and the San Francisco Museum of Modern Art showed a groundbreaking exhibition of her photographic works in 1990. In between times, her works were shown in France, the United States, West Germany, and Italy. As she wrote to Lou Scheper on February 11, 1928: "I would like to have an occupation whose results also arouses others' interest. Standing so lonely and alone before one's works! You understand!"

ULRIKE MÜLLER

• *Florence Henri,* Obst *(Fruit), 1929.*

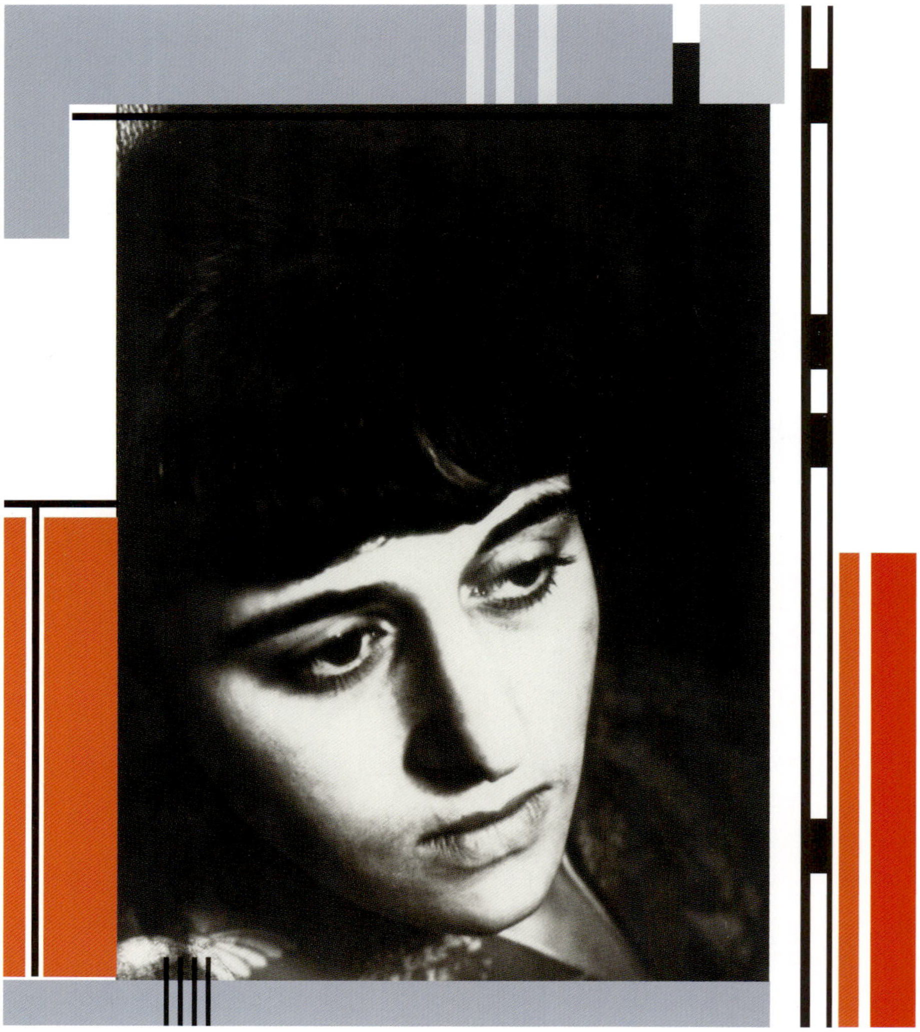

GRETE STERN 1904–1999

"The most important thing was to learn to see photographically. From which perspective do I take the picture? To define the lighting—what should be defined and what undefined—which details should I choose? Only when all of that was decided did one then set up the camera with the help of the screen so that the shot allowed everything to be seen that one wished to show."

Grete Stern, c. 1989

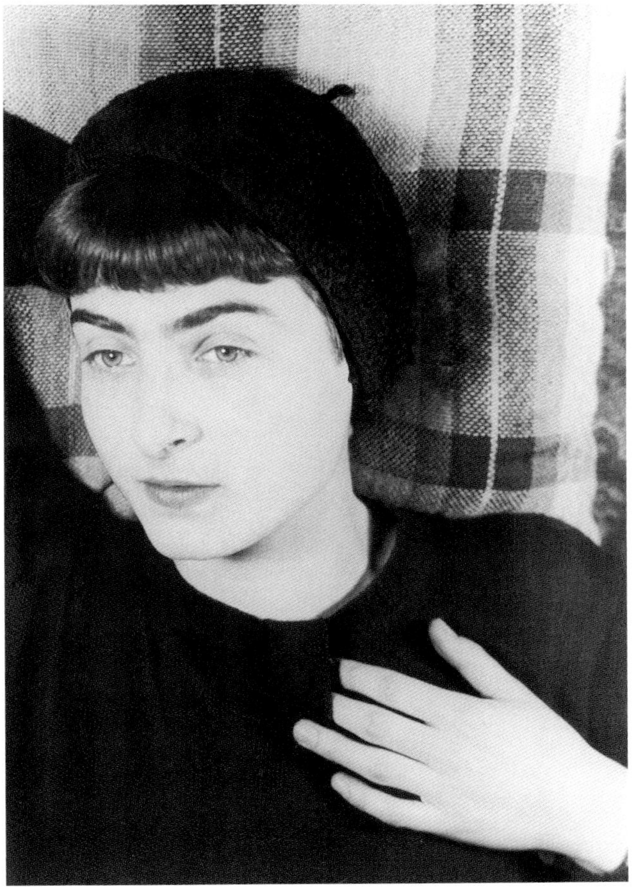

Grete Stern spent over sixty years of her life in Argentina, where she found permanent refuge after the Nazis took power. After the abrupt forced ending of her career as a German-Jewish photographer, she managed to adapt to a foreign country and culture, to develop creative scope, and to find public recognition for her art a second time. At some point she saw herself as Argentinian, but maintained her photographic style. After almost thirty years, a new element appeared in her stringent, extremely meticulously designed portraits, cityscapes, natural landscapes, and photomontages—spontaneity. In a photo-documentary on the life of the Gran Chaco Indians, a poor indigenous people in the north of Argentina, she combined subtle empathy, which was always a trademark of her portraits, with immediate engagement. She spent four months at Gran Chaco in 1964, sharing the worries and needs of the people there and winning their trust. This experience produced around eight hundred photos.

Grete Stern was born on May 9, 1904, in Elberfeld, today's Wuppertal. She spent three years of her childhood in London and attended school there. She acquired her school graduation certificate in Germany after attending high school. She studied graphics and typography from 1923 to 1925 at the Stuttgart Kunstgewerbeschule (Craft School) at Weißenhof, but did not finish her training there. Instead she went to Wuppertal to work as a freelance graphic artist. She went to Berlin in 1927 and worked as a commercial artist, and there she first laid eyes on photographs by Edward Weston and Paul Outerbridge, which so fascinated her that she then wanted to become a photographer. Her brother, who was in the film industry, put her in touch with Otto Umbehr and he sent her to Walter Peterhans. In 1927 and 1928 she was the photographer's only private student. Peterhans, a convinced advocate of the New Objectivity, focused on the painstakingly exact objective representation of reality using the highest photo-technical precision. At the beginning of 1929, Ellen Rosenberg (1906–2004), who had first studied sculpture, became Peterhans's second photography student. When he went to Dessau to teach photography at the Bauhaus he handed the teaching over to his first student. A small inheritance allowed Grete Stern to take over his photo studio. With Ellen as a partner she opened a studio for advertising photography and portraits in 1929 calling it "ringl + pit" after the women's nicknames as children (Grete was ringl; Ellen was pit). From this point on they shared a studio and an apartment, work and day-to-day-life together, and they developed a deep affection for each other. Many original and technically perfect photographic works, which are marked by a fine and often surreal interplay between wit and seriousness, illusion and reality, sobriety and erotica were created by the artistic

• *Facing page: Portrait of Grete Stern, photograph by Ellen Auerbach, c. 1931.*

• *Above: Portrait of Ellen Auerbach, photograph by Grete Stern, c. 1930.*

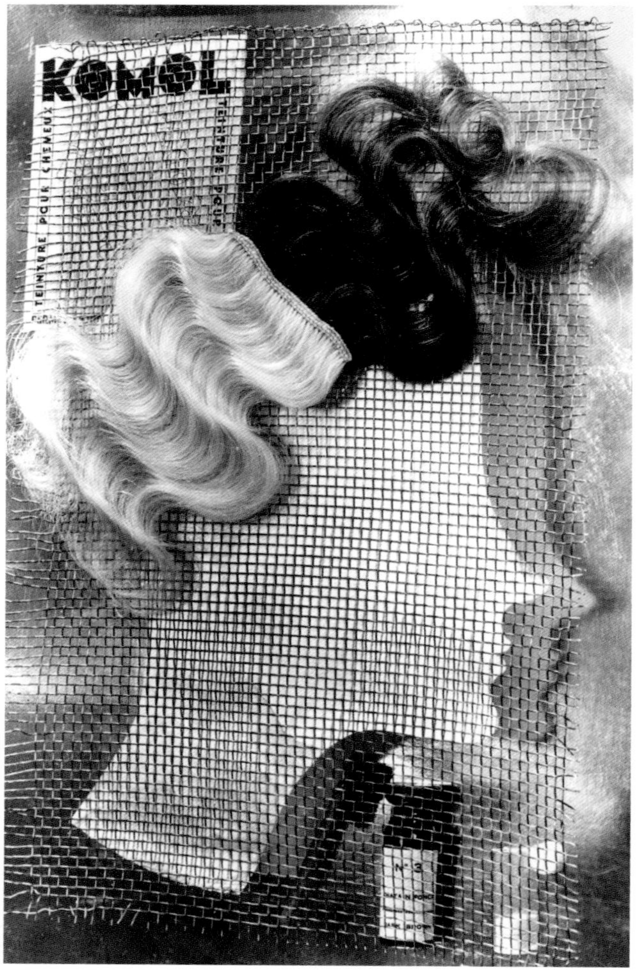

pair. In 1931 they were honored by the magazine, *Gebrauchsgrafik*: "ringl + pit are among the rare photographers, who draw the line of their effectiveness in their work . . . Yet ringl + pit do not seek the extravagant. Only sometimes their young minds are haunted, as in when they title a photographic cloth, *Fragment einer Braut*." Both women entrusted the placement of their work to the advertising agency Mauritius. Thanks to Grete's inheritance, they did not have to earn their living from photography.

Ringl + pit worked chiefly in the studio. Their subjects—people or objects—were always meticulously arranged. Nothing was left to chance, down to the perfect print, and no photo was ever retouched. Grete's acerbic wit and strictness were complemented by Ellen's playful parodies and feeling for the absurd.

Although both worked closely together, each artist visibly maintained her own individuality. In some works, they left it open to interpretation what came from which artist and so avoided any competition, for example, the advertising photo *KOMOL* (1932), for which ringl + pit received first prize at the *Deuxième Exposition Internationale de la Photographie et du Cinéma* in 1933 in Brussels.

Grete Stern studied at the Bauhaus in Dessau for one year in 1930, and from 1932 to 1933 at the Bauhaus in Berlin. Her work shows how much value Peterhans placed on a scientifically grounded laboratory technique. She always proudly stated that she had been his student. Their connection was evident in a passion for fabrics and textures, in the differentiated monochromes, and the rejection of any artificial effects. Some of ringl + pit's works follow typical contemporary themes. Thus their 1930 *Ei des Kolumbus* (in German the "Colombus Egg" is an idiom which describes a very simple and obvious solution to a problem) is in good company alongside works such as Moholy-Nagy's *Huhn bleibt Huhn* (1925), *Foto-Ei Spiegelei* by Aenne Biermann (1931), *Triumph des Eies* (1932) by Paul Outerbridge and the *Fotogramm-Ei* by Man Ray (1946). The "photo-egg" was a favorite subject for still life and photograms at the Bauhaus for almost ten years.

Following the Nazis' seizure of power it was clear to both women that they had to leave Germany. Ellen traveled to Palestine with her future husband Walter Auerbach in 1933 and, following a stopover with Grete Stern in London in 1937, emigrated to the United States. Grete had emigrated to London in the fall of 1933, where she spent three years working as an advertising photographer and also photographed celebrities, using her bathroom as a lab. In 1934 she photographed

• *ringl + pit,* KOMOL, *advertising photo for hair dye, 1932.*

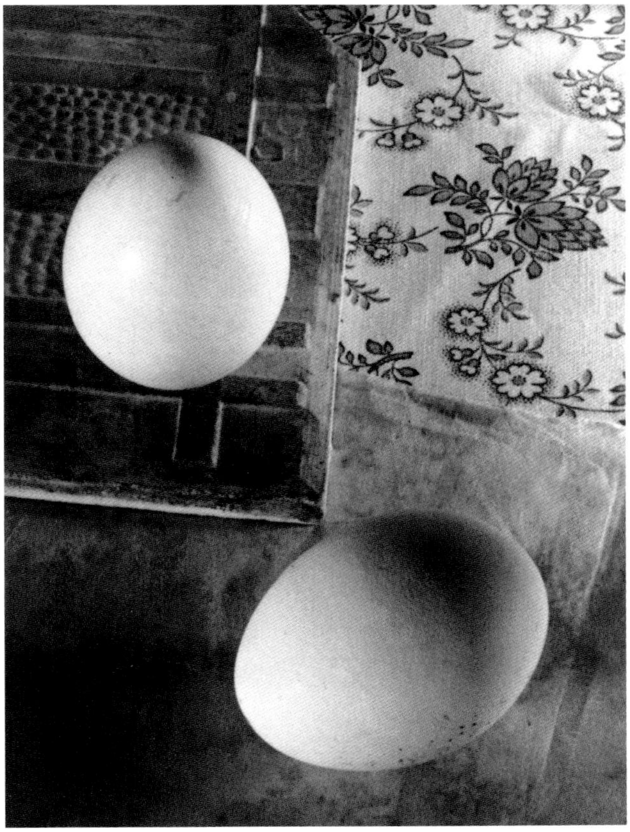

Bertolt Brecht whom she had invited to her "tiny appartment, which had atmosphere nevertheless" (Grete Stern in 1992 in a film by Andrea Lerch).

In 1935 she married the Argentinian Horacio Coppola, one of Peterhans's Bauhaus students and one year later gave birth to their daughter, Silvia. The young family moved to Buenos Aires and opened a photo studio. Following the birth of son Andreas in 1940, their new house in Ramos Meja near Buenos Aires became a meeting point for artists, writers, and intellectuals who, like Jorge Luis Borges and Mariá Elena Walsh, were also photographed by Grete Stern. Sara Facio calls Ramos a "legendary place," a practice room for the choirs in which Grete Stern sang (text from the film by Antonia Lerch, 1992). Following her divorce in 1941, Grete Stern remained in Ramos and designed posters and book covers and gave courses. Between 1948 and 1951, she created a series of 140 dream-photo montages for the weekly publication *El Idilio*, which aimed at giving its women readers insights into psychoanalysis. In 1956 she became official photographer of the Museo Nacional de Bellas Artes. After the death of her son in 1965, she moved back to Buenos Aires and opened another photo studio. She was honored with a solo exhibition by the Museum of Fine Arts while she was in retirement in 1972.

The first show of Grete Stern's work in Germany, following World War II was at the Bauhaus Archive in Berlin in 1975. Further shows on ringl + pit followed, which made Grete Stern and Ellen Auerbach known to the public in many parts of the world including New York (1985) and Vancouver (1991). Furthermore both were portrayed in a 1995 movie by Juan Mandelbaum and in 1992 in a film by Antonia Lerch. The seventy-seven-year-old Grete Stern told Lerch: "I was interested in faces before I became interested in photography."

With increasing age Grete Stern's eyes began to fail her but she did not give up photography entirely until she was over eighty. Grete Stern died aged ninety-five on Christmas Eve 1999.

The artists' collective ringl + pit did not re-emerge following their emigration. The physical distance between the women was simply too great. Yet, whenever they did see each other after years, the old emotional closeness and familiar intellectual "ping-pong" were revived immediately. The following dialog comes from the script of the 1995 film by Juan Mandelbaum: "*Ellen*: We have known each other for 60, 62 years and you know, I do not remember a single disagreement between us. You? *Grete*: Never, no, not at all. *Ellen*: We could start a fight now! *Grete*: What? *Ellen*: We could start a fight now! *Grete*: All right, if you want to (*she laughs*). *Ellen*: See, how can you fight with a person like that?"

ULRIKE MÜLLER

• *ringl + pit,* Das Ei des Kolumbus *(Columbus' Egg), 1930.*

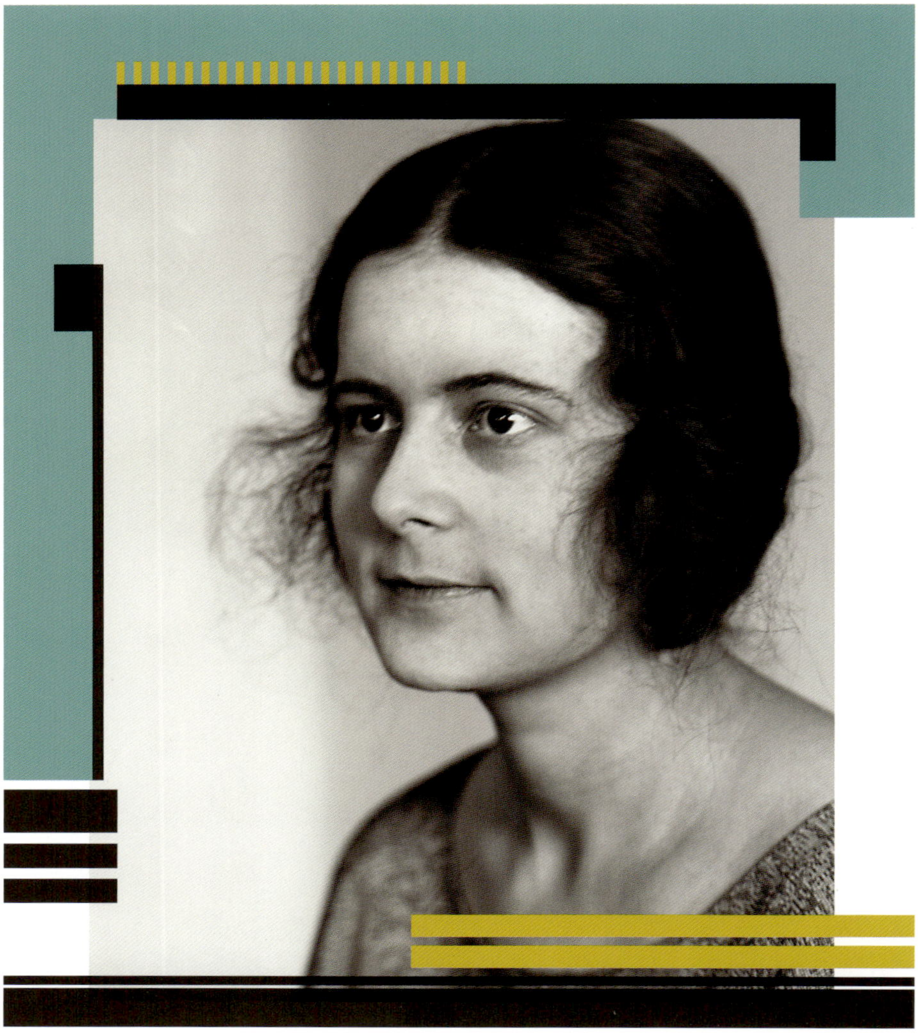

ISE GROPIUS 1897–1983

"Of all movements, cultural developments, etc., that were offered to the German people back then, and which I rejected, only the Bauhaus idea completely captivated me and I urgently wished to make contact with the bearer of the message, without realizing that he had the same wish."

Ise Gropius, addendum to diary, 1970s

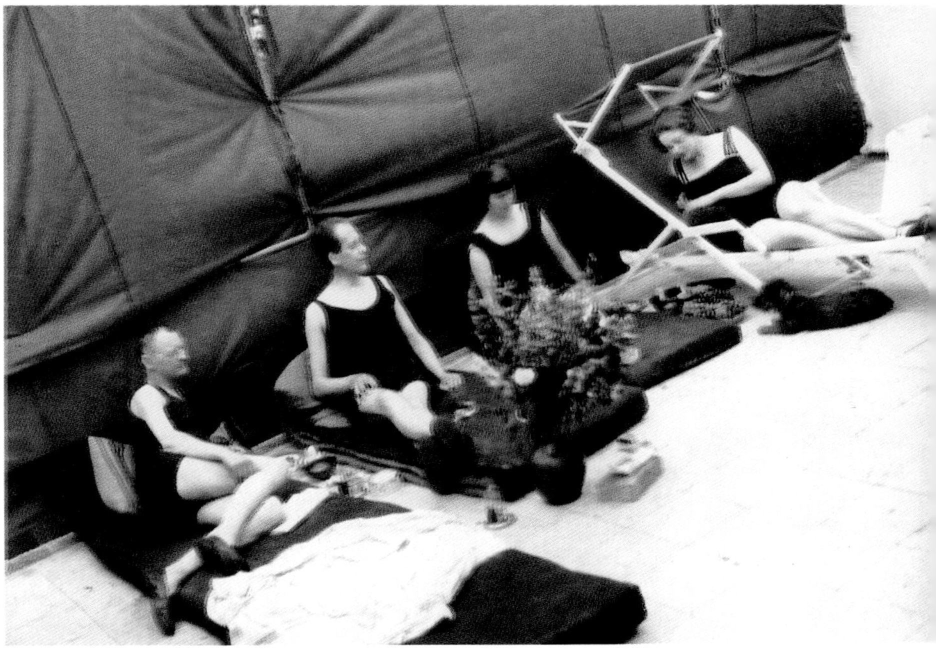

First and foremost Ise Gropius became well known through her dedication to the Bauhaus and to the life's work of her husband, the Bauhaus founder and architect Walter Gropius. From 1924 to 1928, she invested great energy in publicity work, establishing and maintaining contact with the press, sponsors, and supporters of the Bauhaus. "I never entered one of the workshops as my special talent lay more in the realm of literature, which made me a natural employee of my husband" (addendum to diary). In this she clearly developed a high level of journalistic professionalism.

Ise Gropius had also worked as a freelance author and occasionally photographer in the United States and Germany. Following her return from a trip to the United States in 1928, she published a number of articles under her maiden name, Ise Frank: for example, in the magazine *Die Dame*, the gossip column "Wie sieht die New Yorkerin aus?" (How does the New York Woman Look?), and, in *Westermanns* Monatsheften in 1934, a contribution on *Ungarische Hirten- und Bauerntrachten* (Hungarian Shepherd and Peasant Dress).

The texts are reminiscent of reports and features by the Prague journalist, Milena Jesenska, from the early 1920s. With a mixture of incisive, personal observances and entertaining gossip, every-day philosophy and incidental factual information, the imaginary reader is drawn into conversation. She had, in the end, not only experinced something new, but perhaps also almost unnoticed received a little moral instruction. Three of her previously unpublished reports were shown for the first time as part of the exhibition, *Walter Gropius. Amerikareise 1928* (Walter Gropius: American Journey, 1928), which showed at the Bauhaus archive in Berlin and later in Wuppertal until February 2009. Among the reports was *Angst vor Amerika* (Fear of America, 1928): "What is *relaxed*? Relaxed is when a New York traffic policeman smilingly looks into a car in which a tender young couple sits, in the middle of a bustling Manhattan, and says: 'Doesn't look like daddy and daughter!'"

Fittingly for her life as a documentarian, biographical facts about Ise Gropius are scarce, above all about the forty-six years she spent in the United States. She was, nevertheless, not one of those women who became a footnote or completely disappeared having devoted herself to maintaining her man's legacy. In her own way, she belonged to the "New Women" of the 1920s, more because of her progressive attitudes and her modern partnership-style marriage than for artistic endeavor. Ise and Walter Gropius lived and communicated on an equal footing. The thing which connected them, which confirmed their emotional cohesion again and again and at the same time objectivized it was the Bauhaus—as a Utopia and as an active project. To a certain degree, the personal realm was political for her. Added to this was a social way of life, in which love,

• *Facing page: Portrait of Ise Gropius, photograph by Lucia Moholy, 1924.*

• *Above: Walter and Ise Gropius with guests on the roof garden of their master's house, c. 1926–27.*

artistic development and social responsibility had equal place. Both of them were remarkably unpretentious and possessed a rare characteristic which would today be referred to as being "team players."

In the Museum of Modern Art exhibition catalog, *Bauhaus 1919 to 1928* at the Rockerfeller Center (1938) in New York, and in the German edition, Ise Gropius is mentioned alongside Walter Gropius and Herbert Bayer as co-editor; however, the entire work includes only one single photograph of her, in her husband's biography. She is otherwise not mentioned by name. One rich source, however, is the as yet unpublished diary she kept from September 1924 to March 1928. It has, up to now, been used as a source of information on the history of the Bauhaus and Walter Gropius's life. Long passages read as a continuous struggle against hatred from outside but also against increasing egotism on the inside: "9.3.24. Abuse from the *Weimarer Zeitung* regarding the residences for which G. not only spent no state funds but also sacrificed much in private funds. 11.8.26. Young master's entry on great complaints about demotion and very arrogant demands. Its tone is worse than in the Citizens' Association."

The author also discloses details of very unremarkable things about herself, for example, that she often managed to enjoy special moments for herself in the midst of the everyday bustle—a drive in the new car, sunbathing with guests on the roof of the masters' house, a poem by Hölderlin, a dance evening with Gret Palucca, a Bauhaus party. Very personal details are often revealed such as her diplomatic efforts towards her "predecessor," the capricious Alma Mahler.

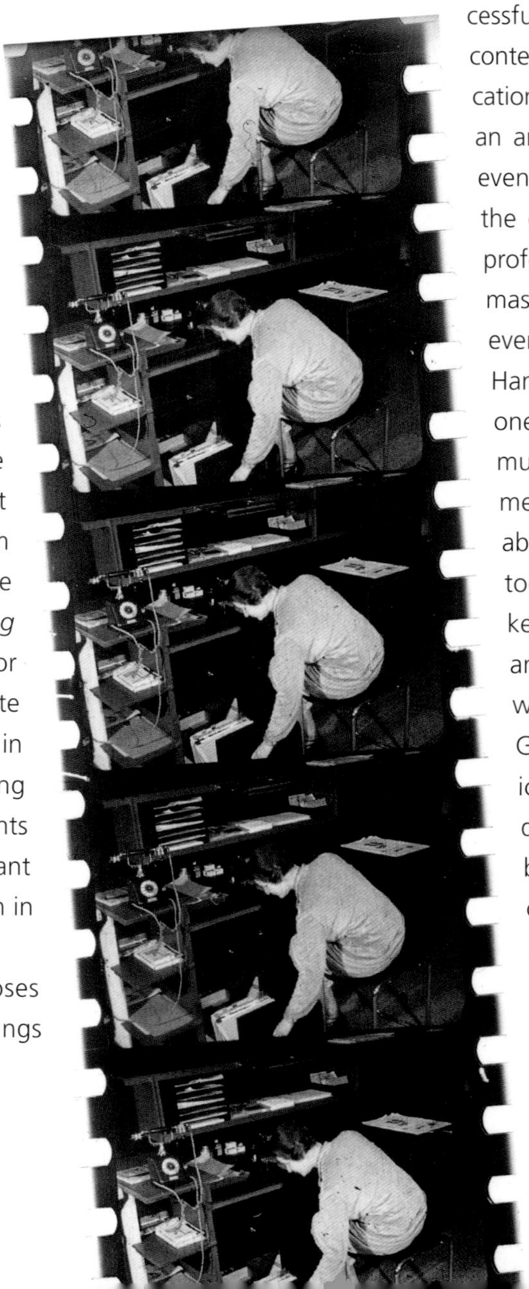

Ise Gropius appeared to have been successful in achieving a balance between contemplative distance and passionate dedication for long periods. Added to this was an anti-bourgeois attitude: "11.21.25. . . . evening lecture from professor spranger in the goethe society. if only these german professors would not show off their schoolmasterly grandeur!" Her criticism does not even stop at the future Bauhaus director Hannes Meyer: "6.23.27. . . . his view that one should not keep a maid . . . is all too much at the cost of the woman, whereas meyer himself would not think twice about having a secretary. . . . in germany today, we are absolutely not prepared to keep a household with children without any assistance, and without the housewife drowning in the everyday." Walter Gropius, who had to deflect much criticism from outside and at times doubted himself, was always defended by her. She shared many of her positive characteristics such as openness and generosity with him. On a few occasions, however, she too lost her composure, and she reached her limits,

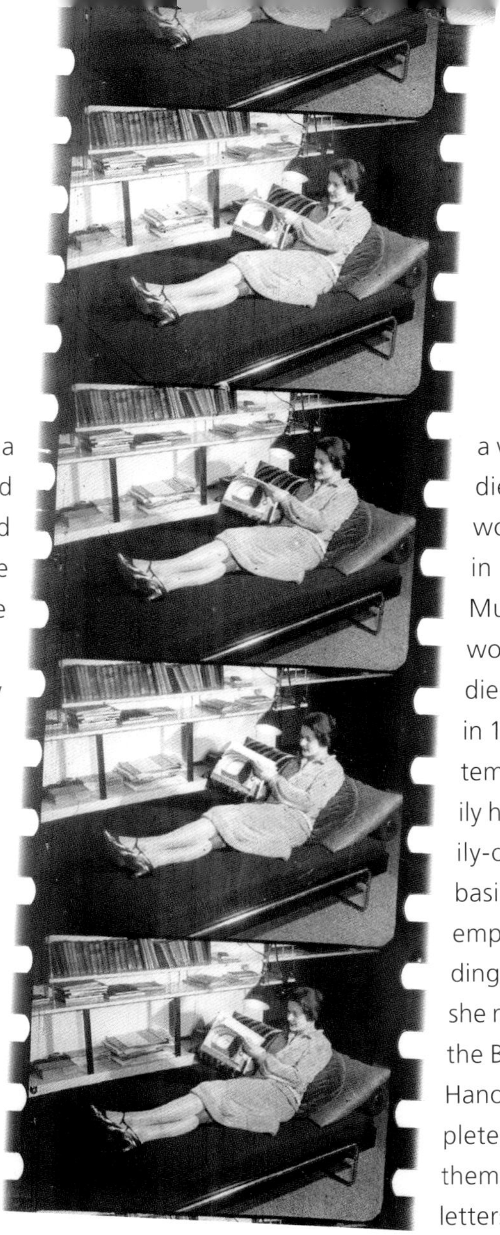

such as when she was annoyed by Nina Kandinsky: "2.19.26. she walks around like a child with a box of matches and causes trouble. . . . her incomprehensible antipathy towards me drives her to the most laughable actions."

Coming originally from a literary background, Ise Gropius developed a deep understanding of design methods, the intellectual concerns, and historical importance of modern art. This is especially reflected in her notes on contemporary music, encounters with artists such as Otto Klemperer, Belá Bartok, or Igor Stravinsky: "11.16.25. morning practise with stravinsky. . . . first the piano concerto! . . . he treats the piano like a percussion instrument and strictly avoids any sentiment. . . . the completely new construction is astonishing and liberating, one feels oneself, our time, our tempo! his pragmatic, rash . . . way, the energetic, lively lack of dogmatism purifies the heart and gives one an unbelievable boost! . . . and yet it became clear how heavy an artist's impact on his own time actually is. . . . this music will be played completely differently in 10 years time! for the present . . . new technology is so absorbing that nothing can predominate."

Following Walter Gropius's death in 1969, Ise Gropius wrote personal addenda to her diaries, from which we can extract some details of her life story.

Born on March 1, 1897, in Wiesbaden, she was the eldest of four sisters and grew up in Hanover. She was a Red Cross nurse in the war years 1917–18, and headed a ward with sick and wounded soldiers. From 1919 to 1921 she worked in a progressive bookshop in Hanover before moving to Munich in 1921, where she also worked in a bookshop. Her father died the same year, and her mother in 1923. She moved back to Hanover temporarily. The sisters sold the family home, and earnings from the family-owned ironworks secured their basic income. Ise Frank's fiancé was employed at the ironworks. A wedding was already being planned when she met Walter Gropius at a lecture on the Bauhaus at the Landesmuseum in Hanover in May 1923. This event completely shook her. It was true love for them both. She wrote one of her first letters to him: "I don't believe I belong to those people who wish to be supported and upheld by you, but I wish with all my heart that you involve me, keep me." Walter Gropius's marriage to Alma Mahler had ended in 1920, but Ise found herself in a tortuous situation. After difficult inner struggles she was able to write to Walter in July 1923: "Hermann and I have separated. I had to decide in your favor." He replied on July 15, 1923: "I have no feelings of guilt and neither should you. The simplicity of your being moves me. Your lack of cant and sense of truth. . . . A garden full of tenderness awaits you. . . . My great work is now saved through you." The fact that she feared she was unworthy of the demands made of her as the wife of the Bauhaus director, delayed her decision. She moved to Weimar, the wedding took place on

• *Facing page: Stills from the silent film,* Haus Gropius *from the series* How to Live Healthily and Economically. *Ise Gropius demonstrates the desk by Marcel Breuer, Humboldt-Film GmbH Berlin, 1928.*

• *Above: Stills. Ise Gropius demonstrates the collapsible sofa, 1928.*

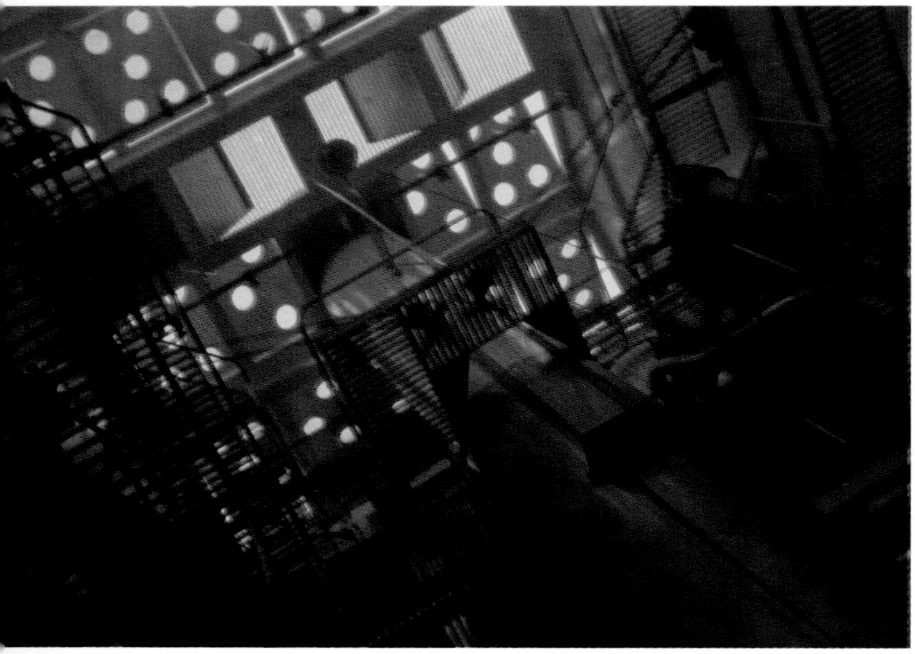

October 16, 1923, and the couple honeymooned secretly in Venice.

While Walter Gropius stood in the spotlight as an educational, artistic, and ideological innovator grappling with politicians, citizens, and press agitation, Ise Gropius stood behind him and the Bauhaus as an unflagging advertising strategist. She also led the Circle of Friends of the Bauhaus for which she organized events. Added to this was her "relationship work" as hostess and in dealing with the other masters' wives and the masters themselves. She undertook yet another task in Dessau: leading tours of prominent guests through Gropius's new buildings in Dessau, and even through her own living quarters. The silent documentary film *Haus Gropius* was made in the Gropius's home at the end of 1926 by the Berliner Humboldt-Film GmbH as part of the series *Wie wohnen wir gesund und wirtschaftlich*. The film sees Ise Gropius, posing as a modern woman and master's wife, at her desk, in the living room, and in the kitchen—and as a result she developed serious eye problems from the artificial lights. She had been subjected to a totally different type of endurance test one year previously. In the fall of 1925, it was discovered that she was unable to have children due to complications after a previously mistreated appendicitis. Her relationship with Walter Gropius was clearly strong enough to withstand such a fundamental disappointment.

Her trip to the United States after Walter Gropius's departure from the Bauhaus in March 1928 was doubtless a highlight. The seven-week tour for architectural research was largely financed by Gropius's benefactor Adolf Sommerfeld. Accompanied by Sommerfeld's wife Renée, the tour was a subject of specialist and public interest from the outset. Structural engineering essays by Walter, reports by Ise Gropius and photographs taken by both of them, chiefly devoted to modern American architecture, were published or offered for publication.

Of the almost four hundred photos taken of the Brooklyn Bridge in New York, Native Americans in the Grand Canyon, and the construction of a grain silo in Chicago, only a few can be attributed to either Walter or Ise specifically. A selection was first publicly shown in the exhibition *Walter Gropius. Amerikareise 1928*. Only the *Maschinenraum der Columbus* taken by Ise Gropius had previously been published a number of times, in 1930 in the *Münchner Illustrierte Presse* and more than half a century later in the exhibition *Fotografie am Bauhaus* in Berlin (1990) and *Abstrakte Fotografie* in Bielefeld (2000). Isa Gropius was not a professional photographer but this picture demonstrates that she could not only handle a camera competently, but also understood photographic design under the perspective of the New Vision. In choosing the ship's machinery she had consciously used a modern technical image, on whose functional construction from basic geometric forms she confers an autonomous constructivist life,

• *Ise Gropius, View of the engine room on the North German Lloyd ship,* Columbus *(Voyage to New York), 1928.*

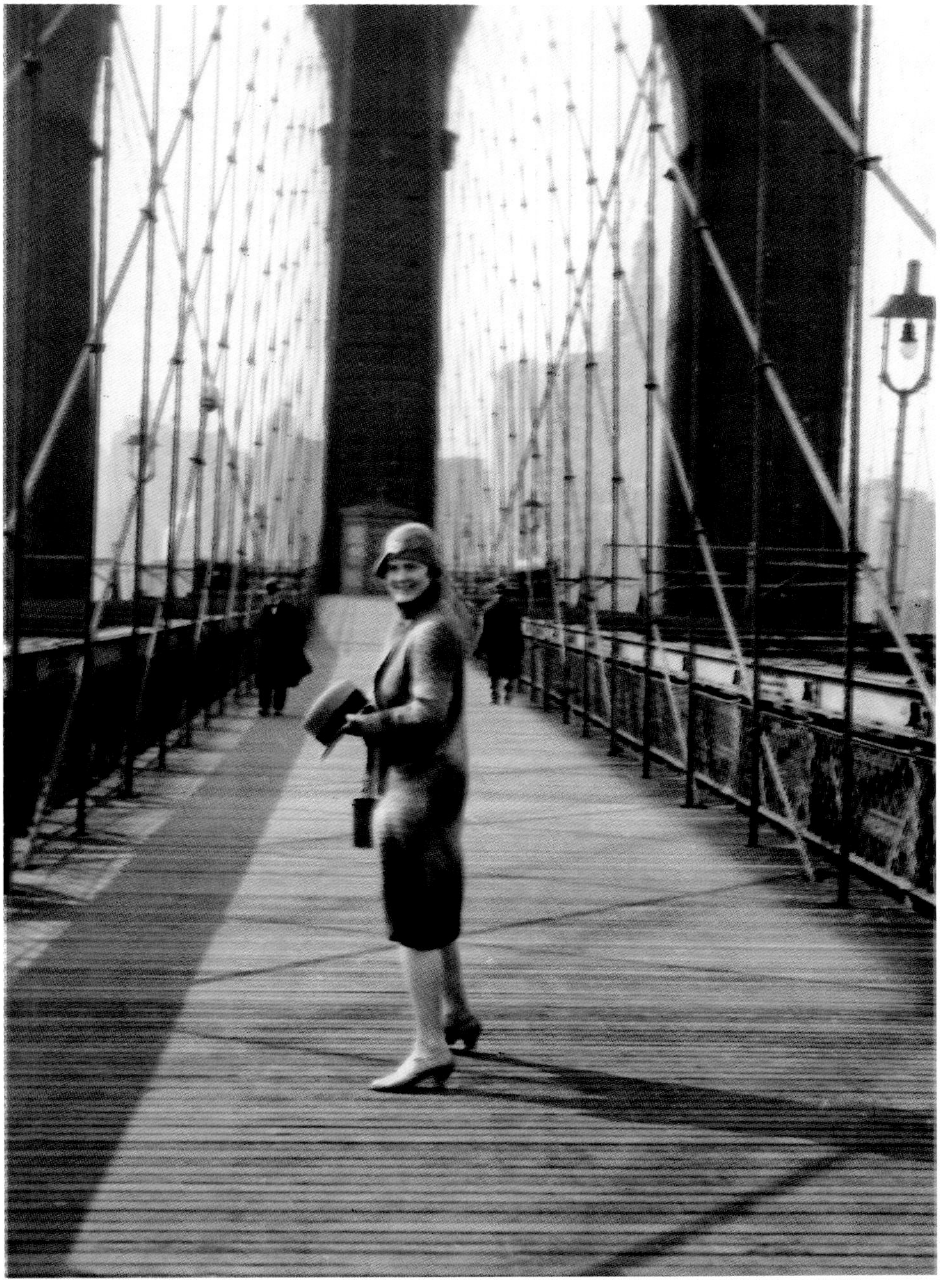

with the help of a tight crop and an extremely slanted perspective, so that it is extracted from the spatial structure and becomes abstracted from reality.

After the Bauhaus period in Weimar and Dessau, and the seven-week tour of the United States in 1928, Ise and Walter Gropius lived in Berlin until 1934, where Ise also worked in the architecture office. Both spent the years from 1934 to 1937 in exile in London. From there, they finally emigrated to the United States and settled in Massachusetts. Walter Gropius became Head of the Architecture Department of the Graduate School of Design at Harvard University in 1938 and built a new house for himself and Ise in Lincoln. After World War II, they re-established contact with former Bauhaus members who were by then scattered all over the world and had survived war and persecution. They set up cross-border communication, which over the following decades made possible many meetings, exhibitions, and publications.

Ise Gropius died on June 9, 1983, in Lexington, Massachusetts. It is indisputable that her work contributed to keeping the importance of the historic Bauhaus and its innovative, socio-critical potential alive, and to reinscribing it in our cultural memory today. She had already warned in her diary of March 19, 1925: "If it should succeed that the Bauhaus is finally brought to its knees, all hope for Germany's artistic future will be lost. Then this will have shown that reactionary ideas have won, and will define all things in times to come."

ULRIKE MÜLLER

• *Walter Gropius, Ise Gropius on the Brooklyn Bridge, New York, 1928.*

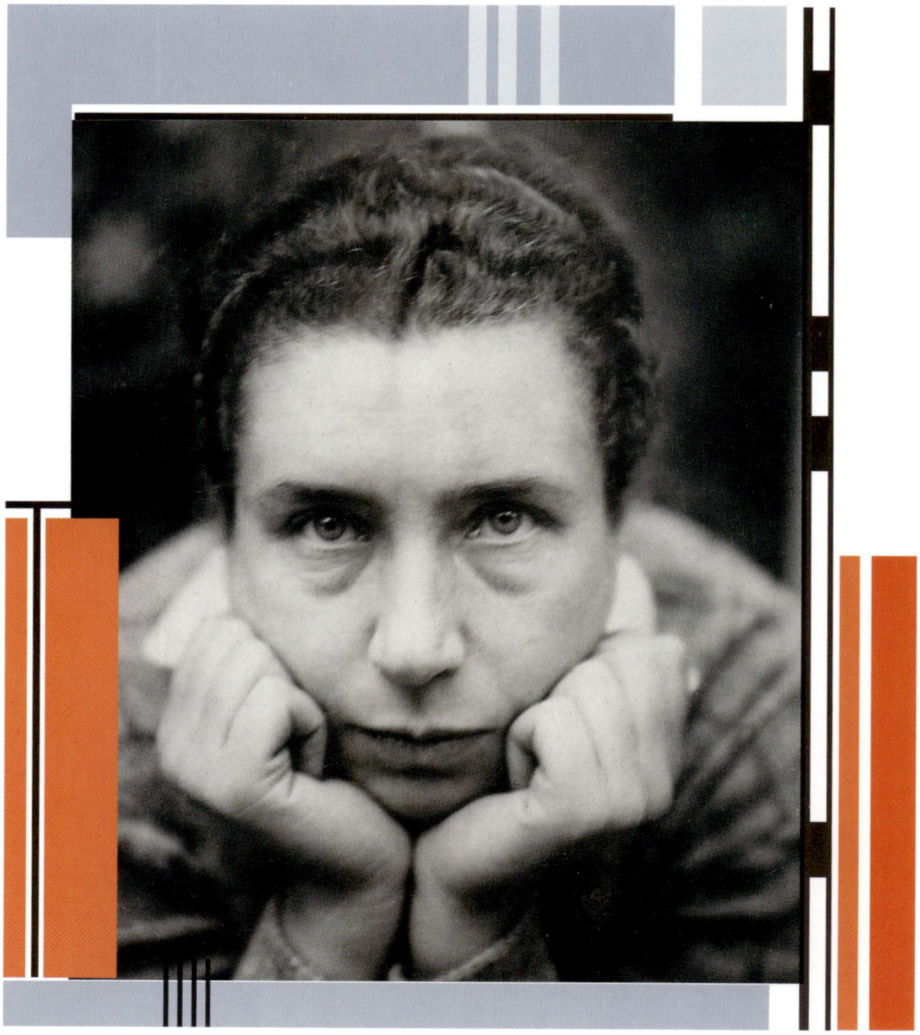

LUCIA MOHOLY 1894–1989

"Photography is a priori *no more art than any other techniques. Someone who paints, draws, etches, or takes photographs must not necessarily be an artist. Technique and tools do not define art, but the person, if he has the talent to create art with these things."*

Lucia Moholy in a radio broadcast, 1958

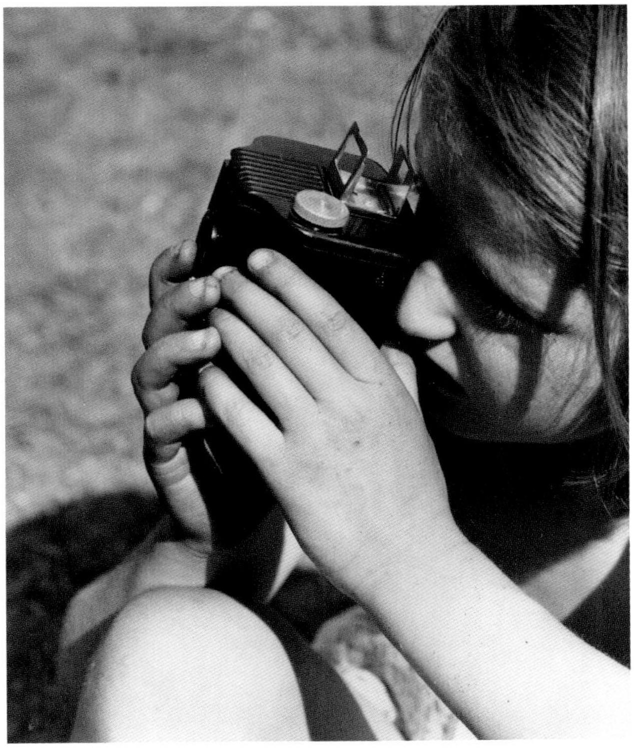

She wanted to observe closely, examine ideas, people, art, capture them in the moment of their importance, not for eternity. "A story-teller with the camera," is how Lucia Moholy was described in a press article. She worked as an editor, copy editor, photographer, documentarian, art critic, and educator. She systematically photographed works, buildings, and personalities at the Bauhaus between 1923 and 1928, and so became the school's "house photographer." Even today, a portrayal of Bauhaus history would be unthinkable without her photographs. When the National Socialists came to power, Lucia Moholy emigrated to London and became a British citizen in 1940. From 1949 to 1956, she worked as a specialist for microfilm documentation of cultural assets for the World Health Organization and UNESCO and built up archives in Iran, Iraq, and Turkey. She gave lectures and published essays about the avant-garde of early modernism, about photography and microfilm, as well as on methodology and possibilities in scientific documentation. She then lived as a freelance journalist in Zurich from 1959. Her photographs have been shown in numerous exhibitions and works on the Bauhaus. She maintained contact with many former Bauhaus members and worked alongside the rediscovery of the school through written contributions which anticipated some of the criticism of the Bauhaus directorship from today's standpoint. For example, she objected to the (self-inflicted) overestimation of the Bauhaus through a mythologizing and ahistorical viewpoint.

Lucia Moholy is viewed as a representative of the New Objectivity, the direction in early modernist photography which developed from a criticism of the experiments of the New Vision. Her objective was to capture her subject, whether person or object, as close to reality as possible, using photographic technique, and to retain this precisely, in the picture, making its form, structure, and mentality—its actual being—visible without subjecting it to spontaneous ideas of form or artificial self-representation. Empathy and reservation, engagement and distance belonged to her work in equal measure. She wrote in the biographical fragment *Frau des 20. Jahrhunderts*: "I believe that I can say with a clear conscience, that if common ambition played any role for me back then, it was a negligible one, my interest was the subject itself. I was deeply involved in it and was suitably critical of it." She is characterized as quiet and discreet but not as a cool intellectual. "Je suis de mon temps"—she quotes this sentence by Honoré Daumier on the title page of her 1939 book on the cultural history of photography. Even in her early diaries her eye for the precisely recorded fact (on May 11, 1907 she wrote: "Grandmother brought Papa three pairs of gloves"), and her empathy and passionate feelings are apparent. The sixteen-year-old records her desires in verse form: "I often believe that I love with hot embers, and sense my happiness, but soon still again, my passion

• *Facing page: Lucia Moholy,* Self-Portrait, *1930.*

• *Above: Lucia Moholy,* Fotografierendes Mädchen *(Girl Taking a Photograph), c. 1929/30.*

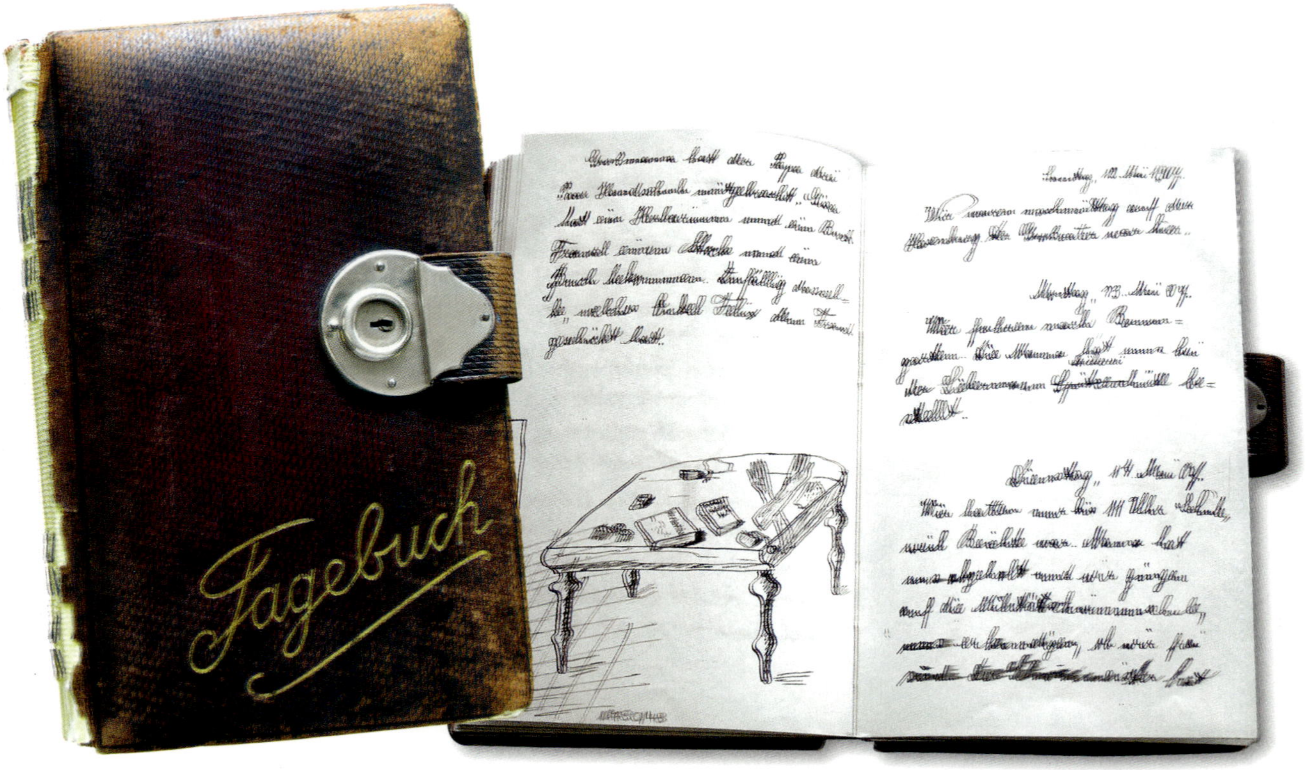

stands, and looks back (December 20, 1910). In later years she portrays climatic impressions of trips (April 12, 1927) as representations of inner moods which recall Rahel Varnhagen's *Wetternotizen*. She was enthusiastic about youth movements and Communism and published poems in the Expressionist style under the pseudonym of "Ulrich Steffen." She paid for a newspaper advert with her first money, in which she applied for a job in order to finally escape her parents' house in Prague. By now, she knew that she wanted to become a photographer. She noted on February 3, 1915, under the heading, *My First Flight into the World* in her diary: "The interest in photography awoke in me. I am a passive artist. I can capture impressions and would surely be able to record everything from its most beautiful perspective, put them through the chemical processes I have learnt and allow them then to appear how they affect me. I am not creative, not productive in myself, but do have a very fine absorption capacity and receptiveness."

We next see Lucia Moholy as a young woman in a work and love relationship in Berlin at the beginning of the 1920s. She filled the traditionally male role of intellectual mentor to a young artist, who possessed nothing but his disorganized, bubbling creativity. According to this role reversal, Lucia earned for both of them. In contrast to him, she had completed her vocational training and had already gained work experience. Fascinated by his creative strength, animated by common ideals, she shared her language, her ideas, her knowledge and her apartment with this young man whose name was László Moholy-Nagy. The couple married in 1921 and Lucia became a Hungarian citizen. Moholy said to his second wife, Sibyl, of Lucia: "Her intellect was like a beacon which lit up my emotional chaos. She taught me to think" (Sibyl Moholy, 1972).

After World War II we experience another Lucia Moholy, one who battled for decades so that her achievements, which she brought to the "symbiotic working group", as she referred to it, with the Bauhaus master Moholy-Nagy, be named and recognized as such. "Omission is symptomatic of the reception of the cooperation between László and Lucia Moholy-Nagy," writes Mercedes Valdevieso in her critical study of the artistic

• *Lucia Moholy, Diary pages from August 11–12, 1910.*

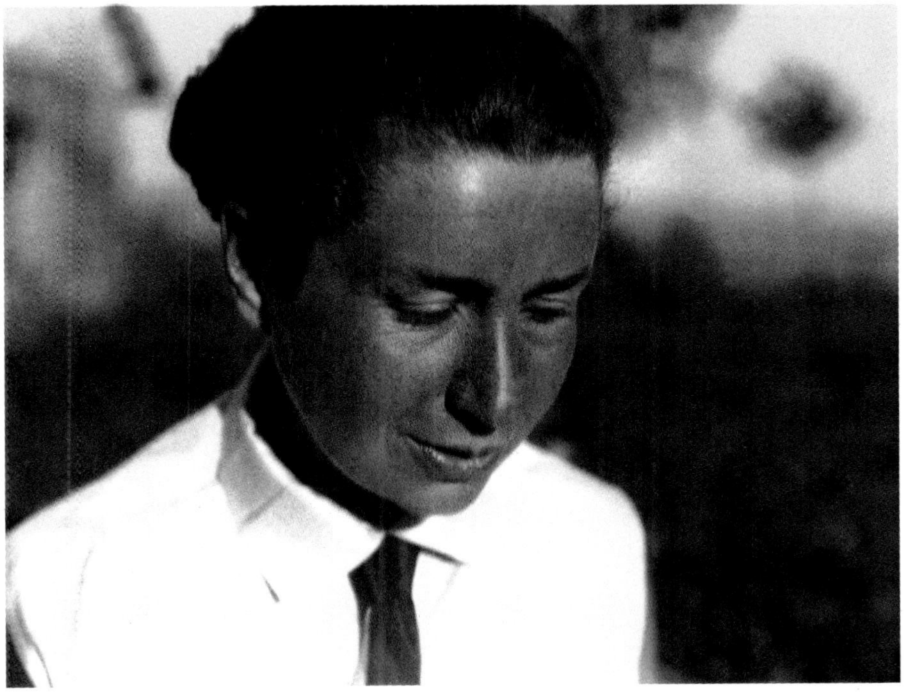

cooperation with Lucia Moholy is in the foreword to the Bauhaus book *Vom Material zur Architektur* (1929): "The manuscript and corrections in this book were resolved and enriched in many ways in thought and formulation by my wife Lucia Moholy."

But to return to the biographical beginnings: Lucia Schulz was born in 1894 in Karolinental, a suburb of Prague, which then belonged to Austria. Her Jewish background played no decisive role in her life until the confrontation with National Socialism: her wealthy parental home was socialist and atheist. As her mother was of German descent, Lucia and her siblings Franz and Gera grew up bilingual and they also learnt French. Lucia graduated after high school in 1910. She studied English, philosophy, and art history at the *k.u.k. Frauenbildungsanstalt* in Prague, graduating with the state examination in 1912. She read philosophy and art history at the University of Prague and helped her father in his law office in order to earn some money. In 1915 she became head of the editorial office of the *Wiesbadener Zeitung* before going to Leipzig in 1917 to work for Kurt Wulff at Hyperion Publishing, where she was responsible for "all stages of production to binding" according to her own account. She spent the summers of 1918 and 1919 at Heinrich Vogeler's Barkenhof in Worpswede, together with Adolf Danath, a leading communist from Bremen. She took her first photographs there. In 1920 she took up a position at the Ernst Rowohlt publishing house in Berlin.

When László Moholy-Nagy was called by Walter Gropius to become a master at the Bauhaus, Lucia

couple (2000). Together they had developed the photogram technique in the fall of 1922, and because the first experiments were one of a kind, Lucia Moholy photographed them for possible publication. However, all the photograms later became famous as the exclusive work of her husband. The book, which they both penned in 1925, *Malerei, Fotografie, Film* appeared under his name. There is a collection of index cards in the Bauhaus Archive in Berlin, on which Lucia Moholy noted by whom, in which work, her photographs were used without authorization and without mentioning her name, and in which texts her work was falsely represented. One senses how she attempted to control this permanent insult—added to concrete loss of earnings—through scientific, objectifying work. The index of errors forms the basis of her work, *Marginalien zu Moholy-Nagy. Dokumentarische Ungereimtheiten*. Here she writes that she was responsible for editing a total of fourteen of the Bauhaus books published by Gropius and Moholy-Nagy. This was not acknowledged in any of these works. Consequently, it was not considered necessary to ask for her consent for the reprints made after the war. Moholy-Nagy's only printed reference to his

• *László Moholy-Nagy*, Portrait of Lucia Moholy, *right, c. 1932.*

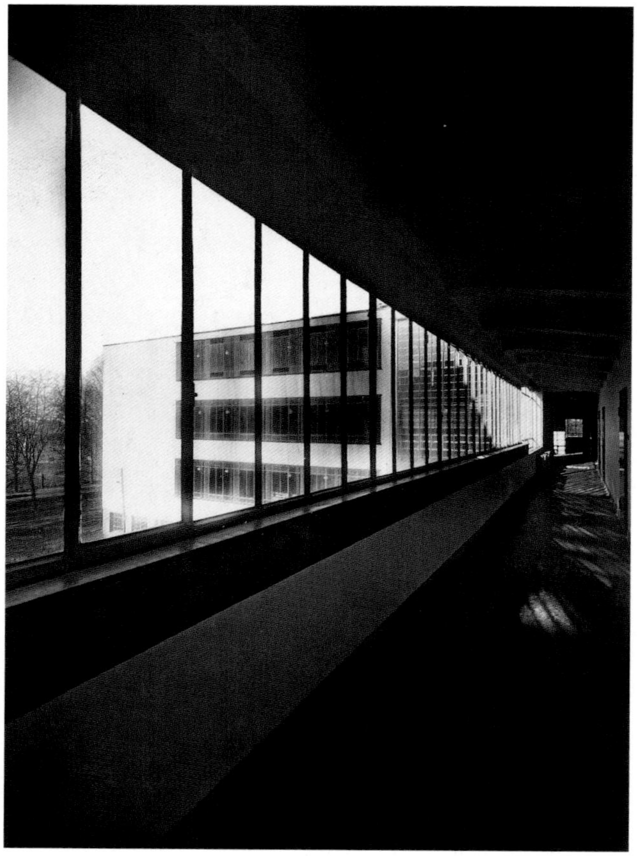

reluctantly followed him to Weimar—she would have preferred to stay in the big city.

While her husband pursued Josef Itten's preliminary course and expanded the metal workshop, she became apprenticed to the professional photographer Otto Eckner, and one year later took courses in reproduction photography at the Leipzig Academy for Graphic and Book Arts. She made her photographic accomplishments and publishing experience available to the Bauhaus without ever being officially employed there. During her Leipzig training period of 1924–25 she had recorded the works produced in the preliminary course and workshops for publications and sample books, which the Bauhaus used to acquire sponsors and advertise to potential contracting industries. For all her Bauhaus photographs she used an 8 x 10 in. (18 x 24 cm) format baseboard camera made of wood and glass plates, typical for reproductions at that time. She transferred the dispassion in her photography of objects to her shots of people. This changed after she began to use a Leica, following its introduction at the Leipzig Spring Show of 1925. She was freer in her portraits which were not for Bauhaus documentation. Here she no longer photographed heads strictly from the side but diagonally from beneath so that they came across as sensitive psychological studies. As Sabine Hartmann, photo-archivist at the Bauhaus Archive in Berlin remarks in the exhibition catalog on Lucia Moholy (1995), Moholy's vintage prints differ greatly from the prints which are made from the same negatives for publication today (modern prints). The vintage prints are less objective and exact, but are remarkable in their strong light/dark contrasts, which have an alienating effect because they "make the pictures look very graphic and also demonize them." Lucia Moholy also frequently retouched her negatives, using a retouching paint for lines and surfaces and changing the negative layer, mostly in order to achieve darkening effects. For all her objectivity, she did allow herself, if only in a limited way, the use of photographic scope, so long as the expression of the subject could be intensified by it. Thus Lucia Moholy showed herself to be a less dogmatic representative of the New Objectivity than Walter Peterhans or Grete Stern, who rejected any manipulation of the negative.

After the Bauhaus moved to Dessau, Lucia Moholy documented the new buildings in numerous photographs in the late fall of 1926. She also carried out all the darkroom work. Ise Gropius reported in her diary: "the requests are multiplying. we cannot produce enough photographs. frau moholy is overworked and works day and night to meet the demand of photos on order" (November 26, 1926). The objectivity in Lucia Moholy's prints corresponded to the objectivity of the new architecture. Every building is shown frontally or

• *Lucia Moholy, The Bauhaus, Dessau, 1926.*

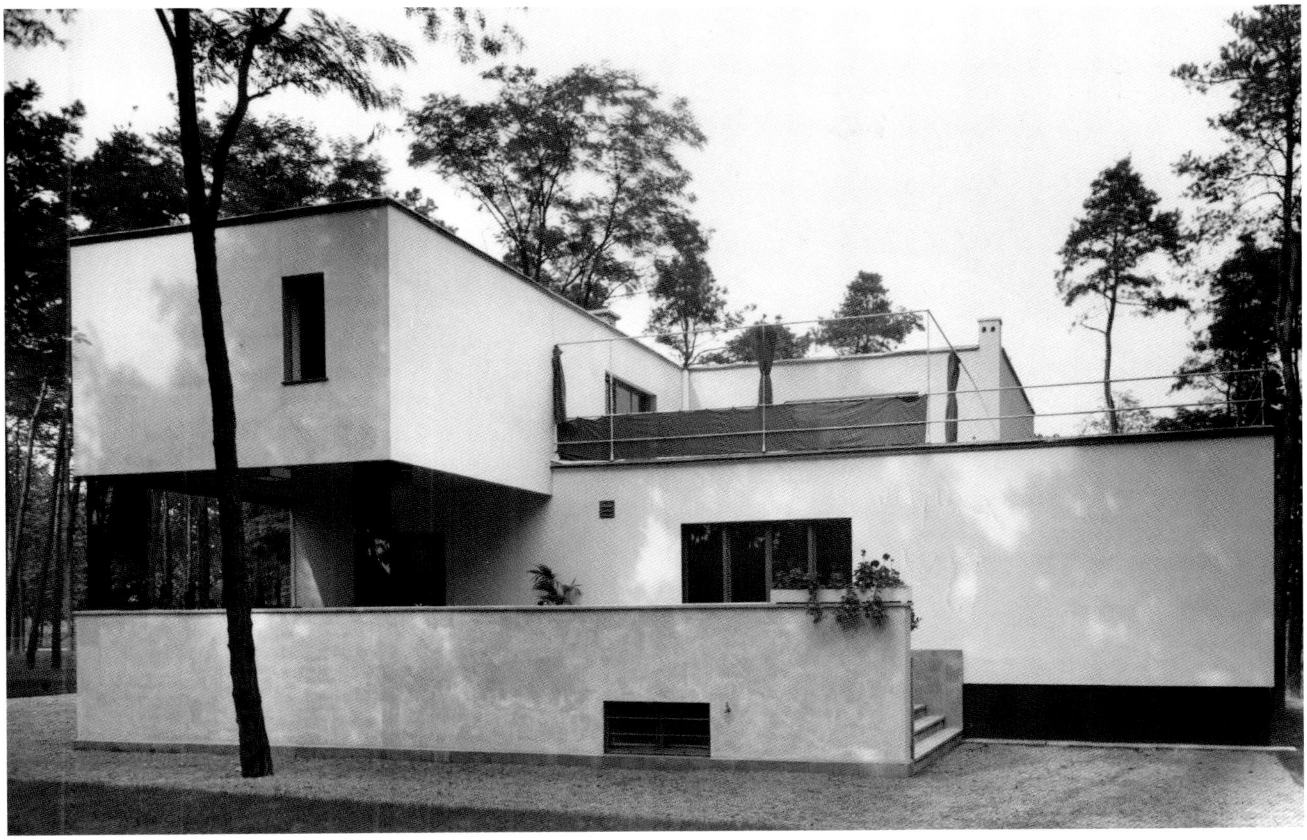

from an angle of 45 degrees at most, mainly in diffused light, and only at times are parts emphasized by penetrating rays of sunlight. The surrounding environment is included where possible.

"Dessau is like a place where one has missed one's connection and has to wait for the next train," noted Lucia Moholy on May 5, 1927, in her diary. She could not stand being there any longer and wanted to return to Berlin. She missed the intellectual and artistic stimulations of the city. In 1928 Lucia and László left the Bauhaus and went to Berlin. They separated a year later and divorce followed in 1934. László had become famous in the meantime and no longer required a mentor. Lucia had gone her own way artistically and was gradually becoming well-known. She had her own photographic studio for portraits, architecture, advertising and arts, worked with the photographic agency, Mauritius, and gave photography courses. In 1929 she took part in the Werkbund's exhibition *Film und Photo*, in Stuttgart and lived with the Berlin Communist assembly member Theodor Neubauer. Neubauer put her in contact with Clara Zetkin, whom she photographed. In 1929, she also became successor to the former Bauhaus member, Umbo, as head of the photography class at Josef Itten's private Berlin art school.

In August 1933, Theodor Neubauer, by now involved in resistance against the Nazis, was arrested in their apartment and taken to a concentration camp. Lucia Moholy managed to flee to Paris via Prague and Vienna. She was forced to leave behind her photo archive, comprising 560 glass negatives, so she entrusted it to the Gropiuses, who emigrated to London in 1934 and fled to the United States in 1937. After Moholy had tried in vain from Paris to help Neubauer using the press, she traveled to London in 1934. In exile in London, she photographed prominent people, gave lectures on the Bauhaus at the Central School of Arts and Design and taught photography at the London School of Painting and Graphic Art (1935). In 1939 her work *One Hundred Years of Photography*, in which, as

• *Lucia Moholy, Masters' Houses Dessau, the Gropius House from the southeast, 1926.*

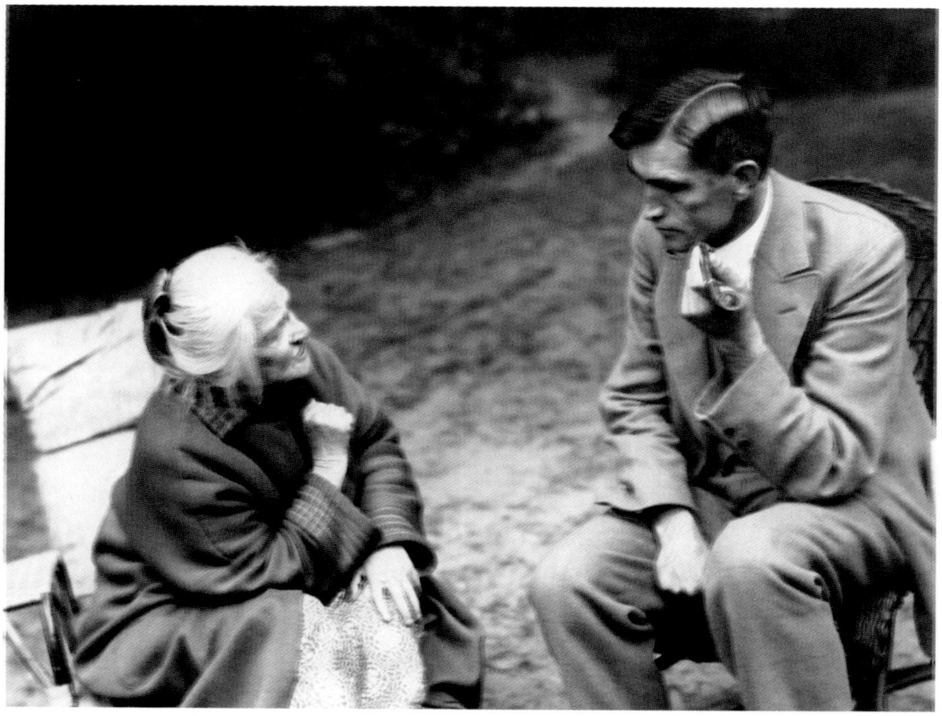

she formulated, she wished to describe "the development of photography from its beginnings as a form of magic art to the status of a world power" was published in an edition of forty thousand.

Despite positive reviews, the book was not reprinted after the war. In 1942 she was given responsibility for the microfilm project, *Association of Special Libraries and Information Bureaux*. Nevertheless, her situation became more and more dismal. The Quaker community helped her in a time of most abject poverty. She made intensive efforts to travel to the United States. Moholy-Nagy, who had been head of the School of Design in Chicago since 1937, tried to help her acquire the necessary visa by inviting her to teach photography. His efforts were in vain.

At the end of the war Lucia Moholy was confronted with two terribly painful losses. Neubauer was murdered by the Nazis in 1945. The core of her work, her negatives, was also lost. The history of Lucia Moholy's photo archive is the stuff of detective novels, and has been shrouded in secrecy up to this day, as so often happens when legacies are to be rescued. Lucia Moholy hoped at first that she would be able to get her negatives back and therefore remained discreet. It was not until her article "The Missing Negatives appeared" in *The British Journal of Photography*, that she voiced her suspicion that the negatives had been deliberately distributed among the Bauhaus masters in order to build their new careers in exile. After the first unauthorized reproductions of her pictures had turned up in the United States during the war, Lucia Moholy began a vehement dispute with Gropius in the 1950s. Ise Gropius sharply rejected the accusations in a letter written on March 4, 1954: Lucia Moholy had never made an agreement to have her pictures returned, back in Germany, but made only "vague arrangements"; "we never knew you wanted them." An accusation of egotism followed, the Bauhaus community, Bauhaus honor, were questioned under oath and in the end fifty negatives from the Busch-Reisinger-Museum were handed over as compensation. One fine day in 1957, they sat safely in a box on Lucia Moholy's doorstep in London. Again, smaller numbers of negatives were bought back from secret sources over the following years. The largest portion, however, remained out of her reach during her lifetime. The Bauhaus Archive in Berlin had access to 230 negatives from the old inventory, alongside from five hundred newer ones, for its Lucia Moholy exhibition in 1995. The treasure of Lucia Moholy's photographs taken for UNESCO, however, still sits untouched in those archives.

The art historian, Rolf Sachsse, who published the first Lucia Moholy biography in 1985, is owed a debt of thanks that she could experience the beginnings of

• *Lucia Moholy, Clara Zetkin and Theodor Neubauer, c. 1930.*

recognition as an independent artist when she was ninety years old. Sachsse clearly understood the difficulties for such a woman as Lucia Moholy, who was married to a famous man, to receive artistic recognition in her own right: "The patriarchal structures are overwhelming in this area." With increasing age, Lucia Moholy herself perceived her negative experience more and more clearly in the context of her social disadvantage as a woman. She fought to be given a professorship, and she battled doggedly for compensation as a victim of Nazi oppression, and time and again for the rights to her pictures. However, at the end of her life, she was not bitter, but reconciled. Visitors remember her joviality and inimitable wit. The Swiss journalist Gislind Nabakowski reported in 1985 in an article, that this over ninety-year-old woman always asked everyone she met: "And what are your plans?" In the end, Lucia Moholy confirmed her own perception of the Bauhaus which she formulated in an article, "Der Bauhausgedanke," for the magazine *Blick in die Welt* in 1948: "Bauhaus is not 'style.' Not a determined scheme, but an expression derived from knowledge of material, form, function, color, etc., which steadfastly develops in time and with time."

ULRIKE MÜLLER, SANDRA KEMKER

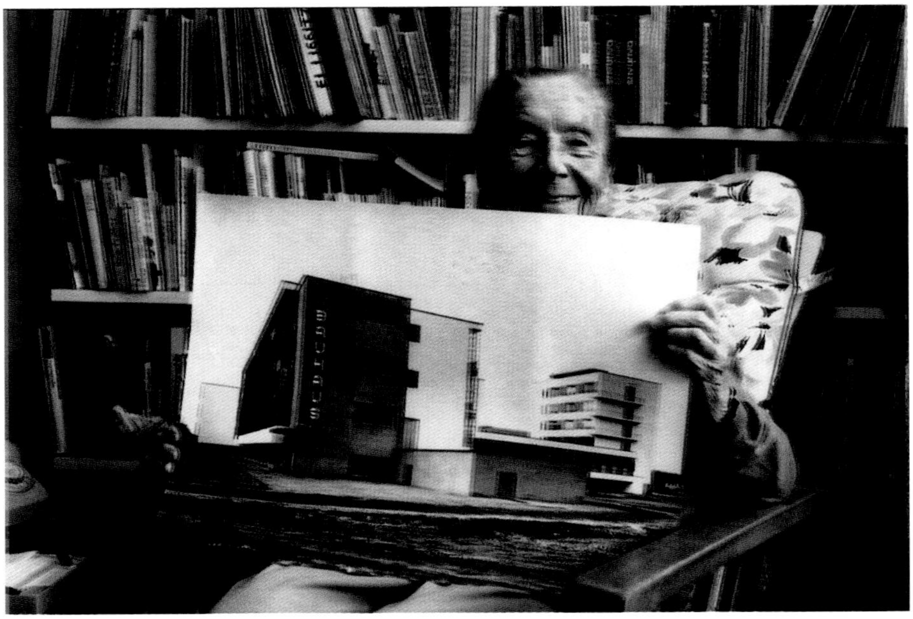

• *Lucia Moholy, photograph by Michael von Graffenried, 1987.*

Bibliography

Albers, Anni. "Die Werkstatt für Weberei." In Gropius, Ise, Walter Gropius, and Herbert Bayer, eds. *Bauhaus 1919–1928*. New York: Museum of Modern Art, 1938.

Albers, Josef, and Anni Albers. *Europa und Amerika*. Cologne, 1998.

ARGE Architektinnen und Ingenieurkonsulentinnen, ed. *Frauen in der Technik von 1900 bis 2000*. Exh. cat. Vienna, 1999.

Bauhaus Archive Darmstadt, ed. *Friedl Dicker – Franz Singer*. Exh. cat. Foreword by Hans M. Wingler. Darmstadt, 1970.

Baumhoff, Anja. "Women at the Bauhaus: a Myth of Emancipation." In Fiedler, Jeannine, and Peter Feierabend, eds. *Bauhaus*. H. F. Ullmann, 2008.

Berger, Renate. *Malerinnen auf dem Weg ins 20. Jahrhundert. Kunstgeschichte als Sozialgeschichte*. Cologne, 1986.

Deutschbein-Oberdieck, Eva. *Erinnerungen "einer alten Dame" an Dornburg*. Bauhaus Archive Berlin, 1966.

Dietzsch and Folke. *Die Studierenden des Bauhauses*. Dissertation. Weimar, 1990.

Dittmar, Monika, and Ursula Hudson-Wiedenmann. *Haël-Keramik – wenig bekannt, bei Sammlern hoch geschätzt*. Exh. cat. Velten: Ofen- und Keramikmuseum, 2006.

Driesch-Foucar, Lydia. "Erinnerungen an die Anfänge der Dornburger Töpferwerkstatt des Staatlichen Bauhauses Weimar 1920–1923." In Weber, Klaus, ed. *Keramik und Bauhaus. Geschichte und Wirkungen der keramischen Werkstatt des Bauhauses*. Berlin, 1988.

Droste, Magdalena. "Beruf Kunstgewerblerin. Frauen in Kunsthandwerk und Design 1890–1933." In *Frauen im Design*. Vol. 1. Stuttgart / Kornwestheim: Landesgewerbeamt Baden-Württemberg, 1989.

———. *Bauhaus 1919–1933*. New York: Taschen, 1998.

Droste, Magdalena, and Manfred Ludewig, eds. *Das Bauhaus webt. Die Textilwerkstatt am Bauhaus*. (Exh. cat.) Berlin, 1998.

Fell, Karolina. "In bester Form. Wie Grete Heymann-Loebenstein in Marwitz aus Keramik Kunst machte." In *Märkische Allgemeine Zeitung* (2006).

Fiedler, Jeannine, ed. *Photography at the Bauhaus*. Cambridge, MA: MIT Press, 1990.

Fleischmann, Anneliese. "bauhausweberei." *Junge Menschen* vol. 5, 8 (1924).

———. "wohnökonomie." *Neue Frauenkleidung und Frauenkultur* 1 (1924).

———. *On Designing*. Middletown, 1959/1971.

———. *On Weaving*. Middletown, 1965/1979.

Frank, Ise. "Wie sieht die New Yorkerin aus?" *Die Dame* 4 (November 1928).

———. "Ungarische Hirten- und Bauerntrachten." *Westermanns Monatshefte* 79 (1934–35).

———. "Wer hat Angst vor Amerika." Breuer, Gerda, and AnneMarie Jaeggi, eds. *Walter Gropius, Amerikareise /American Journey 1928*. Wuppertal, 2008.

Friedlaender, Marguerite. *The Invisible Core: A Potters Life and Thoughts*. Paolo Alto, 1973.

———. *Ein Leben für die Keramik*. Berlin, 1989.

Galerie Bernd Dürr. *ilse fehling. bauhaus bühne akt skulptur*. Exh. cat. Munich, 1990.

Galleria del Levante. *Junge Maler am Bauhaus*. Munich, 1979.

Grunow, Gertrud. "Der Aufbau der lebendigen Form durch Farbe, Form, Ton." In *Staatliches Bauhaus 1919–1923*. Weimar / Munich, 1923. Reprint, 1980.

Grunow, Gertrud, and Achim Preiß. *Der Gleichgewichtskreis – ein Bauhausdokument*. Weimar: Verlag und Datenbank für Geisteswissenschaften, 2001.

Günther, Sonja. *Lilly Reich 1885–1947: Innenarchitektin, Designerin, Ausstellungsgestalterin*. Stuttgart, 1988.

Hahn, Peter. *Bauhaus Furniture: A Legend*. Berlin: Bauhaus Archive, 2002.

———. "Zeichenunterricht in Theresienstadt." *Weimar Kultur Journal* 12 (2003).

Hahn, Peter, ed. *Experiment Bauhaus*. Berlin: Bauhaus Archive, 1988.

Häselbarth, Renate. *Anni Albers*. Weimar, 2002.

Heitmeyer, Hildegard. "Ordnung durch Farbe und Klang. Gertrud Grunows Lehre einer körperlich-geistigen Erziehung" *Die Tat. Monatschrift für die Zukunft deutscher Kultur* (March 1920).

Hudson-Wiedenmann, Ursula. "Von den Haël-Werkstätten zur Greta Pottery. Margarete Heymann-Marks." In Jürgs, Britta. *Vom Salzstreuer zum Automobil. Designerinnen*. Berlin, 2002.

———. "Ein fairer Preis? Zur Vorgeschichte der HB-Werkstätten in Marwitz – eine Erwiderung." *Märkische Allgemeine Zeitung* (2007).

Kemker, Sandra. *Die Rolle der Frau am Bauhaus am Beispiel der Fotografinnen Lucia Moholy und Marianne Brandt*. Dissertation. Bremen, 2004.

Kunst und Kunstgewerbe 7 (1927).

Landesgewerbeamt Baden-Württemberg, ed. *Frauen im Design*. Vol. 1. Stuttgart / Kornwestheim, 1989.

Lerch, Antonia. "Porträt Grete Stern." in *Drei Fotografinnen*, Film and Text Magazine, New York, 1992 (absolut MEDIEN, 2007).

Luckner-Bien, Renate. *75 Jahre Burg Giebichenstein 1915–1990*. Halle, 1990.

Makarowa, Elena. *Friedl Dicker-Brandeis – Ein Leben für Kunst und Lehre*. Exh. cat. Vienna / Munich, 1999.

Moholy, Lucia. "Fragen der Interpretation." In Neumann, Eckhardt. *Bauhaus and Bauhaus People: Personal Opinions and Recollections of Former Bauhaus Members and their Contemporaries*. Van Nostrand Reinhold, 1970.

Moholy, Lucia. "Photographie und Gesellschaft, gestern – heute – morgen" in TV series, *Stimmen der Zeit*, broadcast on Freies Berlin, October 12, 1958.

———. "Marginalien zu Moholy-Nagy. Dokumentarische Ungereimtheiten." Krefeld, 1972.

Müller, Dorothee, and Maximillan Schell. "Conversations with Anni Albers." *Süddeutsche Zeitung* (February 5–6, 1990).

Nebel-Heitmeyer, Hildegard. "Die Grunow-Lehre. Eine Erziehung der Sinne durch Ton und Farbe." *Bildnerische Erziehung* 1 (1967).

Nerdinger, Winfried, ed. *Bauhaus-Moderne im Nationalsozialismus*. Munich, 1993.

Neumann, Eckhardt. *Bauhaus and Bauhaus People: Personal Opinions and Recollections of Former Bauhaus Members and their Contemporaries*. Van Nostrand Reinhold, 1970.

Otto, Elizabeth, ed. *TEMPO, TEMPO! Die Bauhaus-Photomontagen von Marianne Brandt*. Exh. cat. Berlin: Bauhaus Archive, 2005.

Radewaldt, Ingrid. *Bauhaustextilien*. Dissertation. Hamburg, 1986.

Reich, Lilly. "Modefragen." In *Die Form. Monatsschrift für gestaltende Arbeit*. Berlin, 1922. Quoted in Günther, Sonja. *Lilly Reich 1885–1947: Innenarchitektin, Designerin, Ausstellungsgestalterin*. Stuttgart, 1988.

Ringl and Pit. Film by Juan Mandelbaum. Script in Bauhaus Archive Berlin, Boston, 1995.

Rose, Katja. "Erinnerungen an meine Bauhauszeit." In *Katja Rose, Weberei am Bauhaus 1931 bis 1933*. Berlin: Bauhaus Archive, 1984.

Sachsse, Rolf. "Die Frau an seiner Seite." In Eskilden, Ute, ed. *Fotografieren hieß teilnehmen. Fotografinnen der Weimarer Republik*. Exh. cat. Düsseldorf, 1994.

———. *Lucia Moholy, Bauhaus-Fotografin*. Berlin: Bauhaus Archive, 1995.

Schalcher, Traugott. "Fotostudien ringl + pit." *Gebrauchsgraphik*, vol. 8, 2 (1931).

Scheltwort, Sabine. "Sich gesichtet." *Frankfurter Rundschau* (March 7, 1994).

Scheper, Dirk. *Oskar Schlemmer: The Triadic Ballet*. Akademie der Künste, 1977.

Scheper, Lou. "Bäume wachsen in den Himmel." *Athena*, vol. 2, 3 (1947).

———. *Tönnchen, Knöpfchen und andere*. Leipzig, 1948.

———. "Rückschau." In Neumann, Eckhard, ed. *Bauhaus und Bauhäusler – Erinnerungen und Bekenntnisse*. Bern / Stuttgart, 1971.

Scheper, Renate. *Farbenfroh! – Die Werkstatt für Wandmalerei am Bauhaus*. Berlin: Bauhaus Archive, 2005.

Schneider, Katja. "Marguerite Friedlaender-Wildenhain. Vom Bauhaus an den Pazifik." In Jürgs, Britta, ed. *Vom Salzstreuer zum Automobil. Designerinnen*. Berlin, 2002.

Siebenbrodt, Michael, ed. *Bauhaus Weimar: Designs for the Future*. Stuttgart: Hatje Cantz, 2001.

Siedhoff-Buscher, Alma. "Kind – Märchen – Spiel – Spielzeug." *Junge Menschen*, vol. 5, 8 (1925).

———. "kindermöbel und kinderkleidung." *Vivos Voco. Zeitschrift für neues Deutschtum*, vol. 5, 4 (1926).

Steckner, Cornelius. "Die Musikpädagogin Gertrud Grunow als Meisterin der Formlehre am Weimarer Bauhaus." In *Das frühe Bauhaus und Johannes Itten*. Stuttgart / Weimar, 1994.

Stiftung Weimarer Klassik und Kunstsammlungen, ed. *Eine neue Welt für Kinder – Alma Siedhoff-Buscher*. Exh. cat. Weimar: Bauhaus Museum, 2004.

Sykora, Katharina. "Doppelspielerin – Über die fotografische Zusammenarbeit von Ringl + Pit alias Grete Stern und Ellen Auerbach." In Berger, Renate, ed. *LIEBE MACHT KUNST: Künstlerpaare im 20. Jahrhundert*. Cologne, 2000.

Vahl, Volker, and Uta Ackermann, eds. *Minutes of Municipal Bauhaus Masters' Council Meetings, Weimar 1919–1925*. Weimar, 2001.

Valdivieso, Mercedes. "Lucia und László Moholy-Nagy." In Berger Renate, ed. *LIEBE MACHT KUNST. Künstlerpaare im 20. Jahrhundert*. Cologne, 2000.

Verein der Berliner Künstlerinnen. *Käthe, Paula und der ganze Rest. Ein Nachschlagewerk*. Berlin, 1992.

Wangler, Wolfgang. *bauhaus – 2. generation*. Cologne, 1980.

Weber, Klaus. *Keramik und Bauhaus*. Berlin, 1988.

———. *Die Metallwerkstatt am Bauhaus*. Exh. cat. Berlin: Bauhaus Archive, 1992.

Weber, Nicolas Fox. "Begegnung mit Anni Albers." In Schell, Maximilian, ed. *Anni und Josef Albers. Eine Retrospektive*. Munich, 1989.

Website of Architekturzentrum Vienna, www.azw.at

Wilde, Ann. "Erinnerungen an Florence Henri." In Wingler, Hans M. *The Bauhaus*. Cambridge, MA: MIT Press, 1969.

Wortmann-Welgte, Sigrid. *Bauhaus Textiles: Women Artists and the Weaving Workshop*. London: Thames and Hudson, 1998.

Wynhoff, Elisabeth, ed. *Marianne Brandt. Fotografien am Bauhaus*. Exh. cat. Ostfildern: Institut für Kunst und Design der Bergischen Universität Wuppertal, 2003.

From the Bauhaus Archive, Berlin

American press and catalogs of Marguerite Friedlaender-Wildenhain, especially Archive No. 10670/1 and 10670/2.

Archive nos. 11813, 11814, and 11815.

Fehling, Ilse. Letter to Frau E. Steneberg, November of 3., 1911.68. Archive no. 4502/1.

Ise Gropius, Diaries 1924–1928, unpublished, no. 1998/55, and supplements to diaries, 1970s, unpublished, no. 1998/56.

Material relating to Florence Henri, including letters to Lou Scheper.

Material relating to Grete Stern.

Moholy, Lucia. Bequest at Bauhaus Archive Berlin, including diaries (File file 134/135/136); *Frau des 20. Jahrhunderts*, unpublished manuscript BHA Berlin (Files files 3 and 4), undated.

Museums and Galleries Exhibiting Works by Women Bauhaus Artists

AUSTRALIA
National Gallery of Australia
GPO Box 1150
Canberra ACT 2601
Australia
Tel.: +61 2 6240 6501
nga.gov.au

AUSTRIA
Vienna Museum of Applied Arts
Stubenring 5
1010 Innere Stadt, Wien
Austria
Tel.: +43-1 711 36-0
www.mak.at

CZECH REPUBLIC
Jewish Museum of Prague
U Staré školy 1
110 00 Prague 1
Czech Republic
Tel.: +420 221 711 511
www.jewishmuseum.cz

FRANCE
Musée des Beaux-Arts et d'Archéologie
1 place de (place du marché)
25000 Besançon
France
Tel.: + 33 3 81 87 80 49
www.musee-arts-besancon.org

GERMANY
Bauhaus Archives
Klingelhöferstraße 14
D - 10785 Berlin
Germany
Tel.: +49 30 25 40 02 0
www.bauhaus.de/english/

Kunstmuseum Kloster Unser Lieben Frauen
Regierungsstr. 4–6
39104 Magdeburg
Germany
Tel.: +49 391 56502-0
www.kunstmuseum-magdeburg.de

Kunstsammlungen zu Weimar
Burgplatz 4
99423 Weimar
Germany
Tel.: +49 (0)3643 545-0
www.kunstsammlungen-weimar.de

Museum Ludwig
Bischofsgartenstr. 1
50667 Cologne
Germany
Tel.: +49 221 22126165
www.museenkoeln.de

Neue Nationalgalerie
Potsdamer Str. 50
10785 Berlin
Germany
Tel.: +49 30 26557693
www.smb.spk-berlin.de

Neue Sammlung Museum, State Museum of Applied Arts and Design
Pinakothek der Moderne
80333 Munich
Germany
Tel.: +49 89 23805-360
www.pinakothek.de

Sprengel Museum
Kurt-Schwitters-Platz
30169 Hanover
Germany
Tel.: +49 511 168 4 38 75
www.sprengel-museum.de

Staatsgalerie Stuttgart
Postfach 10 43 42
70038 Stuttgart
Germany
Tel.: +49(0)711 . 470 40 0
www.staatsgalerie.de

ISRAEL
Beit Terezin
Givat Haim (Ihud)
Israel
M.P. Emek Hefer 38935
Tel.: +972 (0)4-6369515
www.bterezin.org.il/

ITALY
Peggy Guggenheim Collection
Palazzo Venier dei Leoni
Dorsoduro 701
I-30123 Venice
Italy
Tel.: +39.041.2405411
www.guggenheim-venice.it

NETHERLANDS
Museum Bojimans Van Beuningen
Museumpark 18-20
NL-3015 CX Rotterdam
Netherlands
Tel.: +31 10 4419400
www.boijmans.rotterdam.nl

Netherlands Institute for War Documentation
Herengracht 380
1016 CJ Amsterdam
Netherlands
Tel. : +31 (0)20-523 38 00
www.niod.nl/

NEW ZEALAND
Auckland Art Gallery
Cnr Wellesley and Kitchener Streets
Auckland 1010
New Zealand
Tel.: +64 9 307 7700
www.aucklandartgallery.govt.nz

SPAIN
Institut Valencià d'Art Modern
Guillem de Castro, 118
46003 Valencia
Spain
Tel. : +34 96 386 30 00
www.ivam.es

SWITZERLAND
Museum für Gestaltung
Ausstellungsstr. 60
CH-8005 Zurich
Switzerland
Tel.: +41 (0)43 446 67 67
www.museum-gestaltung.ch

UNITED KINGDOM
British Museum
Great Russell Street
London
WC1B 3DG
United Kingdom
Tel.: +44 (0)20 7323 8000/8299
www.britishmuseum.org

The Potteries Museum and Art Gallery
Bethesda Street
Hanley
Stoke-on-Trent
ST1 3DW
United Kingdom
Tel.: +44 (0)1782 232323
www.stoke.gov.uk/ccm/navigation/leisure/museums/potteries-museum—-art-gallery

Victoria and Albert Museum
V&A South Kensington
Cromwell Road
London SW7 2RL
United Kingdom
Tel.: +44 (0)20 7942 2000
www.vam.ac.uk

UNITED STATES
Art Institute of Chicago
36 S Wabash Ave # 1
Chicago, IL 60603
United States
Tel.: +1 (312) 899-5100
www.artic.edu

Busch-Reisinger Museum, Harvard University Art Museums
32 Quincy Street
Cambridge, MA 02138
United States
Tel.: +1 (617) 495-2317
www.artmuseums.harvard.edu

Cleveland Museum of Art
11150 East Boulevard
Cleveland, OH 44106
United States
Tel.: +1 (216) 421-7350
www.clemusart.com

Cooper Hewitt National Design Museum
2 East 91st Street
New York, NY 10128
United States
Tel. : +1 (212) 849-8400
www.cooperhewitt.org

Cranbrook Art Museum
39221 Woodward Avenue
P.O. Box 801
Bloomfield Hills, MI 48303-0801
United States
Tel.: +1 (248) 645-3323
www.cranbrookart.edu/museum

Detroit Institute of Arts
5200 Woodward Avenue
Detroit, Michigan 48202
United States
Tel.: +1 (313) 833-7900
www.dia.org

J. Paul Getty Museum
1200 Getty Center Drive
Los Angeles, CA 90049-1687
United States
Tel.: +1 (310) 440-7300
www.getty.edu/museum

Metropolitan Museum of Art
1000 Fifth Avenue
New York, NY 10028-0198
United States
Tel.: +1 (212) 535-7710
www.metmuseum.org

Museum of Art and Design
2 Columbus Circle
New York, NY 10019
United States
Tel.: +1 (212) 299-7777
www.madmuseum.org

Museum of Modern Art
11 W 53rd St
New York, NY 10019
United States
Tel.: +1 (212) 708-9400
www.moma.org

National Museum of Women in the Arts
1250 New York Avenue, N.W.
Washington, DC 20005-3970
United States
Tel.: +1 (202) 783-5000
www.nmwa.org

Neue Galerie Museum for German and Austrian Art
1048 5th Ave
New York, NY 10028
United States
Tel.: +1 (212) 628-6200
www.neuegalerie.org

New Mexico Museum of Art
107 W Palace Ave
Santa Fe, NM 87501
United States
Tel.: +1 (505) 476-5072
www.mfasantafe.org

Pond Farm Collection
Luther College
700 College Drive
Decorah, Iowa 52101
United States
Tel.: +1 (563) 387-1111
galleries.luther.edu/artists/wildenhain.htm

Smithsonian American Art Museum
MRC 970 Box 37012
Washington, DC 20013-7012
United States
Tel.: +1 (202) 633-7970
americanart.si.edu

Smithsonian Archives of American Art
750 9th St. NW, Victor Building, Suite 2200
Washington, DC 20001
United States
Tel.: +1 202-633-7940
www.aaa.si.edu

The Sonoma County Museum
425 7th Street
Santa Rosa, CA 95401
United States
Tel. +1 (707) 579-1500
www.sonomacountymuseum.org

Index

Photo Credits

Picture selection and photos taken from archive material at the Bauhaus Archive, Berlin by Ulrike Müller with the collaboration of Ingrid Radewaldt.

Front cover images: left to right: Marianne Brandt, see p.118; Ida Kerkovius, Bauhaus carpet, see p. 30; Marianne Brandt, Teapot, see p. 122; ringl + pit, *KOMOL*, see p. 134. **Endpapers:** Gunta Stölzl, Sketch for carpet, c. 1926. Tempera on paper, Bauhaus Archive, Berlin, see p. 46. **Back cover images:** top from left to right: photo of Bauhaus women, see p. 6; Benita Otte, Nursery carpet, see p. 40; Marianne Brandt and Hans Przyrembel, Hanging lamp with pulley, see p. 119; Ida Kerkovius, *Self-Portrait*, see p. 31; bottom from right to left: Margarete Heymann-Loebenstein-Marks, Jug from the pattern book of Haël Ceramics from 1924, see p. 71; four young woman from the weaving mill: Margret Leischner, Margret Dambeck, Liesel Henneberg, unknown, see p. 6; ringl + pit, *Das Ei des Kolumbus*, see p. 135.
p. 1 Weavers on the Bauhaus steps, Dessau 1927. Bauhaus Archive, Berlin. **p. 4** Gertrud Arndt, see p. 56. **p. 6** Quittenbaum Kunstauktionen GmbH, Munich (2); private collection; Bauhaus Archive, Berlin (2). **p. 8** Klassik Stiftung, Weimar. **p. 9** Photo T. Lux Feininger, Bauhaus Archive, Berlin. **p. 10** Photos by T. Lux Feininger, The J. Paul Getty Museum, Los Angeles. **p. 11** Photo Irene Bayer, Bauhaus Archive, Berlin. **p. 12** Unknown photographer, Bauhaus Archive, Berlin. **p. 15** top see p.17; center see p.25; bottom see p.20. **p. 16** Photo by E. Bouché, Bauhaus Archive, Berlin. **p. 17** Klassik Stiftung, Weimar. **p. 18** Unknown photographer, Bauhaus Archive, Berlin. **p. 20** Kunstmuseum, Bern. **p. 21** Bauhaus Archive, Berlin. **p. 22** Thüringisches Hauptstaatsarchiv, Weimar, Staatliches Bauhaus, Weimar, Nr. 114, Bl. 42. **p. 23** Bauhaus Universität, Weimar. **p. 24** Photo by Louis Held, Bauhaus Archive, Berlin. **p. 25** Colored from black-and-white photo by Lucia Moholy, Bauhaus Archive, Berlin. **p. 26** Archiv Gunta Stölzl. **p. 27** Klassik Stiftung, Weimar **p. 28** Photo by Erich Braunsperger, dpa-Bildarchiv. **pp. 29–32** Bauhaus Archive, Berlin. **p. 35** left see p.62; right. see p.40; bottom see p.47. **p. 36** Photo by Heinrich Koch, Bauhaus Archive, Berlin. **p. 37–38** Hauptarchiv und Historische Sammlung der v. Bodelschwinghschen Anstalten Bethel, Bielefeld. **pp. 39–40** Klassik Stiftung, Weimar. **p. 41** Hauptarchiv und Historische Sammlung der v. Bodelschwinghschen Anstalten. Bethel, Bielefeld. **p. 42–43** Archiv Gunta Stölzl. **p. 44–45** Klassik Stiftung, Weimar. **p. 46** Vorwerk und Co. Teppichwerke. **p. 47–48** Victoria & Albert Museum, London. **p. 49** Bauhaus Archive, Berlin / Musée National d'Art Moderne / Centre Pompidou. **p. 50** Bauhaus Archive, Berlin. **p. 51** The Josef & Anni Albers Foundation, Bethany, Connecticut. **p. 53** Bauhaus Archive, Berlin. **p. 54** The Josef & Anni Albers Foundation, Bethany, Connecticut. **p. 55** Photo by Getuzio Alviani, Milan. **p. 56–66** Bauhaus Archive, Berlin. **p. 67** Städtische Kunstsammlungen, Chemnitz. **p. 69** left see p.74; right see p.83; bottom see p.77. **p. 70** Bauhaus Archive, Berlin. **p. 71–72** Ofen- und Keramikmuseum, Velten. **p. 73** Private collection. **p. 74–75** Ofen- und Keramikmuseum, Velten. **p. 76–77** Bauhaus Archive, Berlin. **p. 78–79** Bauhaus Universität, Weimar **p. 80** Archives of American Art, Washington, Bauhaus Archive, Berlin. **p. 81** Bauhaus Archive, Berlin. **p. 82** Lucia Eames/The Eames Office Gallery **p. 83** Knoll International. **p. 85** left see p.96; top see p.87; right see p.103. **p. 86–88** Bauhaus Archive, Berlin. **p. 89** Bauhaus Universität, Weimar. **p. 90** Matthias Hildebrand/MfK, Leipzig. **p. 91–92** Bauhaus Archive, Berlin. **p. 93** Bauhaus Universität, Weimar. **p. 94** Klassik Stiftung, Weimar. **p. 95–96** Bauhaus Archive, Berlin. **p. 97** Jewish Museum, Prague. **p. 98** Photo by Florence Henri, Scheper Estate. **p. 99** Scheper Estate. **p. 100** Klassik Stiftung, Weimar. **p. 101** Bauhaus Archive, Berlin. **p. 102** Scheper Estate. **p. 103** Bauhaus Archive, Berlin. **p. 105** left see p.120; top see p.117; right. see. **p. 106** Photo by G. Engelhardt, Bauhaus Archive, Berlin. **p. 107–08** Bauhaus Archive, Berlin. **p. 109** Photo by Fritz Schreiber, Bauhaus Archive, Berlin. **p. 110** Bauhaus Universität, Weimar. **p. 111** Museum of Modern Art, New York City. **p. 112** Bauhaus Archive, Berlin. **p. 113** Bauhaus Universität, Weimar. **p. 114** Lore Siedhoff Collection. **p. 115–17** Klassik Stiftung, Weimar. **p. 118–19** Bauhaus Archive, Berlin. **p. 120** Kupferstichkabinett Dresden / Staatliche Kunstsammlungen, Dresden. **p. 121** Bauhaus Archive, Berlin. **p. 122** Klassik Stiftung, Weimar. **p. 123–25** Bauhaus Archive, Berlin. **p. 127** top see p. 131; bottom see p. 134; right see p. 147. **p. 128–29** Bauhaus Archive, Berlin. **p. 130** Bauhaus Archive, Berlin, Galerie Martini & Ronchetti, Genoa. **p. 131–43** Bauhaus Archive, Berlin. **p. 144** Bauhaus Archive, Berlin, folder 134, inv. no. 1170/48. **p. 145–48** Bauhaus Archive, Berlin. **p. 149** Photo by Michael von Graffenried, Bauhaus Archive, Berlin
Attachment and label Vorwerk und Co. Teppichwerke

VG Bild-Kunst, Bonn, 2009
Cover images: Marianne Brandt, Self-portrait; Ida Kerkovius, Bauhaus carpet; Marianne Brandt, Teapot; ringl – pit, *KOMOL*; Endpapers: Gunta Stölzl, Sketch for carpet; back cover: Marianne Brandt, Hans Pryrembel, Hanging lamp; Ida Kerkovius, *Self-Portrait*; ringl + pit, *Columbus' Egg*, 4, 15 center and bottom, 20, 25, 29, 30, 31, 32, 35 left and bottom, 42, 43, 44, 45, 46, 47, 48, 51, 53, 54, 56, 57, 58, 59, 60, 61, 62, 69 right, 96, 105 left, 108, 118, 119, 120, 122, 123, 125, 127 bottom and right, 128, 132 134, 135, 136, 142, 143, 144, 145, 146, 147, 148

The Publishers would like to thank Quittenbaum Kunstauktionen GmbH, Munich for the images on page 7: Margarete Heymann Loebenstein-Marks, Bowl, c. 1930 (16072), *Lidded jar*, c. 1930 (23072), www.quittenbaum.de

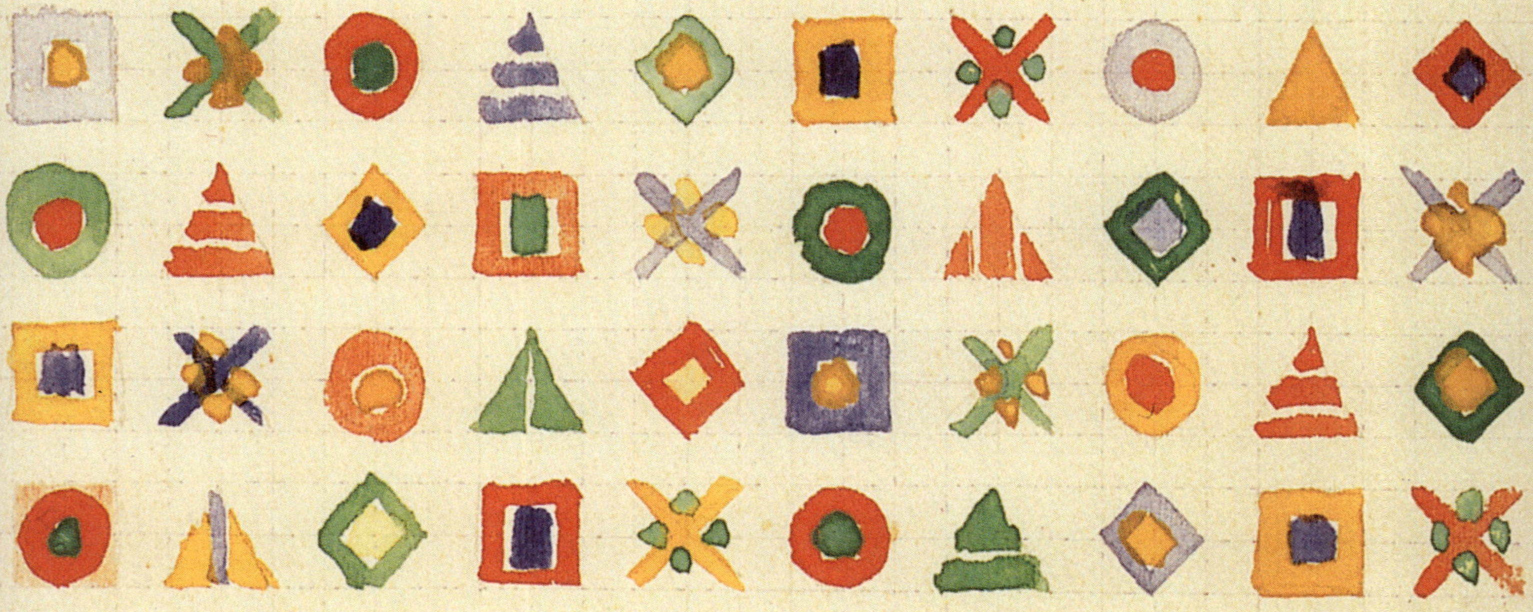